*Confronting Devastation*

# THE AZRIELI SERIES OF HOLOCAUST SURVIVOR MEMOIRS: PUBLISHED TITLES

## ENGLISH TITLES

Judy Abrams, *Tenuous Threads/* Eva Felsenburg Marx, *One of the Lucky Ones*
Amek Adler, *Six Lost Years*
Molly Applebaum, *Buried Words*
Claire Baum, *The Hidden Package*
Bronia and Joseph Beker, *Joy Runs Deeper*
Tibor Benyovits, *Unsung Heroes*
Max Bornstein, *If Home Is Not Here*
Felicia Carmelly, *Across the Rivers of Memory*
Tommy Dick, *Getting Out Alive*
Marian Domanski, *Fleeing from the Hunter*
Anita Ekstein, *Always Remember Who You Are*
John Freund, *Spring's End*
Myrna Goldenberg (Editor), *Before All Memory Is Lost: Women's Voices from the Holocaust*
René Goldman, *A Childhood Adrift*
Elly Gotz, *Flights of Spirit*
Ibolya Grossman and Andy Réti, *Stronger Together*
Pinchas Gutter, *Memories in Focus*
Anna Molnár Hegedűs, *As the Lilacs Bloomed*
Rabbi Pinchas Hirschprung, *The Vale of Tears*
Bronia Jablon, *A Part of Me*
Helena Jockel, *We Sang in Hushed Voices*
Eddie Klein, *Inside the Walls*
Michael Kutz, *If, By Miracle*
Nate Leipciger, *The Weight of Freedom*
Alex Levin, *Under the Yellow and Red Stars*
Fred Mann, *A Drastic Turn of Destiny*
Michael Mason, *A Name Unbroken*
Leslie Meisels with Eva Meisels, *Suddenly the Shadow Fell*
Leslie Mezei, *A Tapestry of Survival*

Muguette Myers, *Where Courage Lives*
David Newman, *Hope's Reprise*
Arthur Ney, *W Hour*
Felix Opatowski, *Gatehouse to Hell*
Marguerite Élias Quddus, *In Hiding*
Maya Rakitova, *Behind the Red Curtain*
Henia Reinhartz, *Bits and Pieces*
Betty Rich, *Little Girl Lost*
Paul-Henri Rips, *E/96: Fate Undecided*
Margrit Rosenberg Stenge, *Silent Refuge*
Steve Rotschild, *Traces of What Was*
Judith Rubinstein, *Dignity Endures*
Martha Salcudean, *In Search of Light*
Kitty Salsberg and Ellen Foster, *Never Far Apart*
Joseph Schwarzberg, *Dangerous Measures*
Zuzana Sermer, *Survival Kit*
Rachel Shtibel, *The Violin/* Adam Shtibel, *A Child's Testimony*
Maxwell Smart, *Chaos to Canvas*
Gerta Solan, *My Heart Is At Ease*
Zsuzsanna Fischer Spiro, *In Fragile Moments/* Eva Shainblum, *The Last Time*
George Stern, *Vanished Boyhood*
Willie Sterner, *The Shadows Behind Me*
Ann Szedlecki, *Album of My Life*
William Tannenzapf, *Memories from the Abyss/* Renate Krakauer, *But I Had a Happy Childhood*
Elsa Thon, *If Only It Were Fiction*
Agnes Tomasov, *From Generation to Generation*
Joseph Tomasov, *From Loss to Liberation*
Sam Weisberg, *Carry the Torch/* Johnny Jablon, *A Lasting Legacy*
Leslie Vertes, *Alone in the Storm*
Anka Voticky, *Knocking on Every Door*

TITRES FRANÇAIS

Judy Abrams, *Retenue par un fil*/ Eva Felsen-
burg Marx, *Une question de chance*
Claire Baum, *Le Colis caché*
Bronia et Joseph Beker, *Plus forts que le
malheur*
Max Bornstein, *Citoyen de nulle part*
Tommy Dick, *Objectif: survivre*
Marian Domanski, *Traqué*
John Freund, *La Fin du printemps*
René Goldman, *Une enfance à la dérive*
Anna Molnár Hegedűs, *Pendant la saison
des lilas*
Helena Jockel, *Nous chantions en sourdine*
Michael Kutz, *Si, par miracle*
Nate Leipciger, *Le Poids de la liberté*
Alex Levin, *Étoile jaune, étoile rouge*
Fred Mann, *Un terrible revers de fortune*
Michael Mason, *Au fil d'un nom*
Leslie Meisels, *Soudains, les ténèbres*
Muguette Myers, *Les Lieux du courage*
Arthur Ney, *L'Heure W*

Felix Opatowski, *L'Antichambre de l'enfer*
Marguerite Élias Quddus, *Cachée*
Henia Reinhartz, *Fragments de ma vie*
Betty Rich, *Seule au monde*
Paul-Henri Rips, *Matricule E/96*
Steve Rotschild, *Sur les traces du passé*
Kitty Salsberg et Ellen Foster, *Unies dans
l'épreuve*
Zuzana Sermer, *Trousse de survie*
Rachel Shtibel, *Le Violon*/ Adam Shtibel,
*Témoignage d'un enfant*
George Stern, *Une jeunesse perdue*
Willie Sterner, *Les Ombres du passé*
Ann Szedlecki, *L'Album de ma vie*
William Tannenzapf, *Souvenirs de l'abîme*/
Renate Krakauer, *Le Bonheur de l'innocence*
Elsa Thon, *Que renaisse demain*
Agnes Tomasov, *De génération en génération*
Leslie Vertes, *Seul dans la tourmente*
Anka Voticky, *Frapper à toutes les portes*

# Confronting Devastation: Memoirs of Holocaust Survivors from Hungary

EDITED BY FERENC LACZÓ

THE AZRIELI FOUNDATION · www.azrielifoundation.org

Cover and book design by Mark Goldstein
Endpaper maps by Martin Gilbert
Map on page xxiv–xxv by François Blanc

Translation of László Láng's memoir on pages 43–45, 119–122 and 339–342; and of Leslie Fazekas's memoir on pages 55–57 and 179–182 by Marietta Morry and Lynda Muir. Translation of Moishe Rosenchein's memoir on pages 123–128 and 343–347 by Vivian Felsen.

LIBRARY AND ARCHIVES CANADA CATALOGUING IN PUBLICATION

Confronting devastation: memoirs of Holocaust survivors from Hungary.
Laczó, Ferenc, 1982– editor.

(Azrieli series of Holocaust survivor memoirs. Series XI)
Includes bibliographical references and index. Canadiana 20190196084
ISBN 978-1-988065-68-7 (softcover) · 8 7 6 5 4 3 2 1

LCSH: Holocaust, Jewish (1939–1945) — Hungary — Personal narratives. LCSH: Holocaust, Jewish (1939–1945) — Hungary — Biography. LCSH: Holocaust survivors — Hungary — Biography. LCSH: Holocaust survivors — Canada — Biography. LCSH: Jews — Hungary — Biography. LCSH: Jews — Canada — Biography. LCGFT: Personal narratives. LCGFT: Biographies.

DS135.H93 A14 2019     DDC 940.53/180922439—DC23

PRINTED IN CANADA

# The Azrieli Series of Holocaust Survivor Memoirs

Naomi Azrieli, Publisher

Jody Spiegel, Program Director
Arielle Berger, Managing Editor
Matt Carrington, Editor
Devora Levin, Assistant Editor
Elizabeth Lasserre, Senior Editor, French-Language Editions
Elin Beaumont, Community and Education Initiatives
Catherine Person, Education and Academic Initiatives/French Editor
Stephanie Corazza, Academic and Education Initiatives
Marc-Olivier Cloutier, School and Education Initiatives
Elizabeth Banks, Digital Asset Curator and Archivist
Catherine Quintal, Digital Communications Assistant

Mark Goldstein, Art Director
François Blanc, Cartographer
Bruno Paradis, Layout, French-Language Editions

# Contents

Series Preface     xiii

About the Footnotes and Glossary     xv

Introduction *by Ferenc Laczó*     xvii

Map     xxiv–xxv

"The Unending Past" by Peter Vas     xxvii

THE CONTRADICTIONS OF DAILY LIFE UNDER WORSENING
EXCLUSION: EXPERIENCES IN HUNGARY BEFORE 1944

Foreword by Ferenc Laczó     3

*Shattered Dreams* by Dolly Tiger-Chinitz     7

*My Surprising Escapes* by Benedikt Korda (Kornreich)     17

*Only When I Laugh* by Imrich Vesely     27

*My Escape to and from Hungary* by Victor David     37

*With Aching Hearts* by László Láng     43

*Hoping in Isolation* by Miriam Mózes     47

*Eviction and Terror* by Sandor (Sam) Grad     53

*Fate and Fortune* by Leslie Fazekas     55

*The Miracle of Our Survival* by Yittel Nechumah Bineth
(Kornelia Paskusz)     59

*Amid the Burning Bushes* by Helen Rodak-Izso     63

DRILLS AND HUMILIATIONS: JEWISH MEN
IN LABOUR BATTALIONS

Foreword by Ferenc Laczó                                          69
*Only When I Laugh* (Part 2) by Imrich Vesely                    73
*My Surprising Escapes* (Part 2) by Benedikt Korda (Kornreich)   91
*Like Slaves in Pharaoh's Time* by Itzik Davidovits             113
*With Aching Hearts* (Part 2) by László Láng                    119
*Two Sorts of Homecoming* by Moishe Rosenschein                 123


HORRORS AND SURVIVAL: IN GHETTOS AND CAMPS

Foreword by Ferenc Laczó                                         131
*Amid the Burning Bushes* (Part 2) by Helen Rodak-Izso          135
*The Miracle of Our Survival* (Part 2) by Yittel Nechumah Bineth
   (Kornelia Paskusz)                                            149
*Eviction and Terror* (Part 2) by Sandor (Sam) Grad             159
*Beliefs under Shock* by Veronika Schwartz                      169
*Fate and Fortune* (Part 2) by Leslie Fazekas                   179
*Hoping in Isolation* (Part 2) by Miriam Mózes                  183
*Apples at Christmas* by Julius Jakab                           189


PERSECUTION AND ESCAPE IN BUDAPEST

Foreword by Ferenc Laczó                                         199
*Shattered Dreams* (Part 2) by Dolly Tiger-Chinitz              203
*The Light in a Dark Cellar* by Susan Simon                     213
*Rowing on Ice* by Kathleen (Kati) Horváth                      227
*Frightful Days* by Katalin Kenedi                              235
*To Start off as a Christian but to Arrive as a Jew* by Eva Kahan   249
*A Time of Fear* by Alexander Eisen                             261
*My Escape to and from Hungary* (Part 2) by Victor David        275

Foreword by Ferenc Laczó                                                   283

*Rowing on Ice* (Part 2) by Kathleen (Kati) Horváth                        287

*To Start off as a Christian but to Arrive as a Jew* (Part 2)
  by Eva Kahan
                                                                          293

*My Surprising Escapes* (Part 3) by Benedikt Korda (Kornreich)            297

*Beliefs under Shock* (Part 2) by Veronika Schwartz                       303

*Amid the Burning Bushes* (Part 3) by Helen Rodak-Izso                    311

*The Miracle of Our Survival* (Part 3) by Yittel Nechumah Bineth
  (Kornelia Paskusz)
                                                                          319

*Hoping in Isolation* (Part 3) by Miriam Mózes                            329

*Hiding from the Germans, Running from the Soviets*
  by Esther Davidovits
                                                                          331

*The Light in a Dark Cellar* (Part 2) by Susan Simon                      335

*With Aching Hearts* (Part 3) by László Láng                              339

*Two Sorts of Homecoming* (Part 2) by Moishe Rosenschein                  343

*As a Free Man* by Mark Lane                                              349

*Fate and Fortune* (Part 3) by Leslie Fazekas                            353

*Shattered Dreams* (Part 3) by Dolly Tiger-Chinitz                       359


Glossary                                                                  365

Author Biographies and Photographs                                        391

Index                                                                     437

# Series Preface:
# In their own words...

*In telling these stories, the writers have liberated themselves. For so many years we did not speak about it, even when we became free people living in a free society. Now, when at last we are writing about what happened to us in this dark period of history, knowing that our stories will be read and live on, it is possible for us to feel truly free. These unique historical documents put a face on what was lost, and allow readers to grasp the enormity of what happened to six million Jews — one story at a time.*

David J. Azrieli, C.M., C.Q., M.Arch
Holocaust survivor and founder, The Azrieli Foundation

Since the end of World War II, approximately 40,000 Jewish Holocaust survivors have immigrated to Canada. Who they are, where they came from, what they experienced and how they built new lives for themselves and their families are important parts of our Canadian heritage. The Azrieli Foundation's Holocaust Survivor Memoirs Program was established in 2005 to preserve and share the memoirs written by those who survived the twentieth-century Nazi genocide of the Jews of Europe and later made their way to Canada. The memoirs encourage readers to engage thoughtfully and critically with the complexities of the Holocaust and to create meaningful connections with the lives of survivors.

Millions of individual stories are lost to us forever. By preserving the stories written by survivors and making them widely available to a broad audience, the Azrieli Foundation's Holocaust Survivor Memoirs Program seeks to sustain the memory of all those who perished at the hands of hatred, abetted by indifference and apathy. The personal accounts of those who survived against all odds are as different as the people who wrote them, but all demonstrate the courage, strength, wit and luck that it took to prevail and survive in such terrible adversity. The memoirs are also moving tributes to people — strangers and friends — who risked their lives to help others, and who, through acts of kindness and decency in the darkest of moments, frequently helped the persecuted maintain faith in humanity and courage to endure. These accounts offer inspiration to all, as does the survivors' desire to share their experiences so that new generations can learn from them.

The Holocaust Survivor Memoirs Program collects, archives and publishes select survivor memoirs and makes the print editions available free of charge to educational institutions and Holocaust-education programs across Canada. They are also available for sale online to the general public. All revenues to the Azrieli Foundation from the sales of the Azrieli Series of Holocaust Survivor Memoirs go toward the publishing and educational work of the memoirs program.

~

The Azrieli Foundation would like to express appreciation to the following people for their invaluable efforts in producing this book: Doris Bergen, Mark Duffus (Maracle Inc), Farla Klaiman, Susan Roitman, Stephen Ullstrom, and Margie Wolfe & Emma Rodgers of Second Story Press.

# About the Footnotes & Glossary

The following memoirs have been excerpted and can be read as stand-alone pieces or sequentially in the sections they appear in. The excerpts may contain a number of terms, concepts and historical references that may be unfamiliar to the reader. Each excerpt may also contain footnotes relevant to the memoir; where works are not cited, the explanations of terms were generated from the Azrieli Foundation's extensive glossary. The common Hungarian terms *bácsi* (uncle) and *néni* (aunt) are not always defined, and may apply to either a biological relation or as a term of respect for an older person. For general information on major organizations; significant historical events and people; geographical locations; religious and cultural terms; and foreign-language words and expressions that will help give context and background to the events described in the text, please see the glossary beginning on page 365.

# Introduction

No other historical event has been followed by as vast and long-lasting a movement to record the testimonies of its survivors as the Holocaust. This unprecedented movement, rooted in earlier Jewish traditions of documenting violence,[1] started even during the Nazi war and genocide.[2] It continued with a major wave of documentation practically immediately upon the unconditional surrender of the Axis in 1945. Survivor testimonies already played a pivotal role in this first major wave and those by Jews from Hungary — where over half a million victims, or approximately every tenth victim of the Holocaust, came from — were prominent among them.[3]

Decades later, aided by the rise of films and videotaped testimony archives, the movement yielded what Annette Wieviorka has

---

1   Laura Jockusch, *Collect and Record! Jewish Holocaust Documentation in Early Postwar Europe* (Oxford: Oxford University Press, 2012).

2   On the frightening and fascinating story of the Oyneg Shabes Archive, see Samuel Kassow, *Who Will Write our History? Emanuel Ringelblum, the Warsaw Ghetto, and the Oyneg Shabes Archive* (Bloomington, IN: Indiana University Press, 2007).

3   For early post-war testimonies from Hungary, see Ferenc Laczó, *Hungarian Jews in the Age of Genocide: An Intellectual History, 1929–1948* (Leiden: Brill, 2016).

famously called "the era of the witness." By the late twentieth century, Holocaust testimony emerged from the margins of Western culture to become a widely discussed and much appreciated cultural form. Following the decades-long painful deafness of the surrounding world after the war, Holocaust survivors would exert a significant cultural impact as the bearers of historical and emotional truths with whom various audiences — members of "communities of connection and identification" in the pertinent phrase of Mary Fulbrook[4] — would finally come to strongly empathize.[5]

At the same time, as Wieviorka has rightly noted, historians have surprisingly rarely drawn on the testimonies of Holocaust survivors and have often treated them with considerable distrust.[6] Only in recent years have some of the major historians of the Holocaust — such as, perhaps most famously, Christopher Browning with the release of his *Remembering Survival* — published research monographs that have taken the documentary evidence offered by survivors as their main basis.[7] A curious and problematic underestimation of the value of survivor testimony remains a pattern among many professional historians today, despite the fact that we are in the possession of a massive and immensely valuable global archive of Holocaust testimonies — testimonies recorded in multiple genres and media, in diverse places and at various distances from the event.

As Noah Shenker reminds us, besides the variety of individual

4 See Mary Fulbrook, "Guilt and Shame among Communities of Experience, Connection and Identification," in *Reverberations of Nazi Violence in Germany and Beyond: Disturbing Pasts*, eds. Stephanie Bird, Mary Fulbrook, Julia Wagner and Christiane Wienand (London: Bloomsbury, 2016).

5 Annette Wieviorka, *The Era of the Witness* (Ithaca, NY: Cornell University Press, 2006), xv.

6 Wieviorka, xiii.

7 Christopher Browning, *Remembering Survival: Inside a Nazi Slave-Labor Camp* (New York: W. W. Norton, 2010).

trajectories and choices, these testimonies have also been mediated in important ways by the specific histories and practices of the major and more minor institutions and initiatives that have provided the framework for their creation.[8] It is therefore important to emphasize that the current anthology draws on the precious and in many ways unique Holocaust Survivor Memoirs Program of the Azrieli Foundation and includes thematically organized excerpts of various length from twenty-one detailed memoirs and one poem written primarily in the late twentieth and early twenty-first century. The present volume contains the autobiographical testimonies of elderly survivors who experienced the Holocaust as young adults or as even younger persons — the youngest authors included in this book were barely teenagers in the darkest wartime years, whereas even the oldest one among them was only in her mid-thirties.

In terms of gender, the volume strikes a fair balance, with nearly equal numbers of men and women among the authors. At the same time, the memoirs clearly attest to the gendered nature of personal experience and not only because labour service (which is covered in section two) was restricted to men but, equally importantly, because the sorrows of liberation (discussed in section five) all too frequently included sexual assaults on women by their nominal liberators in the Red Army — assaults that these memoirs written in Canada repeatedly address, if often succinctly and in veiled language.[9]

This directly ties in with a major issue, namely that the majority

---

8   Noah Shenker, *Reframing Holocaust Testimony* (Bloomington, IN: University of Indiana Press, 2015).

9   On the history and memory of wartime and early post-war sexual violence in Hungary, see Andrea Pető, *Elmondani az elmondhatatlant: A nemi erőszak Magyarországon a II. világháború alatt* [To speak the unspeakable: Rape and sexual abuse in Hungary during World War II] (Budapest: Jaffa, 2018). An English translation is forthcoming. (My English-language review of the Hungarian original was featured in *Hungarian Historical Review*, 2018/4, 842-844.)

XX CONFRONTING DEVASTATION

of memoirs by Jewish survivors of Nazi persecution from Hungary, as from many other places, have been written by emigrants in a permanent state of exile from their country of origin. As Susan Rubin Suleiman has rightly noted, remembering, representing and memorializing the Holocaust in translation has in fact been so ubiquitous that it remains a surprisingly little analyzed and understood phenomenon.[10] It is therefore all the more important to underline the following key aspect of the current anthology: the memoirs excerpted — with the exception of Fazekas's, Láng's, Rosenschein's and Vesely's— have been composed in English by multilingual survivors whose native tongues may have been Hungarian or Yiddish, or — in fewer cases — German, Slovak or Czech, and whose wartime suffering was inflicted primarily in Hungarian and German.

These valuable memoirs were written by Jewish Canadians who, having survived the Holocaust in the (temporarily enlarged) territory of Hungary and within the broader orbit of Nazi Germany, settled, got integrated and acculturated in post-war Canada, typically changing their chief language of communication along the way.[11] Their lives have thus been characterized by two radically different ruptures: the irreparable losses associated with genocide in their youth and their post-war departure from Hungary or one of the neighbouring regions and their ultimately often fortunate arrival in Canada.

This anthology of excerpts, released on the 75th anniversary of the main phase of the Hungarian chapter of the Holocaust, aims to provide an overview of survivor experiences in the country. The excerpts from the memoirs have been divided into five major thematic

---

10 Susan Rubin Suleiman, "Monuments in a Foreign Tongue: On Reading Holocaust Memoirs by Emigrants," in *Exile and Creativity: Signposts, Travelers, Outsiders, Backward Glances*, ed. Susan Rubin Suleiman (Durham, NC: Duke University Press), 399.

11 On these themes regarding early post-war Canada, see Adara Goldberg, *Holocaust Survivors in Canada: Exclusion, Inclusion, Transformation, 1947–1955* (Winnipeg: University of Manitoba Press, 2016).

sections. The anthology begins with insights into the diverse and even contradictory Jewish experiences under worsening exclusion in Hungary prior to 1944. It continues with recollections of the recurrently humiliating and often brutal or even deadly experiences of labour servicemen before aiming to convey, to the extent that this is at all possible, the most devastating experiences in Hungarian ghettos and the Nazi camp universe.

Section four is in turn devoted to the simultaneous but notably different tribulations of Jews in the capital city of Budapest in 1944–1945, experiences that were variously defined by segregation and ghettoization, murderous violence and resourceful hiding, constant fear and hunger, the prolonged siege of the city and — for a comparatively large group — eventual liberation by the Red Army. However, as the excerpts in section five attest, the experiences right after the end of the war could as often be distressing and deeply tragic as liberating or joyous. While the anthology thus covers key facets of Jewish experiences at the time of an unprecedented collective tragedy and trauma, the twenty-one memoirists also reveal the broad diversity of individual survivor trajectories.

Can experiences of trauma and mourning be represented in cultural objects, such as memoirs? If so, how do memoirs of Holocaust survivors grapple with the special problem and notable limits of representing mass violence and their own traumatic survival?[12] More specifically, how have Jewish survivors from wartime Hungary who have become Canadians, and to whose valuable recollections this anthology is devoted, grappled with these crucial questions?

When composing Holocaust memoirs, reenacting the past in the present — reliving the devastating experiences of pain, humiliation and loss — is a constant and threatening possibility. However, beyond

---

12 On this question, see the groundbreaking volume by Saul Friedlander, ed., *Probing the Limits of Representation: Nazism and the "Final Solution"* (Cambridge, MA: Harvard University Press, 1992).

this painful reliving while writing such memoirs, which Dominick LaCapra has aptly called "acting out," there is also another primary goal of memoirists, namely to "work through" their traumatic pasts.[13] Another main motivation of Holocaust survivors to record their personal stories in detail derives from the frequent fear that their experiences are not properly acknowledged in the present and might not be adequately remembered in the future.

Survivor memoirists have therefore tended to compose what James E. Young has fittingly labelled "factually insistent narratives," meaning that their authors are emphatic that, beyond conveying their individual and partly subjective experiences, their memoirs deliver documentary evidence of specific events and ought to stand as testimonial proof.[14] In order to stake this claim to factual representation forcefully, Young notes, memoirists often prefer traditional forms of narration, description and dialogue. The majority of authors in this anthology, with some notable exceptions, indeed utilize the referential function of language more than the poetic.

As Michael Rothberg argues in his book *Traumatic Realism*, beyond the demand for documentation, attempts to represent the Holocaust need to fulfill two further crucial demands: reflection on the limits of representation and wider engagement with the public sphere and contemporary culture.[15] One of the most remarkable aspects of the excerpts is how the factual-chronological narrations and close descriptions are repeatedly interrupted by commentaries expressing shock and incomprehension, and at times also by explicit remarks on or more implicit signs of the incommunicability of one's profoundly traumatic experiences. This tendency of memoirists to break with their main organizing principles under the weight of the experiences

13 Dominick LaCapra, *Representing the Holocaust: History, Theory, Trauma* (Ithaca, NY: Cornell University Press, 1994).
14 James E. Young, "Interpreting Literary Testimony: A Preface to Rereading Holocaust Diaries and Memoirs," *New Literary History* 18, no. 2 (winter 1987): 404.
15 Michael Rothberg, *Traumatic Realism* (Minneapolis: University of Minnesota Press, 2000).

recalled is especially apparent in section three, the darkest core of this anthology, which deals with experiences in Hungarian ghettos and Nazi camps.

Given the sheer, unmitigated horror of the Nazi genocide, the pressure to draw lessons is in many ways irresistible: it is widely agreed among scholars as well as members of the general public that the Holocaust ought to teach us lessons. What this anthology illustrates so well is that the lessons individual survivors have drawn in fact vary a great deal, and it would therefore be unwise if we tried to reduce them to simple formulas.[16] The lessons we ought to learn from the unprecedented *Zivilisationsbruch* (rupture in civilization) that these memoirists from Hungary were so brutally confronted with are much too diverse and complex but certainly no less vital for that.[17]

*Ferenc Laczó*
Maastricht University
2019

---

16 Michael Marrus, *Lessons of the Holocaust* (Toronto: University of Toronto Press, 2016), 6–8.

17 Dan Diner, "Epistemics of the Holocaust. Considering the Question of 'Why?' and of 'How?'" in *Naharaim - Zeitschrift für deutsch-jüdische Literatur und Kulturgeschichte*, 2008/2.

LEGEND

Borders from 1921 to 1938

Borders from 1939 to 1945

0      75      150km

N

Stutthof

WARSAW

Majdanek

POLAND

Neu-Dachs
Krakow

Lwów

Košice

Vízköz

Munkács

Kisvárda

Újfehértó

BUDAPEST
Túrkeve

Debrecen

ROMANIA

Nagyvárad

Cluj

GARY

Hódmezővásárhely

Szabadka

# The Unending Past
# Peter Vas

As soon as I arrived from Canada in Hungary I decided to visit the
    cemetery.
Since the war had ended, fifty years seamlessly have passed me by.
I return to the graves in the country I had left many years ago.
This land was my home, as it is for the trees rooted deep in the ground.
Deceived, betrayed native land, in the eye of mind it lost its grace.
My mind, deeply stirred by looking back,
When I passed under those large wrought-iron cemetery gates,
I thought: "I come only to have a few hours to mourn."
Then a shadow passed me and all the painful thoughts deluged my
    mind,
When I was standing face to face with my deep thoughts at my
    father's memorial site.
I faced the ten-foot-tall tablets of stones, hollow space and empty
    shrines,
Unending names without an ornament.

I feel I am standing here saying a Kaddish; it is my testament
Not only to my father, but to all who died in the war.
To those who were gassed in Auschwitz or beaten to death in Birkenau.
To the women who were raped and shot,

And their infants who were torn out of their wombs.
Men whom they starved and worked to death by the millions,
And who were deprived even of a basic human burial.
And to the children, those uncorrupted souls,
Many of them shot, gassed or cast into the water from the riverbank.
And for those countless victims who died of hunger and distress.
Why would one human do this to another?
What made this assembly-line murder happen?

A four-year-old cannot understand
These questions about life, the reasons, why we are suffering.
I silently witnessed it as a child, a world full of violence.
Someone has to speak for those who are dead.
Someone needs to remind those who try to forget.
This is demanded by the cries of the dead echoing from their graves.
Embedded in my memories is life as it had been.
I need something to hold on to, to restore its legacy.
In Hungary in the cemetery a sign above me says: "Killed by
    abominable hate."

I did not want to acknowledge my father's death;
Later I asked my mother, "Is my father ever coming back?"
I asked because I thought he didn't like us because maybe I was bad
And that was the reason he wasn't coming back.
She picked me up in her arms, held me to her heart, and with a sad
    face she looked at me.
With tearful eyes she said, "Your father is in heaven; he is never
    coming back."

For many years I had blamed him,
How could he leave us, how could he die on us?

Nobody should go through wars and destruction again;
The hate that killed him never should rise up again.
Sad and bitter memories we were trying to suppress.
But it always stays with us, we never really forget.
We remember for this lifetime, and for the future to come.
The bitterness and hate that war can bring should never happen.
This inhuman behaviour God can't justify to humans.
There can be no compensation in this world for such terrible crimes.

The Contradictions of
Daily Life under
Worsening Exclusion:
Experiences in Hungary
before 1944

# Foreword

The Jews of interwar Hungary, and especially those belonging to the dominant Neolog branch of Judaism,[1] tended to be highly assimilated and staunchly patriotic. More in accordance with Western and Central European patterns than was typical in much of Eastern Europe, the majority of Hungarian Jews were strongly integrated into gentile society while also recognizably different from the rest of society in terms of their socioeconomic positions, values and habits.

Hungary almost doubled its size between 1938 and 1941,[2] reconquering significant parts of the various lands it had lost at the end of World War I, and its Jewish population also nearly doubled

---

1 The Neolog branch of Hungarian Judaism, officially called Congress Judaism, was divided from the Orthodox and the Status Quo Ante communities in 1868–71, so Hungarian Jewry had three separate national organizations. Whereas the Orthodox and the Neolog communities were both large, with the Orthodox having more members at the time, the Neolog tended to be more advanced socioeconomically and also more Hungarianized in their cultural practices. The Neolog branch, while not strictly Orthodox, was as close to the Conservative as to the Reform branch of Judaism.

2 This expansion of Hungary took place in four steps: it consisted of the reassignment of southern parts of Czechoslovakia in 1938, the conquest of Subcarpathia in 1939, the reassignment of Northern Transylvania from Romania in 1940 and the conquest of part of the Vojvodina (Délvidék or Vajdaság in Hungarian) in 1941 upon the Nazi German-led attack on Yugoslavia.

to over 700,000 individuals. As a consequence, Hungary included many more Orthodox communities, especially in the northeastern region of Subcarpathia (which belongs to Ukraine today). The new territories that the country had gained made Hungary's Jewish community one of the largest and most diverse in Europe: on the eve of the country's entry into World War II in 1941, its diverse Jewish population covered practically the entire Jewish spectrum in modern Europe, from the wealthy, sophisticated and largely secularized metropolitan elite of Budapest to the Hasidic and Yiddish-speaking Jews in far-flung and barely modernized provinces.

After 1938, the persecution of the Jews in Hungary worsened and their situation became characterized by grave uncertainties. From 1938 until early 1944, in parallel with the country's territorial gains as a result of its commitment to the Axis cause, the authoritarian regime under Regent Miklós Horthy (1868–1957, in power between 1920 and 1944) radicalized its antisemitic agenda ever further. Antisemitism was manifested in multiple acts of legal discrimination against Jews: 1938 and 1939 saw the first two anti-Jewish laws, aimed primarily at discriminating against Jews in the professions, which, combined with a host of more specific restrictions, resulted in the forced economic pauperization of hundreds of thousands. In 1941, Hungary adopted Nazi-style racial legislation, banning intermarriage and sexual intercourse between "Jewish" men and "non-Jewish" (also referred to as "Christian") women.

These years also saw repeated acts of mass violence, including, most infamously, deportations from Subcarpathia to the killing fields of Nazi-occupied Ukraine in the late summer of 1941; mass murder in the re-annexed Vojvodina (Délvidék or Vajdaság in Hungarian) in January 1942, partly targeting Jewish people; and arbitrary executions of so-called labour servicemen (more on the latter in the next section of the book). Committed by representatives of the Hungarian state, these multiple acts of mass violence resulted in the violent deaths of tens of thousands of Hungarian Jews prior to 1944.

These acts of mass violence justify the adoption here of Saul Friedländer's expressions "years of persecution" and "years of extermination."[3] Originally used to denote two major periods of Nazi Germany's relation to the Jews (1933 to 1939 and 1939 to 1945, respectively), we may speak of Hungary's six years of persecution between 1938 and 1944 and a "year of extermination" coinciding with the last year of World War II in 1944–1945. The Hungarian years of persecution prepared the ground for the swift implementation of mass ghettoization and deportations in the spring and summer of 1944 — the fastest large act of genocide committed under the Nazis and their collaborators.

At the same time, even as Hungary was devoted to the cause of the Axis powers, officially joining the Tripartite Pact between Germany, Italy and Japan in November 1940, the large majority of Hungary's Jews — unlike most Jews from across the continent — did not yet have to confront the worst excesses of Nazi violence in 1941–1943. As sketched above, they suffered under severe legal restrictions, socio-economic exclusion and repeated instances of mass violence during these years, and yet most of them still felt comparably free on the Nazi-dominated continent. Although antisemitism was widely endorsed in Hungarian society and was reinforced by the open support shown by state institutions, as the memoirists in this section attest, everyday interactions between Jews and non-Jews ranged from the benevolent and harmonious to the deeply disturbing and murderously violent.

Even though the Hungarian state took numerous measures to exclude its Jewish population in the years prior to 1944, the identification of the Jewish leadership with their country and its leadership

---

3  While we follow Saul Friedländer's terminology here to make an important distinction, we are fully aware that scholars debate the appropriateness of using dehumanizing Nazi terms such as "extermination" to describe the mass murder and genocide committed by the Nazis against European Jews.

6 CONFRONTING DEVASTATION

tended to remain conspicuously high. In 1941–1943, Hungary was surrounded by even more murderously antisemitic regimes on all sides, such as Germany, Romania, Croatia and Slovakia, and could thus be perceived as a relatively safe haven for Jews. Paradoxically, Jewish identification with the country and its authoritarian and increasingly antisemitic regime might even have increased in these years. This surprising trend developed precisely because of the implementation of the Holocaust across almost all of Europe, which turned Hungary into a source of last desperate hopes. Some Jews from other countries indeed sought refuge in the country, only — as the story of Victor David excerpted below shows — to have to flee again in 1944 to what emerged as clearly safer places by then, such as Romania.[4]

Social integration and forced exclusion, a worsening socioeconomic situation and the preservation of a few freedoms, the seeming normality of everyday interactions and mass violence: these are the polarities that defined Jewish experiences during the Hungarian years of persecution between 1938 and early 1944. Stories of the experiences of Hungary's Jews in these years could be remarkably diverse and even contradictory: which of the aforementioned experiences predominated in the life of individuals depended on their social status, age, gender and exact location, as well as sheer luck. The selected excerpts from memoirs of survivors offer precious insights into the contradictory experiences of everyday life, while also showing the worsening exclusion of those years.

---

4 The Holocaust under Romanian and Hungarian rule took place at different times and was committed with different main methods. Whereas Romania was engaged in a most brutal campaign of mass murder during the earliest stages of the Holocaust, resulting in the death of hundreds of thousands, the Holocaust in Romania was practically over by the time the main phase of the ghettoization and deportation from Hungary started in the spring of 1944.

# Shattered Dreams
## Dolly Tiger-Chinitz

Memory is like a stained-glass window. Every little piece fits together, but every little piece should be your own. As the window grows, your personality is formed. You will view the world through this window for the rest of your life. Everything that happens to you that you remember, and the way you place that memory into your window frame, will make you the person you are, different from everyone else in the world. Not only is what happened to you important, but also how you view what happened to you. And while I will try to give a more or less chronological account of what happened to me, where and how, I will sometimes digress and give you a little bit of that coloured stained glass that formed my window on the world.

Life, at first, seemed idyllic: walks in the many beautiful parks of Budapest, or on Margaret Island where we plucked daisies and braided them into wreaths for our hair or picked horse-chestnuts to later fashion into doll-sized furniture; the Gellért Hill with the concrete slides in the summer and sledding in the winter; the beautiful chapel carved out from the rock, complete with a cave where a hermit dwelled. The Korzó on Sunday mornings, where we met other young girls being paraded by equally beautiful and fashionable mothers. But Mari and I were the only twins I can remember, which made us feel very special.

Budapest was a dream city. Tourists crowded the outdoor cafés, the women were chic, the cafés noisy and the air heavy with perfume, excitement and joie de vivre. The Prince of Wales visited, and the city was abuzz with his antics, with the debauchery that was too much for even the fun-loving Hungarians.

Spring was a time when on street corners young girls with round wicker baskets offered tiny bouquets of violets for sale, when the horse-chestnuts and the acacia trees were in bloom, when the amusement park opened its gates again and members of society went to the Gundel restaurant. Winter was the season when elegant people hurried to the cafés, the restaurants and the theatres, when the shore of the Danube River was transformed into a pine forest of Christmas trees for sale, and smells of incense wafted out of churches where the beautiful nativities were set up — our governess smuggled us in frequently. Christmas cards were displayed on the street by heavily clad women, and the smell of roasted chestnuts drifted in the bitingly cold air.

Mother, who we called by our nickname for her, Vinyi, was young, beautiful, extremely charming and popular. Together with her older sister, Elza, who we called Zuli — who was just as beautiful and even more outgoing, rich and scintillatingly intelligent — they were the toast of the town. There were the masquerade balls, the many theatres and cabarets. Every great artist of the day considered it a privilege to appear on stage before the very knowledgeable and discriminating Budapest audience. My mother saw the great ballet dancers Anna Pavlova and Vaslav Nijinsky. She often told us about Pavlova in the *Dying Swan*, when you could have heard a pin drop in the theatre; as Pavlova finished and crumpled in a little heap on the stage, tears rolled down her cheeks. Of Nijinsky in *Le Spectre de la rose* she said, "He did not leap; he floated in the air. It was miraculous." She also heard the singers Amelita Galli-Curci, Enrico Caruso and Beniamino Gigli, and she fell in love with operas as a little girl when her mother took her to outstanding performances at the sumptuous Hungarian State Opera House.

She continued the family tradition and from a very early age we considered it a thrilling treat to attend ballets, operas and special children's theatres. *The Fairy Doll* dazzled us with its colour, the dancing, the music recreating a fairy world on the stage. We simply refused to leave the theatre when it was over. I stubbornly pointed out that the words "The End" had not appeared on the "screen" (we had seen a few movies by then). The tickets that Mother purchased in advance for these performances were pinned on our door, so that if either of us "misbehaved" the tickets could still be removed — the biggest threat imaginable was that of depriving us of a much expected and hoped-for theatrical performance.

Suddenly, there were rumblings closer to home. One day, walking with the governess we chanced on a strange parade. Uniformed boys goose-stepping, throwing little pieces of paper on the ground. We rushed to pick them up. "Don't touch that," she screamed, "it is evil." What could be evil about little pieces of paper, little crosses with the arrows on top? "You don't understand," she muttered and pulled us away hastily from the parade.

But one day school was over, and we were at the railroad station, bags packed, Grandfather in tears, promising him we would come soon and write a lot. We travelled on to Szabadka, Subotica in Yugoslavia (now in Serbia). We moved into a real house with a yard completely dominated by an enormous linden tree. The furniture was familiar and so was the *mezuzah* on the door. But Mother slept in a big bed with Apu bácsi (Uncle Daddy) — that is how we were to call Mr. Paul — and everything else was very new too. I read all the time, probably trying to find something to hold on to. We were told that our name was now Paul, and a teacher came every day to teach us Serbo-Croatian, so we could enroll in Grade 4 by the fall. We also discovered that my mother's niece, Babi, got married and were miffed because the long-expected and dreamed-of wedding of hers took place without our participation. "We are living in historical times," Vinyi said, "it is not proper to make large weddings."

No beautiful Danube, no parks, gardens, theatres or museums; only dust and mud, unbearable heat; and no grandfather, no Zuli. We went often to Palić during the summer, but it was not the same — the long, boring tram-ride on the ancient open carriages, once the novelty wore off, was just uncomfortable. We fished and swam, and we started tennis lessons, but many of our new experiences were simply bewildering. A priest started coming regularly, giving us lessons in catechism. Puzzling new concepts indeed, while new friends we met — children of Vinyi's new friends — were still, comfortingly, just as always, Jewish.

In the fall we started school. None of the friends we had met during previous summers became our classmates. As it turned out, all of them attended the Jewish school but Apu bácsi insisted that we learn Serbo-Croatian in the public school. It proved less daunting for me than for Mari, and soon I became the teacher's pet and thus also the most unpopular girl in class. Vinyi went to Budapest. Our daily life became humdrum: school, study, meals eaten in silence with Apu, served by a surly cook.

When we concluded our lessons with the priest, we were told that we would be baptized and will be Catholics from now on. On the one hand, this seemed wonderful and truly important. On the other, only the maid accompanied us to the church. I thought some physical transformation would take place immediately afterwards, but the ceremony consisted only of a few prayers and a few drops of water.

We now lived in a new country, had new names, a new father, a new religion, a new house and new relatives we hated — everything that was meaningful and important hitherto in our lives was gone without being replaced. I had nightmares of not knowing where I was, who I was, trouble remembering my name, the new language, the new alphabet. The only thing we had was each other, and unfortunately we did not like each other very much.

One morning Apu came to our room to wake us up and told us that Grandfather had died and Vinyi would not be coming home for a while. The nightmare of our existence was closing in. I was unable to comprehend it and could not even shed tears. I asked Apu, "Does that mean I will not be able to go and see *The Son of Tarzan*?" He looked at me and said, "I thought you loved your grandfather." And he walked out of the room.

Vinyi indeed did not return home for many months. The family was sitting shiva to mourn, and they also had a huge estate to settle and a store to wind up. When Vinyi came back she was dressed completely in black, with a black veil on her hat that hid half of her face and went down low on her back. She was pale and thin and coughed and smoked even more than usual and spoke less.

We all survived, more or less, this terrible time of adjustment.

In the fall we were enrolled in a secondary school run by nuns. The choice must have been a bone of contention between our parents, as everyone else of our social standing was in the *Gimnázium* (the classic high school that almost predestines one for university studies). Our stepfather apparently preferred the lower-middle-class aspect of the four-year commercial school. Our studies were continued in Serbo-Croatian, and the friends we made at school were not acceptable to our mother. I remember one girl in particular called Varbai whose name soon became a legend. Her parents were janitors in a building owned by one of our parents' friends.

On our walk home from school one day, Varbai spotted a piece of rubber on the pavement that looked like a discarded balloon. She asked us whether we knew what this was. We, of course, did not. At this point she happily launched into a convoluted explanation about how babies are made with the help of a small rubber balloon and the parts of our bodies "down there." We were astounded at this newly acquired knowledge, and while we firmly believed that this was classified information, we confronted Vinyi to confirm the story. She was livid, denied any such goings-on among human beings as means towards procreation, and we were never allowed to speak to Varbai again. She also complained to her friends for whom Varbai's parents worked, and the parents almost lost their jobs. Our popularity among our classmates did not exactly skyrocket.

We heard the ominous wailing of the air raid sirens for the first time on Palm Sunday in 1941, on our way home from church. We ran home and stood in the garden, frightened, while a seemingly lost German plane, flying low, machine-gunned the town. There were no casualties; however, from that moment on the war was a palpable daily reality for us. The next day, Yugoslavia surrendered unconditionally to the Germans, and a few weeks later our part of the country was delivered lock, stock and barrel as a gift to Regent Horthy. There was some resistance in our town, some street to street fighting and sniping from rooftops by the Chetniks[1] or the Partisans (who hated each other though both of them hated the Hungarians), so we spent a good deal of our time in the cool cellar with Vinyi. She taught us how to play the card game Gin Rummy.

Regent Horthy arrived on a white horse one balmy spring day, and we were torn between jubilation (we are Hungarians again!) and the frightened disdain expressed by all the grownups around us.

When we went back to school, all the lessons were switched to Hungarian. Towards the end of the school year we came home rather upset and agitated. I questioned the cook about something the priest had told us during religion class: "What happens to someone when he is hanged?" She started wailing for our mother to come quickly to the kitchen and turned to the stove, heaving with sobs, stirring the pot frantically. "What did you want to know?" Vinyi asked. "What happens to someone when they hang him?" I repeated. "Where did you hear this?" she wanted to know. I told her that the priest told us that a bunch of communist Jews had been hung yesterday, the rabbi's son among them, and I would like to know what happened to them.

---

1   Yugoslavian insurgents who opposed their country's surrender to Germany.

Vinyi called my stepfather and asked him to return home from the store. Shouting ensued, during which there was a lot of crying by the cook and us, and we learned beyond doubt what happens to those who are hanged. We never went back to that school. While rumours of atrocities in Novi Sad were on everyone's lips, it was only much later that we found out what those atrocities in early 1942 actually were. Hundreds of Jewish males of Novi Sad were lined up at the bank of the Danube. To show their sympathy and their outrage, the Serbian men came and stood with them. Every tenth male was shot and thrown into the Danube. This was called "decimation."

We were on a train to Budapest within a few days and spent a very pleasant summer in a hotel in the Svábhegy district of Budapest. We saw a lot of our family again. My mother's sister, Zuli, and her husband, Uncle Imre Tieberger, were happy to have us around, and I fell in love for the first time. The boy's nickname was Szatyi, which was derived from his family name. He was very handsome, tall, sixteen years old, and actually talked and walked with me in the happy boredom of a summer resort. One evening as we were sitting on a bench arguing about the state of the world, he leaned over and kissed my cheek.

My sister and I started private lessons to help us integrate into the new school they were planning to send us to in Budapest. Although the convent of our choice did not accept children of Jewish origin, another one was found, humbler and cheaper, where they did accept us in spite of our parentage. Vinyi received a long list of clothing requirements and started shopping and sewing labels to prepare us for our entry. Puzzled by one of the items, she visited the convent and asked Sister Superior what a "bath shirt" was. The sister gently asked, "Madame, what do the little girls bathe in at home?" Vinyi replied, "In the bathtub." Sister blushed, "Well, yes, of course, but what are they wearing in the bathtub?" It was Vinyi's turn to look puzzled. "Nothing." The Sister patiently explained that wearing nothing in the bathtub is a sin, that one should not view one's body, so in the convent little shirts are worn.

So we started another grade of our middle school in a convent in Budapest. We wore uniforms, which eased our embarrassment of always being dressed alike: here everyone was dressed just the same. My sister and I drifted further and further from each other, making friends with different groups of girls. Our life, completely regimented, was also placid, peaceful and felt somewhat unreal. From an ebullient, loud, emotional environment, we had been plunged into the silence of the convent, with its strict restrictions on talking above a whisper, silently gliding nuns with their sombre habits and baby-like bows under their chins. At every turn there were nuns leaning over slightly to greet us and each other with a bow, saying in Latin, "Laudetur Jesus Christus." (Praised be Jesus Christ.)

Then the regular air raids started.

In the middle of the night we had to get out of bed, freezing, shivering with fright, sleepy, marching in pairs down to the basement shelter while waiting for the "all clear" to sound. The bombings were scary, but they became a part of life's routine, accepted like so many other very unpleasant things had gotten accepted lately. Life went on.

Then school was over, and it was summer again — a summer I have difficulty remembering. There were trips back and forth between Subotica and Budapest, and the tension and anxiety continued. We were not at the centre of the universe any longer.

~

Late in the fall of 1943, Vinyi and Mari and I went to Budapest. There we joined Zuli, Imre bácsi and a widowed friend of theirs with her fourteen-year-old son, Bubi, in order to drive to the Mátra Mountains for the High Holy Days. We drove under cloudy, rain-darkened skies. We were thrilled, singing all the way, as an exuberant holiday mood permeated our little party.

A room in our hotel was designated as the synagogue, where the men prayed, swaying and chanting, wrapped in their large prayer shawls. We took long walks, breathed the marvellous mountain air, enjoyed the springy, pine-needle-covered paths under the gigantic pines, the good food and the company of an older boy. Bubi was gloating with self-importance to be the indispensable tenth man at the prayer gatherings and could not make up his mind which one of us he preferred. We all marched down to the little brook and emptied our pockets of crumbs, in the traditional *taschlich* ceremony, and tried for the first time to fast on Yom Kippur.

Schools did not reopen on time that fall. Because clustering children in schools, all in one place, might expose too many of them to excessive danger, a wait-and-see attitude was adopted by the government, and lessons for children were broadcast every morning over the radio. In the meantime, the Allies were steadily advancing, so the news about the war was good, as we heard that it may finally be winding down.

Our family had gathered once more in Subotica during the previous months of the summer: Zuli, Vinyi and Babi congregated in Vinyi's sumptuous light-blue satin-bedecked bedroom. We were called in solemnly and enlightened with new information. We were told the "facts of life," a completely new concept to me: all of this has to be done in order to have babies; it is done on the wedding night ("Nicholas did that to you, Babi?" — I was nonplussed); it is all very unpleasant and painful, and women bleed every month in preparation for future child-bearing. Mari haughtily declared that she knew all about it already, culling her facts from various books and encyclopedias. I was aghast at the plethora of new information and her prior knowledge. I went to Marcel, our cook, to check out the story. She blushed and confirmed it. We were thus prepared to face approaching adolescence.

But the talk among the adults was chiefly about the war. They discussed the likelihood that Hungary could avoid the destruction suffered wholesale in other parts of Europe. And they worried about whether we could avoid organized "action" against the Jews, rumours of which reached and frightened all of us. The young men of our town, including Nicholas, were already in forced labour brigades, and some others had become POWs during the short-lived Yugoslav war against the Axis.

News reached us only sporadically while everyone dreaded the approaching winter. Zuli — ever practical, shrewd, pragmatic — decided that what we needed most at this time was Christian friends. She established a solid friendship with two women in Budapest. One was a widow of a very high-ranking army officer, who had a son, also called Bubi, who was a cadet in a good military school. The woman was young and pretty, now living with another high-ranking officer whom she did not marry so as not to lose the pension from her first husband. We drank in these little snippets of delicious gossip with glee. Her other new friend, Júlia Szentirmay, was also a widow with a son, Gyuri. Júlia was a once wealthy and now somewhat impoverished woman, who was awed by the friendship offered by Mrs. Tieberger; she would do anything for any of us, should the need arise.

In mid-October, we were back in the convent. School life had to go on, and a sense of normalcy seemed to be returning to our lives. The food was worse now, even scarcer than it was the previous year. Rumours were rampant about what was going to happen to Jews (there was only one other Jewish girl in the convent). Bombing raids intensified in ferocity and number, and there was hardly a night we could sleep undisturbed. We became experts at guessing whether it was the Soviets or the Americans bombing. I slept with a miniature teddy bear.

However, as the nuns reassured us, all was not lost, and we could all be redeemed with even more prayer and self-sacrifice. They told us to dedicate our lives to Jesus for the many sins committed by our parents and grandparents (your mother got divorced! Jews don't go to heaven!). Frightened, passionately trying to do the right thing, I promised to become a nun.

# My Surprising Escapes
# Benedikt Korda (Kornreich)

It was not my intention to stay in Hungary and especially not in Munkács. I had good reasons for that. I was known as a Czechophile and a leftist. In wartime Hungary, those were sins that could be used against you. News travels fast, even through airtight borders, and I already knew that some of my former friends had become active Nazis. Two of them became notorious as brutal torturers in the Hungarian political police. I also knew that the worst atrocities were now over and that some normalcy — whatever that meant in conditions of war and under German pressure — had returned to Hungary. In fact, as I learned later, liberal elements in the Hungarian political elite were far from dead. Alas, in 1944, when the Nazis invaded wavering Hungary, all their efforts came to naught. Anyway, in my reasoning Hungary was not my goal: it was just a stage in a longer journey out of the German orbit. But things often don't turn out as one plans.

My journey to Budapest was an adventure I wouldn't want to repeat. At noon on December 23, 1942, I boarded the express train from Prague to Vienna with connection to Budapest. After the fact, it still remains a mystery to me how I got on that train. There were no reservations in those days. You had to just buy a ticket and fend for yourself. It was my fault that I didn't take into account the simple fact that the Christmas season is the busiest time of the year, especially in wartime. Thousands of soldiers and "volunteers" working in Germany were travelling on furlough. To say that my train was already filled to capacity when I arrived would be a gross understatement. There was no room to sit and no room to stand either. The cabins, the corridors, everything was full; one couldn't drop a penny. Somehow, I managed to push my way with my luggage to the middle of the corridor. I felt terrible pain as human bodies squeezed me from all sides. Because of the luggage standing in front of me I couldn't straighten out. I was scared, too, since a worker on the train could kick me out if he found out that I was a Jew. Who would dare to help me?

In spite of all that, I tried to reassure myself. It's only a few hours, just hold out. But the train wouldn't move. It was long past departure time when the train started moving slowly, and a new concern crept into my mind. I was worried that leaving late meant I would miss my connection to Budapest. It was indeed too late for the connection when we arrived in Vienna; it was past midnight, and the Budapest express was long gone.

What now? The railway station was full, and I was not the only one who had missed their connection. There were thousands there, with police mingling among them looking for deserters. Twenty hours in this stench, without sleep, with no food or drink? I was numb, I was desperate. The first light of dawn was already visible when I noticed a slowly moving Hungarian freight train with some passenger cars attached to it. Such trains stop everywhere, so they are, as a rule, too slow. But what the hell — it was still better than this rotten station. I enquired. "Yes, we are going to Budapest. Yes, we can take you. We'll be leaving in about fifteen minutes." It was fantastic. On the move again. It was a tremendous relief to be able to sit down, to stretch or even to lie down on a wooden bench. The train was half-empty. Not many people travel at night. Most importantly, I was able to wash off the long day's dirt and it washed off my sleepiness as well.

The passengers were all Hungarian. I listened to their conversations and, as a stranger, asked some questions. I knew that life was more relaxed in Hungary, but still I was surprised. They spoke relatively freely. It was obvious from the conversation that they were quite well off (the German war effort caused an economic boom in the neighbouring countries). The kind of food supply problems we had in Prague they, apparently, didn't know. "Well, we have ration cards too, but for bread only. Even that's not serious. You can get as much as you need." I made a fool of myself. We had a stop at a small town and I noticed in a shop window a huge pile of beautiful apples. "That's not rationed either?" My companion had a good laugh. Fruit rations in Hungary? What a foolish question! Well, tough luck too. Shops are closed on holidays, so I couldn't taste the good apples.

At last the train stopped in Budapest. I knew Budapest from hearsay only, but I had never set foot there before. I heaved a sigh of relief. It could not be worse than Prague, anyway. I knew for sure that it would be much better than in Prague. I felt some sadness too. What I left behind was a piece of my life, all my friends and my kids. Would I ever see them again? I also had to cope with some feelings of insecurity concerning my future. A new phase in my life was about to begin and it started with some surprises.

Budapest had a large Jewish population. I already knew from numerous stories that Dohány Street was a Jewish street and that the hotel there (which I believe was of the same name as the street), was patronized predominantly by Jews. After my experiences in Prague I wouldn't have dared go elsewhere. "Can I help you?" "I hope you can. Have you got a room for me?" "How long are you going to stay?" "Let's say a week." "Hmm, I have nothing for tonight, but I have here two young men from Munkács who have a big room with three beds, I'm sure they won't mind sharing it with you." They didn't. The two guys were about twenty, much younger than me. I was glad to be with them. I craved company, especially Jewish company, to get some interesting information. After all, I was in a new country. They were in Budapest on business, but I don't remember what kind of business. What I do remember was that their first concern after arriving in Budapest was girls. Well, that wasn't going to be a problem to arrange in Budapest. The concierge had a list of call girls, and as it turned out, my boys already knew some of them from prior visits.

So what, one might say. Boys are boys and sex was not invented yesterday. True, but my mind was still in Prague. No Jewish man would dare approach a gentile girl of a certain profession there. As we talked, in Hungarian and partly in Yiddish, they surprised me more and more. Business is good, they told me. Hungary, like Slovakia and other German satellites, was enjoying a wartime boom. It seemed to me that their business success was the only thing that interested them. What if their business deals helped the German war effort? I am sure such questions never occurred to them. Business is business. Did they know about the fate of Jews in neighbouring countries, especially in countries as close to Munkács as Poland or Slovakia? Of course, it was impossible to remain completely ignorant. But I had the impression that they either knew very little or didn't care. What's going on there, over the hills, is sad. But we are here, it's relatively calm here and business is good. For a newcomer from another planet, which I was, their unconcerned attitude was astonishing. They were far from alone, and soon I met many others with the same attitude.

Another surprise came in the restaurant where I went for supper. The waiter who took my order asked me almost apologetically whether I had ration cards. "You don't? Never mind, I have some extra cards." "What do you need ration cards for, anyway? Is there any rationing here?" "Yes, bread is rationed." "Oh well, I don't need bread at supper." For a Hungarian waiter, it was hard to conceive of supper without bread. "I'll bring you some in any case."

Supper was good and food was plentiful. As I learned in the days to come, nobody in Hungary took food rationing seriously. This shouldn't have surprised me — Hungary had been a significant food producer and exporter. But I still remembered the end of World War I, when there was rationing and food shortages. Now, in the fourth year of the war, the supply situation still seemed to be close to normal. What a sharp contrast to Prague.

The biggest and most pleasant surprise was the political situation of the country. I did expect a more relaxed situation than in Prague, albeit not much more. But the difference was striking. Let me start with the press. The paper I bought in the morning was refreshing. There was still some freedom of the press. They rigorously questioned government policies, including war policies. From the papers, I got some insight into the workings of the parliament. The exchanges in the parliament were sometimes lively, like in the good old days. This suggested to me that democracy was not dead yet. I remember one parliamentarian saying, "Our fellow citizens of Jewish extraction who fell on the fronts while fulfilling their duties in labour units are war heroes, the same as other fallen soldiers." To me, such utterances sounded like voices from a different planet. The deputy in question was familiar to me from pre-war days, when he had been a journalist in Czechoslovakia and an outspoken antisemite. Apparently, he retained a measure of human decency. I had a number of such pleasant surprises. It was also surprising that Hungarian papers printed obituaries of Jews who "died the heroes' death" somewhere on the shores of the Don River. Sad and cruel as the whole story of those Jewish "mine-sweepers" on the Don front was, I considered the printing of those obituaries in Hungarian papers remarkable.

But I don't mean to exaggerate. Freedom of the press and the workings of the democratic institutions were far from perfect in Hungary in those days. The fact that Hungary, which was subservient to the Nazis, still had an elected and working parliament was, in my view, remarkable. There were such parties in the parliament as the Social Democratic Party and the Smallholders' (Peasant) Party. The latter did an especially good job. Its courageous leader, Endre Bajcsy-Zsilinszky, was murdered in 1944.

Let me explain why the "liberal" atmosphere in Hungary surprised me so much. There was a sharp contrast between the atmosphere in Hungary and the one in Germany and occupied territories and puppet states like Slovakia and Croatia. In the latter, the press, for example, had been tightly, even absolutely, controlled by the Nazis. Not only was it impossible to print any independent opinion, the news itself was scrutinized and deliberately manipulated. The Germans coined the term *Gleichschaltung*[1] for that tight control of the press. I didn't know then that a new Hungarian government was installed in 1942 in Budapest and inaugurated real changes in policies. This government, headed by Miklós Kállay, was less subservient to the Nazis and more liberal than the former one. Such "unpleasant" news items would have never appeared in the German press.

Regarding the political scene in general, the contrast was even sharper. There was no trace of democracy left in Germany. The Nazis openly despised democracy as a degenerate system. Their one-party system (similar in this way to the Soviet one) was totalitarian, with all aspects of life controlled by the government. Though the Hungarian political system was far from ideal, there were at least elements of democracy in it. It was miles away from Nazi totalitarianism, more different from it than I had expected.

Hungary was Nazi Germany's ally, even if sometimes a reluctant one. I think that the main reason they allied themselves with the Nazis was their own desire to reconquer the vast territories they had lost after World War I. The rise and rapid expansion of Nazi Germany provided a good opportunity. Thanks to the Nazis, Hungary gradually recovered virtually all the territories lost to Romania, Czechoslovakia and Yugoslavia (not quite all of the territories, since the Nazis found it more useful to create two "independent" countries, Slovakia and Croatia, both fascist and virulently antisemitic). I was at that time

---

1   This German word was used by the Nazis to refer not only to the control of the press but to the entire process of coordination by which all aspects of German society were aligned with Nazi goals and ideology. Using laws, propaganda and purges, Hitler brought arts and culture, the economy, government and education under Nazi control in his first years as leader.

under the spell of leftist slogans, which oversimplified things (just as they do today). According to these slogans, Hungary was simply "fascist," regardless of who was at the helm. Some facts seemed to support such a view, but reality is always more complicated than slogans.

There were excesses in the reconquered territories, the worst and bloodiest of which were in Vojvodina (a region taken from Yugoslavia), where many Jews and Serbs were massacred. There were atrocities in Munkács too. Fascist and antisemitic elements seemed to get a free ride. The worst and saddest anti-Jewish atrocity of that period was the deportations of the so-called stateless persons, people with no citizenship (Jews, of course). There were thousands of those unfortunate ones (many from Munkács and its environs), men, women and children, who were rounded up in the summer of 1941 and deported to Nazi-occupied Ukraine. There, they were mostly massacred by Nazi Einsatzgruppen. Only a handful survived.

Hungary introduced a number of anti-Jewish laws too. (How much of that anti-Jewish legislation was due to pressure from Germany is irrelevant, and for sure not all of it was.) One of these laws relegated all Jewish males of military age to forced labour. Since this is part of my story, I have to tell more about it. I was in Prague, and news in those days didn't travel as fast as it does today. Jews were expelled from the army (military service was mandatory for males of certain age groups in all European countries) and put in labour camps. It was not called forced labour. Allegedly, it was just a substitute for military service called Auxiliary Labour Service. The inmates were organized in battalions under military supervision and discipline. They had the same paybooks as soldiers and the same pay as privates (which meant pennies). They didn't get uniforms, just an armband, but were paid for the wear and tear on their clothes (again, no more than pennies). The labour companies were managed by a commandant and his deputy, both officers, and a handful of sergeants or privates, the so-called *keret*, frame in English, who supervised the work.

The problem was that in some of those units, especially in remote places, the "frame boys" had absolute power over the inmates, and more often than not they used it to satisfy their sadistic inclinations. I heard numerous stories from former inmates of such companies about beatings, torture and death. The situation was especially bad in units sent to the Soviet front to clear the terrain of mines, which was cruelty of the highest degree. Those labour companies were neither trained nor equipped for mine-sweeping work. They were not even outfitted for the hard Russian winter. Many of them died, killed by exploding mines, by Soviet bullets and also by simply freezing to death, as well as at the hands of Hungarian sadists. Among the dead were a number of people from Munkács. One of them, a friend of ours, had the misfortune of having a good winter outfit, including fine custom-made boots coveted by one of the frame boys. He refused to give up his boots and was shot in cold blood. Our brother-in-law, Tibor, was on the Don front too and was shot there, but miraculously, he survived.

There is no free lunch, and Hungary had to repay the favours from their German benefactor. Hungary sent a sizable army to the Soviet front, where they got a good licking. This loss had a sobering effect on the political elite and led to a rethinking of Hungarian policies. When I arrived in Hungary, the worst atrocities seemed to be over. Not only that, there were debates in the parliament about some of the past excesses. Investigations and judiciary procedures were started in some of the cases. How they ended and whether the perpetrators were ever punished, I don't know, as I soon found myself in one of those labour units and was not able to follow up on things.

But I started to learn about the subtleties of Hungarian politics. The Hungarian political elite was far from unanimous in joining the German side during the grave drama that started to unfold in the late thirties. The opponents of the alliance with Germany apparently got a boost when the fortunes of war started changing in favour of the anti-German alliance. Part of the Hungarian political elite was convinced, especially when the United States had entered the war, that Germany was going to lose. Allegedly, even Regent Horthy belonged to this category. Whether it was true or not I'll never know, but the fact is that early in 1942 he appointed a new government with Miklós Kállay as prime minister.

Kállay was an old fox, a liberal politician. He introduced a measure of civil liberties, including some increased freedom of the press. The situation for Jews also improved under his premiership, since Jews received a degree of legal protection. When I arrived in Budapest, I didn't know much about any of that. That's why the Hungarian press surprised me so much. I was lucky that I was not in Munkács in the early days of Hungarian rule. I could have been caught in the nets of their secret police, as many of my friends had been. They were as brutal as the Gestapo.

Labour service for Jews remained in place, but some of the most brutal excesses subsided. There was a new problem there too. Who is a Jew? The Hungarians had adopted the Nazi concept, which is racial, without realizing that they didn't fit in the Nazi scheme of "Aryan" dominance over the world. Hungarians did not qualify as "Aryans." Their origins are different. At first, for Hungarian antisemites, Jewish was a purely religious concept and identity. For pious Hungarians, it seemed improper to treat converts to Christianity, and especially their children, as Jewish. A dilemma arose over how to treat Christian Jews, those Christians who were now classified as Jews. The solution to the dilemma was illogical, almost funny. But who would bother with logic in that strange time period? They simply organized two types of labour camps distinguished by the colour of armbands the inmates wore. The "Jewish" Jews wore yellow armbands; the "Christian" Jews had white armbands. The whites had it somewhat better than the yellows. No wonder, then, that many young (and not so young) Jews tried to get into the ranks of the white armbands by any means, most frequently by purchasing baptismal certificates. Well, that's the law of the market: where there is demand, there is supply. Some clergy were so kind as to make the mitzvah of "instant baptism." That they were rewarded with some cash already in this world is beside the point. I would end up among the white armbands too.

# Only When I Laugh
# Imrich Vesely

The trip to Budapest was normally a simple matter. One would board the express train in Bratislava, have dinner in the dining car and arrive a few hours later in Budapest with the taste of Hubertus liqueur still in the mouth.

However, in November 1938 there was no such thing as a normal train ride. I anticipated considerable hassle at the Hungarian customs, so I thought I would make a detour to my hometown first and seek the advice of some relatives who lived near the old border.

The train was packed with refugees and my doubts about ever reaching my destination grew with every mile. Sure enough, after an hour's travel, the train stopped in an open field. We soon figured out why. A bunch of Hlinka[1] thugs came aboard and started throwing people out of the cars by the dozen. There was a lot of shouting, shoving and yelling, mixed with the cries of the victims, as the motley crew of pimple-faced adolescents and grown men drunk with the glory of power brandished their weapons and decided the fate of the people on the train. The passengers — young, old, rich, poor, men, women and children — were helpless.

Citizens yesterday, cattle today, and tomorrow? "Identification!" barked a voice. Two storm troopers stood before me.

---

1   The Hlinka Guard was a Slovakian paramilitary force that persecuted and terrorized Jews and other individuals.

A shorter trip than I expected. I thought it was all over. There wasn't a remote chance of escape and in all my papers the word Jew was mentioned prominently. I slowly reached into my pocket.

"Come on, come on!" yelled the smaller of the two. "We haven't got all day!"

Why put it off any longer? It was best to get the damned thing over with. I took out my wallet and opened it.

"Hey, what do you want from that one? I've checked him out already," yelled another voice.

A third storm trooper stood before me. I did my best to look at him with a blank face. His name was Durshansky, and he was a former fellow clerk from the hardware store. I suppose he looked rather stupid in his improvised Nazi uniform but to me he looked like the most intelligent and most attractive fellow in the world. Everything is possible in a madhouse. It's even possible to find a human being inside a costume with Death written all over it.

Years later, Durshansky stood trial before a special tribunal that handled the cases of former Nazis. On the strength of my testimony, he was given a light sentence.

Many of the passengers never returned to the train. They were herded into a group guarded by armed louts. Their luggage was removed by eager hands and put on a truck. How noble it is to fight under the banner of a grand ideology, especially when one's loyalty to the cause can be demonstrated by looting and brutalizing the weak.

It seemed an eternity before the train started to move again. It was seven o'clock the next morning when I reached my transfer point. What was normally a two-hour trip had taken eleven hours and I now had to wait twenty-three hours for my next train.

It was cold, windy and raining. All the hotels were full — not that it mattered, for I had very little money — so I tried to find shelter inside the door of a hotel. It was paradise short-lived. In a minute or so, the porter appeared. Since it was obvious he was about to throw me out, I decided to do the honours myself. It was less humiliating that way. I started towards the street. The porter called after me.

"Hang on, son, I see you're cold. I go on duty in a few minutes and you can sleep in my bed." He didn't have to say it twice. I jumped into his bed and I was fast asleep in no time.

The next morning, I took the train to my hometown, Šurany. The whole town was upside down, with everybody scared, mixed-up and hysterical. The good citizens had woken up one fine morning to discover they were now part of Hungary, and the forced replacement of state personnel, the so-called "changing of the guard," was under way. The new Hungarian authorities were exactly as disorganized as their Czechoslovakian counterparts who were in the process of leaving. Everything was hanging in mid-air and nobody wanted to take any responsibility. Chaos reigned.

Of one thing I was sure. I could sleep under a roof that night since my relatives owned the local hotel. Actually, the place had been built for them by my father; my sister and I were supposed to have shares in it.

My relatives must have thought that I had come to collect from them, for they received me without a trace of enthusiasm. I promptly decided not to outstay my welcome. The relatives were greatly relieved when I said that I didn't want a thing and, with a bit of luck, would leave them the next day. Their guarded behaviour turned to overt expressions of great joy. With a grand gesture — what the hell, the world was coming to an end anyway — they bought my railway ticket to Budapest. It was a good way of making sure that I wouldn't change my mind about the time of departure.

Ah, the warmth that a family can provide… Unfortunately, I considered the train ticket to be the least of my headaches on my way to Budapest.

Since nobody knew what to do, government bureaucracy operated under the old rules — most of the time. I knew that trains were still being stopped at the old border crossing point, at Komárom, to check passports and visas. Those without proper papers were held up or turned back, including those who had come from places that were by then under Hungarian jurisdiction.

Little did I know that the day wasn't too far away when I would remember those chaotic times as the good old days of peace...

The next morning, I took leave of my relatives. They all came to see me off at the station — no doubt to make sure that I was really leaving. When both my feet were on the steps of the train, Uncle Vilmos gave me a twenty-pengő bill as yet another grand gesture.

I arrived back at Érsekújvár, my transfer point. By that time, Hungarian troops were in charge and certain attempts had been made to establish some sort of order. As the civilian authorities were still in limbo, I went to the army headquarters. I told the commandant who received me after hours of waiting that I was Hungarian, born of Hungarian parentage, and that I couldn't find work and wanted to go to Budapest and try my luck there.

I must have been fairly convincing because he immediately gave orders to prepare travel and entry permits for me. The officer who was preparing my documents looked up from his desk.

"Are you Jewish?"

My heart stopped. If I said "No" and he checked my papers, I'd be in big trouble — probably bigger than if I said yes. I made what seemed the smarter choice. I nodded. The officer looked at me a long time, pen in hand. Then, without saying another word, he signed the papers. Why? Did he like me? Was he sorry for me?

What motivates people in authority to decide in favour of one person at one moment and against another at the next, without any good reason?

～

There was a Room to Let sign on the gate of a mid-town apartment building and I decided to take a look. Apartments in middle-class neighbourhoods all had a maid's room and badly paid civil servants or teachers — or their widows — would often rent out this small room. The one I looked at was an extraordinarily unattractive little rathole but it had one important characteristic: it was cheap.

I gave ten pengős advance to the landlady and with that I was a Budapestian with an address. I unpacked quickly, washed myself and went back to the street. I bought myself a bag of French fries and a movie ticket and sat down on the plush seat like a playboy without a worry in the world.

What about a job? What about food? What about a roof over my head next week? Who cared about petty things like that when the glittering, silver marquee outside held a million dancing light bulbs that spelled out the magic words, Errol Flynn in *Robin Hood*? I was bursting with optimism and joie de vivre. Why not? I was twenty-one, damn it!

After living under the freely rampaging Slovak Nazis, I saw Hungary as a dream-like oasis. In spite of the fact that the country's economic and political life were greatly under Berlin's influence, the government had gone to great lengths to maintain the appearance of independence. Apart from the obvious propaganda angle, there was a very solid reason for not hugging Hitler openly. The centuries-old hatred of the Germans was still very much alive in the hearts of many Hungarians, even if it appeared as though their national rebirth came as a result of the German presence.

The streets of Budapest and smaller towns and villages were still fairly safe but the dams had been cracked and the flood was only a matter of time. Nazi hoodlums weren't on the loose yet, as in Slovakia, but their party was growing steadily. Their newspapers, fashioned after their great example, *Der Stürmer*, did their best to emulate the vicious tone of their German masters. Hatred, mainly against Jews, permeated their pages and they seemed to enjoy immunity from all rules and laws, written and unwritten.

Their systematic attacks and accusations against Jews were not without results. Legislation had been passed to curtail the role of Jews in the economy. A new law called for a quota system. The so-called Jewish Bill in 1939 limited the employment of Jews to six percent of the workforce — slightly higher for labourers. Also, Jewish owner-ship of businesses was drastically reduced.

Of course, I didn't worry myself too much about the Jewish Bill while watching Errol Flynn as Robin Hood in colour. It was the first time I saw colour on the screen.

He must have given me some inspiration, or else I was born under a lucky star, because the next day at nine in the morning I got a job. I became a labourer in the stockroom of a hardware store. The salary was lousy, twenty pengős a week, and the work was hard, but it was a job and I had something to live on. I was in no position to be choosy. I sat down immediately to write to Mother about my good fortune. I didn't mention what the job was. It would have made her sad.

Unfortunately, I didn't have to hide the facts from Mother too long. One morning my boss told me that a man of "Aryan" back-ground had applied for my position and he had to let me go. I was quite upset and so was my employer. He tried to console me by saying that a good-looking lad like me would find another job in no time. What else could he say or do?

I wasn't in a mad rush to get home. As I walked the streets slowly, my head down, a man stopped me and asked if I would help him across the road. He was old and had trouble seeing and was scared in the traffic. I helped him and he thanked me profusely. I looked at him and thought how happy he would be to change places with me and take all my troubles if he could only have my youth and strength as well. The fact that I wasn't the most miserable, lowliest pariah of Budapest gave me a little lift. I straightened my back, looked up and enjoyed the lovely, late autumn sunshine.

Beautiful as the autumn sun was, it couldn't prevent the dwindling of my money supply and the rent was due. I looked for any kind of job. Nothing. Then I tried the other side of the Danube, Buda, hoping to have better luck there. In one of the streets, a group of road-menders was working. I quickly figured out which of them was the foreman and asked him if he could use one more man. He sized me up. "Do you have work clothes?"

"This is my only suit but I'm willing to start right this minute."

It didn't take him long to see that I was in trouble and needed the work. He gave me a sledgehammer and a pair of leather knee protectors and in a few minutes I was breaking stones on the pavement of the ancient capital of Hungary.

~

I found another ad in one of the evening papers: "German-Hungarian hardware firm is looking for bilingual, certified clerks. Aryan background." The ad was tailor-made for me — except for the "Aryan" part, but nobody's perfect. Aryan or not, the next morning I took a bath, put on my best clothes and went to apply. The firm was located in the old downtown of Pest. It was a district of large, stately townhouses and sedate apartment buildings. The stores were expensive and glamorous, their clientele a mixture of patrician, upper middle class and nouveau riche. Somehow I got a job offer and started working in the company's big warehouse, near the docks where the freighters arrived to load and unload. The store rooms were filled with merchandise that was hard to sell. My job was to keep the place in order and sell whatever I could.

Soon I was so involved in my work and so happy at my successes that I almost forgot what kind of a world I was living in. I was busy running here and there, meeting buyers and suppliers as if it were the most natural thing on earth for a Jewish refugee kid from Slovakia to hold a well-paid, high position — even though unofficially — in a company with strong German ties. Following the Sunday luncheon, my boss had invited me several times to his house. I was treated as a family member by him and his wife.

What stronger proof was there of my boss's trust in me than the fact that he had put me in charge of the export and import business that had to go through the German consulate? Our firm dealt with representatives from a number of German companies and, through them, we received numerous orders for materials used in the German war industry. We would ship out entire trainloads of barbed wire and other hardware. It was my job to keep records of what was sent where and when and what else was to be shipped. Because I was fluent in German, I was soon given the job of taking the orders as well.

I developed a very good relationship with one of the consulate's chief clerks in the commerce department. He was a very important person for us, because he was in charge of checking quotations and tenders and it was up to him who got the order.

Shortly after I entered the picture, my boss noticed, with surprise, that the guy at the consulate had hardly a word to say about prices whereas before he had been a pain in the neck who would find a flaw in everything and bargain like a Baghdad street vendor. Well, the change in his attitude wasn't quite accidental. Every time I submitted a quotation to him, it was accompanied by a small token of my friendship, which, in turn, probably helped him to come to the conclusion that the German Reich and its beloved Führer would somehow survive in spite of him paying a few pennies more for a metre of wire. The small tokens of my friendship included a shotgun with inlaid silver decoration, a gold cigarette lighter and other choice expressions of esteem.

I had no reason to complain about my financial situation. I had been with the firm for a year and my bank account showed a balance of ten thousand pengős. In winter, I wore a fur-lined coat. I had ten suits as well as the necessary shirts, shoes and accessories. I took a larger room from my landlady. In short, I lived well.

An invitation arrived one morning in the mail. My friend at the German consulate had sent it to me. It was for the annual German Ball, held at one of the most luxurious hotels in Budapest. Me at the German Ball... Some joke. I decided to write a polite note of regret, with an even more polite excuse, and stay home. My boss, however, disagreed.

"Just go and buy yourself the proper evening clothes, white tie, everything...." He spoke as if complying with the dress code was my only problem in attending the ball. It was one thing to conduct business on behalf of my employer's well-connected firm and quite another to hobnob with dangerous people. Awkward questions could be asked and a slip of the tongue could bring big trouble on everybody concerned.

The boss remained stubborn. I saw that there was undeniably a grotesque, humorous side to it all.... Naturally, in the end I decided to go through with it, come what may.

The full impact of my childish prank didn't dawn on me until I entered the posh ballroom and stared right into Hitler's moustache. The Führer's portrait, the size of a movie screen, stared back threateningly. I was sure that at any moment he would pounce on me off the wall. As if that wasn't enough, the man presiding over the VIP table was none other than the infamous Nazi propaganda minister, Joseph Goebbels — not in portrait, in person.

My friend from the consulate came to greet me and took me to his table to introduce me to his wife. After the customary exchange of niceties, I was about to withdraw but he wouldn't hear of it. He invited me to join them at their table as their guest and we ate the lavish dinner together. Unfortunately, I couldn't fully enjoy the meal because I had a great deal to be nervous about. How many of the several hundred guests might know me? Hitler's portrait and Goebbels' presence also failed to increase my appetite one little bit. My presence at the ball had suddenly lost all the humorous aspects I had seen before I accepted the invitation.

If I felt rotten during dinner, guess how I felt during dessert. My friend told me, with great excitement in his voice, that he had arranged a surprise for me. In order to reciprocate all the favours I had extended to him, he was going to introduce me to Goebbels.

He couldn't have found a more shattering climax to an already disastrous dinner, and bowing out with any excuse would have been more than suspicious. It would have been an affront. It was a thoughtful gesture on behalf of my friend who had every right to expect me to be thrilled by so great an honour.

With the same joy one feels on the way to the dentist's chair, I followed my friend to the head table. To my surprise, Goebbels didn't exactly fit the Teutonic Warrior image the Nazis were so fond of projecting. He was neither tall nor blond nor blue-eyed. He reminded one more of an underdeveloped chimpanzee, with the notable difference that chimpanzees aren't vicious.

The honourable minister shook my hand and greeted me cordially. My friend told him briefly about our dealings. His Excellency listened attentively, then, loudly enough for the whole table to hear, said how splendid it was that the cheating, conniving Jews had been pushed aside so that our two nations could enjoy a pleasant, trouble-free business relationship as this "fine young gentleman" was there to prove.

Thus, with one sweeping stroke, I had become a fine young gentleman as well as the very embodiment of "Aryan" business ethics. It's all in a day's work....

During the rest of the evening it became apparent that members of the Supreme Race were very good at consuming liquor but not so good at holding it. Much as I love music, drunken Germans bawling tavern songs and patriotic marches are not my kind of entertainment, so it was time for me to discreetly leave.

# My Escape to and from Hungary
# Victor David

I was born David Mojzesz in 1922 in a Polish town called Przemyśl,
but I spent most of my childhood in Lwów (now Lviv, Ukraine). In
September 1939, after the war started and Poland was divided between the Germans and the Soviets, eleven members of my close
family were deported to Siberia, where most survived. But of the remaining fifteen, I am the only survivor. For years I kept wondering,
"Why me?"

The Germans came to Lwów at the end of June 1941, singing as
they rode through the city on motorcycles and trucks. I felt no immediate fear, but the next day the Ukrainians staged a pogrom, and
within days anti-Jewish policies were brutally imposed. It didn't take
long for us to realize that we were in danger unless we could obtain
certain documents stating that we were working in industries necessary for the war effort.

The Germans created the so-called *Judenrat,* an organization that
was supposed to represent us and to whom the Nazis directed their
demands. Then the community had to supply thousands of Jews each
day for various cleaning and construction projects.

After several weeks of back-breaking work at the airport and train
depot, my high school friend Rysiek Gruder told me that a German
SS unit was hiring workers to help in the warehouses for the fighting
battalions of the SS. I gladly joined him there, as I thought that employment for the SS would result in my protection.

The work conditions were a great improvement; we were given half a loaf of bread weekly, and later, a good thick soup for lunch. Most significantly, they provided us with special documents that protected us from the constant *Aktionen* of the Ukrainian militias. We were also told that we would be protected from the threat of deportation.

Eventually I was given another assignment to work for four soldiers, shining their boots and leather belts and bringing in the coal to keep the fires going in the ovens. One was a young soldier named Stigler, who spent much time resting because he had been wounded in his leg. We would talk — speaking German so well helped me — and through our conversations, I found out that I was the first Jew he had met personally. He only thought in stereotypes, and he had acquired his antisemitic hatred from his father, who had supposedly lost a business to Jews. Under the bizarre circumstances of those times, our relationship could be characterized as almost friendly, a strange indication of the warped age in which we lived. Yet Stigler was violent. He could hit a Jew and then come back and talk to me as if nothing had happened. One day, three Jewish leaders were hanged. Stigler told me that he, too, had shot a Jew that day. But I, he said, was "different." This forced me to realize that fate was closing in on us. How could men like Stigler be so contradictory? One workday, I witnessed the SS walking among Jews lying in fields, shooting randomly. I sat on a railroad track, not so much afraid as appalled, witnessing the murder of my people. By August 1942, some 65,000 Jews had been taken from Lwów to the Belzec death camp.

During my conversations with Stigler, he told me not to delude myself with the idea that working for the SS would make it possible for me to survive the war. He confided that they had an order to "finish off" all Jews by the spring of 1943. Stigler told me that he'd heard that Jews lived under free conditions in Hungary, and said if I managed to cross the border, some one hundred kilometres away, I might survive.

∼

In September 1942, I managed to flee from Lwów and arrive in Stryj, where my uncle lived. He told me I would not find any help to get to Hungary, and that I would be arrested and sent back. Dejected, I was on my way to the Jewish community offices to find out if I was able to get a permit to travel back when a middle-aged man approached me and asked me if I knew where to exchange pengő. I knew that the pengő was the Hungarian currency. Being curious, I asked him where he got the money from. He told me that he was a Jew from Czechoslovakia who had escaped, with his wife and brother, from his home to Lwów in 1940, where he could live safely under Soviet rule.

After the German invasion of Lwów, they realized that they would not survive if they stayed there. Speaking Hungarian, and having some relatives in Hungary, they wanted to cross the border back to Hungary. But they made a mistake in boarding the train too close to the border. Their documents were inspected, and they were caught without the proper ID papers. They were arrested and handed over to the Germans on the Polish side. They were then put on the same train that took the Jews from Stryj to Belzec in an *Aktion*. He alone managed to jump out of the train and had also survived being shot at by the armed guards.

I asked him what he intended to do, and he explained to me that he needed some local currency to buy food and a place to rest, and then he would try again to go to Hungary. But this time he would walk to the big city of Munkács, some eighty kilometres from the border.

I realized that this was my chance to survive. I told him to keep the pengő. I would finance his stay and the trip to the border if, in exchange, he took me along and let me stay a day or two with his family until I found a way to orient myself.

We were on our way. We took a chance and walked along the highway. We did not carry any luggage and were dressed as peasants, hoping not to be recognized as Jews. After some time, we saw a *csendőr* (Hungarian gendarme, or military police) walking towards us. As my partner passed by him, he greeted him in Hungarian and we continued walking. After some fifty metres, I turned my head to look back and saw him standing and watching us, but apparently, we must have been dressed properly, because he continued walking.

In the evening, we arrived in a village and found a synagogue where the evening prayers were being said. I don't know what my partner told them in Hungarian, but one family took us in, gave us dinner and let us sleep in the barn. In the early morning, they gave us breakfast and we were told that the milkman who was delivering milk to Munkács would allow us to go with him.

Once in Munkács, we went to the Jewish community office, but they were not prepared to give us any assistance. It was Friday afternoon. We went to a synagogue where we rested. Meanwhile, the Shabbat services had started. There is an old Jewish custom to share the Shabbat dinner with strangers in town. The *shames*, the synagogue's caretaker, asked us where we were from and arranged an invitation to a family.

My partner had told me not to reveal that we came from Poland and say only that we were from a town on the Romanian-Hungarian border that had been part of Romania until 1940. He could then explain to our hosts that I had been going to a Romanian school and that was why I didn't speak Hungarian. In the middle of the meal they somehow realized who we really were, and told us to leave the house.

We found our way to the railroad station, where he discovered that there was a train leaving soon for Budapest, so he bought tickets for us and kept the remaining pengő in his pocket. The trains at night were poorly lit. To avoid any eventual questions from other passengers, I pretended to be asleep. In the early morning, when the train was on the outskirts of Budapest, I realized that my partner had disappeared with the pengő. I left the station without knowing a word of Hungarian, without any local currency or an address to go. I was completely lost.

Realizing that this was Saturday, I approached a passerby who looked Jewish and asked him in Yiddish for directions to the nearest synagogue, which he gave me. It so happened that the very large Conservative synagogue on Bethlen Gábor Square was not far away.

During the services, I started crying from desperation. When members of the congregation asked me why, I explained my situation in German, which some could understand. They told me to go to a small Orthodox synagogue where I might find help. In the meantime, I got some warm food in the synagogue from the open kitchen for needy Jews. Without knowing the language or the city, somehow I found the small synagogue where a *minyan* came in the evening for the so-called third meal and prayers. I told them my story, and they delegated one man to come with me to try to find a place for me to sleep.

We went to the Jewish section of Kazinczy Street. He took me to several different places that used to rent beds for the night, but none of them was willing to accept me without papers. Finally, he gave up and left me in the middle of the street. I was desperate and found my way back to the large synagogue, where I now hoped to be able to stay overnight. But everything was locked up by then and I couldn't get in.

When passing a police station, I was almost at the point of going in and surrendering. Then I noticed a building across the street with an open front door. I went in, went down to the basement, and found one room open, which was used as an air raid shelter. I spent the night there, and the next morning I returned to Kazinczy Street and found another synagogue. From there, I was directed to a communal eating-place where I had free breakfast and made the acquaintance of a young, enterprising Jewish boy.

After hearing my story, he told me to come and stay with him. He had a bed in a large room he shared with four other people. The bed sheet was black from dirt. I asked him where I could change some currency and he took me to an apartment where the resident happened to be a Jewish refugee from Poland. I got some pengő from him — I wasn't sure whether he gave me the right amount in exchange — and he informed me that there was a Polish office serving as an unofficial consulate. Upon receiving a document from them, Polish refugees could get permission from the Hungarian ministry to legally reside in Hungary. However, they were not giving such documents to Jews.

Then he took me to the Jewish community offices. In Hungary there were two main Jewish communities, one Orthodox and the other reform. The reform was sending me to the Orthodox, which sent me back to the reform one. The boy arranged for someone to sell me some identity papers stating that I was from the part of Hungary that had previously belonged to Czechoslovakia, which was meant to explain why I couldn't speak Hungarian. Much later on, I realized that for official inspection these papers were worthless. They did allow me to find a place to sleep though.

I decided to find my companion who had run away with the money. I knew only that his family lived in a border town called Nagyvárad. I decided to go there, and I soon got a job offer and began to work in a workshop. Having been assured three decent meals a week, plus earnings, I was able to settle into a comfortable, peaceful life in comparison to what was happening in Poland. Eventually I could speak Hungarian quite well, and I spent summer days on the beach and made several friends. During the night, I had occasional nightmares that I was back in Poland and the Germans were still there.

In late November 1943, I found out that I could receive documents from the Polish office in Budapest that would confirm that I was a gentile refugee from Poland and could thus secure from the Hungarian authorities a legal permit to reside in Hungary. I went to Budapest and obtained the documents under the Polish name of Wiktor Smalski. Smalski was the name of my Polish friend from elementary school, while Wiktor, or Victor, I assumed as symbolic of what I hoped would be my victory: my survival of the war.

# With Aching Hearts
## László Láng

Translated from Hungarian by Marietta Morry and Lynda Muir (2013)

In 1940, my father decided that I had to learn a trade, because by that time boys of the Jewish faith were not easily accepted into institutions of higher learning due to antisemitism. My father travelled to Budapest, and with the help of a friend of his, he managed to arrange for me to be accepted in the apprentices' hostel of MIKÉFE, the Magyar Izraelita Kézmű és Földművelési Egyesület (Hungarian Jewish Craft and Agricultural Association)[1] at 49 Hermina Street. Being a disabled veteran, he got 50 per cent off the fee, so that he only had to pay fifty pengős per month. My father came back and told us about it with glee. I was less happy about this arrangement because I loved my parents and wanted to stay with them. My father told me that we would be leaving in a couple of days. The distance between our village and Pest was more than two hundred kilometres, a huge distance for me in those days.

---

1 This society was formed in 1842 with the goal of integrating Jews into Hungarian society by helping them become agricultural peasants and guild craftsmen, as well as by promoting the Hungarian language among Jews. MIKÉFE was the longest-running non-religious Jewish organization in Hungary and operated until the Holocaust.

I knew that a three-year apprenticeship was no simple matter, but I accepted the challenge. The first weeks were the hardest. I was tremendously homesick and really missed my mother's affection. But as time went on, this also abated. I had lots of really good friends at MIKÉFE. I was great at soccer, and I was also admitted into the Turul scout group, whose members had been staying at the hostel for a long time. I started to feel good at both my workplace and MIKÉFE. In the meantime, the political situation was deteriorating by the day, and we didn't know what lay in store for us. Perhaps it was a good thing that we didn't.

~

One fine day in 1943, we were transporting finished work from the shop to Wesselényi Street using a small cart pulled by two apprentices. The transport consisted of two jobs: the delivery of the merchandise and, on the way back, the picking up of material, namely tin and other types of metal. I entered the store and spoke to the man whom I had always called Uncle Duci in previous encounters. After we had exchanged greetings, instead of asking what we had brought, he asked me if I knew how to play soccer. I replied yes. Then he asked me to come and play with his team because he was the team's captain and he was a few players short. I told him that I had two good friends who wouldn't mind playing either. I was thinking of Gyuri Stern and Miklós Moskovitz. Uncle Duci told me that his team was called Compactor and that it belonged to the bookbinders' association. I had never heard of this association before, but that didn't really make a difference for me. Uncle Duci told me to come over to the soccer club the same evening, because he needed to get some certificates ready.

I told my two friends about the team and they agreed to play, so we went over to the soccer club where Uncle Duci was waiting for us. We quickly filled out the forms and attached our photos. By Saturday afternoon, we were all set to play on the team. The other players didn't know us, but we won the game and made Uncle Duci happy. He asked us to come again the next week for another game. We agreed. We didn't get any compensation for the game, but we were glad that at last we could play soccer on a team. We returned to MIKÉFE tired but happy. However, the Hungarian government kept pronouncing anti-Jewish laws so quickly that people couldn't even keep up with reading them. When we went to play again the following week, we were already in the changing room and half-dressed for the game when Uncle Duci informed me, in a voice that was practically wailing, "My Lacika, I received a letter from the league stipulating that Jewish players are not allowed to be part of the team."

This was the first time in my life that I experienced the injustice of humanity. The Hungarian government was trying to paralyze Hungarian Jewry step by step and strip us of all our human rights. We started undressing in silence, without a word. Our hearts were aching, and I was thinking what it meant that Hungarian citizens of the Jewish faith were not even allowed to play soccer any longer. How low had our civilized world sunk? Surely this was a beginning of the Final Solution designed by that madman Hitler and his cohorts and gladly supported by the Hungarian government.

In April 1944, the building that housed MIKÉFE was seized: from one day to the next, a fascist organization kicked us out. I remember it as if it were yesterday. One morning, once everyone had been body-searched, they all started off with a little bundle to look for a place to live. Not everybody managed to find a place on such short notice. My sister, Katalin, who was working as a hairdresser in Pest and who had a larger circle of acquaintances, found me a small room in Zugló, at the house of a Jewish widow who lived with her two daughters and had an extra room to let. Soon after, another so-called Jewish law was decreed that forced more men to enter labour camps. There were posters that announced when each person needed to sign up, according to alphabetical order. By this time, it had already been decreed that Jews had to sew a yellow star onto the left side of their outer garments.

# Hoping in Isolation
## Miriam Mózes

By 1942, I had many worries and unresolved issues on my ten-year-old mind. After a very restless night, I was glad to wake up, even if it was to the scary sound of loud thunderstorms. I jumped out of bed and peeked through the window curtain. The sky was covered with heavy clouds; fierce lightning illuminated the dark sky, accompanied by continuous thunder. It looked as though heavy rain was ready to pour down and flood our neighbourhood. I felt very uneasy and for no specific reason thought that the scary, dark sky was a premonition of what I could expect in the near future.

Over the previous few days I had been thinking about the new phase of my life I was stepping into with my first day in a new school. It was a very prestigious Reformed (Calvinist) Gimnázium in our city. I was proud to be accepted — mind you, my parents had to pay about five times more than any non-Jewish kid's parents did. I felt this was really unfair and, for the first time in my life, felt that I was different and discriminated against. I felt uneasy and helpless.

My thoughts kept jumping in all directions, to the present, the past and the unpredictable future. All my life I had lived in a well-protected, privileged environment; I had attended Jewish kindergarten and elementary school and all my friends and all my parents' friends were Jewish. The only non-Jewish people I had ever met were my nanny, the cleaning ladies and the cooks who worked for my parents. How was I going to fit into this new environment? Was I ever going to have a non-Jewish friend? How were we going to relate to each other, representing two such different worlds? How would my new teachers relate to the only Jewish girl in the class? Would anybody discriminate against me and, if so, how should I react? Should I be humbly bent down or should I stand erect, express my objection and fight back? I did not have answers, nor did anybody I asked appear to have any.

What made my new move so difficult was that it followed the start of Hungary's cooperation with Nazi Germany, as declared by the Regent, Miklós Horthy. I shared my uneasy and unhappy feeling with every Jew living in Hungary; we all felt very helpless. There was nobody to turn to for advice. Everybody avoided discussing the future of Hungarian Jews, the horrific possible consequences of that co-operation.

That's why my first day in the new school was tainted with two very different feelings: excitement about starting the new intellectual phase of my life at a prestigious school and uneasiness about meeting people from outside my familiar Jewish community.

At seven-thirty, Mom knocked on my door with a big smile on her beautiful face. As always she was very elegant, wearing a colourful silk gown. She looked as if she had just stepped out from a hairdresser's salon. She hugged and kissed me, then took from my cupboard my new navy-blue pleated skirt and blazer with the matching fancy white blouse. "Marikám, it is probably one of the most important days in your life," she said. "You are growing up," she continued, "and today is the first time you'll step out from your overprotected family circle and try to become part of a much broader community. You will be in a minority as a Jewish girl in your new school." Her eyes looked sad and I could feel the worries in her trembling voice. I gave her a big hug and promised her to do my best. To reassure her, I added, "I know how to behave and you can trust me." I put on my fancy uniform and combed my hair. I did not feel hungry, so I skipped breakfast and was ready for the big day. The school was close by, so I walked to the carved wooden gate of the beautiful old school building. A guard in a uniform opened the gate, and I entered the building that became my second home for the next two years, until 1944.

The Grade 5 classroom was very big, with about thirty ten-year-old girls. They were all well-dressed and cute as they crowded together in small groups. As I learned later, they were the daughters of doctors, dentists, lawyers and businessmen, the so-called "elite" group of our town, Hódmezővásárhely. I really thought that I could easily become an integral part of the class. I would just have to be a little more outgoing, not so shy, and I would find a few good friends. It sounded simple, but it was not so easy.

I was anxious to join one of the groups but none of the girls invited me. What's worse, nobody even asked who I was, what my name was or where I came from. So I stood alone for a few minutes, not knowing what to do. Luckily I met a girl named Margaret, who was not part of any group either. She seemed to be an outsider as well. I really could not figure out what made us different and why both of us were ignored. It took us a few weeks to figure out.

I was relieved when the bell rang and the teacher, the head of the class, an elderly, distinguished-looking lady, entered the room. We all ran to our desks and stood up to greet Mrs. Kovács. She was a kind-looking lady with a warm voice and we all felt comfortable listening to her. She briefly told us in a firm manner what she expected from us. "You have to behave well, be obedient, do the best you can, respect your teachers and friends, and stick to the rules posed by the school and teachers." Nothing extraordinary, I thought, I can follow those rules. I felt ready to start my new school.

At the beginning of the day, Mrs. Kovács read our names and asked each one of us which school we had attended before and what our favourite subject was. When my turn came, I answered proudly that I attended the Jewish day school and I loved all the subjects taught there. I looked around and I noticed that the girls were staring at me with weird expressions on their faces. Even Margaret seemed to be a little surprised. She leaned towards me and whispered into my ear, "Are you really Jewish? You do not look like a Jewish girl." I felt very upset. It was good that Mrs. Kovács did not react the same way as the girls did. I thought it was a good sign as I was really keen to become part of my new school.

The first few days were quiet and uneventful. We met the teachers, who seemed to be smart and kind, if strict. No chattering was allowed during the class; we had to be quiet, pay attention and be ready to answer questions at all times. So there was tremendous pressure on us to listen and absorb whatever was taught. It seemed difficult, but it was a good method to train our young brains to be focused. As a matter of fact I enjoyed being challenged and alert all the time.

The recesses were much more difficult to handle. I just did not belong to any of the cliques gathered at different spots in the huge yard. Margaret was my only companion; she remained my friend for many years to come. She was a chubby little girl, with dark eyes and long dark braids. She looked Jewish but belonged to the Unitarian Church, a branch of Protestantism. We were both outsiders in the Református Gimnázium.

As I learned later, she was also different from most of us because she came from a poor family. Her father was a blacksmith who owned a small store at the outskirts of the city. Margaret had been accepted to this elite school because she was a very smart girl, an excellent student with straight A's, so she received a scholarship to attend the *Gimnázium*.

Slowly we became good friends, but our friendship was limited to the school. I never visited her, and neither did she come to our house. We discussed everything related to our school life but at first we avoided discussing family matters or anything related to our private lives. She never asked me about my faith, and I never asked about hers. That worked well for the first few weeks, but later we became more open with each other.

One cool, breezy, sunny October morning, I arrived at school a little early, dressed in my winter uniform. Glad to have a few minutes to relax and enjoy the nice autumn colours before starting class, I sat down on a bench and watched the girls arriving, hoping that somebody would join me to have a little conversation. I got excited when I saw a few girls approaching me. I was very happy, thinking finally the ice has broken, I thought. Then a girl named Magda stepped very close to me and whispered something that I'll never forget: "I am glad that you are attending our school, and we decided to give you a cute, cuddly name, *Kis Zsidó*, little Jew."

It was terrible; it felt like somebody stabbed me. I did not know how to react — should I cry, shout, keep quiet or humbly accept my new name? There was nobody there to ask those questions, so I had to make my own decision. I felt that I did not have a choice; my schoolmates were the majority, so I did not say a word. My day was ruined, and I could not concentrate on anything. The only thing I wanted was to go home to be with my parents and brother and get some comfort and encouragement from my loving family. There was nothing I could do to change the girls' attitude, so *Kis Zsidó* became my nickname until the German army occupied Hungary and we were deported to the Strasshof transit camp in Austria.

The first time I entered the classroom with the mandated yellow star on my clothing was even worse than when I got that nickname. Everybody looked at me with curiosity. Nobody openly remarked on it, but from that day on my life changed. Girls left me alone most of the time; they hardly talked to me and did not play with me during breaks. Even my best friends ignored me. I became an outcast and felt lonely and helpless.

The teachers were a bit friendlier than the students; they involved me in class activities and continued to call me Marika. No wonder that I preferred to stay in the classroom, even during the break, to avoid my classmates. Soon I realized that the only way I could improve my status in the school was to work hard and become the best student in the class. And I succeeded. I learned some useful lessons:

keep focused, pay attention to details, set new goals and never give up; try to do the best you can, always be positive and hope for better times to come.

In early June, after I finished my year at the high school with excellent marks, all the Jews from the town were deported to a ghetto in Szeged, from where some were sent to Auschwitz and others to work in Austria. Wearing the yellow star and being called a little Jew in Hungary were nothing compared to what followed our deportation to a slave labour camp.

# Eviction and Terror
## Sandor (Sam) Grad

World War II officially broke out when Germany invaded Poland in 1939. For a few years, Hungary was spared the brunt of the Nazi war and terror machine. My family and neighbours knew a little about what was going on, since news and rumours trickled in from outside the country. Still, the atrocities and crimes being committed by Hitler's Third Reich were too far removed for my family and others to be concerned.

What little of it I knew as a child was gleaned from the workings of my father's cherished — yet illegal — shortwave radio, which was kept hidden under his bed. The radio would pick up BBC transmissions in Hungarian and other assorted news stations, allowing my father a glimpse into the world outside Vásárosnamény. But I was sworn to secrecy about it by my father.

Throughout the course of my youth, my father was called into the service of Hungary's standing army, as part of his civic duty. But as the 1930s ended and the 1940s began, he and other Jewish men began to be conscripted into a Hungarian forced labour army that bore little resemblance to the one they had been proud to participate in before. This forced labour was a harbinger of the end of the peaceful way of life for us and for the other Jews of Hungary.

During the war, Jewish children in Hungarian day schools were often segregated from Christian children and put into special classrooms away from their peers. They put two and sometimes three grades of Jewish children together in one classroom. Jewish classes of mixed grades could not learn together and were not being taught with the seriousness required. By this time, everyone was aware that there was plenty of antisemitism in Hungary, and quite naturally the Christians knew this too.

I felt degraded by these events, and school was never the same for me again. In my last year of day school in 1943–1944, the school curriculum was severely cut due to the war. By the time we were taken away in April 1944, the school year had already finished, and because of the Hungarian war effort, children were required to go home to help their parents in the fields or work otherwise.

# Fate and Fortune
# Leslie Fazekas

Translated from Hungarian by Marietta Morry and Lynda Muir (2018)

The real horrors of the war didn't touch us until March 1944. Of course, we heard and knew about everything. We listened to the English radio broadcasts every day and followed the troop movements on the map that hung on the wall of our room — first, into the Soviet Union and later out of the Soviet Union when the Germans started to retreat in order to "shorten the front." We heard about the Warsaw Ghetto Uprising in 1943, and we knew that the men who had been sent to the Ukraine for labour service would often not make it home alive. We also heard about the total defeat of the Hungarian army at Voronezh, and that those who survived it were fleeing back to Hungary whichever way they could. We heard about Stalingrad and knew for certain that the Germans were going to lose the war. The one thing we didn't know was what fate awaited us and whether we Hungarian Jews would survive this world conflagration. Our teacher Dr. Gonda phrased the situation as follows: It's true that Hitler is about to kick the bucket, but first he'll kick us.

In the meantime, we kept on going to school, and our major preoccupation was whether we were adequately prepared for the next day's math or literature quiz. Our school and our parents shielded us from the horrors. Both we and our parents were hopeful that what had occurred elsewhere in Europe would not happen in Hungary.

We courted girls and enjoyed an active social life. I started dating Judit, my wife-to-be. We would go to the movies and the theatre, study together, read books, discuss politics and debate important topics. From time to time, we played bridge, and if we misplayed a hand, we got upset. We tried to remain as normal as possible in an upside-down, abnormal world.

$\sim$

My father was called up for labour service in 1940. He arrived at an assembly point near Debrecen with the requisite amount of gear. It was summertime. We didn't hear from him for weeks, and then the message came that we could visit him if we wished. My mother took me along. We boarded a train early in the morning and arrived before noon in the village where my father was being detained.

It was a very strange visit. My father was made to stand on an elevation behind a barbed-wire fence, while we stood on the other side of the fence, watching him standing motionless and mute on top of the little hill, looking at us. It was forbidden to talk or wave. We could only watch him, a person bound for death. I don't remember what went through my mind at the time. This "meeting" must have been horrible for my parents.

Unexpectedly, my father was allowed to return home a few days later. Perhaps it was because of his age, since he was already in his forty-eighth year. That's how he survived: as a result of the strange and incomprehensible games that fate plays.

In Debrecen, my age group was not called up for labour service. This amounts to another incomprehensible thing, because people who were born in 1925 were conscripted in other locations. In 1943 my class matriculated, and I applied to the Science Faculty of the University of Debrecen, where I was admitted as a "guest student."

Jews were no longer being admitted as regular university students, but four of us enrolled this way. We studied together and all four of us did well on our exams.

Beginning in March 1944, upon the German occupation, we were not allowed to enter the main building of the university. However, some of our professors relocated the lectures to a secondary building for our sake, which took quite a bit of courage on their part.

# The Miracle of Our Survival
# Yittel Nechumah Bineth
# (Kornelia Paskusz)

A pall hovered over Hungary in the years between 1941 and 1943. By this time, the Nazi Party had dominated Germany for several years. Their aim was to make the world *judenrein*, to wipe out the entire Jewish population. Their methods and plans defy human comprehension and baffle the mind. The German system for mass murder included gassing living people and then burning their bodies in crematoria, shooting, starving, torturing and degrading people both physically and emotionally. German Jews were already being deported in those years. Germany had invaded Poland, where Jews were forced into ghettos and sent to camps. Hungarian Jews received some information about these horrifying developments, but they did not believe that the same would ever happen to them.

In our case, the atmosphere became increasingly tense in 1943. Close to midnight on a Sunday, we suddenly heard heavy banging on our large, bolted front door. Mother, Renee, Meshulem and I all stood frozen by our window. As the noise of the banging increased, we started yelling and crying out for help. We saw people outside strolling home from their evening entertainment. To our horror, they were oblivious to our plight and ignored our cries. We were terrified!

Meanwhile, we heard glass being shattered. They were breaking our veranda windows! Our hearts were pounding. Our terror was indescribable. Mother directed us to the back door. I was only four-teen years old at the time and followed my instincts instead. Without anybody's instructions, I jumped out the front window in my night-gown and ran as fast as I possibly could to the police station, one kilometre away from our house. My head was throbbing, and by the time I got to the police station I was crying and shaking.

I could hardly utter a syllable but did manage to beg them to save our lives. With the mercy of heaven, they believed me, and two po-lice officers took off on their bicycles, pedalling as fast as they could. They reached our home just in time to catch the criminals inside the apartment adjacent to ours. The blood on their hands from the broken glass made it clear that they were guilty. The gangsters were apprehended just as I arrived home. Mother kissed and hugged me, calling me her little "heroine." My reward was to watch the men get handcuffed and taken to jail.

Unfortunately, this was not the end of the episode. There was a wartime curfew law in effect stating that whoever broke into a house during the night was subject to capital punishment. The Hungarian thieves were apprehended and jailed and were liable to be executed. This caused great anxiety among the Jews of Csorna; antisemitism was rampant, and the Jewish community was afraid that the fam-ily and friends of these criminals would take revenge upon innocent Jewish people. The Jews were so intimidated that they went through the difficult process of raising a huge sum of money to bail out the bandits. This involved complex negotiations and a depletion of the community's monetary resources, but the kehilla, the community, felt that this would be the lesser of two evils. Their efforts were successful, and in an ironic turn of events, they managed to have these criminals set free.

It was a very cold night in January 1944. I was tossing and turning in bed, unable to fall asleep. I sensed something unusual happening in the house, and I was both curious and frightened. I listened very carefully. Mother was in the other room with our youngest brother,

Meshulem, and they were packing things into boxes. I dared not go out, afraid to find out what the packing was all about. At just about midnight, when all was quiet and nobody was around, they carried the boxes out to the backyard where we had our shed. Meshulem dug a huge hole, and together they buried all the boxes in the ground. With her foresight, Mother knew that time was running out and that she had to do whatever she could to save as many of our belongings as possible. Later I found out that these boxes contained our cherished and valuable silverware and jewellery.

As time went on, antisemitism continued to thicken in Hungary. In spite of the growing tension, Mother tried to continue her work, which involved constant travel. She left on one of her business trips as usual just as the Nazi soldiers were invading Hungary. The moment that everyone had feared and tried so hard to deny was now taking place. Mother, unaware of the danger, was at the train station when the station manager approached her and said, "Paskuszné, go home immediately. You have very little time, and it is very dangerous. Do not waste a minute." This man saved her life. By the time she arrived home, Csorna was full of soldiers. All of us were deeply worried, and we were thrilled when Mother finally walked through the door.

The Germans had occupied Hungary on March 19, 1944, and were issuing new commands almost daily. The situation in Hungary went from bad to worse. The Nazis swarmed over our cities and villages, carrying out oppressive and frightening new edicts. The tension was becoming unbearable. Jews had to sew yellow stars onto their coats to identify themselves. Jewish businesses were forced to shut down, and the yeshivas had to close their doors. A new order was issued, commanding all men and boys eighteen years old and older to report to labour camps in various parts of Hungary. My brother Binyomin came home from yeshiva and got ready to leave for the labour camps.

My heart is pounding again as I write this because I so vividly remember his coming home from yeshiva and how he prepared to leave. The boys had been commanded to cut off their *peyes*. As he stood by the mirror with the scissors, his hands were trembling and he was sobbing. I looked up and saw for the first time that dear Mother was sobbing too. How we all cried!

Binyomin then picked up his knapsack and headed for the door. Mother quickly regained control of herself. She consoled him by telling him that no harm would come to him. She beseeched him to have faith in *Hashem*[1] and to be very strong, and reminded him to be as "frum and ehrlich" (righteous) as he was at home. She put her hands on his head and *bentched* (blessed) him with the *posuk*, verse, "Yevorechecho Hashem Ve'Yishmerecho" (May God bless you and keep you). After that, he closed the door behind himself and left.

---

1   A Hebrew word that literally means "the Name" used by some Jews to refer to God to avoid explicitly using God's name.

# Amid the Burning Bushes
## Helen Rodak-Izso

On February 1, 1942, I married my long-time best friend, Ernő. Those few months that we had to ourselves were spent hiding and waiting for the dreaded draft call. Ernie was twenty-seven years old, dependable and of good character. We had mutual friends and interests, both loved music and books. Since we enjoyed outdoor activities, we often spent the weekends on hikes in our beautiful countryside and mountains.

Soon those joyful hours came to an end because the dreaded draft cards started to arrive, which we knew was a serious warning. In those years, even before the gates closed down around us, we realized with bitterness that our future was doomed, hopeless. We couldn't talk or think about anything else at the time. We spent our time either trying to keep hoping for a better future while feeling incredibly hopeless or else trying to figure a way out of our situation. We felt trapped and frightened beyond words.

~

Ignoring the hints in the letters that we should not dare to come to the labour camp, we decided with my friends Ella and Magda Young, whose husbands were at the same place as Ernő, that we still wanted to go to see for ourselves what the situation was there. They never elaborated on what kind of troubled life they were living there, and we could never have imagined what really went on.

On a Monday, we prepared and packed the most important and practical things for them, such as warm clothing and some food, and left. On the train we met and befriended an older woman, who was already familiar with the conditions there. She looked like a person with good intentions, so we were thankful for her counselling. She tried to warn us to look modest. We shouldn't wear hats, just a kerchief so we could mingle with the rest of the passengers. She told us that when the train reaches its destination, we should walk off separately. We, of course, didn't know anything about what had happened there on the previous Saturday.

The station, Tiszalök, was full of Hungarian gendarmes, who were known for their cruelty. They could be seen everywhere with their distinctive big rooster feather in their hats. I was lucky that when the train stopped, the gendarme who was supposed to be in front of my door to watch every single passenger leaving the train happened to look somewhere else, missing the opportunity to see me.

We walked to the restaurant closest to the station, carrying a heavy suitcase while still making sure to keep enough space between us so that it didn't look like we were going there together. The owner of the restaurant, a Jewish man, met us with dismay and horror. He didn't cover up his displeasure and anger, because, as we found out, we were all in danger. We finally heard the story about the past week's events and we realized that we had come into a lion's cage.

We regretted our thoughtless trip, but it was too late. There was nothing to do, other than to wait for the next train to go back. Unfortunately, this train was leaving only in the afternoon, so this poor man, seeing our disappointment, tried to help us after all.

He sent a message to the camp, and soon enough a young boy came from the blacksmith and we had to follow him. Again we walked separately, and luck was still with us, because on the way we met several high-ranking SS officers busily talking. Thank God that somehow they didn't notice us. We just walked past them as if this would have been the most natural thing for us to do. The truth is that we were trembling. Our suitcase was heavy, but it seems the fear gave us some extra strength.

When we arrived at the blacksmith's place, my husband, Ernie, was on guard at the gate in front of the building and saluted me like a total stranger and directed me to the nearest village house. I looked in the yard, where I spotted the familiar faces of the camp mates, many from our hometown, Košice, also known as Kassa. They were all busy with one horse, trying to horseshoe the poor animal, which didn't understand the sudden concern. There were sixteen people around him. The minute I stepped into the house, all the camp mates, guided by Ernie, came in to hear some news from home. But the first question they all asked us was, why did we come?

Only when we spotted the huge posters with large black letters did we understand their bewilderment. The posters clearly stated in bold and clear words a serious warning against anybody who would try to help Jews in any way. After reading this warning, we hurriedly gave these men the items we had brought and prepared ourselves for a quick departure. This village had only rough roads leading to the barracks and to the railway station. Luckily, we reached the train in time and came home safely. We had not expected such a dramatic trip.

We found out later, now at a safe distance, more details about what had happened in that village before our visit. The camp had made an announcement that relatives from nearby places could come to visit on a Saturday. Of course, many mothers, wives and other family members came. When everybody arrived and was let in, the air and mood abruptly changed. Every inmate of the camp who had visitors was violently humiliated, so the visitors could see and hear. The victims were tied to a tree with their feet up and when the person lost consciousness they were splashed in the face with water. This went on while the guards enjoyed themselves, laughing aloud. When this torture was over, they turned to the visitors and ordered them out, marching them straight to the station with the most obscene, indecent language and shouting.

None of the visitors had been able to talk to their husbands or sons and they had to return home with everything they had brought and prepared with such loving care.

The terrible thing was that our visit was unnecessary, because two weeks later they all came home for warm clothing and blankets. We had carried the heavy trunk for nothing. We knew only too well what this meant and what would come next. This was in 1942, around October, and I never heard from Ernie again. My wait for good news continued for long years, but unfortunately my husband had just vanished from this earth.

# Drills and Humiliations: Jewish Men in Labour Battalions

# Foreword

In several respects, the antisemitic radicalization of the Hungarian regime during World War II closely resembled that of Nazi Germany, even if this process unfolded with a certain delay in Hungary. For instance, Nuremberg-style racial laws were adopted in Hungary in 1941, six years after their introduction in Germany. An equally striking example of Hungary "catching up" with the persecution and violence inflicted by Nazi Germany occurred in early 1942 when members of the Royal Hungarian Army — many of whose members had observed the merciless conduct of war by the Wehrmacht since Hungary had entered into the war as a belligerent in the spring of 1941 and some of whose own troops also actively participated in acts of mass murder on the Eastern Front — initiated and committed mass murder within the country's enlarged territory. In raids conducted under the pretext of an anti-partisan crackdown in Vojvodina in early 1942, about 3,000 individuals — mostly of Serb ethnicity, with a substantial minority of Jews among them — were murdered.

Along with such forms of involvement in Nazi-style mass crimes, Hungary's antisemitic radicalization also led to the establishment of specific policies and institutions. Perhaps most infamously, Jews and other distrusted elements were excluded from military service but were not relieved from having to serve the country and its army. They were conscripted as slaves, to employ the apt phrase by Robert

Rozett:[1] compulsory labour service (*kötelező munkaszolgálat*) was established by law in 1939 for individuals the regime deemed unreliable and it targeted mostly Hungarian Jews. By 1940, there were some sixty units consisting entirely of Jewish labour servicemen.

The enrolled individuals were not allowed to carry weapons and worked mostly on construction sites and in mines. Upon Hungary's entry into the war in 1941, labour servicemen also often had to perform life-threatening tasks during combat, such as clearing minefields. This specifically Hungarian institution had only inexact parallels in other countries and tended to result in the painful humiliation and general misery of the overwhelmingly Jewish *munkaszolgálatosok* (labour servicemen), with tens of thousands of them perishing during the war.

Treating labour servicemen in a relatively humane manner was rare but not unheard of. Slight improvements in national policy in the middle of the war allowed more servicemen to survive. However, the basic framework of this peculiar institution clearly facilitated and regularly condoned violent excesses. Ultimately, how labour servicemen fared largely depended on the responsible military personnel and their choices — as well as the sheer luck of individuals. As the excerpts from Benedikt Korda (Kornreich), Moishe Rosenschein and Imrich Vesely attest, the widely varying personal backgrounds, mentalities and coping strategies of individuals would also significantly influence, if not the types of experiences themselves, at least how victims experienced their tribulations.

Such diversity of individual coping aside, the conscripted slaves of the Hungarian army were recurrently assigned dangerous or downright life-threatening tasks, especially once they got transported to

---

1   Robert Rozett, *Conscripted Slaves: Hungarian Jewish Forced Laborers on the Eastern Front during the Second World War* (Jerusalem: Yad Vashem International Institute for Holocaust Research, 2013).

the Eastern Front. Amidst the fiercest battles recorded in human history, they continued to serve on the front lines of the aggressor armies without being in the possession of military equipment. As Itzak Davidovits' recollections illustrate, the Hungarian Second Army was overwhelmed and largely eliminated during the Battle of Stalingrad in the winter of 1942–1943. As a consequence, many labour servicemen perished alongside their unequal peers in the army, whereas others were captured by the advancing Soviets with diverse and often tragic consequences.

The Hungarian army was involved in strictly enforcing discriminatory measures during the war years. Army representatives brutally and arbitrarily mistreated Hungarian citizens whom the authorities collectively placed under suspicion. Members of the army even committed several acts of mass murder. However, the Hungarian army was not among the chief partners in the systematic annihilation of Hungarian Jews in 1944.

It is one of the ironies of the Holocaust in Hungary that the discriminatory and life-threatening institution of labour service, which was clearly among the worst places for Jews to be in Hungary prior to 1944, would contribute to saving the lives of numerous Jewish men under the drastically worsened circumstances. If labour servicemen remained or newly came under the authority of the Hungarian army upon March 19, 1944, they could be spared the experience of the Nazi concentration and death camps — just when most members of their families would likely have been deported and murdered. By continuing to enroll Jews during the most fateful months of genocide, the Hungarian army effectively saved them — without having a humanitarian motivation for doing so.

Although the number of casualties was in the tens of thousands during the war years, a significant number of labour servicemen managed to survive the war, which had major consequences for the way the Holocaust in Hungary has been remembered since. Along with the horrific suffering of Hungarian Jews in Hungarian ghettos and Nazi camps in 1944–1945 and the anarchic and traumatic Arrow Cross terror of late 1944 and early 1945, the often harrowing and deeply tragic but also rather diverse experiences of labour servicemen have also been recurrently narrated, analyzed and commemorated. The recently deceased Randolph L. Braham (1922–2018), the towering historian of the Holocaust in Hungary for many decades, is a famous example of someone who had to undergo such experiences and later on dealt extensively with the history of Hungary's forced labour service in his research.[2]

The personal stories here offer intimate perspectives and numerous intriguing insights into this unusual and sinister institution.

---

2  See, for example, Randolph L. Braham, *The Hungarian Labor Service System, 1939–1945* (Boulder, Col.: East European Quarterly, 1977).

# Only When I Laugh
## Imrich Vesely

In early September 1940, I reported to the labour corps. Although I was now in the Royal Hungarian Army, under the command of army officers and NCOs, I wasn't called a soldier. I was called a labour serviceman. To add insult to injury, all the recruits had to go through the official swearing-in ceremony and take the oath of allegiance to a country that was about to strip them of all human rights and dignity.

From the original assembly point, we were transferred to another location for primary training. We had to supply our own clothes, blankets, canteens and other necessities of life but, in a splendid show of generosity, the Hungarian state supplied the yellow armband we had to wear all the time. I had never been chauvinistic about my Jewishness — I wasn't even religious — yet I wore the yellow armband with a certain pride. It was designed to brand and humiliate but I chose to see it as the distinguishing mark that announced loud and clear to the world that the wearer did not belong among the masses infected with the loathsome disease of fascism.

The world was rushing towards catastrophe like a tidal wave. On the furious, stormy sea, the individual was a helpless, fragile toy boat.

The Hungarian army had marched into Transylvania and Yugoslavia to reclaim lost territories. The country paid a tragically high price for the few chunks of land tossed its way by Hitler: Hungary had become a German satellite. In practical terms that meant the full exploitation of Hungarian agriculture and industry and the loss of tens of thousands of young men, who died to save German lives in hopeless battles fought without the benefit of up-to-date weapons, transportation or equipment.

In the camp, the labour company was put through the obligatory marching drills and other usual army fun. After a few days, rumours started about a transfer. (Rumours were the only reliable means of receiving news and one soon became efficient at separating the plausible rumour from the common or garden canard.) Then, one morning, we got our orders to pack our gear and get ready. We obeyed. And next morning again. And the next. Finally, on the fourth day of readiness, we were loaded onto trucks and driven to the freight yards where the cattle cars — and one passenger car for the officers and NCOS — were waiting. Another eighteen hours later, the train actually started to move.

The train took us to Transylvania and, immediately upon our arrival, we were given a chance to test our newly acquired marching skills. The thirty-kilometre-long winding mountain road took us to a small sawmill somewhere in the Carpathian Mountains.

The work was strenuous and dangerous. Each man had to carry an eighteen-foot plank from the mill to the Soviet border, about ten kilometres away, where the engineers were busy on several constructions. The load was heavy and awkward on the treacherous mountain paths with crevices and canyons dropping away as much as five hundred feet. Each plank was a foot wide and could easily turn into a sail whenever the wind decided to become playful.

It didn't take too long for our company to turn into a gang of elderly invalids. Many a great man has had some elevating words to say about the benevolent effect of hard work on the human soul. Obviously, none of them has ever carried lumber in the Carpathians. Shoulders, arms and hands became lurid with colour — green, blue, yellow, red. Soon, many of us were unable to work because of illness or exhaustion or both. Our masters had no choice but to declare every second day a rest period. Those were the easy, early days when the Hungarian authorities still believed that a living slave was more useful than a dead one.

⌒

Our work now basically consisted of road building. Of course, it involved cutting down giant trees, clearing thick — and very wet — bush and other activities previously unknown to us. But it was better than carrying the planks. To my surprise, we got used to physical labour quite quickly even though the majority of the boys had never tried it before. There's an old Hungarian saying (no, the Chinese do not have a monopoly) — work makes you noble. I never appreciated the full stupidity of it until those road-building days in the pouring rain.

The work was better than the plank business, but it was far from being pleasant. There was also a large measure of humiliation inflicted upon us by our commanding officers and NCOs, who all made sure that we didn't forget we were the scum of the earth, traitors, bloodsuckers. And those were the nice words they used. Hungary may not be very rich in a number of material commodities but the language's wealth in abusive terms and swear words is unsurpassed. And army personnel, especially NCOs, have always been extremely well versed in the art form.

The local people in the Carpathian Mountains knew their district like the palms of their hands. As in most border communities, they had always been engaged in a little contraband activity and, like all good businessmen, they had done their research. They knew every bush, every branch, every crevice, cave and nook. They knew the streams, the paths and the swamps. They knew the schedule of the border patrol better than the patrol and we heard rumours that they had helped several men from previous work parties to escape.

Many of the guys in our company were seriously considering the move. I was the only one there who spoke the language of the natives — a distinctive dialect that was a jolly mixture of Czech, Polish, Russian, Ukrainian, Romanian and God knows what else — so of course everybody was after me to act as interpreter for the negotiations.

All was going well until the Hungarian border patrol nabbed two guys who were trying to sneak through to the Soviet Union. After a few interrogatory punches, the prisoners named a Ruthenian peasant as their guide and me as their interpreter.

The next day, two civilian gentlemen arrived from the special investigative branch of the Ministry of the Interior to look into the illegal border crossings. Neither of them looked particularly friendly. Shortly after their arrival, two gendarmes put in an appearance. I knew that we were heading for trouble. My name was announced. Quickly and swiftly and in all sorts of hurry, I leapt forward and stood to respectful attention with what I hoped was the world's most innocent expression on my face. They, in turn, were not in the least respectful as they grabbed me by the shoulder and shoved me towards the little wooden cottage in which the investigators from the Ministry had set up shop.

The two gentlemen of Budapest had set the stage skillfully. They had positioned themselves behind a table, and the scene didn't look too great from my point of view. One man stood motionless beside the table, with his back to the wall. The other, who was of higher rank, was seated at the table and was rocking his chair on its hind legs. This gentleman held in his hand a rubber club which he was softly tapping on the edge of the table in a measured, monotonous rhythm. To further dramatize this threatening gesture, there was also some very expressive background music improvised from the bone-shattering cries and screams of the Ruthenian peasant who was being beaten to a pulp by a group of gendarmes.

The investigators let me stand there a while to take in the picture fully. When they thought I got the message, the one behind the table spoke to me gently, to emphasize that he was a refined and distinguished gentleman, and asked if it was true that I was the go-between and interpreter for the Ruthenian peasant and the deserters.

I didn't have too many options. If I admitted everything, I'd be beaten up and executed. If I denied everything, I'd be beaten up and executed. In my dilemma, I remembered another old Hungarian saying: he who gains time, gains life.

"I don't know any Ruthenian peasant."

The hangman behind the desk still played the subdued gentleman.

"I see. Well, if that is so, why did your own comrades say that you were their interpreter and go-between?"

"Probably because they tried to talk me into going with them and I refused. They just want to implicate me out of sheer revenge."

The soft-spoken gentleman rose slowly from his chair. "We'll find out about that soon, won't we?"

He started for the other room, obviously intending to bring in the Ruthenian and make us face each other. He stayed away quite a long time. I guessed they were trying to revive the Ruthenian a little for the face-to-face confrontation. The other investigator stayed in the room with me.

As I had not much to lose, I started to talk to him.

"I'm sure I've seen you before. I'm from Budapest." He didn't hit me so I went on. "I live near the National Theatre."

"I live in Zugló, in the suburbs. We have a house there."

The ice was broken.

"That's a nice place. The air is better than in the city."

"Yes. It's better for the children. They can play in the garden instead of on the street."

Keep talking, keep talking…As long as you keep talking about your kids and your house in the shady street of Zugló, you won't hit me. Who knows, maybe you'll even like me a little and, who knows, maybe I'll get to stay alive a little….

"Oh, you're absolutely right. Fresh air is very, very important for children. And they shouldn't have to play on the street. It's better for the grown-ups there too. They deserve a bit of quiet after a hard day's work."

"You can say that again. I've got ulcers. That needs a lot of rest."

At this point, the door opened and the pleasant social chatter came to an end. The gendarmes pushed the Ruthenian into the room — or what was left of him. His face had been, shall we say, altered beyond recognition, and he could hardly stand. The gendarmes propped him up.

As soon as I saw him, I yelled in his own language, "If you want to stay alive, you don't know me!"

The investigators immediately wanted to know what I had just said. "I told him to come nearer so that I could look at his face."

Frankly, I don't think they believed me, but I was the only interpreter within a hundred miles and if they wanted to communicate with the Ruthenian by words instead of billy clubs and fists, they needed me.

The interrogation went on for hours. I managed to convince the Ruthenian that we were both better off if we stuck to my story about the deserters trying to involve us in hope of lighter punishment. The poor guy was not quite conscious half the time but kept nodding at the right places, bless him, and supported my story.

I was very fortunate that the investigator with the house in Zugló, the ulcers and the kids he tried to keep off the street was more than ready to believe most of my answers. To everybody's great surprise, I walked out of the cottage unharmed. The poor Ruthenian was far from unharmed but they let him go, too.

After this incident, escape attempts stopped.

The Wise Men among us came to the conclusion that we had a better chance of surviving hard labour than of living through beatings and executions.

~

The frightening, terrible news in June 1941 of a war between the Nazis and the Soviets, two aggressive dictatorships, came as a harbinger of joyous tidings to our labour company. We had such a dim view of our future that the expansion of hostilities seemed our only hope. The more fronts the Germans had to fight on, the sooner they would be defeated. That night our batteries were recharged.

To us, war wasn't whistling bullets, diving airplanes, relentless tanks, frozen feet, torn limbs, devastation and the bankruptcy of humanity, but a knight in shining armour, a parade of heroes on white horses who would save the downtrodden victims of one of history's major injustices. Why do people always believe that the projected death of millions of others is the only way to achieve peace and quiet for themselves?

The next morning, business was as usual. Well, not quite. Our keepers seemed to be under great stress as a result of orders arriving from headquarters every half hour or so. Every new order cancelled the previous one only to be contradicted again by the next. Something was about to happen, either a transfer or some other kind of reorganization, because the Hungarian army always operated on the same principle: keep doing something no matter how useless, stupid or suicidal.

Indeed, three days after the declaration of war, orders arrived to be ready to move. We packed. Two days later, we marched to the station. There stood a train of cattle cars and one passenger car. Fourteen hours later, the train pulled out.

The rumour was that we were going to Budapest. It sounded too good to be true and we refused to believe it until we arrived at the outer yard of the Eastern Station in Budapest. We marched straight to our next place of work, Shipyard Island, at the north end of the city. As we trotted through the gates of the compound, we couldn't help noticing the soothing, inspiring motto above the entrance: "Prepare for war because lasting peace exists only in the graveyard."

We braced ourselves for even tougher work and rougher treatment but, bless the army brains, nothing ever goes according to common sense. The day after our arrival at Shipyard Island, we got a one-week furlough. With the speed of bullets, we shot out of the compound and rejoined the human race. After so many months, we were about to live like civilized people again for one whole week. Baths. Electric lights. Flush toilets. Food on plates. Knives and forks. Sheets, pillows and beds. Women. Movies. Human speech.

Too much!

My room had been paid for a year in advance so I went straight home. My landlady greeted me warmly and I headed directly for the bath. I could have sat for hours in the warm water but I had other urgent matters to attend to. I dressed with care. Shirt, tie, pressed pants, jacket, shoes. What luxury! I took a cab to Weingruber's restaurant.

When the waiter placed the menu before me, it took all my discipline not to tell him to bring everything, from the top of the list right through to the last item. But I was a well-brought-up young man so I simply ordered beef stew with dumplings. I ate, paid and left. Fortunately, I still had a tidy sum in the bank. Then I went straight to a nearby restaurant and ordered a Wiener schnitzel. I thought it was best not to order two meals in the same restaurant.

Thoroughly scrubbed, properly groomed and well-fed, I now turned my attention to matters of the heart. To my greatest dismay, I learned from neighbours that my girlfriend, Lili, had gone home to visit her sick mother. Without wasting much time, I took a cab to the railway station and managed to catch a train to Lili's hometown within the hour. Hitler, Stalin, the war, the labour company had all faded away into the foggy distance. Maybe they were just a figment of the imagination… I couldn't think of anything but Lili, who would soon be in my arms.

The cobblestones of the quiet street had a slightly sobering effect on me. As I walked towards the house, it struck me that Lili might be annoyed at my following her. What if her parents knew nothing about us? All I knew about her family was that her father was an architect. I had no idea what kind of a man he was, what his political views were, whose side he was on…. What if he refused to let me in at all?

A girl in her early twenties answered the door. I knew immediately that she was Lili's sister. She looked at me questioningly and, in a few seconds, she flashed a very pleasing smile.

"You must be Imre."

I nodded. She offered her hand in a friendly welcome.

"I'm Lili's sister. I'm very glad to meet you. I can't wait to see Lili's face when she sees you."

As soon as I entered, Lili jumped up and kissed me in front of everybody. I suddenly felt quite fine. She hung on my neck and kissed me again and again.

Friendly faces greeted me on all sides. It was a nice house. Lili's parents made me sit down at the dinner table and they asked me a million questions. They wanted to know everything about the man their daughter loved.

A discussion on politics was more or less inevitable. Obviously, the parents were aware that I was Jewish, and they showed absolutely no hostility on that account. Nevertheless, they strongly believed in the cause of the Germans and Lili's father in particular had a high opinion of the Nazis.

"There is no question that the Third Reich will soon run Europe," he declared. "The Allied powers are weak and indecisive. They have ruled too long and there's a need for fresh blood."

An unfortunate turn of phrase.

It's never very good manners to contradict one's elders — especially the father of one's love — but I was very annoyed at what he said and I had also had a glass of wine and every drop of it had gone to my head.

"Excuse me, sir, but it seems that the new blood has so far only succeeded in trampling others under foot."

"That's right, son, but you must appreciate that a major power has to get rid of its enemies before it can establish itself and do some good."

The debate grew more and more heated. He stuck to his views and I to mine. I stated that so much hatred and so much bloodshed couldn't possibly lead to happiness — which may not have been the most original philosophical discovery but it was a hell of a lot better than his maxim that if you want an omelet, you have to break eggs (that, by the way, is not a Hungarian saying). I was about to trump that with a strong reply when I caught Lili's eyes. She looked worried and confused. I quickly came to my senses because the last thing I wanted was to turn her father against me. He wasn't a bad guy, only blinded by the catchy slogans of the Nazis that seemed to shine more convincingly with Hitler's initial successes on the battlefields. I stood up and turned to him with all the politeness I could muster.

"I respect your opinions, sir, but I hope you're wrong. Because if you're right, I won't have the pleasure of discussing the matter further with you."

Lili's father stood up and embraced me. "I like you, son. Let's shake on it."

From the corner of my eye, I saw Lili relax and smile.

A few wonderful days followed. I spent practically every minute with Lili. We never said it out loud but we both felt that it would be a very long time before we saw each other again — if ever.

On the last evening we stayed up very late. There was no way I could face the parting scene so I decided to leave quietly in the morning before anyone was up. I rose at five and walked to the railway station. Before I left, I scribbled a few words on the clean side of an envelope. "Sorry to sneak out like a coward. I've no strength for goodbyes."

On my arrival in Budapest, there would be a telegram at my door. "I'll wait for you forever. Lili."

The train ride to Budapest did not take too long but it was long enough to give me plenty of time to think. I did my best to occupy myself with the scenery on the other side of the grimy window, but I saw nothing. The clatter of the wheels exploded in my head and the hard sound of steel hammered out a series of questions.

What if I had listened seriously to the American woman at the nightclub who wanted to take me home with her? Maybe I should have gone to America. Maybe I could have taken my mother and sister along as well. Of course, in America I wouldn't have met Lili. Now that I had stayed, would I see Lili again? Would I ever see anybody I cared for again? What if I had assumed another identity, taken another name, another religion, another place of birth, other parents and tried to outlive the Nazis as another person? Would I be better off? Would my chances of survival be greater? What if, what if, what if?

~

One evening, about a week after we started work in the brick factory, a sergeant came to our quarters.

"Attention!"

We stood rigid in honour of his greatness. He cleared his throat.

"Men, from now on you'll be taking a course. An ensign from the corps of engineers will come every evening, direct from the District Headquarters, and will give you instruction on the mechanism of landmines. Understand?"

"We understand!"

When the sergeant left us, we stayed rigid, in deadly silence, frozen with fear. So that was the plan. Somewhere, in the snow-covered fields of the Ukraine, they were going to chase us out to pick up landmines left by the Soviet army or the partisans. Where were the mines? Simple! Wherever a Jew was being blown to bits.

As promised, the young engineer arrived every night to acquaint us with various members of the landmine family. He lectured on the subject with great enthusiasm, as if he were discussing ways to prepare our favourite gourmet dishes instead of telling us how to kill ourselves. Were those people so evil and cynical that they enjoyed rubbing our noses in their dirt or were they just criminally stupid in following the eternal rules of Kafkaesque bureaucracy?

Eight hundred and fifty of us left for the Soviet front. Eight hundred and fifty healthy, bright, life-loving, strong young men.

Three of us saw our homes again.

On the way to the Eastern Front, we worked ourselves into the proper mood. At our first stop we got a little preview of things to come. A middle-aged man was being escorted towards our train by a group of gendarmes. The rather distinguished-looking man was followed by some members of his family and, before he was about to join us in the cattle car, he tried to embrace his wife and daughter. That highly provocative gesture prompted two gendarmes to beat him up severely in front of his family and other onlookers. I learned later that the gentleman was the head of surgery at the local hospital, a respected citizen in the entire region. Four weeks after the incident, he was killed near Voronezh by an exploding mine.

It was a four-day journey to the marshalling yard in Gomel, previously part of the Byelorussian Soviet Socialist Republic and now under Nazi occupation. An hour after we left the train, orders came to meet up with a company of engineers to help them build a bridge. We were soon standing up to our necks in water and handing beams and poles to the engineers. It was summer and the weather was warm but standing all day in the fast river, tied to a pole to prevent us from being swept away by the current, wasn't my idea of fun in the sun. On top of extreme physical exertion and discomfort, we also had to suffer under a non-stop barrage of choice insults hurled at us by the noble Hungarian soldiers.

While still in Budapest, we had heard of atrocities at the front and we were more or less prepared for difficult times. Yet, when the whip cracked on our own backs (that is a Hungarian saying), the effect was crushing. It was one thing to hear terrible news while one was still in relative comfort and safety and quite another to see in person that Jews and other inferior races were systematically killed in a business-like manner and that the massacre of certain people was simply one more branch of Nazi industry.

We had heard, of course, of concentration camps in Germany and of Jews being stripped of their rights, and we knew that the same process had started in Hungary and the other satellite countries, but only when we stepped on foreign soil did we take in the terrible reality of our total helplessness.

Without ignoring the facts, for some reason or other we had felt reasonably safe in Hungary. Cruel treatment alone didn't alarm us because treating soldiers — Jewish or not — like animals was an old Hungarian tradition. We got slapped in the face, soldiers got slapped in the face. The NCOs kicked us in the stomach, they kicked regular recruits in the stomach. That was the law of the land and, since soldiers were seldom beaten to death, we also weren't afraid of getting killed.

At the Eastern Front, things were different. Human life was cheap and death walked among us every day, morning to night, night to morning. What could I expect from soldiers who themselves didn't know whether they would live fifty years, five months, five days or five minutes?

Standing up to one's neck in cold water, tied to a post all day and heaving heavy beams around is a damned good way of opening one's eyes and gaining instant wisdom. Unfortunately, with wisdom came the facility to catch a much closer glimpse of human nature than one would have liked.

When we finally got out of the river, we marched. This was no drill anymore. This was the real thing. Thirteen hundred kilometres of it. The invigorating walk ended near the Ukrainian town of Voronezh. There was no need for neon signs to advertise that we were near the front. The constant thunder of heavy artillery explained everything.

We were given quarters in a place that resembled an archeological excavation site more than the hamlet it once was. The houses had never been really suitable for human use — and to think that we used to consider our own villages primitive and poor — but by then we were no longer fussy. Being dead tired, we simply collapsed on the floor.

Work began the next day. We had to dig tank traps. It was murderous work and by the time we had learned a few tricks and gained some experience, the food had grown thinner and thinner and so had we. The little nourishment that was available went first to the Germans — after all, they were the superior race — next to the Hungarian officers, then to the NCOs, to the soldiers and only then, a mile below the bottom of the pecking order, to the labour servicemen. The good news was that we had no worries about obesity. There wasn't a speck of fat in our food and as the weeks and months passed, the situation got slowly worse.

Then came the first casualties. Physical exhaustion and psychological breakdown brought on by malnutrition and humiliation proved too much to overcome. Every morning, more and more boys were found dead. They couldn't stand it any longer. Without the strength or desire to live, they gave in and died.

None of them was over thirty.

As our strength diminished, we found it harder to work. We sank lower and lower by the day. Those of us with enough strength to think wished we hadn't. There wasn't enough optimism in the whole world to convince us that there was any chance of getting out of that hellhole alive. It was clear that our masters didn't regard us as human beings and that as long as we were alive, we would work, and when we died, they would bring new Jews, and when those died, they would bring more.

Under such circumstances, it was obvious that our only hope was to make it to the other side, never mind how risky that was. Nothing was riskier than staying put. The far side of the Don River was in Russian hands and freedom was one swim away. One only had to make it to the river, preferably under the protective blanket of darkness, and swim across. No big deal. Many of us had swum across rivers before, for fun.

This was no summer fun, however. Most of the guys were patho-
logically weak, damaged in body and spirit. They never made it to
the other side. They drowned in the fast, relentless current. A few did
make it, however. The percentage wasn't good, but it gave encouragement to the rest of us. Unfortunately, it also gave encouragement
to our keepers to tighten the already tight screws. As the desertions
increased, so did the cruelty. It was obvious that the Royal Hungarian
Army wasn't going to stand by with folded arms while their slaves
disappeared.

One morning, an unusually large number of soldiers came and
joined our crew at roll call. We were much too tired and lethargic to
speculate why they were there. We started the daily routine of counting ourselves.

One, two, three, four, five, six, seven, eight, nine, ten…

"Step forward!"

Eleven, twelve, thirteen, fourteen, fifteen, sixteen, seventeen,
eighteen, nineteen, twenty.

"Step forward!"

The coin finally dropped. A murmur ran through the rows.
Decimation! So that's what it was like. The game continued
monotonously.

Thirty-eight, thirty-nine, forty…

"Step forward!"

There they stood, the condemned. Their numbers grew by one
every ten seconds. What was their crime? They were tenth. Does that
warrant the death penalty? According to the rules of the game, yes.
Why them? Just because! Who made up the rules? Oh, it's a very old
game, with traditional rules — we don't make them up, we only play.

We were neither shocked, nor scared. Like sleepwalkers, we
moved mechanically and accepted everything that happened around
us. Maybe deep down we wanted to end the whole thing one way or
another. Death is one form of escape, after all.

The brave Hungarian soldiers went to work. They quickly grabbed the condemned men and dragged them to improvised gallows. Laughing, swearing, pushing, cursing, the soldiers hanged the boys and cracked great jokes as the bodies twitched. We didn't find it funny but many of the guys may have, in a way, envied the hanged ones. For them, the pain was over.

There was one more decimation. I was eighth at the first, sixth at the second.

All punishments, including the executions, were ordered by our company commander and carried out by his men.

~

An officer from the engineers arrived with two soldiers who were carrying a wooden crate. The box contained two Soviet-made landmines and the officer duly proceeded to tell us how they worked. He held them up, one after the other, so that we could examine them from all sides. He was probably afraid that we might mistake one for a box of fine Swiss chocolates. The course ended with the officer telling us how to defuse the little monster — providing we could get it out of the ground without blowing it up.

The fascists must have had an extremely high opinion of our mental abilities and mechanical knack because after an hour-long demonstration we were pronounced experts in dismantling mines. To show how much we were trusted, we were immediately sent out to the minefields.

It would be unfair not to mention that we were given the best equipment available. Every man received a short spade and a long stick. According to Royal Hungarian Army logic, if we came across a mine we couldn't dismantle for one reason or other, the following procedure came into effect: utilizing spade, labour serviceman digs one hole deep enough to accommodate himself. Labour serviceman climbs into hole. Utilizing long stick, labour serviceman pokes at mine until explosion of same occurs.

And to think that the genius who planned this has remained anonymous! The plan allowed for all eventualities: If mine blows up and Jew doesn't, Jew can proceed to next mine; if mine blows up and Jew blows up, that's okay, too.

Fortunately, the cute little gadget that hid itself neatly in the ground and made such a fuss if stepped on occupied our minds fully and left us little time and energy to think about our situation. Just as well. Behind us were the Hungarian guns, ahead of us were the minefields and beyond them was the Soviet army, which nervously started to fire like mad after each explosion from us.

As a further show of trust, our keepers generously allowed us to go out there all by ourselves, without guards, to defeat the Red Army with a short spade and a long stick.

Needless to say, it didn't take us long to come up with a great idea. Since there were no guards, why on earth should we pick mines? Nobody could see us, so why couldn't we go out there, lie flat for a few hours and then go back and report that we hadn't found any mines? We might even stay alive....

Alas, the strategists of the Royal Hungarian Army outsmarted the conniving, shrewd Jews. Did we have a good scheme? They had a better one! How can one make the Jew pick mines without an armed guard watching over him? Simple! If the Jew doesn't bring in a dismantled mine, the Jew doesn't eat.

The first night produced four dead. They survived the explosion but fell in the ensuing Russian fire.

Walking at night in the Russian winter in rags with no gloves on the hands and no food in the belly isn't much fun. When said walk takes place in a minefield, it's decidedly unpleasant. Even mother earth becomes an enemy. She's frigid and unwelcoming, full of holes and mounds and furrows. Tanks, armoured cars and exploding missiles had ploughed the surface into an abstract relief that made our difficult task even more horrendous. Every bump and every pile of frozen dirt could turn out to be a mine.

# My Surprising Escapes
## Benedikt Korda (Kornreich)

My departure to Kassa (now known as Košice in Slovakia) in April 1943 was the first step in a new chapter of my life. From then until the end of the war, all of my possessions were in my knapsack. You can hardly imagine how precious some of those possessions were, even just a comb or a toothbrush. In the wilderness, where we spent most of those two years, there was no way to replace such luxuries. I was quite upset when I lost them alongside my hat. In September 1944, they fell prey to a German tank. Foolishly, I had carried them at that time in a small bag on my shoulder, not in the knapsack. But let me proceed from the beginning.

The former cavalry barracks of Kassa was turned into a gathering point and a kind of distribution centre for inductees into forced labour. My introduction to this place was (or was meant to be) a scary one. More than a thousand of us were herded into a small yard. On an improvised podium, a corporal wielding a heavy bludgeon welcomed us. He must have been an illiterate farmhand who enjoyed his new-found power to scare, insult and humiliate people. His long talk must have been very boring, because I soon lost track of it and stopped paying any attention. I just remember him babbling about "you Jews are going to listen here" and similar threats.

I already had some information about that place from friends who had been there before, especially about its notorious commandant.

Lo and behold, I remember his name — first lieutenant (promoted later to captain) Milakovics. He was the absolute ruler of the place. There was no appeal against his rulings, against the punishments he meted out. He was the "emperor," as his court Jew called him. This "court Jew" was no fool. He just played the fool to avoid labour assignment. It seemed to me that both he and the "emperor" liked the game. The commandant was presented to me (and not only to me) as the incarnation of evil. Well, I guess I have to be more charitable. He was not as bad as his fame would have it. Perhaps he liked to scare people and he took pride in his fame. But my experience with him was not bad. In 1944, when the deportations of Jews to Auschwitz started, he issued hundreds of urgent summons, which saved many Jews from Auschwitz — or at least that's what a friend of mine told me who was personally helped this way.

The second day was reserved for registration. Tables were set up in the big courtyard to process the rookies. One of the tables was reserved for "Christian Jews." Well, it was very attractive to get into this group, and in some cases it meant as much as saving one's skin. Getting into this group required a baptismal certificate, a hot commodity in those days. I didn't have one. But why not try it in any case? I watched the goings-on from a distance and then at a moment when there was no traffic I approached the clerk, a normal-looking young reservist, and asked him to register me. "Your baptismal certificate?" I expected that request and was prepared for it. I told him that I had come from Prague just a short time ago, that I'd had to leave in a rush and had forgotten my baptismal certificate. I told him that I had married a Christian. Perhaps a marriage certificate would do? He hesitated, but I noticed that he was a softie and I was sure that some persuasion would suffice.

Alas, something unexpected happened. Suddenly one of the notoriously cruel guys appeared behind my clerk. He must have already been there for a minute or so, as was clear from the tantrum he fired off. Yes, it was him, master sergeant Kerekes. The night before, one of my seasoned roommates had given a perfect description of him with a warning: "He is the fright of the barracks. Do not cross his path if you can help it." I don't have the vocabulary to repeat his abusive language, but the gist of his very loud logorrhea was that anybody could come with such stories and that I should "buzz off, or...." There is not much anyone can do in such a situation.

I made an about-face in a soldierly manner and retreated, though not too far, continuing to watch the scene. When the air cleared, as soon as Kerekes left, I returned and started talking to the clerk again. Apparently, he was a nice guy, but he said that there was nothing he could do. "You heard my superior. I cannot defy his order." As I went on with my attempts at persuasion, he told me that the only way open to me was to report to the commandant, to Lieutenant Milakovics. When I heard the name, I lost my courage, since I already knew about him from my friends back in Munkács. Here, too, I had heard only the worst things about him. I had already seen him. "That's him," I was told when he walked about. Not a promising figure, so why bother? I just played the innocent and told the scribe that I didn't know him. "He walks here every few minutes, a stocky, rather short man with a moustache. Or you can find him there in that big building." I thanked him and virtually gave up. But who knows, maybe it was worth it to play such a high-stakes game to the end. I talked to some people but didn't get any wiser.

By chance, my brother Béla appeared. What was my brother doing there? Well, he had been inducted before me, but he was in a special position. He was not assigned to any specific unit. They just used him as a construction technician and sent him out on special assignments. Since they valued him as an expert, he had a great degree of freedom of movement. Well, he was never a talker and was brief this time too: "I think you should try. It cannot make things worse."

That was clear advice, so I set out to the old, gloomy three-storey office building at once. "Where to?" asked the armed guard at the entrance. "To Lieutenant Milakovics" — I stood at attention. "Third floor" was all I got from him. It was not difficult to find the right door. I knocked. A sweet voice answered, "Come in." A good-looking blond in her forties behind the desk asked me what I wanted. "I wish to report to Lieutenant Milakovics." She was even less talkative than the guard downstairs. With a simple gesture she indicated the door I had to enter. I knocked again. This time a strong bass voice answered. Yes, it was the "emperor" in person, sitting behind a big desk. I sprang to attention as elegantly as I could (I admit I rehearsed those *meshuga* moves beforehand) and started to bombard him in a clear voice, first with the required formula and then with my request to be registered with the white armbands.

"So why don't you go to that table?" He showed me the registration table from the window. I explained to him in the same voice that I had been there, and then I repeated the whole blue lie I told the clerk. To my amazement, he didn't scream, and neither did he try to question my statement. "Where is your paybook?" The question surprised me; I didn't know that a paybook had already been prepared for me in advance. "I didn't get one." "What's your name?" I told him my name. Without a word he stood up, went to the door and asked the woman to find my paybook. He went back to his desk and kept me waiting without saying a word. It was a long wait, I don't know how long, but for me it was an eternity. Finally, she returned, unhappy that she couldn't find it. Without saying a word he left again and I kept waiting. This time I didn't wait too long. He came back with my paybook in his hand. As he leafed through it, I succeeded in reading the company number I had been assigned to. (As I would learn the next day, that company had left just that morning for the Soviet front.) He tore the book to pieces, wrote a new one and gave it to me. All that without a word. I thanked him and made an elegant about-face and, in no time, I was out of the building. Thus started my Christian career. The comedy of "fearless, soldierly" behaviour worked. My paybook is still with me, though not in the best shape.

Somehow it survived fifty years of adventure. It was probably destined by Fate to be saved for posterity.

Some people might question the morality of my actions. I am no expert in the field of morality, but in my view one basic tenet of morality should be accepted by everyone: Don't do to others what you wouldn't like to be done to you. Most of the rest is open to discussion. In those days, nobody reproached me for anything; we just had fun playing the game. To illustrate this, I recall one of my friends in the barracks, a bearded man about thirty years old whom I befriended because he was very lonely. I used to see him daily in the yard. We spoke Yiddish, since my Yiddish was still quite good in those days. He claimed to be a rabbi, although not officially recognized as such, which is why they had not let him go. Food was not kosher there, so his diet was very meagre. As our stay stretched out, I asked him why he had been there so long. Well, he had tried everything possible, without any success, to get an exemption from the service. Now he had his last chance. He had faked some disease (I don't remember what) and was granted a medical checkup. "And why have you been here all this time?" he asked me in return. "I'm a meshummad" (a rude word meaning apostate), I told him with a smile. No one should say such a thing to a holy man, I thought to myself; why break up a friendship? But once the words were out I couldn't take them back. Fortunately, all went well. His reaction was not what I expected. He returned my smile and said, "Also good."

⁓

The one place in Hungary proper where we had to perform a serious job was Hajdúböszörmény (I am sorry about the name, I realize it is impossible for non-Hungariana to pronounce). There we were supposed to build a military airport or rather just an airstrip but never finished anything. Hajdúböszörmény was a God-forsaken backwater on the fertile Hungarian plain. It had a population of almost 35,000 and was thus bigger than Munkács, however, it was just a large village, practically still stuck in medieval times with no modern amenities. The bulk of the population consisted of farmers, and even the tradesmen were part-time farmers.

As I got better acquainted with the new environment, life in Hajdúböszörmény became somewhat more interesting (or let us say less boring). First of all, I learned more about gentile Hungarians. I must admit I was quite prejudiced against them and afraid of them too. I was suspicious that every Hungarian could do me in. It was a kind of paranoia based on my experience with Hungarian propaganda, with anti-Jewish laws and with the atrocities committed during the reconquest of lost territories. And there were indeed many fascists among Hungarians, especially within the army and the political elite. Some of my former friends even turned out to be fascists and virulent antisemites when it was opportune. But still it's not right to generalize.

In the rural environment of Hajdúböszörmény, my experiences with Hungarians were quite good. They knew who we were and they knew that we were not supposed to leave the grounds of the camp, but nobody cared and nobody ever denounced us. We had normal, friendly conversations with them. It seems to me that common folks are mostly harmless and rather friendly. They are more concerned with their everyday business than with politics or with tormenting innocent people. But again, let's not generalize the other way around either. Anyway, as soon as I got acquainted with the environment, I started to move about freely, not only in the town but also outside of it. It was all risky.

One nonsensical episode scared the hell out of me, but it ended quite happily. Bozenka, my wife, who I had first met in the Czech lands and who came to stay with me as much as that was possible, felt that she needed her hair done. This shouldn't be a problem, we thought, since there was a hairdresser in town. The problem was language. How could Bozenka explain what she wanted? She needed an interpreter. Though it's not a job to my liking, what choice did I have? I didn't realize that the barber business had its own terminology, which remained unknown to me. Worse than that, they looked at us as if we were from another planet. In the Hungarian plains, people almost never hear a foreign language, and meeting somebody who doesn't know Hungarian is the sensation of a lifetime.

"What language do you speak?" The question caught me off guard. It occurred to me that it might be inappropriate to answer that we spoke Czech. Czechs and Hungarians were archenemies. For more than twenty years, Hungarians had read in their papers that the bad Czechs robbed them of a big chunk of their territory. I didn't want to take on the role of an enemy, so I answered quite mechanically, "We speak Swedish." It was indeed a mechanical reaction, because in the old days back in Munkács, when we talked about Czechs (with Czechs present), we called them Swedes. This time the camouflage was revived in a funny way. There was nothing special in our conversation at the barber's, so we forgot it before the hairdo was finished.

We went home to prepare some supper. No sooner had we sat down to eat than somebody knocked at the door. A strange thing, because the etiquette of giving notice of your arrival was rather unknown there. Neighbours either came in without knocking (the luxury of doorbells was virtually unknown) or they would call to you from the street. I answered the door. A man about my age entered. I knew his face. I had seen him several times loitering around the perimeter of our compound. He introduced himself and showed me some ID, but I didn't catch his name, nor the name of the agency he worked for. It was clear, though, that he was a plainclothes officer, and he scared me. After all, I had no business being there. He started with some roundabout questions (I don't remember a thing about them) and left me guessing what his visit might be about.

Then came the bombshell: "Do you speak Swedish?" I felt some tickling in my belly and I had difficulty holding back loud laughter. At last I understood what had led him to our place. Ah, I should have realized that the barber was not familiar with our Munkács slang. I explained to him what Swedish meant in our jargon. Fortunately, the guy was not stupid. He already understood that the whole thing was nonsense. As a form of apology, he explained to me that the Swedes had built a plant not far away and some might come back to spy there. He left with a friendly handshake. I was still somewhat concerned, as I was wary of Hungarian officials. But the next day, I talked about it with my friends. Lévai, a lawyer, told me that he knew the guy and there was nothing to worry about.

I was working in the kitchen when we got a new arrival, a master sergeant whose name I have forgotten, a rotten, bad guy. At least that was my impression from his own bragging. He came from the Soviet front, from the Don River where a number of my friends perished. They died not only from mines, "enemy" bullets and extremely cold temperatures, but also often from mistreatment by their own supervisors. I got the impression that this man was himself one of those brutal guys. I wouldn't have paid attention to him, but I overheard the company number he served in. It was the same company where my brother-in-law, Tibor, was and my sister Blanka hadn't had news from him for more than a year. I thought maybe this sergeant could give me some information.

When he came for lunch, I gave him a good portion of meat and asked him, "So you served with company no. 42 (might have been a different number). Incidentally, did you know one Tibor Ney, a well-built, tall guy?" "That gangster, that scoundrel!" he exploded. "We shot him dead. He stole a wagon with a horse and ran straight to the enemy, but he didn't succeed. He was about halfway to them when we shot him, that traitor." You can imagine how I felt. It was not the information I'd hoped to hear. But should I believe this guy at all? There was also the mysterious message Blanka had gotten from an unknown person who rang the doorbell, left there a scrap of paper with "Greetings from Ney" on it and ran away. I figured that it was a message from Tibor sent from the other side of the front. The two pieces of information didn't match, did they? Anyway, what could I have done with such new information? I decided to keep it to myself.

One and a half years passed before I learned the truth. It turned out that the sergeant was right, though not exactly. Tibor was truly shot when he tried to escape with a wagon. But he was not killed, only seriously wounded. His left shoulder was totally destroyed. He fell unconscious and was captured by the Soviets. Fortunately, there were some good Jewish doctors there, who brought him back to life. His shoulder was lost and his hand became a useless appendage. It was a kind of a miracle that he survived there, since the conditions in those Soviet field hospitals were far from the best.

~

The next serious assignment we had was at a place called Lăpusna. Though Lăpusna is labelled on maps, I never saw a village there, just a huge compound of wooden structures, houses, barns and other utility buildings. The buildings had apparently not been in use for years. Decay was visible everywhere. Swallows had a perfect, undisturbed nesting ground there. They nested not only on outside walls, but also in a number of rooms. The compound used to be, we were told, King Carol's hunting castle, but after the Romanians lost Transylvania to Hungary, he no longer had access to it. Not far away uphill was a new brick and stone building, also huge. It was Regent Horthy's hunting castle. Apparently, the two archenemies had similar tastes for wilderness (let me add that their taste was not bad). I just imagined how nice it would have been to see both rulers hunting there and feasting together and then settling the question of sovereignty over Transylvania the old-fashioned way, by the sword.

Otherwise, this place was in the wilderness. It was not as romantic as the village of Botiz, where we had previously stayed, but charming nonetheless, with wide spaces and a river (who could remember all their strange names?). The accommodation was not too bad either. I settled with a group of friends in one of the small rooms. In the old days it would have been a servant's room, I guess. When we moved in, the only occupants were a family of swallows. Their nest was in the middle of the ceiling. The swallows seemed unperturbed by our presence. We watched with the curiosity of city kids as the pair fed their offspring. They flew swiftly out of the building and in no time they were back with some goodies to feed their young. It was quite a spectacle, until one of the boys became too curious and wanted to have a closer look. As he climbed on a table and tried to peep in the nest, the swallows were frightened; they packed up their offspring and left, never to return. I was terribly sad and very sorry for them. Our own fate and that of many others came to mind. We had to leave our nests too.

Our mission in Lăpusna was again to build a road, this time, though, a real road for motor vehicles. We could only guess what purpose it would serve. Rumour had it that the Germans had planned a new offensive in that direction. It was now summer 1944, when the myth of German invincibility was already long gone and the war was, for all practical purposes, lost by them. I am sure the German generals, or at least most of them, were aware of that. What kept them fighting was fear of that sickly corporal Hitler and his entourage, who had no choice but to believe in miracles and fight up to the last German.

To plan an offensive under those circumstances along a road that didn't exist yet (I am sure it doesn't exist to this day) must have been the brainchild of some desperate general. I would have viewed it as comedy if not for the tragic situation we were in. But I am no expert in military matters, so perhaps my judgment is biased.

I was out of the kitchen. Actually, to use military jargon, I was "dishonourably discharged" from that prestigious job. Well, there were serious complaints against me that I was favouring my close friends. Perhaps those allegations had some merit. Who knows? We always have some biases. But that couldn't have been the real background of the complaints. Under normal conditions, such misunderstandings could have been settled in a friendly manner. But conditions were not normal, and as psychologists will tell you, people under confinement act strangely. Some get very nervous and look for scapegoats for their misery among fellow inmates, usually among a group of "others." Divisions always exist in such groups. I realized all of this, and so I was not too disturbed. Fortunately for me (and for us all), commandant Gyenge was a reasonable man and not a bad guy. The conflict came to an end with my dismissal. I didn't mind at all: a rest from that ungrateful job was just fine with me. At least I can tell you more about the charade called road building.

Building a road in the Carpathian wilderness is not a simple matter under any circumstances. Building it without any machinery and with no materials requires real ingenuity. Our first task was to prepare material. There was, of course, plenty of wood around to cover our needs. However, to fell those huge trees with no power tools was a hard job, and for soft-skinned city boys like myself it was a terribly painful one. My skin was gone after pulling the saw for half an hour. Once, as we felled a tall fir tree, we spotted a squirrel's nest in a cavity. The big squirrels had fled, leaving a bunch of tiny squirrels huddled together. They were cute, still without fur, but with fleas feasting on them. I was sorry for those little guys. They were doomed.

What we needed most was stone, lots of it. But there was no quarry nearby, and the only possible source was the river. We had to wade in the river and harvest stone from the riverbed. Well, that's not a very bad job as long as you can take your time. However, some of those crazy guys set for us a daily norm that was impossible to fulfill. I don't remember what it was, maybe three cubic metres of stone, maybe five. It was definitely too much. There was no arguing with those military men, but with some ingenuity and courage people can fulfill impossible requests. When no guards were around (which occurred quite frequently, because everybody likes a rest), we quickly assembled a few big logs and built around them nice pyramid-like piles from stones we collected. You might say it was a risky game, since somebody could discover that those piles were almost 90 per cent wood and this obviously would have been discovered as soon as we started building the actual road. Well, to be sure, there is always some risk involved in such an enterprise. But we weren't too concerned with such an eventuality. We were confident that it'd never come to that. It was already five to midnight or, as we used to say, it was time for *ne'ila* (a saying we used that referred to the closing service of Yom Kippur). Only fools, alas very dangerous ones, considered it still possible to turn the tide of the war.

Another preliminary task consisted of surveying the future road, which is a technical job. The engineers responsible for the job came from a sapper battalion stationed not far away. There were three of them, all lieutenants. Two virulent bastards about my age were directly in charge of the measurements. I didn't know the function of the third one, a tall, rather impenetrable old man. I just noticed that he became friends with commandant Gyenge. I watched them from a distance, talking very seriously. Not once did I see a smile on his face. By chance I learned that his name was Margittai. I imagine that for most people there's nothing special in that name. Well, it was quite different for me. Actually, it is a very unusual name, and I'd call it an artificial one. The family's name was originally Morgenthaler and they were Germans. There were two German villages adjacent to Munkács. Some of the Germans became Magyarized (adopted Hungarian culture) and changed their names.

How did I know all that? Simple: during my years in high school I had a math teacher named Margittai. I knew him really well and I was his best student. Now I noticed a similarity between the two Margittais and I became curious whether and how they were related. I approached him one day and introduced myself. It was unusual for a forced labourer to approach an officer without due cause. So what, I thought, he wouldn't kill me. Indeed, he didn't. However, it seemed to me that he was loath to talk to me. He didn't react to my name, though everybody in Munkács knew the Kornreichs. Well, I thought, to hell with that antisemite.

Still, to satisfy my curiosity, I told him about my math teacher. I also told him that I used to be his favourite student. Not a single muscle moved on his face. "Aren't you related?" I asked at last. "Yes, he was my brother," he said very reluctantly, at least so it seemed to me. He used the past tense, meaning that his brother was no more. I didn't ask any further questions as I had had enough of the conversation. I didn't know what category to put him in. Was he really a bad man, or just one of those who didn't want any problems?

People who live normal lives can hardly understand how brutal regimes can affect people's attitudes. I lived for almost three decades under the two most brutal regimes of modern times. In my experience, there are always zealots who, for one reason or another (not necessarily egotistic), are ready to stone you, to bury you alive in support (real or imagined) of a dictator. They are the pillars of the regime, but they are only a minority and not sufficient on their own for the survival of the regime. Then there are those who are ready to fetch a stone and hurl it at you, not because they want to, but because they are told to do so and don't have the will to resist such orders. They are very dangerous because they are numerous and because one can't be prepared for them. You never know from which direction the blow might come. Your best friend, and even your spouse or your own child might betray you. Then there is a much larger group of those who, for fear or convenience, look the other way. They don't want to hear or see what's going on and refuse to get involved. There are always courageous people too, and, believe me, under those regimes it required courage to reach out to someone who was made into an outcast. Margittai was probably not a bad man, after all. I would say he belonged to the third category.

He didn't stay long with us as he was soon discharged, I guess for age. Sometime later, in early June 1944, all those from Munkács and its environs were summoned to commandant Gyenge. He had a sheet of paper in his hand, a letter from Margittai. Gyenge told us in a somewhat broken voice that he felt it was his duty to read us part of the letter, however sad. I can't recall the words, but Margittai wrote about how all the Jews from Munkács and the surrounding areas had been herded into a brick factory and deported a few days later. "It's a tragedy, but unfortunately those are the facts," he wrote.

There is no way to describe how we felt. The thought that so many people were squeezed into that brick factory was horrifying. The rest I knew from my experience in Prague. Gyenge tried to comfort us, telling us that the Nazis already knew their time was up, that they were just taking hostages in order to barter for some concessions in case of capitulation. It was good to hear such soothing words from a Hungarian officer. They revealed a lot about Gyenge. He was definitely on our side, but his words were no consolation for me. Unfortunately, I knew too much about deportations to unknown concentration camps from which nobody was supposed to return alive. It was horrible to think of that, but as I recall those events now, it seems I got used to unspeakable cruelties. I took them for granted as the way of life under the Nazis. It seemed futile to ask why.

However, this time it was different. My whole family was there in Munkács — my father, my mother, my brothers, my sisters and my playful nephews. I was quite pessimistic about their fates and didn't believe I would see any of them again. I was bleeding inside as I stood there listening to Gyenge. I tried to visualize all those men, women, infants and old people squeezed into those brick factories. I knew those factories: just dirty walls and dust inside, mud outside, without the most elementary facilities. It was all beyond my imagination. The scum of humanity, Germans and Hungarians, armed to their teeth, displayed their power over defenseless people. I don't like to show emotion, so I tried to remain calm when Gyenge read that letter, but I could not hold back my tears.

I learned the general facts later when I was back in Munkács and some of the details only much later. All the Jews of Munkács were gone by mid-May 1944. They were dispatched to Auschwitz-Birkenau. Those over fifty and children with their mothers were murdered right away, gassed and cremated. That's how Father, age sixty-four, died. My stepmother (forty-nine) went to her death with her younger son, Miki (eleven); Sára (thirty-nine) with Norbert (nine); Blanka (thirty-five) with Tamás (seven); and Piroska (thirty-seven) with her prodigy son, György (five). We shall never know the exact date of their deaths. It happened probably sometime at the end of May. Jóska, Béla and András were sent to other camps to work. András, who was seventeen, did not survive either. Ten members of my family out of the twelve present in those fateful days in Munkács were thus annihilated. Our family was no exception; many families were completely destroyed.

~

Although our mission to build a modern road in the wilderness remained unaccomplished, just as we had anticipated, the military still had hopes that the narrow, winding dirt road that we worked on could be fixed and used, if not for attack then at least for the inevitable retreat. The main roads, as I learned later, were jammed and under German control. A well-sheltered road like ours, even if very narrow and in poor shape, could come in handy for the retreating armies. To make it passable, if only for light vehicles, required lots of work. In our judgment, it was too late even for that. The military planners didn't ask for our opinions, but I am sure that they too (at least some of them) already realized the futility of that new initiative.

Anyway, we were sent over fifteen kilometres southeast to build a bridge where the road crossed a river. This time we were fully under the control of the sapper battalion, which was terribly unpleasant. The sappers understood their job and expected real results from us. Cheating on a grand scale, as we used to do, was out of the question here. This time we had to work very hard around the clock. As before, we had only hand tools, and our only raw material for the bridge was the tall fir trees growing around us. To fell those trees, five feet and more in diameter, with simple flat saws was a bloody hard job. It destroyed the skin on the palm of my right hand. Removing the branches and the bark was perhaps less demanding on muscle power, but it was a nasty and boring job.

Worst of all was moving the timbers to the construction site. Though the distances were small, moving such a heavy and big body by our own strength alone was a difficult task and not without dangers. Moving such an object requires at least twelve people of about the same height and their movements have to be closely coordinated to avoid accidents. It was fortunate that the sergeant who supervised our job was experienced in both lumbering and carpentry. His clear commands made our job somewhat easier. He was not a career soldier, but he wanted the job done and he was tough. Otherwise, he was not a bad guy, not a racist like so many in the officer corps. He was one of the few sergeants with whom we could have meaningful talks.

Surprisingly, the work itself went ahead without a hitch. In no time, the skeleton of the bridge was ready. That's all we did there. Whether the job was ever finished, I don't know — I assume not. The way we understood the situation, the southern Carpathian front line was moving quite rapidly in our direction, more rapidly than the military planners were ready to admit. In spite of our isolation in the wilderness, we were well informed in those days and up-to-date about the situation on the front, especially on our section of the front. How we got our information, I cannot recall anymore.

We were on the move again. We didn't go far, less than a day's march down the same winding dirt road. Judging from the job we were given when we got there, we were helping to prepare for retreat. The section of the road we had to fix was periodically washed out in the rainy season and became virtually impassable. It was the worst place of our odyssey. I don't know the name of the place or even if it had a name at all.

We were in the bottom part of a very narrow mountain pass, steep slopes on both sides. Sunshine never penetrated there. Our quarters, a big wooden structure with no divisions (just four walls and a very leaky roof) and some dirty straw on the floor, was the worst I ever had. It was also miles away from our job. Fortunately, we stayed there for only two days. Our job consisted of digging drainage ditches, spaced about four yards apart. We had to dig six-to-eight feet deep in that stony terrain and then fill the ditches with gravel. It was a bloody bad job. We were each assigned one ditch a day.

Our supervisor, a young engineer, was undoubtedly from the fascist school. But his bark was worse than his bite. He too had already received the message that it was no longer advisable to mess around with inmates. I was ready with my ditch ahead of time and wanted to enjoy a good rest, like a number of others. I then noticed my neighbour sweating profusely, just halfway down the ditch. I jumped down to help him. Lévai was a lawyer about two years older than me. He was a sharp debater, and a very witty man. But handling a pick or shovel was beyond his capabilities. He was glad that I came to help him, actually to replace him, since there was not enough room in the hole for both of us. I let him climb out for a rest, which I regretted later. As it turned out, he didn't deserve my help.

It was too late when I found out that his ditch was a very bad one, too rocky to dig. It was impossible to use the pickaxe more forcefully, lest the whole ditch collapse. I realized too late that I couldn't be ready in time with that bloody job. I had just intended to climb out when the supervising engineer arrived. It was the end of the shift and he had come to make sure the job was done. It was, except for the one hole I was in. Try to explain to a Hungarian officer that it's not your hole or that the ditch you are caught in is out of the ordinary. I had no intention of doing that, since I knew the futility of such efforts.

The verdict was swift — you stay here until you finish, he told me. I was already tired and hungry. Supper time was about an hour's march away. It didn't occur to Lévai that he should at least stay with me. On the contrary, he found it funny that I had been trapped. He left with a big smile on his face. I must say I was quite desperate. I was tired and didn't know how I could finish the bloody ditch before dark. But then I realized I was not alone, since an inmate couldn't be left alone in such a remote place even if he wouldn't know where to run from there. Rules are rules.

The bloody lieutenant assigned one of the "frame boys" to guard me. To my satisfaction, I was guarded by a peasant in his forties. He was a mild-mannered man who hated soldiering. His mind was far away, concerned with his small farm in the Hungarian plains. He was as eager as I to go for supper and to lay down. He enticed me first: "Don't play with it that much, finish it." Then, as it started growing dusky, he looked at the ditch and told me: "Well, that's good enough. Let's go." I felt relieved.

It was a long way home, not only because I was tired, but because of an unexpected obstacle on our way back. As we reached a sharp turn about halfway to our quarters, we found our way blocked by a mountain of rocks and there was no way around it. We had to climb the loose rocks, a very unpleasant and tiring exercise. What exactly had happened there, I couldn't tell. When they blasted the rock, they probably applied a charge of dynamite that was bigger than necessary. To make things worse, it started raining. It was dark by the time we arrived, and we were wet. But I had a very warm reception. The boys had waited for me. They saved me my supper and kept it warm. How, you might ask. Well, the tailor and the cobbler shared a small shop there and they still had a fire burning. The tailor needed it to heat the iron to press uniforms. I gobbled up my supper right there in the workshop and then left to get some sleep.

～

The air raids intensified. The Soviets wanted to hinder the ordered retreat. And how could they distinguish between marching Germans and us? To be sure, the raids were not so bad. For one thing, the

Soviets didn't have many planes on our front, and compared to modern bombers, the planes they had were small, clumsy and inaccurate. It still became dangerous to march in broad daylight — maybe even more so for the horses than for us. There was no activity at night because of the then current military technology. So we would rest during the day and march at night. There was no way I could have objected to this logic, though it was hellish for me. I couldn't rest in the morning, because I was back to cooking. At least I was granted the privilege of not having to carry my own knapsack. My bag travelled on a wagon with the kitchen.

The human body is a marvellous system. Its adaptability is just fantastic. On the second night, I found myself sleeping during the march. I kept pace with the others, while at the same time I slept and dreamed. I occasionally woke up during the march, noticed that it was still pitch dark and told myself that there was plenty of time to go on sleeping. I remember that in the old days I had heard such stories from veterans of World War I, but I could never believe them. Those night marches didn't last long, just a few days. They stopped as soon as we were far enough from the front.

One day as we were walking on a highway in our usual relaxed and, I'd also say, disorganized manner, a group of Hungarian senior officers appeared from nowhere. They didn't like what they saw. One of them, a general, started screaming choice Hungarian curses (it's like poetry, impossible to translate) and threats. He summoned the commandant and gave him a loud dressing down. "How do you command that gang? You'll be court-martialled!" He repeated that threat several times. Poor old Gyenge was standing there at attention without uttering a word. When the tantrum was over and the officers were out of sight, he turned to us and said, "You see those assholes, they are drowning, they are up to their necks in shit and still they are grandstanding. To hell with them."

The court martial never occurred; it was too late for that. But the crazy guys still decided to punish us, to turn us over to the direct control of the Germans. This form of punishment actually turned out to be a blessing, not unlike the biblical Balaam's curse but without the talking ass, of course. We arrived at our final destination in Baia Mare (known in Hungarian as Nagybánya) and in addition to our "frame," we got two German supervisors. They proved to be harmless and nobody was overworked. Apparently, they were quite happy that they could chat with us in German. One day, when we were already well acquainted, they told us, Jew or non-Jew, "das ist für uns ganz egal." (It doesn't make any difference to us.) "We are Austrians, not Germans." It sounded to us almost as if they had said: "The end is close, so remember who we are." We indeed noticed significant improvements. We started to get our supplies from the Germans, which was a change for the better. We got German military rations, no more old beef and beans everyday. Everything was suddenly top grade, since the Germans cared for their army.

Our impression was that Baia Mare must have been prosperous. It used to have a Jewish community, like all the other towns in the region. I even found a shop sign bearing the name Mihály Kornreich. The shop was locked and nobody was around. Who knows what happened to the owners. In a few days we were well acquainted with the town and with some of the townsfolk.

We decided that Baia Mare was an ideal place to depart from the group and wanted to make sure it would be safe. In the chaos generated by the approaching front, it was relatively easy to blend with the locals and wait until the Soviets arrived. We were not the only ones who had this idea. We noticed that Gyenge, too, was busy scanning the local elite for their attitudes. He even tried on a civilian suit at one point. It was too hot in our uniforms, and we wanted to relax a little. We didn't have to wait long for the opportunity to escape.

It was to be expected that after Romania switched sides in August 1944 and joined the Allies, Hungarian politicians would be busy exploring ways to extricate Hungary from the lost war too. The Hungarian situation might have been more complicated than the Romanian, but that's not for me to judge. Most importantly though, and unfortunately for the remaining Hungarian Jews, Regent Horthy was not King Michael of Romania. Horthy was a soldier with a soldier's ideas about honour. Soldiers do not simply sneak away. Instead, Horthy notified the Germans about his intentions and went on the radio to address the Hungarian people on October 15, 1944.

As many people had radios in Baia Mare, we learned about the speech right away. The two German supervisors even brought a radio. They sensed that something important was going on because the same message was being repeated. They wanted us to translate. We did it with pleasure. Their reaction was curt and simple: "That's the end of it. We'd rather disappear." And that's precisely what they did. We never heard from them again.

We had been orphaned, so to speak. We were quite lucky, as everything went smoothly. However, not all the labour battalions were lucky like us. In a unit not far from us, they celebrated the event quite openly with wine and one of the frame boys, a Hungarian corporal, got mad and started shooting indiscriminately. Two of my childhood friends, one of them a talented physician, were shot dead on the occasion.

We learned about the tragic consequences of Horthy's cavalier and utterly stupid approach to getting out of the war only much later. But we knew the next day that Horthy was removed from office and an Arrow Cross government led by Ferenc Szálasi was installed. The Arrow Cross was the epitome of an authoritarian movement and it was virulently antisemitic. Döme Sztójay, who as prime minister of Hungary did the dirty job of deporting masses of Jews for the Germans in previous months, was apparently not harsh enough. The Arrow Cross never gained respectability in Hungary. They were installed by the Nazis to continue fighting and finish off the remaining Hungarian Jews (the Jews of Budapest). We didn't expect them to last more than a few days. Alas, they lasted more than two months, long enough to commit unspeakable atrocities. Both Sztójay and Szálasi were executed for their crimes after the war, too late for the hundreds of thousands of their victims.

# Like Slaves in Pharaoh's Time
## Itzik Davidovits

In 1941 I arrived in Pétervására and was taken to an open field in an abandoned village. There were barns all around the fields. I couldn't wear my own clothes. I was given a uniform and a hat, but no shoes, so had to use the shoes I was wearing. There were only Jews here, and we had Hungarian soldiers watching over us. I quickly started to realize that I was not in the army as a soldier, but instead was a prisoner of forced labour, like the Jews who were slaves in Pharaoh's time. Sentenced to hard labour by the Hungarians, I was forced to build their roads and dig their trenches, with little food and shelter and under inhumane conditions. We were routinely beaten and tortured. The Hungarians told us that we had no privileges except to die.

The Hungarians didn't like it if we didn't speak their language, but I couldn't speak Hungarian; I spoke only Yiddish and Romanian. Every day I would write letters home to my mother and to my girlfriend, and every day I hoped and prayed that I would receive letters back, but I never did. Then one day the Hungarian soldiers showed us what they were doing to our mail. It was a letter from my girlfriend. They brought it to me and showed me that they had this letter from her and then they ripped it up in front of my eyes. They said that if our mail wasn't written in Hungarian they would tear it to pieces.

Up until July 1942 we still had army clothes, but that all changed when we reached Jolsva (now Jelšava, Slovakia), our last stop before the Soviet front. We were given orders to write home to our families to ask them to send us civilian clothing. We each had to have our own suitcases with our names on them and we had to get blankets from home. The only things they gave us were a cap and boots. When our suitcases arrived, I had to give in my uniform and change into the civilian clothes my mother sent me.

One night after dinner, the head officer in charge of our division came out and lined us up. He was our new commander, and would prove to be more brutal than our last one. He proceeded to say that we had been selected to go to the front to dig trenches for the Hungarian and German soldiers. He said that it was our duty to obey orders, and that whoever did not follow orders would be punished or shot. He was speaking directly to us, the Jews. He turned to the Hungarian soldiers who were not Jewish and said, "Your duty as Hungarians is to make sure that the Jews get their work done and that they obey your orders. If they don't obey, make sure they are punished or shot." He also told his officers that the sooner they kill all the Jews, the sooner they will return home to their families in Hungary.

The first day, we marched all night. By morning, ten of us had been beaten to death for no reason at all. Then we arrived at the front near the edge of the Don River. There were landmines everywhere, which we were ordered to clear for the Hungarians. We proceeded very carefully so as not to get blown up. We then started to build roads for the Germans and dig trenches with our shovels and picks. We dug trenches deep and wide enough to hide a tank. We had to work very hard as the ground was like concrete. We worked through the night so that we would not be seen, and during the day we marched about one and a half kilometres back to a village. We slept during the day in dilapidated, abandoned houses left behind by civilians.

Later on, we were caught in the line of fire during the day, with bullets going both ways across the river. We knew that the Soviets were on the other side of the river and we could even hear them. The Soviets knew we were there too and shot at us and bombed us. We never saw any Germans, even though we had heard they would be there to fight with us. I only saw members of the Hungarian army.

When the retreat started, there was no way I was going to march back with the Hungarian soldiers. They warned us that if the Soviets arrived they would shoot us, but I was more afraid that the Hungarians would shoot me. So I remained down on the ground. They did give everybody a piece of bread that was supposed to last for the three days of the march because they couldn't take the field kitchen with them. They were in a hurry to get out of there.

Two hours later the company came back. I asked them what had happened, and they said they couldn't get through because we were now surrounded by the enemy. We were somewhere near the city of Voronezh and it was January 1943. After the war, I heard that out of the 800 men in my unit, 669 had gone missing or been killed by that time.

Everybody returned to their lodgings and were told to wait for another order. At around one o'clock in the morning they blew the horn telling everyone to line up again, and then the Hungarians left. This time they left for good — I never saw them again. When I woke up in the morning I saw there were eight others with me. I wasn't alone, after all. It was quiet, no bombings, gunshots or any noise. We started to see Soviet civilians coming in carrying bags with food, having taken what was left behind in the kitchen. They must have known that no one was around and that the fighting had stopped for a while. We had enough food for three months. One guy took charge of the kitchen and made sure that we didn't take too much, because we were undernourished and our bodies could not have handled it. Some of the men died from eating too much, too quickly.

We were there for three days and we didn't see anybody. We were happy. Then two Soviet soldiers on little horses but without guns came towards us. They talked to us very politely and even gave us cigarettes to smoke. They asked us some questions to find out who we were and why we were there. They said they would come back for us. They told us not to worry and then explained what would happen to us: "It's war, and you will be like a prisoner of war. You will work for us. You will have enough food and you will go home after the war, so don't worry about it." I thought that my situation would be better with them, and so I waited for them to come back for me.

Soon, we had to march to a camp where they were holding prisoners. I couldn't walk because my feet were swollen and my shoes didn't fit. It felt like they were frostbitten. My two friends had to carry me with their hands under my arms. When we arrived at our destination, the soldiers there were disorganized, drinking vodka and singing. There were a couple of officers, who told them to search us. There were prisoners from across Europe there, Germans, Italians and others. We were told to put our hands in the air as they searched us. We had to give them everything, including all our watches, knives, cigarettes and even our shaving tools.

My feet were frozen and I had *shmattes*, rags, wrapped around them, and my shoes were tied with a string hanging over my shoulders. They took away even these shoes and other supplies I had brought from the army kitchen that the Hungarians had left behind. I had a coat from a Soviet soldier, which I had found somewhere. When an officer saw that I had this Soviet coat, he said I must have killed a Soviet soldier for it. I thought I was going to be punished or killed because of that coat, but I wasn't. The officer took it away from me and threw it onto the pile with the rest of my things. It was freezing cold and I had no shoes and no coat.

~

We were soon marched to another camp, where all the other captive prisoners were being kept. The roads were snowy and treacherous, and I saw hundreds of frozen corpses along the roadsides. This frightened me and showed me how brutal the Soviet soldiers could be. Eventually, the Soviets marched us further and then just left us in an abandoned village in a house with other sick people; they probably assumed we would die there, without food and water, and all of us being so sick.

After six weeks or so only five of us remained alive. I told myself I had to get up or I would die of starvation. A lawyer friend asked to join me and we walked to a bigger town where we would have a better chance of gathering food. When we got there, we spotted a house on top of a hill. I knocked on the door and a middle-aged woman answered. She was with another woman whom I believe was her sister.

She took a look at us and started to ask questions. I told her I was a Hungarian Jew who had been in a forced labour camp and was left to die but then captured by the Soviets. I told her that we had no food and were starving. She wanted to know if I had a wife. I said yes. She asked me if I had any children. I said yes, three children. I had a beard and my hair had already grown long and had lice in it, and she looked at me and shook her head in despair. She kept repeating, "Bozhe, Bozhe" (Oh my God) and put her hands together in prayer. "Don't worry," she said, "the war will be over soon and you will return to your family at home."

She then asked me how old I was. I told her to guess my age. She said that I looked like I must be sixty or sixty-five years old. I was in shock. I thought she was kidding, but I could see that she was serious. It had been a couple years since I had seen my own reflection, and I knew I must look like some wild man-beast since I hadn't been able to shave or cut my hair. But I never would have thought that I looked so old. Did I age so much? Would I ever regain my looks? I had been robbed of my youth.

I tried to hold back my tears, but I simply had to cry and I blurted out, "No, no, I am not sixty-five years old, I am only twenty-three, and I don't have a wife and I don't have kids." I started to tell her the truth. She clasped her hands together and said *Bozhe, Bozhe* again, and she broke down and cried. I had a bag with me and she filled it up with food. She felt so much pity for me and gave us whatever she had. She told us to go in peace and keep safe.

We left and walked down the hill to the road. There was snow all over, and behind the road was a ravine. When we got to the road I heard a loud voice yell out, "Stoj! Stoj!" (Stop! Stop!) All I could see was a shiny officer cap, and I knew right away that a high-ranking Soviet officer was standing in front of me. I remained still, and so did my friend. He approached us holding a small handgun and as he walked around us he screamed at us, calling us all kinds of dirty names and swearing at us. He accused us of robbing the civilians and raping their women. He called us enemies and murderers and said that he was going to shoot us right then and there. He told us to line up on the edge of the steep valley behind us, so that when he killed us our bodies would drop into the ravine below.

The woman whom we had just visited came out of her house and down the hill to a well to fetch some water with her buckets over her shoulders. She immediately heard and saw the officer and dropped her buckets and started to scream. She frantically ran over to where the officer was standing and pushed him, all the while screaming, "No, no, stop! Leave these poor men alone. They mean no harm, they are innocent, they didn't do anything wrong and they are not the enemy. Let them go! They are poor and hungry people. Don't waste your bullets on them as the real enemy is out there, not these men." She was just like an angel. She saved our lives.

He stopped and said we were free to go, but that we would not be so lucky if he ever saw us in this town again. We had escaped, but my friend got increasingly weaker from hunger and couldn't hold on. He died a few days later.

# With Aching Hearts
# László Láng

Translated from Hungarian by Marietta Morry and Lynda Muir (2013)

The atmosphere was deteriorating by the day, and my life had gotten so much worse. My parents were first deported to the ghetto in Kassa and from there to Auschwitz. They would never return. I don't know anything more of their fate. I received a postcard from my mother, in which she wrote that they had been deported and she didn't think we would ever see each other again in this life. She said goodbye to me. Unfortunately, my mother turned out to be right. I don't have any other memento of her, not even a picture. This was the first major tragedy of my life, to be left without parents. Out of my extended family of fifteen people, not a single person returned from Auschwitz.

When the call-ups reached the letter L, it was time for me to pack my little knapsack and show up in Vác, from where we were transported to Mosonmagyaróvár. We were all young men, several hundreds of us, because older men had long been serving in labour camps on the Soviet front. A few weeks later we were taken to an oil refinery in Szőny. The factory had been shelled, and since it was considered an important war factory, the Hungarian government wanted to have it repaired.

At first we were housed in a half-finished building within the factory. I met three boys from MIKÉFE there, the carpenter Gyuri Weisz,

László Friedmann and Pál Hartenstein. I was a metalworker by trade, and on the first day in the factory, we were asked if there were any metalworkers among us. I put up my hand right away and told the others to do the same, because this would mean indoor work, and I would be directing them. "You have nothing to fear," I told them. And that is what happened.

~

Our situation deteriorated further after the new Hungarian fascist government seized power in October 1944. The winter became more severe too. We labour servicemen started off again, this time towards Sopron. On arriving at Sopron, we were placed in a brick factory, and on occasion smaller groups of men were taken to do work outside. I was lucky because on one such occasion we ended up in a military camp where we were supposed to tidy up a big clothing and shoe warehouse. During this job I quickly and deftly managed to exchange my boots and my clothing for new ones.

One day, the head of the warehouse, who was a sergeant, came over to me and told me to go to his apartment and clean it up. He gave me the keys to the apartment, and I went there. It consisted of one room, which wasn't dirty. His mess tin was still full from his dinner the night before, and I ate it. There were many pieces of bread on the table. Those I took with me and shared with my friend Gyuri Weisz. Every bite of bread was welcome, because the food we got was sparse and lacked nutrition.

Another day, when my friend Gyuri's feet had gotten too chafed by his shoes, he said he would stay behind and go see the doctor. I asked him to come to work instead, but he chose to stay inside. In the evening, when I returned, I didn't find Gyuri, because those who stayed behind sick had been picked up by the Hungarian soldiers guarding us and sent to the concentration camp at Mauthausen in the territory of Austria. After the war, when I was in Israel, I met a boy called Smuél Weisz, whom I knew well from the labour camp. He told me that he had seen Gyuri Weisz in Mauthausen sitting beside the wall of the barracks, and that's where he died of starvation. I experienced one of the most difficult hours of my life when I heard this, because had he listened to me, he might have stayed alive. Thus I lost a good friend who had been in MIKÉFE with me, and we'd also been scouts together in the Turul pack.

About a week or two after this, we were forced to move on because the Soviets were approaching. After we had walked for a day or two and were already on Austrian territory, our guards were replaced. The Hungarians handed us over to the Germans, so we were no longer under Hungarian command. The German Wehrmacht soldiers were old and they behaved quite well towards us. The cruelty of the Hungarian guards had been harder to bear.

In Austria, the accommodation in a former school building was quite adequate. The village we stayed in was called Windisch-Minihof. It was seventy to eighty kilometres from the city of Graz, quite close to the Hungarian border. Our job was to build tank traps, which consisted of digging a wide ditch between two hills. The aim of these traps was to impede the forward movement of tanks and trucks, and thus to stop or slow down the advance of the Soviet army towards Germany. However, this only worked in theory. It was already winter, and with our primitive methods in the frozen ground, the work progressed slowly, in spite of the fact that four or five hundred people were working there, including Austrians.

After a few months of work, around the end of April 1945, the Soviet front got near. Our health had deteriorated — we were covered with lice and there was no possibility of cleaning ourselves, no hot water at all. One day, I came down with a high fever. Our doctor said it was typhus fever. All he could recommend was that I go to the forest where there was a hunting lodge that already had a few sick boys in it, and report there. The doctor told me that because of the advancing Soviets, the company had been issued an order to move on. "And you," he told me, "would be in no condition to march with such a high fever."

I took the note the doctor wrote for the person in charge of the sick and I found the place after walking for half an hour. The good-looking young man who received me was not a doctor, but rather a pharmacist by profession. He was from the Felvidék, now in Slovakia, and spoke several languages. He directed me to a place on the straw-covered floor, where about twenty boys were already lying. I no longer recall the orderly's name, but he was a good-hearted soul. Unfortunately, however, there was no medicine, and things weren't easy, as there were some very sick people among us.

One morning the orderly came to tell me that he had received a notice from the German headquarters. They would be coming by to carry out an inspection because they thought that we were suffering from endemic typhus, which is a highly contagious disease. Someone from the nearby village must have reported to the German command that there were patients with endemic typhus in this place. The next morning, the orderly announced that the German delegation had arrived and that I should go outside to be inspected.

I was a bit worried because I was surrounded by four or five high-ranking officers, who must have been doctors. I quickly removed my shirt. They examined my body, looking for spots, but they found none. I had always played sports, and my body was in good shape despite the fact that I hadn't had a decent bite of food for almost a year. The inspection lasted for about ten minutes, and finally they turned around and left. Had I actually had endemic typhus, I wouldn't be writing this memoir, because they would have finished me off right then and there. In this instance, we all stayed alive.

# Two Sorts of Homecoming
## Moishe Rosenschein

Translated from Yiddish by Vivan Felsen (2015)

In early 1944, after many travels, we arrived at Repenye (now Repynne, Ukraine). Twenty-four of us were put into a small room. We scattered some straw on the floor and lay down exhausted. We didn't have much food, but we had no choice and made do with what we had. Those who had money bought what they could. Whoever did not was forced to trade the little they had. Every day we walked some eight kilometres to our place of work in the mountains, where we dug artillery trenches and bunkers.

I wrote a very angry letter to my sister in Pápa because she had not met me at the train station. Two weeks later I received an answer, a long letter in which she responded that she had been sick at the time I sent her the telegram. Nevertheless, she had baked some things, packed them with warm clothes and came to the station. She had waited for me from the afternoon until midnight. A train came by with some workers, and she asked if anyone knew me and whether I was on the train. Someone called out that he did, and so she gave him the package, but I never received it. After that she sent me a large food package.

On the eve of Purim I said to my friend Pinchas, "Do you know what? I don't want to go to work today. I'm going to hear the Megillah."

He tried to dissuade me, but I didn't listen. I broke away from our brigade and ran over to the *beys midrash* courtyard where I waited until the brigade had left. In the evening my comrades came back and told me that during the roll call the corporal had noted that I was missing. That night it was announced that Rosenschein was to report to the corporal in the morning.

When I went to report, the lieutenant asked me why the corporal had requested me, as the corporal was too sick to be present. "Because my shoes were not properly shined," I said. "Good," said the lieutenant, "tomorrow after work you will shine a hundred pairs of army shoes." I walked out and started laughing with my friends. The lieutenant came over and asked why I was laughing. "Because I know there aren't a hundred pairs of shoes in the entire storehouse." At that moment, the lieutenant also started to laugh.

~

It took less than an hour for us to cross the border and arrive in Vízköz. The army gave us something to eat. We were then led a few kilometres away, where we stopped. We were ordered to remove the snow from the road. Right away we began shovelling. The officers told us that when it was done, we would go back home. Everyone did his work well so we could go home faster. At 8:00 p.m. we were done. We wanted to go, but were not allowed to. Instead, we were taken to another place to work. It was now 12:30 a.m. Tanks, machine guns and other weaponry arrived. The Germans and Hungarians wanted to conduct an offensive into the Soviet Union from all sides.

The soldiers who passed by would beat us. We were Jews, after all, so we could be beaten just like that. When a wagon came by and the horses were not strong enough to pull it, they took off the horses and harnessed us to their wagon. And we had to move, because their weapons were behind our backs.

~

When I arrived back from work one day, all of our belongings had been put in front of the barn. What was happening? No one knew at first, but soon we got the answer. At the roll call, which took place every day after work, the lieutenant informed us that as of July 1 no labour camp Jews could live under a roof but instead had to live separately in the open air. Whoever disobeyed this order would immediately be sentenced in the military court. We were taken to the woods nearby, to an enclosure they had built, and we put our things down there.

We were given some soup to eat. We lay down to sleep but I could not fall asleep. The ground was very cold, and I had only one blanket. I didn't know whether to spread it out under me or use it to cover myself. Finally, I got an idea. I said to my comrade, "We'll cover ourselves with your blanket and I'll spread mine out underneath us."

In the morning we were woken by the impact of thick truncheons. Whoever failed to get up immediately had to wipe blood off himself a few minutes later. Everyone tried to avoid this because it was easier to just go to work. There was no water to wash with, but not far from us was a small ditch with some water, so we could wash ourselves once a week. God helped us.

I had only one single shirt. I had nothing else to exchange because little by little I had sold everything to try to satisfy my great hunger. Now I was being eaten up completely by lice. Many nights I couldn't sleep because my body was full of bites, but there was nothing I could do. I lived with the hope that God would help me survive this and I would tell all about it to my mother in peacetime.

～

One day an order was issued that we had to return to Poland. Whoever was not healthy had to visit the doctor. I went to the doctor and he recognized me. Ten boys remained in the village, and the rest went back. Two hours after our comrades left, one of them came back and told us that when they were leaving, he went to hide, and after they had left, he came back because he did not feel well enough to join them.

Around 5:00 a.m. our lieutenant arrived on a horse, very upset. He came into our shelter and shouted at us, "Where is the boy who ran away yesterday?" The boy stepped forward. The lieutenant told him to go outside. He led him to a small hill nearby, and then we heard shooting. I ran out and found our comrade dead on the ground. The officer told me to call out another boy. He ordered us to dig a grave, then take off our dead comrade's clothes. We put his body, which was still warm at the time, into the grave.

An hour later, the lieutenant ordered that all those who had remained here with the doctor's permission should present themselves to him. The ten of us stood in a row. He commanded us to turn to the wall. We all obeyed him. He took out his revolver and went over to the first comrade and asked him, "What is your last wish before you die?" The boy started sobbing that he was sick and begged to be let go.

I was next in line. He walked over to me and asked me the same question and started shouting, "You dirty Jewish traitor, you don't want to fight for our country. You are pretending while Hungarian soldiers are falling at the front." I showed him my bandaged foot. He shouted, "That's nothing! You can go to the front like that!" He began to hit me, mostly on the head, and also started to beat the rest of the boys. All of us were soon lying on the ground half-dead. Two soldiers came in and poured cold water over us. They bandaged us and then sent us to the border to join the rest of our comrades. When my friend saw me, he was horrified. I calmed him down by saying that I had fallen off the wagon.

～

On the eve of Yom Kippur we arrived back in Repenye. We prayed and then went to sleep on the floor. On Yom Kippur day we walked a long way through the mountains to go to work. As soon as we arrived at our destination, we recited the prayers for half an hour instead of a midday break. Then we began to work. In the evening I got home from work and broke the fast.

The next day we walked until we came to Zhulitse near Munkács. I told my friend that we should try to run away. We got up at 4:00 a.m. and snuck through the fence and walked through vegetable plots until we came to a peasant woman who offered to hide us in her barn. The Soviets were not far away, she said. I gave her one hundred pengős. She led us into her barn and took our little food to cook it for us. We stayed there covered in straw and filled with fear. Every day she brought us food. At night I couldn't sleep because I was so anxious. Whenever I heard noise or some movement, I thought someone was about to discover us. On the third day the woman came in and told me she was going to Munkács, but she had instructed her little girl what to do. At around four o'clock, the girl came into the barn and told us that we had to get up quickly and run away, because the Hungarian military police had learned that we were hiding there and they would soon be coming for us. Terrified, we got up, dressed and left the barn. Outside I saw four other comrades from our camp. They told me that they had been hiding just like us, that they had also been betrayed and that we had to urgently flee.

The owner of the place where they had been hiding guided us into a forest through the vegetable gardens. Once in the forest, the peasant told us that we should stay there and that he would bring us food, and when the Soviets came, he himself would come for us. Then he left. It began to rain, and I took shelter under a tree.

We were seven boys, each of us desperately worried about what would happen to us now. First of all, what would happen if the peasant did not bring us food? Secondly, it was pouring rain, and at night we would not have anything to cover us. It turned out that our fears were not mistaken. No one brought us food, and we sat all night in a tree because the ground was so wet we couldn't lie on it. My heart pounded with the rustle of every leaf, because human beings have frightful imaginations. That night felt eternal; time seemed to stand still. Finally, God sent daylight, and we cast lots among ourselves to decide which of us would go into the village to find us something to eat. The task fell to me.

As I began walking out of the woods, I was stopped in my tracks, astonished to see not far from me a group of tattered soldiers with weapons. I threw myself on the ground and crawled on my belly back to our comrades to tell them. Everyone was of the opinion that they were coming for us. We began to think about what to do. We decided to continue sitting on the ground because we couldn't go into the village and we couldn't go deeper into the forest either.

A few minutes later a soldier came, saw us and asked us who we were and what we were doing there. Our answer was that we were Jews, and we were lost. To that he replied, "You don't have to deny that you ran away from the work camp. We also ran away from the front. We didn't want to fight anymore." He went to call the rest of the soldiers. They took out some whiskey and we all drank. "Here. We can already feel that the Soviets are not far away, but we are starting to worry about what will happen to us." We consoled them by saying that we would be together with them and everything would be fine.

The next day, October 16, 1944, the peasant who had taken us into the forest came running over and was very happy to tell us that the Soviets were in the village. We began to dance with joy.

# Horrors and Survival:
# In Ghettos and Camps

# Foreword

March 19, 1944, the day Hungary was invaded by its German ally, is a key date in the history of the Holocaust in Hungary. This fateful date is deeply engrained in the minds of many Holocaust survivors, and its significance as the beginning of the Hungarian "year of extermination" is illustrated in the following memoir excerpts.

The most devastating phase of the Holocaust in Hungary followed shortly after March 19, 1944. It took the Hungarian and German perpetrators less than two months after the invasion of Hungary to launch mass deportations of Hungarian Jews. Unlike the more widely known case of occupied Poland, for example, where ghettos would survive for months and sometimes for years (with the Lodz ghetto, at the end of the spectrum, existing for over four years), the ghettos that were established across Hungary in the spring and early summer of 1944 were quickly abolished, as their inhabitants were collectively deported. The German occupation of its seemingly "unwilling satellite" — to reproduce the overly benevolent phrase used by John Flournoy Montgomery, former US minister to Hungary — was one of the main triggers of this ruinous process.

However, only the enthusiastic cooperation of practically all the relevant Hungarian authorities, from the national level to that of tiny localities, could have made the genocide possible in the radical shape it took. By 1944, Germany's defeat looked ever more certain, and the

German experts in the business of genocide in Hungary were few in number with limited resources of their own, whereas the Jewish community of Hungary was vast, consisting — according to the racist definition of the perpetrators — of more than 800,000 individuals. The ghettoization and deportation of Hungarian Jews could only have been implemented because practically all relevant representatives of the Hungarian state altered their behaviour after March 19, 1944, and started to actively participate in the German-led genocide — there was no way the German occupiers could have implemented such a massive program on their own.

As László Karsai, a leading historian of the Holocaust in Hungary, sardonically remarked, the German occupation may have been meant to pre-empt Hungary's abandonment of the Axis cause, but as the smooth unfolding of the actual occupation showed, the Germans responsible for the decision to invade the country might well have overestimated the Hungarian leadership's willingness to exit the war. Hungarian perpetrators in fact seized the opportunity provided by the entry of their German allies to swiftly launch an extended genocidal campaign.

The main phase of the Holocaust in Hungary that followed was utterly devastating: in a mere fifty-six days between mid-May and early July 1944, the majority of Hungary's sizable Jewish population, about 437,000 individuals, were deported, nearly all of them to Auschwitz-Birkenau. In the course of this last major chapter of the Nazi genocide, most of those deported were murdered practically immediately upon their arrival there. The camp complex of Auschwitz-Birkenau had to be extended to implement this most barbarous act of genocide, and its crematoria could still not cope with the unprecedented rate of murder — the corpses of many Hungarian Jews were eventually burned in the open air.

As a result of this frightening efficiency on the eve of Germany's defeat, Jews from Hungary constituted the single largest group of victims — about every third victim in total — of this most infamous

Nazi camp. The mass murder of Hungarian Jews in the late stages of the war greatly contributed to making Auschwitz-Birkenau into a widely used synecdoche for the Holocaust worldwide.

Only a small fraction of Jews deported from Hungary in those months were sent to other camps. The largest group within this minority, nearly 21,000 individuals, were sent to Strasshof in today's Austria, among them memoirist Leslie Fazekas. This special arrangement was the result of a highly controversial deal. Adolf Eichmann aimed to extort goods from the (Zionist) Relief and Rescue Committee of Budapest and offered lives in exchange. As the most important result of the ensuing negotiations, which have remained heavily debated since, in June 1944, Hungarian Jews were transferred from the ghettos of Baja, Debrecen, Szeged and Szolnok to Strasshof. The conditions under which this minority had to struggle were significantly better than those of the large majority transported to Auschwitz-Birkenau, and their chances of eventual survival were much higher too.

The approximately 100,000 Hungarian Jews who survived the initial selection round in Auschwitz-Birkenau — and all our memoirists recalling this most infamous camp complex by necessity belong to this minority — were to be used as forced labourers and were often transported further. Nazi policies of previous years were aimed at creating a Germany "free of Jews" and the Nazis declared the goal accomplished in May 1943. By the summer of 1944, however, the Germans began their retreat and started clearing out the camps in the East. They did not want to leave witnesses of their murders behind and intended to continue to exploit a human labour force within Germany (and Austria).

As a result of this reversal of Nazi policy, the minority of Hungarian Jews who survived Auschwitz-Birkenau were often moved deep into the Reich's territory — some 28,000 Hungarian Jews were transported to Dachau and its subcamps alone. Usually, they had to persevere through multiple torments in a host of additional camps to have any chance not to perish. As Nikolaus Wachsmann shows in *KL*, his imposing monograph on the subject, the system of Nazi concentration camps in fact never held more inmates, over 700,000, than in this last phase of the war — right before the death marches would have engulfed the inmates of these camps in the middle of Germany and Austria too.[1]

As many camps were evacuated amidst the final collapse of the Third Reich to pre-empt their liberation by the fast-approaching Allies, their gravely weakened inmates were forced to march towards destinations unknown to them and often undefined. Just before the remaining camp survivors would have been liberated, the Nazis unleashed another lethal and unfathomable wave of violence, killing many of them.[2] As Helen Rodak-Izso's memoir attests, these shocking, often extended and utterly unpredictable marches left deep scars on those who survived them. The disturbing memory of such deadly marches would often prove to be as traumatic as those of the camps.

1  Nikolaus Wachsmann, *KL: A History of the Nazi Concentration Camps* (Boston, MA: Little, Brown, 2015).

2  On the death marches, see Daniel Blatman, *The Death Marches: The Final Phase of the Nazi Genocide* (Cambridge, MA: Harvard University Press, 2011).

# Amid the Burning Bushes
## Helen Rodak-Izso

We felt numb to the terrible events happening around us — nobody knew what the next minute would bring. I find it so difficult to explain what we were going through and felt; who could understand it now? In the current peaceful and quiet atmosphere and after so many years, talking about such disturbing times makes me feel so far from what was happening. What is it to live in danger, in constant fear?

We hear all the easy criticisms now, such as the idea that we should have tried to get away. But where would we have gone? And how? It was too late, too risky. Some lucky ones escaped, but many just tried in vain. Many committed suicide, entire families. We just couldn't or didn't want to believe all these horror stories at the time. Who can believe that in the twentieth century people can go mad and behave like animals? They let their sadistic fantasies go free and nobody stopped them in time. It all happened in the wide open for the whole world to witness. Unfortunately, the easiest answer was to look away. We also didn't believe that Miklós Horthy, Hungary's regent, would let us be taken away. We trusted him naively.

We were just hoping that the war would come to an end, so we would be spared from this horrible plague of violence and persecution. I still see my father with a map always open, tiny flags marked on it following the events. We tried to hope right until the tragic day of March 19, 1944, when the German army marched in — the beginning of the end.

No words can describe the dead silence, the numbing fear that like a dark cloud descended on our homes and the whole city. We were panic-stricken; the streets were completely empty.

Our parents were solemn; they tried to show us that they remained calm. The truth was that we were all covering up, and something was building up in our hearts. Something terribly frightening was in the air. We didn't have to wait long to find out what.

Somebody rang the doorbell from the main entrance and nervously shouted the terrible news: The plant is on fire! This was my father's cork factory. Adding to the panic, there were huge posters warning us that after seven o'clock Jews were not allowed to be on the streets. The fire was visible from the back porch of our home, so after a little impatient waiting and helpless watching, my father decided that he had to go there against the Nazis' order.

Uncle Martin, my father's partner, came as well, and the two of them were standing there, watching how the fruit of their many years of tireless work was destroyed. The fire blazed out of control all night. It started on all four corners of the building, so it was clear that this was not accidental. The cork itself is highly flammable, but there were also other flammable materials. Soon the Gestapo arrived and started the interrogation and strict investigation: Who are the owners? If the owners are Jews, it must be sabotage! Following this ruthless announcement, the Gestapo took my father and uncle away to an unknown location.

We found out later that our father and uncle were taken straight from the fire to the Gestapo headquarters, which was in the largest and nicest hotel, Schalkház, in our town. They were interrogated for the whole night, standing in a corner facing the wall.

After being detained at the police station, they were taken in a truck, which drove around the city in many directions in an attempt to disorient them. First the truck drove south, and then suddenly the driver changed speed and went in another direction until they arrived at an abandoned boarding school, which was in the suburbs in the north. The height of the truck made it difficult for these elderly gentlemen to get on and off, and my father injured himself when he jumped off.

The place was totally empty, with just a cement floor. There were about a hundred hostages. The families of the hostages were ordered to furnish the ice-cold building with the most important materials for day-to-day living. A table was placed in the middle of the room with four machine guns on it pointing in four directions. The hostages were given the strictest orders to follow the regulations. We sent a collapsible bed, clothing, bedding and other necessary items. My father and uncle were there for three weeks.

Unfortunately, there was no way to help them. There were no visiting privileges or other possibilities for help. But we had to do something — we couldn't just wait with folded hands. People who wanted to help established a public kitchen for the hostages.

We didn't know what else to do. There was sheer panic.

A long line of Jewish people seeking refuge arrived in our town in both small and large groups. We realized the bitter truth that unwelcome intruders were taking Jewish homes, homes where people were still living. The owners of these houses had been given five minutes to get ready and were then forced to leave as soon as they were dressed. They left everything behind. Everybody was shocked and distraught.

After this came an even worse catastrophe: the order to wear the yellow star. Students were no longer allowed to attend schools, and people were arrested for all kinds of reasons. Wearing the yellow star made us feel stigmatized and as though our destiny was sealed. Hit with blow after blow, we didn't have a chance to analyze our bitter feelings.

To our unspeakable horror and heartache, we found our dear aunt Ella from Abaújkér in a group that arrived from a neighbouring region. From a well-to-do family, she now owned only a single outfit of clothes, the clothes she had been wearing since she was found in her home. She arrived with nothing, absolutely nothing, having left everything behind. All she had now was the same miserable, tragic and uncertain future as everybody else.

When people were forced to leave their villages, they tried to grab whatever they could carry. Everyone, young and old, sick or able, tried to save whatever was most important: medicine, clothing, toothbrush or hairbrush. With children, the situation was always more complicated. People who had kept a clean and comfortable home were suddenly thrown out. All their treasures were hurriedly packed in suitcases, rucksacks or bags.

There were constant air raids, and we had to run to the basement, where we would tremble in fear, sometimes for hours. There were rumours that a certain part of the city would be segregated (isolated) for the Jewish population, where we could go on with our lives. We hoped that the end of the war was getting nearer and we would survive under these conditions. Most of all, we hoped that we wouldn't be taken away and that they would not separate us.

~

The tragic day arrived when our street was to be emptied. We were being deported. We felt that we were looking around our home for the last time. We had to be ready to leave, since the Hungarian police were waiting for us, but we weren't aware of what was happening around us. We were being forced to leave this place, where we had been together, where we had had our meals, talked, read books. Our life was being halted for some reason, but why? We had spent so many happy hours here, simply living the life of a family. We looked around to say goodbye to the familiar furniture, pictures, walls, and all of a sudden everything came alive and felt important. We discovered things that we hadn't bothered to look at before. Oh, how it hurt to close the doors behind us! Once more we looked down at the garden, which was blooming in the usual spring colours. The sky was blue, but for us everything was grey.

My sister Olly was placed in a hospital. My father had prepaid and arranged for her to stay there as a patient, hoping she could live through the dangerous times there. Many families tried to hide or save young girls this way. Unfortunately, we were wrong to hope she would be safe there. The sad day would come when all the hospitals had to give up their Jewish patients. There was no mercy!

Our younger brother, Laci (László), was already at a forced labour camp. My other brother, Sanyi (Sándor), was in British Mandate Palestine and was beside himself, because he didn't know anything about what was happening to us. There was no way to correspond. The official Red Cross letters had to be very short: only the signatures as signs of who was still at home and alive.

The Hungarian police officer startled me out of my silent meditation with his rude order: Get moving! Take a last look at your door, because you will never put your feet through this doorway again! His southern Hungarian dialect and his inhumane message is still in my ears today and will be forever.

The yards of the synagogues and Hebrew schools were full of people from out of town. It was a horrible sight, so many crying children and desolate parents trying to find some way to soothe their children's discomfort and pain. At last we heard that we were going to be stationed in the brick factory, which was at the west end of the city.

The factory blocks had no walls; they were wide open. These were the buildings where the bricks were placed to dry, and it was also our destination. The place was full of coal and brick dust, and we were without water. My father put some nails into the wooden slope of the roof so we could hang up our coats. When the wind was blowing, the clothes danced on their nails. Without walls, we were at the mercy of the elements — the wind and rain came in freely.

This part of our struggle was the darkest time for me, despite all the misery that I went through later. To see my parents in such circumstances was really unbearable. We had to watch them suffer the daily struggles in this factory, lining up for coffee or, even worse, lying down wherever they could. This was far too much! There was nobody we could hope to turn to for some help or relief. Simply, there are no adequate words to describe the situation.

Looking back on those intolerable, difficult days, I have to mention something that we didn't even notice at the time: our parents never complained about the inconveniences or other problems until they looked at us and were worried sick by what we had to endure and also about what the future might bring. This helpless, hopeless feeling paralyzed us, because we couldn't do anything to soothe or ease their tragic plight. It is unforgettable how heroically they behaved in this chaotic situation.

The bar mitzvah of my little cousin Imike (Imre), the son of Aunt Clara and Uncle Marci, took place in this factory ghetto. There could hardly be a more sorrowful place for such a joyful occasion. His grandmother, Aunt Mariska, and her daughter Ágnes were allowed to come over from the other side of the road. The rabbi from Abaújszántó participated and Imi said his Haftorah beautifully. It was incredibly moving and no eyes were left dry. The rabbi didn't have to say much, as the situation spoke for itself.

We felt that people can sometimes be stronger than steel, but weaker than a single hair.

Imi's older brother, Ervin, was there too, about eighteen years old at the time; tragically, neither of them returned after the war. Both sides of the family adored them. Clara's family got permission to participate in the bar mitzvah for a few hours, but then she rushed back to their place. Little did we know that this was the last time we would see them. To our great shock, we heard the bad news the next day: the deportation on the other side had taken place. All we found out was that all those who had attended the bar mitzvah a day before, Clara's family and other relatives and many friends, were gone. We never heard from them again. This was the middle of May 1944.

A new panic set in on our side, because we knew it was just a matter of time and we were going to be the next in line unless some miracle happened, for which we still were praying and hoping.

The next tragic date was June 2, 1944, and it arrived just like the dreadful day of an execution: it was now the turn of our group, the fourth and last one in Kassa. We were forced to leave our hometown and enter occupied Polish territory.

From the moment of our entry into Auschwitz-Birkenau, we were frightened all the time, wondering what more could come next. We kept on thinking all the time, yet we were trying to avoid the question we feared the most: what had happened to our dear parents upon our arrival?

We were too afraid to believe what we had heard on the *Appellplatz*. The dreaded notion that we had been deceived slowly crept into our minds, and with closed eyes and trembling hearts we tried to hope against hope. We were not awake; we were in a daze, just moving about mechanically. We didn't grasp yet what was going on, that we had lost our family, our home and everything.

Even the little bag with our most cherished family pictures had been brutally and senselessly taken away from us. It dawned on us that we had no right to anything anymore. There was no way out, and it felt as if a dark curtain had descended in front of us, blocking the view to the outside world. The gnawing pain became unbearable, but this was not the place or time for emotion. We were deprived of everything that makes a human being into a person.

Meanwhile the gas chambers were working full time.

～

One morning after an early alarm we had to march to the railway station, where a long row of wagons waited for us with open doors.

We were taken to Kaiserwald, a terrible concentration camp in the suburb of Riga. We learned many new things there, such as how to mix cement and how to straighten and widen the road. One day our supervisor came by and told me that if I could be very careful, he would give me another assignment and I could take another girl along. He sent us ahead on the road to check the work and prepare the measurements of the width of the highway. We went ahead and sat down to relax a little. I have recalled many times since how we were talking to each other about our dearest ones there who were always on our minds. We also discussed our constant problem, our acute hunger.

Since now we were working in the countryside, we knew we could at some point come across somebody from the village. I had the idea that we could try asking the people passing by for some bread. My friend agreed, but gave me the first opportunity. I was polite and told her to take the first step. While we were debating who would try first, a village woman showed up, and my friend pushed me forward. As I got closer to the woman, I changed my mind and decided that I would tell my friend that the woman had nothing. It just didn't come out of my mouth to ask for food. But this brave woman from the village was faster. As she saw me approaching her, she quickly took something out of her basket and threw it on the ground before me. I quickly picked it up and took it to my friend. We opened it, and there were two pieces of beautiful, home-baked brown bread wrapped in a newspaper. Without even looking at me, she quickly disappeared. The experience was bitter, but it felt good to bring something back. Hunger is a big boss and doesn't allow anyone to be proud!

~

Is this all happening to us? Are we the same people here in the forest who recently lived in homes and could come and go the same as everybody else? We are now prisoners of some sort, only we don't have the slightest idea about the reasons why. It just cannot be that in the twentieth century something like this could happen. The world must have gone berserk!

All of this was happening out in the open for the whole world to see and hear. But the simplest action was to look away. We were treated this way in a country that used to be the centre of culture and knowledge. We watched the birds and bees flying all over, freely. Where did these people learn all these devilish skills? And how did they have the brutal strength, the plain physical strength, to inflict all this barbarism day after day?

~

From Kaiserwald we were sent to Ḳurbe and then to Rechlin, where we were assigned to work in a huge SS vegetable garden. One SS man, who was watching my work, came closer, bent down and used his beautiful pocket knife to cut off some of the vegetables I was working with. It had a distinct taste and smell, like mint. He ordered me into the SS kitchen with the green leaves.

To my surprise he wanted me in his office, which was full of guns on the walls, and then he ordered me to sit on a chest, which must have been full of ammunition. I didn't feel safe at all among all these unfriendly and strange things, and with my host, a real SS man. Of course, I didn't have any idea what his plans might be, but it was better not to guess. I just sat there, frozen and motionless, waiting for my fate.

He left me alone and then suddenly returned with a bowl of warm milk soup, which he carried with both hands. It was a real delicacy, and he ordered me to eat it with the spoon he provided, in front of him. The green mint vegetable was used in this heavenly meal, which made the soup even better. My first thought was to share with my sister, but he yelled at me, told me that I had to finish right there under his watchful eyes. With trembling hands and heart, I finally took two or three spoonfuls — I couldn't eat any more. He urged me to finish it, and with the most severe and strict look he warned me that when he let me go I had to keep my mouth shut, otherwise I would see the consequences.

I walked out into the sunshine, dazed and sweating, partly from the meal and partly from excitement. I was so weak, perspiring profusely. My starved body was not used to normal meals anymore. He must have known that the first meal for a starved body should be light and small, otherwise it amounts to torture. The whole situation was unbelievably difficult for me, because he didn't stop watching me and I didn't know if I would get out alive. I also felt terrible that I had had a chance to eat but was not able to share with my sister. He must have been a sadist to force me to finish the whole bowl in front of him.

$\sim$

Our next journey was not any easier. Our destination this time was Glöwen, a subcamp of Sachsenhausen. Every day brought new problems there, which were even harder to bear than the previous ones. For a short time, my sister Olly was the kapo. My sister never dreamed that there would be someone among the SS guards who understood our language. One Sunday when they sent us to work, she bitterly lamented out loud that even on a Sunday they wouldn't leave us alone. A Hungarian in a German uniform heard her and gave Olly's number to the people in charge, who were just waiting for such news.

When we came back from work, the whole Lager was called out for *Appell*, and Olly's number was called. She was threatened with serious punishment and the very next day she had to stand barefoot at the entrance gate for the whole day. Since it was winter, this form of punishment was intensely harsh but at least they didn't kill her. It was another miracle that she somehow came through this trial. For me, it was really a trying time to watch her, since I was not able to help. She was punished because she had supposedly used the word "barbarians" — how much can a person endure?

On one occasion my group was assigned to move bombs, ammunition that we were to hand from one person to the next. The bombs weighed about fifty kilograms. We started to be concerned not just about our physical health but about our mental state too, because our life had become nothing but fear, mental and physical anguish, hunger, thirst and dirt. We decided to check our minds to see if they were still working. The game we created involved walking with heavy burdens, the bombs and other ammunition, until we met the other labourer halfway. We would then hurriedly ask questions, and the other person had to answer quickly. If the question was too difficult, they would answer at the next turn. The questions consisted of names of actors, actresses, plays, books, titles or authors. We even tried geography, just to think a little bit. We also tried to create some kind of social gathering on Sunday afternoons when possible. There were girls who knew some poems, recitals, singing — they were ready to perform anything just to get away from the gnawing, painful existence.

We left Glöwen. With heavy hearts we started another long journey into the unknown. This one lasted three long weeks, laboriously walking day and night. Step after step, we tried to keep pace with each other, never daring to hope we could get out alive. Our guards were still with us, although some suddenly changed their uniform for civilian clothes. Hope and fear were constantly with us. Since we were working on different *Kommandos*, working groups, we all knew that the road we had just started on was full of danger. Underground and on both sides, the bushes and trees were covered with hidden explosives.

The road was beautifully asphalted pavement, and the march went on seriously and quietly. We didn't need any warnings not to talk. We didn't utter a word; we just walked and didn't dare look at either side, because the briar bushes were on fire already. The Bible story with the burning bush came to my mind. We walked among the burning rose bushes, and the bombs were coming down, and soon everything was engulfed in flames, and we were in the middle of all this, just walking. It was an unforgettable experience. It was a miracle that we escaped this part relatively unharmed.

We were in constant danger, with air raids and hunger escorting us everywhere. If the air raids came too close, we had to hide in the ditches as deeply as possible and lie on our stomachs. Of course, hunger was the worst part as there was no hope for food, no place to get something to eat. The grass was all we had. Hunger is a big master, as we discovered again and again. We discovered with great satisfaction that some of our guards wore civilian clothing and didn't have such a big voice any longer. The road was full of people, civilians of all kinds, others like ourselves, families with children, old people trying to save themselves and some of their belongings. We just followed everybody else. It seemed like the whole world was on the move.

We eventually reached another camp called Ravensbrück, a women's camp famous for its brutality. The real chaos came towards the end. We could now see fear in our guards' eyes — they were probably contemplating what was in store for them.

The situation became more uncertain each day. In this camp, we had another chance to look for relatives. As we looked around the camp, we saw a large pile of stiff, naked bodies stacked along a whole length of a crematorium wall. I looked at those bodies with deep-seated anguish, afraid of what I might find. My dear mother had an operation in her younger years that left a mark that was visible all her life — I was scared I would come to see this mark now.

Suddenly there was a call that they needed a few people to perform some tasks. We never knew what to expect, but our meagre situation was pushing us to try. Poor Olly, my sister, unfortunately fell into a *Kommando* where the work was much too hard. She, along with other girls, had to gather the remaining parts of the bodies piled against the crematorium and carry this heavy load in little wagons to the end of the Lager near to the river. There they had the sorrowful task of burying everything and raking the top. Finally, thank God, Olly got away from there, but it was a terrible experience. I was working somewhere else. On the way back, Olly found a powder case, which she gave to the kapo in exchange for two slices of bread. It was a lifesaver.

After a short stay in Ravensbrück we had to march again. It would be very difficult to describe what we saw on the road. After some unspeakable hardships, we reached some place, but nobody quite knew where we were.

We were not aware how close we were to the battle zone, but very shortly this became all too evident. Fortunately, a man wearing a Belgian uniform noticed us and offered his guidance. We followed his instructions and suddenly found ourselves at the edge of a place looking down on a beautiful, quiet meadow with farmhouses. It looked like fairyland to us and was totally abandoned. When we soon found ourselves in front of a farmhouse, we simply entered. In our shocked state of mind, we did not realize that the owners of the house must have just left because of the alarm signals.

It was unthinkably beautiful there. The rooms were warm — they even smelled clean and offered a taste of family life. My only wish was to find a small pillow, and I was lucky to discover one. With one hand hugging the pillow, a real treasure, my other hand clutched the bucket containing our would-be supper. We could not stay there forever though, so we started to prepare ourselves to leave this beautiful place. The meat was distributed so that each of us had a parcel to carry. Some of the girls took a camera or bicycle, and then slowly, quietly, we left. Nothing was pushing us, but the time seemed ripe.

Suddenly our brains started to function again, because we found ourselves face-to face with the owners of the house. It dawned on us how thoughtless we had been. They started to return from their shelter and met our group holding their belongings. They were a whole group of people, mainly women but also a few men with rifles in their hands, ready to use them at any minute. They were angry, and their yelling was truly frightening. They demanded that we put down their belongings. For me it was hard to part from my pillow, but I had no choice, and the bucket had the same fate. They were so much stronger and healthier than us, and there were so many more of them. We were weak as flies, and anybody could have overpowered us, so we gave up everything and started to leave.

We were able to reach the forest, where we lay down in the rain-soaked grass and didn't care about anything anymore. We were certain that those German people with all their anger would follow us any minute and finish us.

# The Miracle of Our Survival
# Yittel Nechumah Bineth
# (Kornelia Paskusz)

In May 1944, all the Jewish people of Csorna were forced to abandon their homes and move into a ghetto. Our house faced one of the main squares of town and stood in the middle of the Jewish community. Our apartment was in the front of the building, with four others in the back. We occupied five rooms, as well as a kitchen and a bathroom. It was considered a very spacious and well-furnished home.

The Jewish ghetto was created where we were living; therefore, our apartment had to accommodate a different family into every room. These people were forced into our quarters, and we had to give up our rooms without any say in the matter. This created enormous problems. We had only one kitchen and one bathroom, which we now had to share with other families. We needed a great deal of organization and cooperation in order to live together. Each family did their own laundry and cooking, but even with such a system in place, living like this was barely manageable. The noise alone was almost unbearable. Little did we know that this was heaven compared to the hell we were yet to witness. We were utterly depressed and frightened, yet we could not imagine what was being planned for us.

By then, rumours of deportation had spread. We hoped that if we Jewish girls could prove that we were able and ready to work in the fields and make contributions to the economy of the country, then we could possibly avoid deportation. Girls aged twelve to eighteen quickly filled out the necessary applications to sign up for work on farms. I was assigned to Pál Major's farm, which was located in the little village of Dör, about six kilometres from Csorna. During the week, we lived and worked on the farm. On our first day, we did back-breaking work, bending down to the potato plants till the evening hours. The second day we had to clean the corn fields. Again, all day long we were bending down to pick the corn. Our hands became rough and were full of blisters from too intense use of the tools.

Every day I had to travel to Csorna by bicycle at precisely one o'clock midday to pick up the homemade kosher food for all the Jewish girls. This was a frightening experience because there was a curfew in effect for Jewish people. We were permitted to be on the streets only at certain designated hours. Each time I travelled, I turned my coat lapel inside to hide my yellow star. With my heart pounding from fear, I pedalled my bicycle as fast as possible to avoid being stopped for questioning. By the time evening arrived, we were so exhausted that we fell onto the straw mattresses like limp dolls.

In the Csorna ghetto, our troubles multiplied. Hunger set in. We could not get enough food. This desperate situation lasted for several weeks, but our tormentors were still not satisfied. We received a new order: on Monday at 10:00 a.m., every man (most of whom were already gone to the labour service), woman and child had to line up in front of their ghetto house. Each person could carry only one small piece of baggage and had to be prepared to travel. No destination was given.

Nobody slept a wink on Sunday night. Our heads were throbbing with questions: Where would we be going? What was our fate going to be? We all sensed that greater evil awaited us. We tossed and turned all night long, hoping that a miracle would save us. Somehow the long night passed; the sun rose and the dreaded morning came. The first thing we did was pray to *Hashem* to help us. We then ate the little food that we had in order to store up some energy. At 10:00 a.m. on June 19, 1944, we stood in front of our house.

Soon we arrived at the train station, where a long train was waiting for us. We all had to squeeze in, about one hundred people in each cattle car, like animals. German horses actually rode in better accommodations. We were still not told our destination, but after about two hours we arrived in Sopron, a larger city that served as a ghetto for Jews from the surrounding villages. We were taken to a large, unfinished school building, which had no floor and no windows. We were told to sleep on the bare earth. Food was scarce too. We stayed in this place for two weeks, suffering and praying to *Hashem* for help.

One day Mother disappeared. I was devastated, but luckily I still had my sister Renee and brother Meshulem to comfort me. They reassured me, saying that she was surely coming back.

As it turned out, the Germans had a list of the ten wealthiest residents of our town, those who paid the highest taxes. Mother was fortunately, or now unfortunately, on this list. These arrogant Germans had the audacity to search for Mother and take her back home to Csorna so that they could force her to reveal where her treasures were hidden.

Mr. Schlesinger was the wealthiest man in town, the owner of a brick factory. After lining up the other nine people, the Germans ruthlessly beat up this innocent man in front of everybody. They did this to intimidate the others, so that they would offer no resistance. All the others, including our mother, instantly directed the soldiers to the relevant spots and handed over their treasures, which were not only very valuable but emotionally important beyond imagination too. These treasures had been saved from generation to generation, passed on from father to son and from mother to daughter throughout the ages. What a heart-breaking experience this must have been for Mother! Yet everything is relative — this was still an easy task in comparison to those of mothers who were forced to hand over their darling babies to these barbarians.

For three days and three nights we travelled at an unusually fast pace. It seemed to us that we were going very far, but we did not know where. We slept in the cattle car on the floor, leaning on each other for lack of space. The only food we had consisted of the few supplies we had brought with us. Unfortunately, this was very little.

Finally, after an exhausting three days and three nights, the train came to a sudden stop. This was the seventeenth of Tammuz (July 8) 1944, a day fated for sorrow in Jewish history throughout the centuries.[1] We were hurried out of the wagon in a chaotic manner. We got out in a frenzy. We noticed a tall wire fence surrounding the entire vast area.

Dear Mother was horrified, but she did not lose herself. Her first concern was for her children. In the chaos, all the people around us were asking for members of their families, and Mother did so too. She questioned everyone in sight, asking whether they had seen Yozsa, Lici or Dóra among the multitudes of people. Finally, through a miracle, two of the sisters appeared, and we were all united — all except Lici. This was a very ecstatic if brief reunion.

We were told much later that Lici was taken to a huge brick factory in Miskolc, which served as a gathering station for Jews before they were to be deported to Auschwitz. Lici gave birth to her third baby under the unspeakable conditions of this factory. Witnesses from Miskolc related to us that when she came in front of Josef Mengele, *yemach sh'mo* (may his name be obliterated), she was holding her three-day-old baby boy in her arms. The barbarian doctor wanted to grab the infant, but Lici would not let go. He ruthlessly ordered that she be sent to her death together with the baby. Lici was a beautiful woman in the prime of her life when she was killed. Her other two children were murdered in the same manner.

Upon arrival in Auschwitz, Mother, Yozsa, Dóra, Renee and I were ordered to enter the rows of five that were being formed. After

---

1  A day of fasting to mark the breaching of the walls of Jerusalem by the Romans in 69 CE, which led to the destruction of the Second Temple.

we had walked for a while, the line was cut and we had to stand one-by-one. We were ordered to appear in front of Mengele for so-called selection. We were told that children under sixteen and women over forty were to go to the left because they were not fit to work. The people ordered to the right would be sent to labour camps.

This infamous doctor glanced at those lined up in front of him, and within a moment he determined whether the person merited life or death. Of course, we know that these decisions were actually made by *Hashem Yisborach*, blessed God, alone. Those of us who survived have countless stories of *nissim*, miracles, that are a clear testimony to *Hashem's* presence and direction in the midst of the worst horror, the Holocaust. However, this barbaric Mengele was the *shaliach*, messenger, who enacted the hideous murders that took place in Auschwitz-Birkenau.

The first among us to face Mengele was my sister Renee, who was ordered to the right. Not until later did we discover that this meant life. Then it was my turn. He quickly observed me from head to feet and said, "Right." When Mother stood before the beast, he started questioning her. It seemed he wasn't sure. "What is your name and what is your occupation?" he asked. She answered, "Housewife." "How old are you?" he continued. Mother remembered the warning from the *Häftling*, prisoner, and answered that she was forty, although she was older. It looked like this satisfied Mengele's doubts, and Mother was also ordered to the right. With *Hashem's* help, Yozsa and Dóra followed right behind us.

*Hashem Yisborach* had mercy on Mother and me, for when we entered the dreadful room with showers, water came out of the faucets. We actually welcomed the shower. Then we were each given one prison dress and nothing else. The dresses were given out at random, from the pile that others took off — they did not care about the size nor the condition of these dresses. Some were much too big, while others were pitifully small. Poor Renee ended up only with a blanket to wrap herself in. Our meagre possessions were never returned to us, but we never mourned those mundane belongings because we had far more grave reasons to mourn. The only things returned to us were our shoes. Mother was the recipient of a special kindness at this time; somebody recognized her as being a very special, *frum*, devout, woman, and gave her a shawl to cover her head. She was *zoiche*, merited, to keep her head covered during the entire time. Not only that, but someone else found a *siddur*, a Jewish prayer book, and gave it to her.

Evening came and we were finally led to our barracks in Block 3, which was to be our sleeping quarters. This was actually a gigantic, empty stable that did not even have straw on the floor. Dear Mother's response was to keep thanking *Hashem* for the fact that we finally had a roof over our heads. She was able to search for the positive in all situations. She maintained a constant awareness of *Hashem*'s goodness, even in the most trying circumstances.

Even in these horrific circumstances, we managed to daven, pray, *Shacharis*, *Mincha* and *Ma'ariv* (the morning, afternoon and evening prayers) every day, using the *siddur* Mother was given. She shared the *siddur* with everyone who wished to use it. She also knew a lot of *tefillos*, prayers, by heart.

The first Shabbos came. It was Friday night, and Mother invited all those who wished to daven to come to the back of the barracks and pray together. She even managed to get two candles. The girls formed a huge circle, with Mother and me in the centre. Mother davened aloud, and all the girls repeated quietly after her. We were very careful not to draw the attention of any SS guards, for this would have put our lives in danger. After davening, dear Mother spoke to us and told us about the setbacks the Germans were having. She told us that in certain areas they were already retreating, hoping to instill faith and hope into those who were downcast and pessimistic.

The girls frantically asked her, "Paskusz néni, how do you know?" She responded, "I have my sources." We never really found out about the sources, but we didn't really need to either. Strengthening our *emunah* and *bitachon*, our faith and trust in *Hashem*, was vital at that time, for after only a week we were already beginning to succumb. We were all defeated in body and spirit, stricken with pain, suffering from exhaustion, hunger, heat and rain.

～

Once again, we found ourselves face to face with Mengele, the "Satan." They hurried us along the camp grounds without any explanation, until we found ourselves at the train station again. We travelled continuously for an entire day and night. We arrived at a small German town called Hessisch Lichtenau. Our final destination was a new concentration camp.

Originally, the Lager in Hessisch Lichtenau had been built for the German army — it was not intended for Jewish prisoners. There was a huge munitions factory here called Dynamit Nobel. By this time, most of the German workers had been drafted to fight on the fronts, and there were not enough people to operate the factory at full capacity. Therefore, the Germans had brought the Jewish prisoners here to work as slave labourers.

Every morning we were forced to walk twenty minutes to the train station. Then we took a train ride to a part of Hessisch Lichtenau called Fürstenhagen. From this station, we had to walk another thirty minutes in our wooden clogs up to the top of a mountain. During the winter, walking in the snow was absolute torture. By the time we arrived at the munitions factory, we were already exhausted.

The factory was very carefully concealed. It was built entirely underground, with evergreen trees growing on the rooftop. The Germans had planned everything very carefully. Nobody would have guessed the awful plight of the people doing slave labour under the beautiful garden of evergreen trees.

Although our living conditions had improved somewhat, we were now slated to suffer the punishment of working beyond our physical and emotional limits. There was an even worse pain to bear: we were forced to produce materials that were being used to kill and maim our own people. Under immense pressure, we spent the whole day manufacturing cannon powder for German weapons. The powder was yellow and bitter, and the air was so saturated with it that our hair and bodies were constantly yellow. It was dangerous to inhale this poisonous powder, and we were given flimsy masks to minimize the hazard. In spite of the masks, two of our workmates, both young girls, died from inhaling the poison.

Our lunch consisted of a small piece of stale bread, which tasted bitter because of the powder. Often the German officers would throw leftover pieces of dried bread on the floor. We would very eagerly pick up these pieces.

At night, when sleep did not come, we pondered our situation. Were we prisoners or were we slaves? We could not be prisoners, because prisoners are not forced to do such hard labour. We could not be slaves, because slaves are given a proper meal at the end of the day. We knew only that we were a downtrodden, abused and humiliated people.

～

The holy days of Rosh Hashanah, Yom Kippur and Sukkot were approaching, and we wondered how we could observe those awesome days. Mother was there to make the plans. She first approached Manci Pál, our kapo and ally, to ask her to excuse us from work on these days. Manci Pál was a Jewish woman with a good heart, so she gave us permission. We were forever grateful to her for this special privilege.

Our meagre food was the same on Rosh Hashanah as on any other day, but we ate the bread especially slowly so that it would serve as a *seudah*, a holiday feast. Mother had written down the *tefillos* of Avinu Malkeinu[2] in block letters so that each of us could follow her correctly. We prayed all day, beseeching *Hashem* to help us and return us

---

2   A Jewish prayer recited during Rosh Hashanah and Yom Kippur, as well as on other days of repentance and reflection.

to our homes and our families. On Yom Kippur we fasted. This was not so difficult because we were always hungry anyway. Again, we prayed all day. We were physically powerless, and our grip on life was slipping; we were sustained only by our faith in *Hashem*.

We constantly thought of home and worried about our loved ones, wondered what might have happened to them. There were no means to communicate with anybody on the outside, and we did not have the slightest clue about the fate of our family. I was so lucky to be together with my dear mother and kept asking her how we would ever survive this horrible ordeal.

We were becoming weaker and weaker. Our bodies were shrinking, and our energy was failing. Mother covered up her real worries. When I despaired, she always reprimanded me by saying that we must not think negative thoughts and that we must keep faith. Eventually we would go home, she promised, and be reunited with our entire family. She continued to plan for our family's future and thought about how all her children would soon be of marriageable age. They would marry and set up beautiful new homes. After hearing such wonderful plans, I felt as if new blood was flowing in my veins.

By mid-April 1945, the atmosphere remained extremely frightening but a definite feeling was in the air that Germany's defeat was now imminent. The Germans were very anxious to finish the process of mass murder as quickly as possible. Although they were obviously confused and disorganized, they never lost sight of their vicious goal.

# Eviction and Terror
## Sandor (Sam) Grad

The Germans entered Hungary in March 1944 as an ally. The Hungarian government almost immediately made policy changes to accommodate the German government's plans for the Jews.

This was the year I turned thirteen and was to celebrate becoming a bar mitzvah. But about ten days prior to my bar mitzvah party, my father was called in to the Hungarian slave labour army yet again, and the bar mitzvah party had to be postponed until after Passover that year. That party would never happen. Still, I remember learning my *D'var Torah*[1] in anticipation of the event.

Hungary passed a law on April 5, 1944, that the Jewish population needed to wear the yellow star anywhere they went in public. Later that year, on the last day of Passover — Saturday, April 15, 1944 — rumour spread that the Jews of Vásárosnamény were about to have something terrible happen to them. Sure enough, the town crier soon announced to the village that no one should go out in public.

On Sunday, the very day following Passover, two Hungarian police officers entered our home and told us to get ready to leave within two hours. They told us to bring only basic necessities. All valuables needed to be left behind. I put on several layers of clothing, and my

---

1  A talk on a section of the Torah, often given by a rabbi after the Torah reading, and which is likely to carry a life lesson.

family members — father, mother, David, Herschel and baby Irwin (born April 1943) — all tried to do the same to take as much as possible. We had to walk to our designated gathering place, where some people were searched for valuables (which were taken), though I don't remember if we were searched.

All the Jews were then moved to the town hall, which was lined with horses and wagons, and there we were told to load up all of our remaining belongings before being forcibly moved to a temporary camp outside the town.

When they took us away from our house, just after Pesach, it was shocking. At thirteen, I was still a child. I didn't have to figure out what to do. My parents did. My mother told me what to put on and what to bring and so on. I did what my parents told me. We knew we had to go and that we weren't supposed to take any valuables. The non-Jews watched from their homes. I felt humiliated.

Our lay leaders thought this would never happen to the Jews of Hungary. How could it? We were an integral part of the community, loyal Hungarians. It's really hard to express how it felt when arbitrary laws and persecution were suddenly enforced against us. The atmosphere in our town, the apparent attitudes towards Jews, was no different from where I live now, in Toronto. The population was not openly antisemitic. Just as when I speak to my neighbours now, they are friendly and say "good morning" and "hello" to everyone, our neighbours in Hungary were friendly to us. Basically, until they took us away, there was little visible antisemitism.

But this was just the start of the terrible things I would endure over the course of the next year. The Nazis took about ten thousand of us Jews outside the city to a dormant brick factory, which actually belonged to my mother's uncles. I don't think most people knew where we were being led. That isn't to say that some of the people there hadn't already heard rumours of the camps. After all, it was 1944, and for a while now, the Nazis had been committing mass murder of Jews from Poland, Germany and other countries.

But I didn't know where we would be going or understand what was happening. My parents probably didn't want to burden me with this information. While the Hungarian local police took us from our home, my one thought was, "I'll never come back to this place. No matter what." I was so humiliated.

When we got to the brick factory, we realized the building was not designed to house people. Nonetheless, we were all gathered there and put into makeshift barracks, areas typically used to hold bricks. The only thing resembling shelter at the factory was its roof. There were huge pillars holding the structure up, but no side walls. There were no bathrooms, kitchens or hygienic facilities either. When we arrived there, people were forced to create makeshift latrines by digging big holes covered by planks for sitting. People also designed some cooking facilities somehow.

As a young kid, I had no idea what an incredible feat that was and what kind of labour went into making this factory fit for humans even on a basic level. All I knew was that I still had food, and on some level, I even enjoyed this new condition because I no longer had to go to cheder or school. We kids got to fool around all day, and I had a lot more freedom in some sense than I had ever had before.

Although we had been warned not to bring any valuables with us when we were removed from our homes, there were, of course, people who did bring valuables and tried to hide them from the authorities. One morning, the Nazis came to the factory and announced that anyone still harbouring valuables or jewellery should deposit it in special barrels set up for collection. After this, they announced that they would do a person-by-person search, and anyone found still hiding valuables would be shot on sight. The barrels were filled up quickly and taken away; nobody got shot and no real search was made. Many barrels of jewellery were hauled away. Other shocking events occurred at the factory too, but I was too young to really take note of them.

Some of the people in the factory started a committee, in which my father was involved, and were able to petition the city to allow my father and others to go back to Vásárosnamény to get some supplies for our factory ghetto, which he did. On one such excursion back to town, when visiting our old house, my father found out that he had been called back into the Hungarian forced labour army. He had a choice to make, and in thinking about this, he decided that going back into the army would perhaps prove to be a better opportunity to keep in touch with the outside and could maybe help us in some way.

My mother, brothers and I remained in the factory until May 23, 1944. Two groups of people had been transported out of the factory by train prior to this, and on Tuesday, May 23, we were among the third transported out. Once again, we didn't know where we were being taken. The trip there was difficult. We received some water, but two days and nights without food were hard, particularly on my mother and my thirteen-month-old brother. I was the oldest child, so it was a little easier for me. Still, we were a mass of people pressed together. We were hot, cold, hungry and crying. Nobody knew where we were going or what was going to happen to us. As it turned out, we were being led to nightmares.

～

The Neu-Dachs forced labour camp in Jaworzno, which was a sub-camp of Auschwitz-Birkenau, had two kinds of working groups: one worked at a coal-mining facility, others were sent to an electrical plant that was being built. I was chosen for the latter. The first job I was assigned to consisted of unloading bricks from train cars. We worked in a human chain, passing bricks from hand-to-hand. The work didn't bother me at first, though it was hard.

After working in this chain for a couple of days, a Nazi assessor came by and realized there were some young kids in our work group, including me, and took us away to a complex that housed repair shops, locksmiths, blacksmiths and various metal works.

I worked there with the blacksmiths and locksmiths until I was taken away to yet another workplace where they made us work with ceiling plate tiles. This work wasn't hard. We'd mix water with a type of plaster and make casts and manufacture a lot of plates at once. In fact, in order not to lose this easy job, we prisoners would try to stretch out the production so it looked like we were working harder than we actually were.

One of us was constantly watching to be able to warn us to start working if the SS or kapos came. Still, one day our precaution failed and the Nazi assessor came in and realized we were taking it easy. For this, our French Jewish foreman — who was an artist and a mensch — received twenty-five lashes with a whip while the rest of us got one each. After this incident, I was sent to a carpentry shop. I got along well with the people in this shop and worked there until the end of 1944.

Although we got little food, we did get our rations regularly. We got black coffee every morning, soup at noon and bread in the evenings, sometimes with a piece of salami or other spread. I always made sure to leave a bit of bread for the next morning, so I could eat something before starting my work. But we were starving. Whether prisoners lived or died often had to do with what work details they were assigned. Being able to work in a "lighter" camp meant that your chances of survival improved because your body did not have to work as hard. But this also depended on whether the kapos, who would beat you at will, liked you more or less.

I witnessed a lot of these beatings. I was punched a few times, but luckily, I never got beaten up too badly. And being young, I had some protection from older prisoners. Another thing working in my favour was that I was a Hungarian who could speak Yiddish. Many of the kapos were Polish and spoke Yiddish too. They would often chide the Hungarians for not being real Jews because they could not speak Yiddish. In cheder, our lessons were in Yiddish, so my Yiddish was pretty good. I made sure to befriend some Polish boys in the camp to pick up their Yiddish accents. In this way, I managed to stay on the kapos' good side. To them, I was a Hungarian Jew, but I wasn't like the other Hungarian Jews.

Despite the lack of food, this particular camp wasn't so hard for me, because I was able to work inside and do light work. I witnessed many people who worked on the outside detail get sick. Many sick or weak people were taken away to Auschwitz, and while we didn't know what was done to them, by then, I suspected that they were being murdered.

My problems really began when the Neu-Dachs camp was evacuated in January 1945. The Soviets were coming, and the Nazis decided they had to take us further inland. Everyone who was able to stand was lined up and told that we were leaving. However, the sick and immobile were told they could stay. Still, many of the sick decided to try to line up, because they figured if they stayed, they'd likely be killed. I later found out that those who stayed behind in the camp actually survived and were liberated by the Soviets shortly after we left.

The Nazis packed up their goods in wagons, and since there were no horses, prisoners were required to push the wagons. I was one of these prisoners, because at this point I was in barracks No. 1, which was right next to the front gate. For the first day, I was pushing the wagons. Then we started to walk. We walked without rest for two days and nights. People began to drop. All those who could no longer walk and fell got shot, and their bodies were then put on wagons and pushed along with the rest.

After a while, the walk became tough for many of us, and our path turned into a killing field. Anyone who walked out of line was shot. Soon enough, the dead were being left on the side of the road instead of being put on wagons.

I was able to walk with three friends, two brothers and the man who was my supervisor at the carpentry shop. We stayed together and locked arms so that if anyone was sleepwalking, which we did a lot, none of us would walk out of line or fall. This greatly helped our survival.

After two days and nights of walking, we were put up in a barn, which couldn't accommodate all of us. There was no room to sit and there were no washroom facilities either. We were all exhausted and there was no food for most of us. However, my friends and I were lucky enough to be pushing a wagon full of food and cigarettes. We managed to steal some food to eat (and even some cigarettes to trade), so we weren't starving as much as others.

The night was supposed to be a time of rest for us. Instead, it turned into a nightmare. With unsanitary conditions, no food and no possibility to sleep, we were more tired than ever.

In the morning, the Nazis lined us up and announced that whoever could not keep going should step aside. Those who could not walk were left behind with a squad of soldiers and given tools for digging. Those of us continuing on our march knew that they would be digging their own graves. We heard the gunshots from a distance.

We no longer marched on the road, but instead walked through the snow across fields. The third night was again a nightmare, with the SS shooting many at random. It no longer mattered if someone walked in line or not or if they were strong or not — they just shot people when they felt like it. Hundreds were killed on the whim of our Nazi guards. There were about three thousand of us left on that fourth day. It's hard for anyone who didn't go through it to imagine how tired and hungry and cold we all were.

We finally arrived at the Blechhammer camp on that day. Blechhammer was a big forced labour camp located between the German and Soviet war fronts. The camp was half-empty when we got there because the Nazis had already evacuated a lot of the inmates. That night, we heard constant firing of shells between the German and the Soviet armies. When we woke up the next morning, all the Nazi guards were gone. The two barracks where the sick were housed were burned down with the patients still inside. The burning corpses could be seen from the outside.

We scavenged for food and looted the German storerooms. We found potatoes and meat. My friends and I (a new friend had joined the brothers and the supervisor from the carpentry shop) moved into an empty barracks near the Blechhammer camp's front gate and built a fire that night and cooked goulash. However, I decided not to eat because I felt sick and thought to myself that it was better to wait until morning to see how my stomach was.

The night was finally quiet on the war fronts, and I slept for what I thought was a long time. But I was woken up by the words "Get up quickly! You're being moved to a new camp!" We were especially surprised because we had seen Soviet tanks in the distance and had thought the Germans had left us. We thought we had already been liberated. However, some German soldiers returned to the camp at night to take prisoners with them. Since we were close to the gate, we were the first ones they grabbed.

About 250 of us were marched from the camp and another large transport was marched out as well. The Germans didn't have the time or the ability to get the rest of the prisoners out of Blechhammer. Those who were left behind were liberated by the Soviets the next morning, including one of my friends, who managed to stay behind when the Nazis came back for us.

Unfortunately, I was one of the unlucky ones.

This march lasted three and a half weeks. Every day we walked in the cold and snow through mid-February. Every evening we would be taken into a barn so our guards could rest. We would be given a cup of soup brewed by whichever farmer was housing us.

The death march took on the same character as before: we walked, and anyone who stopped walking was shot dead. While we walked, we could see the limbs and corpses of those who had been marching ahead of us. Feet, hands, heads… all sticking out from the snow.

At the end of this march, those of us who survived were taken into the Gross-Rosen concentration camp. We were cautioned by the other Jews in that camp not to tell the camp residents that we were Jewish. We had to hide the fact from the Polish or Ukrainian gentile inmates, because it was rumoured that they would sometimes kill Jews.

We didn't stay there long and were soon squeezed into open train cars. The train cars were so crowded that there was standing room only; we were in exposed freight cars while the temperature was freezing, and this train ride would last three days.

We had been given a chunk of bread and some salami before being put on the train. Many ate their rations immediately. I was always careful to ration my food, not knowing how long any journey would take or when I might get my next morsel of food.

After just one day of travel, there were maybe forty dead people in the wagon next to mine, and I wasn't sure how many had died in my own. Every day they'd unload more dead bodies. And whenever someone died, others would search the body for food rations or anything of value.

I had more luck on this trip. Nobody had any food left, but I was still with my three friends. Unbeknownst to the rest of us, one of the brothers had managed to keep a plain wedding ring on him throughout our travels. On the third day of our journey, he showed it to the SS guard on our train, who miraculously took it in exchange for half of his sandwich. We split that sandwich. For the four of us, that piece of bread was a lifesaver.

At the end of the third day we arrived at the village of Leitmeritz. Those who were able to walk were taken off the train. We were marched through the village while the villagers watched; many of our group were shot dead on their streets just because they were unable to continue walking.

We were marched into the Leitmeritz concentration camp, which was a tough subcamp of Flossenbürg, and only a short distance away from the Theresienstadt ghetto and concentration camp. At the time we had no idea where we were. The camp was infested with lice and there was less food than at our previous camps. For a while, I was assigned to pick potatoes. This allowed me to steal some potatoes from time to time, which I divided with my friends. It helped us survive, but it was a very dangerous thing to do.

We were at the camp until late April 1945, at which point the Nazis asked all the Jews to step out. At this point, the Germans were so disorganized that they did not know who was Jewish. I decided not to volunteer my religion, but it was soon discovered, and I was taken out of Leitmeritz with many others and walked a few kilometres to Theresienstadt.

As soon as we got there, we received a big bowl of soup. We saw Jewish people in civilian clothes. We found out that this was the Nazi "model camp," where Jews were treated well for the media to deflect attention away from the real death camps. The camp had a theatre and a canteen to buy goods. When we arrived, we were skin-and-bones and scared the Jewish children there because we looked like ghosts.

We stayed there until the Soviets liberated us. Once we were liberated, hundreds of former prisoners became sick from eating too much too quickly after starving for so long. Others contracted typhoid fever, and many died. The illnesses were so rampant and there was so much human waste that the Soviets had to quarantine the camp. Despite all this, it was a very happy occasion to see the Soviets. I was lucky not to get sick.

Why did I survive when so many others did not? I really don't know. I was young, fit, I didn't need to eat as much as others, I had some good luck and I got some help from other prisoners. I can't tell you that I spent a lot of time trying to figure out, or understand, why I survived. I focused on getting on with life instead.

# Beliefs under Shock
## Veronika Schwartz

Cruel laws and rules were forced upon us day after day. It was extremely painful to realize that we had been overly optimistic for too long. It was shocking when I visited one of our tenants, the Posner family, who were of Russian origin. They used to have a maid, a Roma girl (we called them Gypsies at the time) who I liked talking with. She was always happy and cheerful. I had asked where she was and was told that she was forcibly taken away and drowned with many others. "How is it possible to kill innocent people? They must have sent them to work somewhere," I told Mrs. Posner. She said softly to me, "I wish you would be right."

Whenever my father went to the Orthodox synagogue in our town, Kisvárda, he came home with dreadful news. He heard that a prominent doctor and his entire family committed suicide. When I walked down the street to try to find out about some more news, I was pelted with rocks. My mother used to love going to the mikvah, the ritual bath; it used to be one of life's pleasures for her but now she could no longer do that. We were not even allowed to listen to the radio anymore.

I heard a lot of whispering. I overheard my parents talking about an escape route but they would not have been able to execute the plans. It was too late. Jews were not allowed to travel. My mother would never agree to any escape route unless the whole family could escape together and that was impossible. We carried home a lot of merchandise (furniture, yard goods) from our store. Our sheds were dug up and we buried the yard goods and clothes in wooden boxes.

On March 19, 1944, the German army marched into Hungary. Beyond the Germans' expectations, the Hungarians welcomed them and fully cooperated with them. We felt trapped.

I remember Mr. Fekete, who came to our house to read the electricity meter. When he walked in, he looked at all of us. He started to walk towards my parents and it seemed as though he would have liked to talk to them, but he was so overcome with emotion that he started to cry. He just kept on crying and walked out. He knew that something terrible was going to happen to us. Sure enough, a few days later, one young man came to our house and my grandparents' home. This young man lived on our street. My grandmother and his grandmother were friendly with each other. His name was Bajor and he was authorized to take inventory of our belongings. It did not take long to find out that we would have to leave our homes and move to the ghetto in Kisvárda. All of us tried hard to comfort each other.

My parents felt that my brother should enlist for a labour camp. Perhaps he would have a better chance to stay alive there. He listened to them and left to enlist. It was heartbreaking to see him go.

My parents entrusted our livestock to the people who used our property to cross into town. Even though they promised to take good care of all the animals, it was hard to leave them behind — the baby goats whom I adored, the beautiful horse I loved to ride, the cows, geese, ducks and chickens.

My mother worked frantically to prepare a soup base, a mixture of flour and oil or chicken fat. She said that as long as we could get some water at least we could make soup. I saw her break down and cry. I begged her not to cry. Her answer was, "I am not crying for myself, I am crying for all of you. I love you all very much." I tried to tell her that our departure was only temporary. She hugged and kissed me. She was always very brave, but my parents were experienced and I was naive. They knew how irrational people could become through hatred, jealousy, vengeance and power.

My parents worked very hard, never taking a vacation. They never smoked or drank and saved every penny. Because the custom was to give girls a dowry when they married, they had bought precious jewels, diamonds and gold for the three of us so that when we eventually got married we would have the means to start a new life on our own. Now my father called us and we all went down to the cellar. He removed some of the bricks from the wall, hid the jewels in a bottle and repaired the wall. So we all knew where they were. He hid some of our jewellery in the attic. The Fishers, our neighbour from across the road, hid some of their jewellery in our attic too.

Around the middle of April 1944, we were transported to and imprisoned in the ghetto in Kisvárda. We were taken under the cruellest conditions by the Hungarian gendarmerie and then all of us were crammed into a single room — my grandmother, my parents, Aunt Margit, Uncle Ernő, and my two sisters, Klára and Éva. Below our room was a cellar. That's where people were brought to be interrogated, to find out where they had hidden their money and valuables. It was always the head of the household who was interrogated. At first they tortured the very wealthy and later the members of the middle class. It was horrible to hear the screams.

We also worried about our father. Food was scarce so my dad would sneak out before sunrise. A gentile family gave him eggs, milk and bread. He took a tremendous risk to improve the quality of life of his family. The people who gave him the food were also very special, unselfish, kind and willing to help others in need. It was a courageous act. They could have gotten into trouble for helping Jews. Good people like them gave us the incentive to try hard and go on with our lives. It was a joint effort to do the best we could. We supported each other, sharing the household duties. We were free to walk anywhere within the ghetto. I walked a lot with my sisters and everyone else in the family, talking to our friends and neighbours, trying to find out about political news.

One morning, there was a knock at our door. My mother answered, and a young man introduced himself and asked if he could talk to me. My mother spoke to him for a few minutes, and then she called me. She introduced him to me; his name was Ainsley. We went for a walk and we talked. He told me that he wanted to get to know me and asked if I would be interested in him. Well, I was most surprised. He was very good-looking, slim, tall and very polite. I couldn't figure out why he would be interested in me. I asked him, "Why me?" I pointed out all my shortcomings and offered to introduce him to some beautiful girls from Kisvárda. He just smiled and told me that he had seen all the girls in the ghetto but had no desire to go out with anyone except me. He did seem very honest, so I agreed to be his girlfriend. I enjoyed his company very much. He introduced me to his mother, who turned out to be a very nice lady.

I was happy. However, a few days later, a young boy (the son of our tenant) handed a message to my mother. The note had come from a Hungarian gendarme and it stated that he wanted me to go to the end of the ghetto by the fence, alone, and meet him on the empty field. If I refused, all the older men would be tortured. I looked at my family. I will never forget the look on my mother's face — it reflected fear, terror and helplessness. I knew that there was just one thing to do — go. I told my family not to worry, that I would speak to this young man, everything would be fine, and I would be back soon.

I went on my own to meet him. We talked for about fifteen minutes and then my boyfriend appeared with a letter from a doctor saying that I had gotten my appendix out and that I was not allowed to be out walking; I must stay indoors and not be on my feet. The gendarme gave him a stern look and told both of us that we could leave. As soon as I got back, I lay down just in case the gendarme decided to check on me.

The next morning, Ainsley came to see me. All of us were shocked to see him — his arm was in a sling and he had black eyes. He had gotten badly beaten up. It was horrible to see him like that. I felt responsible for all his suffering. He told me not to worry, that his injuries would heal. And he brought me a book to read, *Gone with the Wind*. He was my first boyfriend and I really liked him a lot.

Once again, the news was frightening. And once more our hopes that the war would be over soon and we would get back to our homes and businesses, and be able to resume our lives, were shattered. People were saying that the Germans were going to transport everyone to work camps. The ghetto became like a funeral parlour; people were openly weeping. Everyone there was scared. It didn't make sense that Germany would want grandmothers, pregnant women, babies, sick people and children to work for them. What would happen to us was the question on everyone's mind.

I was brought up to respect everyone, no matter their religion. So it was difficult to comprehend the complexity of human hatred. I did believe that the Germans would be taking us to work. My grandmother worriedly asked me, "What type of work can I do for them? I am too old to work." "Well," I said, "you could help out in the kitchen, like peeling potatoes, or in a hospital preparing bandages. We could all do some work."

On May 29, 1944, my boyfriend didn't come to visit me. I became panicky and told my mother I must go to see him. She agreed. So I went but he and his family were gone, taken away with the first transport. I felt horrible. I couldn't even say goodbye, but I was hopeful that I would see him again after the war.

My family and I were taken on May 31, 1944. About eighty people were herded into each wagon of the cattle car. We weren't allowed to take anything, only the clothes we wore. There was a pail of water, the doors were shut, and our journey towards an unknown destination began. My father, my mother, my grandmother, and my sisters, Klára and Éva, Aunt Margit, Uncle Ernő — everyone was quiet, sad and speechless. I tried hard to cheer them up. I found a little space where I was able to look out and watch the scenery. I asked everyone to come and watch. No matter how hard I tried, no one was interested. My grandmother kept repeating that she was too old to work. Had I

known what was to happen to them, I would have spent every moment kissing and hugging them and would have tried my best not to
get separated from them.

Finally, the train arrived in Auschwitz-Birkenau, Poland. The
doors opened. Somehow I was pushed out in such a way that I found
myself standing alone and a long line was forming behind me. I
looked everywhere but I could not see anyone from my beloved family. Fear and panic hit me. I sobbed and threw myself to the ground,
thinking to myself that I would not get up unless they reunited me
with my family. I didn't care if I got shot. Behind me in the line were
the two Fried girls from our street, Vár utca. They were crying too
but they lifted me up and begged me to stay on my feet. They told me
that their mother was pregnant and they could not see her anywhere
either.

We saw the barbed wire with a high voltage security fence. We saw
a lot of people inside. It was a scary sight. Some people walked with
long sticks and were beating up others. People wore rags. We couldn't
imagine what this place could be. Some people were saying it must be
a mental asylum. But how could they treat mental patients so badly?

We found ourselves inside the Auschwitz-Birkenau camp. This
was the worst day in my entire life. My heart ached, not knowing
what was happening to my family. Where were they? I searched as far
as I could see, in every direction, even imagining that I was seeing my
father in the distance.

It started to rain and was cool. We didn't get any food all day but
we had to stay in line and wait. We were mentally and physically
drained. Finally, an SS officer came and told us that he would try to
get us some tea. It was no comfort to me. I was a lost soul.

Later on, we had to be disinfected. At this place, they shaved our
heads. We had to strip naked. They put us through humiliating tor-
tures. Our clothes were taken away and we had to get dressed from
a pile of rags. As I walked around this disinfecting area, like a sudden miracle, I noticed my first cousin from my father's side, Magda

Klein. She noticed me at the same time. She told me that she had no one from her family with her either and that we should try to stay together. I hoped we would be able to do that.

We were later led over to the C Lager in Birkenau. We had to wait outside at first where a kapo came to talk to us. She told us her name, Toska. I believe she was a Polish girl. She seemed very honest. She asked if we had any questions. Many people asked the same question, "When will we be reunited with our family members?" With tears in her eyes, she pointed to the crematorium. She had a difficult time talking. After regaining her composure she said, "Like you, I was brought here with my family, but now I am alone." She warned us to be alert; it would not be easy to stay alive.

After that, we were herded into the barracks. There was another kapo there whose name was Éva. She was mean. She was a good-looking Jewish girl, who behaved shamefully, using a stick to control people.

We were squeezed into a very tight sitting position for the night. In my misery, I decided to heed the rabbi's advice: to hope and pray. Every night, I recited prayers in Hebrew. I knew them well and I included every member of my family and, of course, Ainsley. Somehow, my religious background gave me strength. But I also had a guilty feeling, "Why me? Why am I alive and my family gone?" I tormented myself with such questions.

Before sunrise, we were awakened by a loud whistling sound. We had to rush out and line up for inspection. A couple of times a week, we had to march into the barracks naked in front of the doctors, Mengele and some others. This was called selection — if someone was taken out of the line, it meant death. So we tried to look our best.

We received a slice of bread and about a teaspoon of jam in the morning. In the afternoon we took turns picking up our tiny bits of tasteless food. There were no dishes, no cutlery. So we lined up and drank from the same cup. In the afternoon, we again had to stand in line for a couple of hours just to be counted. One morning after the lineups I lay down on the ground. An SS soldier stepped on my stomach. A day's survival was an achievement. Sometimes I saw corpses at the fence that were burnt like charcoal. It was horrible. About three or four weeks later, we were lining up one morning to have our identification numbers tattooed into our forearms when my cousin Magda was taken away. Once again I felt lost. I wanted to remain with her so badly, so I crouched down and crept to a window. I climbed through it and found Magda. I lined up after her. We had no idea what would happen to us but once again we were together and that meant a lot to both of us. Sixteen people were there. We got into little boxcars pulled by a tractor. After travelling three to three and a half hours, we arrived on a farm.

We were given shelter in a shed. We slept on straw on the ground. Later on, the supervisors put up some bunks for us. When it was getting dark, the door was shut and we were locked in. At 6:00 a.m. the doors opened again. We received some food and were driven by truck to the fields to work. We had to gather wheat or oats, form bunches, tie them up and put them in an upright position. We had two supervisors. The man was nice; if someone had difficulty doing the work, he tried to help and was never angry. The woman disliked all of us. I overheard her telling the male supervisor that we were Jews and that we didn't deserve any help.

All of us tried to do our utmost. This place was definitely better than Auschwitz. On Sunday, we were given mashed potato and a slice of ham on a regular plate for supper. This meant a lot to everyone.

One day the owner rode up on horseback to where we did our work. He called me and another girl over to talk. He told us that instead of working in the fields we would be working in the kitchen. The other girl was only thirteen and she was mostly polishing shoes, as far as I could tell. I ended up helping the two maids peel vegetables, fruits and so on. It was a better job than working the fields. I managed to fill my clothes with apple skins. Sometimes I managed to hide some carrots or small apples and shared them with all the others.

On Sundays, I would see the entire family of the owner going to church. It reminded me of how I used to go to synagogue with my parents, brother and sisters, and other members of my family. I was not jealous of them but I was badly hurt. The injustice was too horrendous. Here I was working like a slave. Why? I hadn't done anything wrong. They were born into the Christian faith. I happened to be born into the Jewish faith. They had kept everything they owned while everything was confiscated from us. Their family was alive. I didn't know what had happened to mine.

How could this crime be allowed to happen in the twentieth century with not one single nation trying to rescue us? Where was God? Had he fallen asleep? I was losing my faith in humanity. I questioned the existence of God. After all, I could see the crematorium smoke all the time while I was in Auschwitz. The sadistic cruelties that I witnessed gave me few reasons to believe that I would see everyone from my beloved family again.

After working in the kitchen for about three months, I overheard the two maids expressing concern about how close the Soviets were and what would happen to them. To us it meant hope, that the hour of our freedom was getting closer.

One afternoon after work, when I entered the shed, there was dead silence and everyone was looking at me. I asked, "What's going on?" It was explained that one of the women was in her sixth month of pregnancy and she worried about losing her baby due to working in the fields. The maids had agreed to let her work in the kitchen if I was willing to take her place in the fields. There was no question of debating the issue. The next morning, I went to work in the fields.

The Soviets were inching closer. We had seen gunfire explosions. Our lives were now additionally at risk. Everyone was scared. We continued working a couple more weeks but one morning, instead of being driven to work, we were transported back to Auschwitz. It was very difficult to hope anymore.

The people in Auschwitz looked like skeletons, and they were jealous that we had spent time working on a farm. They were telling us that there was an outbreak of typhus. People were dying all around me. I cannot find words to explain the intensity of the crime. By this time, it looked like we were mere remnants of a people. I kept telling myself not to give up — if anyone from my family had survived they might need me. This feeling of responsibility to my family and to our people kept me struggling to stay alive.

The hunger, filth and torture continued. One morning, to my amazement, I received a small package. The kapo who gave it to me told me that she had to bring back a reply. I opened it: there was some bread, a pencil and a note that said, "I was born in Poland. I am not Jewish. I publicly expressed opposition to the ruling government; therefore, I was sent to Auschwitz. I am a doctor. I would like to know if you would marry outside your faith."

It didn't take me long to reply. In my heart, I knew that I would not marry outside my faith, out of respect to my parents. Also, I had not given up on Ainsley yet. So I expressed my thanks to him and stated my reasons. I never heard from him again but it gave me a tremendous boost to believe that there were some decent people out there.

# Fate and Fortune
# Leslie Fazekas

Translated from Hungarian by Marietta Morry and Lynda Muir (2018)

On the first of May 1944, I wound up in a labour camp. Decorated Jewish veterans of World War I were accorded special status in the labour service and the father of a good friend of mine, Tomi Szemere, was an exempted lieutenant. He could arrange for his son, along with a few of his son's friends, to be in Haláp under his command and work in the forest there. Compared to people in other labour camps, we lived like lords. We were billeted in a farmhouse, where others cleaned and cooked for us. All we did from morning till night was "cricketing," which meant freeing the roots of felled trees from the soil. We worked with shovels and pickaxes, and after four weeks, all beefed up, tanned and healthy, we had to return to Debrecen.

In June, we were sent to the Debrecen ghetto and then we ended up in a brick factory, from where we were deported to Vienna. In the Debrecen ghetto, each family was allocated one room, which they filled with all the belongings they wanted to salvage, so there was hardly any space left for the people. Since it was June, everyone was out on the streets most of the time. The few city blocks into which Debrecen's Jewish population had been crammed were now teeming with throngs of people.

After a few weeks, the ghetto was evacuated, and everyone was herded to the brick factory carrying only small knapsacks. It was late afternoon when we started off. We were moving westward, and the reddish sun slanted its rays at us. It was close to dark when we arrived at our new quarters. The gendarmes herded us up to the attic of a barn. By then it was completely dark and everyone tried to secure just enough room to lie down. There was quarrelling and fighting all around, and it was a long time before the four of us could spread a blanket on the dusty floor and finally lie down.

The first thing I did the next morning was leave the attic and look for some place to stay outdoors. Judit's family squeezed even closer together, and when it looked like four more people could fit in, I went back to the attic for my family and we all moved over. Fortunately, it wasn't raining, because our spot was underneath the eaves, and the eaves only covered half of our "apartment," which consisted of a blanket with four bedcovers and four pillows. The pillowcases also served as our knapsacks.

Both in the ghetto and in the brick factory, we were surrounded by friends and acquaintances. And Judit was always there. We couldn't even imagine what might lie in store for us and didn't even dare think about the future. We lived only for the present; everything else was relegated to the background.

We didn't spend many days in that place, but every day was filled with atrocities. The wealthier citizens of Debrecen were taken to the Gendarmerie station and tortured until they disclosed where they had hidden their gold and jewellery, if they possessed any. Gradually the prospect of leaving this place behind began to seem like redemption to us, no matter the destination. The first transport had already left and we wanted to get on the next one at all costs. We succeeded in that.

The first transport set out in the direction of Auschwitz, but for some reason it had turned back and then started off towards Vienna. It took the train four or five days to arrive at Strasshof, which was a transit camp just outside Vienna. Those of us in the next transport headed west right away and reached Strasshof after a two-day journey. In the railcar there was just enough room to sit, so we tried to sleep while sitting. The night was filled with wailing, crying, moaning and bickering. For the purpose of relieving ourselves, a bucket was supplied, which you couldn't really make use of in the dark of the night. Another transport, which consisted of doctors, lawyers and others who had been staying in the attic, was taken to Auschwitz. Three other transports left from the vicinity of Debrecen, all to Strasshof.

It was late in the afternoon of the second day when our train arrived at its final destination, Strasshof. German soldiers surrounded the train and made us exit the cars quickly. My family and Judit's had travelled in the same car, and the first thing I did on arrival was set out with Judit in search of water, a pail in hand. We found water nearby, filled up the vessel, and returned to our families. By the time we reached them, there was no water left in the vessel. We were so thirsty we drank it all on the way back.

Strasshof was a transit camp, and the Jews who arrived there were directed to various workplaces. We were sent to a tank factory; Judit and her family were sent to do farm work. In the Lager of the factory we lived amid different nationalities and worked at night, until the end of the war.

We have learned that the German soldier is the horribly perfect creation of Hitler. If ordered to kill, he would kill; he would kill a child or a defenseless woman without any particular emotion or feeling of guilt. If he didn't receive an order, he wouldn't kill.

Something we experienced may serve as a case in point. During our deportation, we were not under the jurisdiction of the SS. Right beside our Lager, however, there was another Lager behind barbed wire where Jews just like us, as well as others, were kept under the authority of the SS. In the last month of the war, every evening five of us from our Lager went to work in the same factory as the "stripers," men wearing striped prisoner uniforms. The only difference was that the stripers were escorted by SS men, who would surround them with weapons at the ready and put them under floodlights to prevent their escape. Three SS officers marched behind the group, and behind the SS officers came the five of us. We had no guard and no supervision. We only used the light of those floodlights to help us avoid falling into bomb craters. Sometimes the SS officers would turn to us and begin to engage us in conversation. The yellow star was there on our chests in case they didn't know that the only reason we were working in the factory was because we were Jews. If a Jew among the stripers stepped out of formation, the same officer who was discussing the story of that day's air attack with us would have shot the escapee without hesitation, simply because he had been ordered to do so. They didn't have any instructions concerning us, so we could do as we pleased. We weren't their responsibility, and even though we were Jewish, that wasn't their problem, only ours.

# Hoping in Isolation
## Miriam Mózes

In February 1944 we were still living in our beautiful home and were waiting for miracles: for Dad's homecoming and the return of happier days. All my friends, along with every Jew in Hódmezővásárhely, were worried about our unpredictable future. People were spreading rumours like, "This is only the beginning. There are concentration camps in Germany, Poland and Austria, and probably we will also be deported soon."

Peter, my best, though rather overly smart, friend, always told stories about those camps: "Those are the most horrible places one can imagine. People live there in dirty barracks, starving, sleeping on the floor, hugging each other to keep warm at night. They look and act like ghosts. Those camps are equipped with gas chambers," he said, "to burn the Jews alive." I was terrified when listening to Peter, but in my mind these were mere horror stories — I never believed them.

One morning in March 1944, we woke up to a very loud noise. We could not figure out what it was. I was scared to death, thinking that there was a bomb attack. The noise kept on and on for hours. We sneaked out from our room to find out what was going on. We met a few scared people on the street. One elderly gentleman told us that we had lost our freedom completely, that German tanks carrying soldiers had marched into Hódmezővásárhely. We did not have to wait too long for them to take over everything in our town. The next morning they occupied our house. The Nazis set up their headquarters there and kicked us out.

We had to move, leaving everything behind, into a small office at the back of the building. My father had owned a business involving grain cleaning and trading, and a building for the business was connected to our house by a corridor. There was no washroom and we had to use an outhouse and a washtub. The only good thing was that the office was attached to our old home, so it almost felt like home. We were lucky that the room had a huge glass window facing our beautiful garden. My mom loved flowers and the flowers were so nice and colourful that when we looked at them, we almost forgot how miserable our existence was.

There was only one bed in the room, so my brother, András (Andrew), and I slept on the floor on very worn-out, thin mattresses. There was no table and no chair to sit on, so we had to sit on the floor. I remember that I was always very hungry, since there was not much to eat. Once a day, we got a watery hot drink, a so-called soup, from the Germans who had occupied our house. For the first time in my life I realized how terrible it was to be hungry all the time. Luckily I found a soapbox full of cookies Mom had hidden from us under her bed. Once in a while I managed to steal a few delicious cookies while singing a song we had made up, "Lanolin Baba," to divert her suspicion. Gobbling them made me feel a little better.

There was not much to do all day, as Mom forbid us from going out, since the huge backyard and the garden were buzzing with German soldiers. These were the most boring days in my life, as there was nothing to do except look out the window and watch the German soldiers walk, talk and laugh all day long. However, Mom tried to keep us busy, telling us stories about Dad and our grandparents and their lives together. I was fascinated by these stories, and Mom's calm disposition and optimistic outlook made me forget the severity of our situation and our hopeless future.

In June 1944, after spending a few days in the city's synagogue, the Jews of Hódmezővásárhely had to march to the railway station and were squeezed into cattle cars. I was pushed so hard by the crowd that I lost my balance and fell down. I managed to regain my balance but was terrified that I'd lost contact with my mom and Andrew. I started to scream, "Anyu, Anyu, where are you?" so loudly that even in the crowded car, my mom heard me and crawled towards me on the floor. I still vividly remember how seeing my mother helped me regain hope. "Anyu is there for me forever," I thought. The heat, the crowded space, the smell, the darkness and starvation were unbearable, but having my mother at my side and clinging to her gave me security.

The train ride in the cattle cars lasted a few days, but the only thing I remember of it vividly was my aching stomach. I was starving and so thirsty the whole time that my mind was in a continuous haze. Andrew and I were clinging to our mom. She kept hugging us and telling us stories about the happy life we'd had in the past and the hope for the future. Now and then I felt somewhat relieved but the pain of starvation just would not disappear.

It was dark when we arrived in a large, empty place that looked like a gymnasium. We had to take off our clothing and everybody was standing naked there, waiting to get into the shower. Nobody knew what was waiting for us, but everybody was scared to death. The rumours circulating were really very scary: most people talked about gas chambers, final moments and the end of life. Somehow I did not believe these scary stories. My mom agreed and kept her optimism high. "Do not worry; God will help us through these terrible times," she said. "We just have to believe that we'll survive and we will." Her firm belief and optimism influenced us, and we ignored the rumours.

It was the first time in my life that I saw naked people, especially naked men, walking around. They looked terrified but seemed to find some comfort in talking to each other. I found it very weird, but my curiosity kept me wandering in the room to observe everybody, mostly the men. After a short while, I lost interest and accepted the strange situation.

After waiting in line for a while, we were guided into a huge room, equipped with hundreds of showers. I was so glad to have a shower after so many days of being dirty that I almost forgot where I was — I was completely absorbed rediscovering the pleasures of a hot shower.

My recollection of the ten months after deportation to Austria is very vague; I barely remember any details of these horrific times beyond a few frightening events.

Towards the end of the war, we were transferred to Theresienstadt. We arrived there from Linz in March 1945 after three weeks of marching, mostly through deserted, spooky side roads. It was a long and gruelling trip without much food or rest. When we finally reached our destination, dead tired and starving, we were taken to a huge barracks equipped with hundreds of beds. We would end up spending three months in this camp.

One morning after we finished our meagre breakfast, a small slice of bread with a cup of soup that tasted like water, my friend Éva ran to me and pulled me aside, "Did you hear the latest?" "No," I said. "What happened?" She paused for a moment and whispered in my ear, "There are a few rumours circling around in the camp. One of them is good but the other is all the more terrible. The good news is that the Soviet army is very close by so we could be liberated within a few days. The bad news is," Éva continued, "that the Germans do not want the Jews to survive the deportation and tell their stories to the world. That's why they are planning to kill all of us in the gas chambers."

I was devastated. I cried all day and could not eat, no matter how hungry I felt. I walked restlessly up and down in the barracks, trying to figure out how to handle the situation. Obviously there was not much I could do to influence the outcome of events. Towards the end of the day, I somehow managed to convince myself to be more optimistic and felt more positive about our chances of survival. I did not share the secret with my level-headed mom and my calm, nine-year-old brother. I did not want to upset them with unfounded rumours.

When I went to bed after a scant so-called supper, I still felt restless, but deep in my heart I was reassured that soon we'd be free, we'll return home and our life will be back to normal. After tossing and turning, with my thoughts running all over the map, I finally fell asleep. My dreams moved back and forth from survival to death. I dreamt that we were standing in a long line in front of a newly erected gas chamber, close to our barracks. When I came close to the door I could not face my inevitable death, so I stepped out of the line and ran away as fast as I could. I kept running for a long time, until I almost lost my breath. Then I suddenly stopped, hoping that I had escaped my imminent death. Opening my eyes to check where I was, I looked around to find myself on the barracks bed shared with Mom and Andrew.

To have to face death was unbearable for a young girl, so I tried to escape reality by forcing myself to close my eyes again and dream happier dreams. When I realized that I was too agitated to fall asleep, I started to daydream instead. In my daydream, it was March 15, my dad's birthday. His handsome features, blond hair, blue eyes and tall, slim body came so vividly to my memory that I felt I was really sitting beside him, while he was hugging me and talking to me. I wished him well on his birthday and prayed for his health and for his safe return from his captivity. An optimist all my life, I hoped that he was alive, well and healthy somewhere, just as we were, my mom, my brother and me, a restless, hopeful, ambitious little thirteen-year-old. I was confident that soon all of us would be together again.

# Apples at Christmas
# Julius Jakab

The whistle blew at the end of the day and in no time we were ready to go back to the Kaufering concentration camp. The trip back to Kaufering was uneventful, except for our attempt to smuggle small tree branches into the camp to light a fire in our little stove in order to warm up the barracks for the night. We were lucky — the wood was not detected and we were all excited that we could build the fire. If all went well, we hoped to cook on it in the future.

The lineup for dinner was uneventful except for the change in the menu: the soup was only made of turnips that day, and we were also given three potatoes and a miniature slice of hard jam. We went into our barracks and started to eat the soup. I didn't like the taste of it. I couldn't eat it. I asked Joe if he was ready to eat the awful soup. Joe said that it wasn't that bad. So we made a deal that I would trade him my soup for one of his potatoes, plus some of his soup from the next day. He was worried that I would be losing crucial calories in this deal, but after I insisted, he agreed. We ate slowly, trying to enjoy every spoonful, every bite. After I ate my potatoes plus the one Joe gave me, I was feeling better.

When we finished eating, we made our beds and took off our shoes. We got into our beds and suddenly Joe said to me, "Surprise!" He had lit a wooden match and stuck it into a boiled potato and started to sing "Happy Birthday" to me. It was my twenty-first birthday.

Just three short weeks before, I had thrown him a party for his twenty-first birthday in Budapest. What a difference a few days can make. We never thought then that we'd be up to our necks in this almost hopeless situation. But Joe and I made a promise to each other that we would be strong and that we were going to survive, no matter what. We started a fire, and even though it was just a small stove it made a big difference. There was smoke in the air we were breathing, and the little fire and celebration made us feel homesick.

The fire was a huge success. We now needed to get some matches, and the only people who had matches were our Organisation Todt guards, so we had to be on good terms with them. This meant that we had to finish our quotas, so we did, even if it meant more work for us. Before six o'clock, I asked Fritz, our guard, if we could have a few matches. I explained to him that we wanted to start a fire in our barracks because it was bitterly cold during the night, adding that if we slept in a warmer place we would work better. Fritz contemplated whether my request could get him in trouble. He gave us five matches and warned us that if we got caught he'd pretend he didn't know anything. We told him not to worry and that we would be careful. There was plenty of firewood around us, mostly branches, but we had to break them into small pieces so that they would fit into our pockets. When we got back to our barracks, we all emptied our pockets around the stove and looked forward to the warmth the fire would provide.

The hunger we experienced in a KZ — Konzentrationslager — is what I call absolute hunger, being hungry without even the hope of getting any kind of food. Our brain was feverishly computing all the possibilities, the sources of food available, including stealing, fighting, cheating or any possible way to satisfy this incredibly strong urge overpowering our bodies. Nothing else mattered to us! This was what we felt every day, from sunrise to sundown and beyond.

The rations of mostly ersatz food that we had been given daily provided maybe five hundred calories. Considering the hard work we were forced to do, it was completely inadequate. We were forced to stand outside in the cold for hours, jumping up and down just to stay warm, expending precious energy and causing us to lose even more weight. We lost approximately one pound a week. When we left Hungary, we were fairly well fed, so we had some reserves of calories in the form of fat and muscles. I had weighed approximately one hundred fifty pounds and had been considered a skinny person, but when the war ended I weighed only eighty-five pounds. The American army in Augsburg, Germany, weighed me after liberation. I was in good shape compared to others in my situation, because I had received extra food, without which I would not be here today to write these memoirs.

Getting better after a sickness made us believe that we could beat the odds and actually live to see another day. Even with our daily suffering and desperation, we still didn't feel ready to give up. It's unbelievable how much strength we could muster to stay alive, even under such abominable conditions. I didn't meet anybody who wanted to die or commit suicide. The three who were electrocuted didn't want to die — they were desperate to live. They thought they'd try to escape, thought that maybe they would get lucky and could face the future on the outside.

The minds of the prisoners were short-circuited, in a sense, and most of the time nobody could think straight. The preoccupation with daily survival could have driven anybody crazy, but surprisingly most people in our camp stayed mentally stable. Everybody was always conspiring about how they could get their hands on some extra food. That was the thought on everybody's mind, not suicide!

It was the middle of December 1944, and Christmas was coming soon. Even though we were Jewish, we had happy memories of December celebrations: Hanukkah, Christmas trees decorated with ornaments, candles and presents wrapped in shiny boxes. We knew that this year there wouldn't be any candles, trees or presents for us, but somehow we imagined what it could have been like, which boosted our spirits. Our imagination gave us hope that we might survive this nightmare and that the day would come when World War II would finally end and we'd be free again. We could tell everyone about our imprisonment in the KZ.

However, most of the survivors I know didn't tell anybody about their experience, except for close relatives, because somehow they were ashamed to talk about it as if it were their fault. It took me exactly fifty years to do what I should have done decades ago, but for some reason I just couldn't. It took many years of psychotherapy to heal my soul.

~

The kapos blew their whistles, indicating that it was time for our shower, and told us not to bring any valuables. That was not a good omen, and we were worried it could mean that we would not come back again. We had no valuables, since everything had been taken away a long time ago. All we had were pictures of parents, brothers and sisters that some people had managed to hide. I had a photo of my family and was determined to keep it no matter what.

Christmas Eve somehow affected the kapos, and they were more tolerant than usual. We were led towards a larger building, which we hadn't known existed. The building was made of wood and had a chimney; next to it was a smaller one, which we assumed was probably for laundry. We were led into the first part of the large building, ten guys at a time. We were told to undress until we were naked and to throw the uniforms, shirts, shoes, scarves, gloves and socks through a window into the laundry room. We then had to walk through the next door, holding our hands up, and throw everything from our hands on the floor. I had to drop the picture of my parents on the floor. I then went over to a soldier and begged him to let me keep my picture. What harm could there be in keeping a simple picture?

"Nein!" (No!) "Du wirst es nicht mehr brauchen! Los!" (You won't need it anymore! Go!)

He pushed me through the door into the shower stalls, as he yelled, "Five minutes!"

Everybody got a square of soap. There were ten showerheads, and each of us had to position ourselves under one of them.

The soldier yelled, "Achtung!" (Attention!) "Los!" (Go!)

At this point we still didn't know whether water or poison gas would come out of the showers. Then the water sprayed out, nice hot water. It had been about three months since we had had a shower, and we had already forgotten how a shower felt. It felt unreal. We rubbed each other's backs, washed our hair, beards, feet, hands. We felt like the parts of our bodies we had so rarely seen were being reinvented. Some guys were singing, and others were crying. A yelling soldier interrupted us. We had thirty seconds left of our five minutes. We had one towel to share between two guys and one minute to dry ourselves.

When we heard the whistle we had to proceed through the next door to where our clothing would come out of the washing and de-lousing. We had to get dressed quickly. We went through the last door that opened to what appeared to be an open garage. But our clothing was not there. We were standing shoeless and completely naked in freezing cold weather, having just had a hot shower. Our skin was still steaming. It was a desperate situation.

I said to Joe, "If we don't catch lung disease now, we never will!"

We started to bang on the door where the showers were.

"We are freezing! Open the door! We need our clothing! Please!"

There was no answer! We tried to break down the door. We panicked, thinking we were going to freeze to death on Christmas Eve, of all days. Suddenly, the door opened and uniforms, including five shirts, socks and caps, were thrown on the icy floor. We grabbed them and realized that they were not our uniforms. But we put them on anyway while we kept searching for our own.

Neither Joe nor I could find our uniforms, so we decided that we'd take what we could get and try to find the people who had our uniforms the next day and trade. We picked up a pair of shoes and ran back to the barracks. We were almost frozen. The clothing from the laundry was still wet and soon it froze on us. When we got into the barracks, we had to undress and dry each piece. We were lucky because we had some wood and charcoal briquettes hidden for emergencies, and this was definitely an emergency. We kept the fire going all night. We had our first day off the next day. Thank God! This was the first thing that we had to thank God for after all the suffering.

Our Christmas dinner held a pleasant surprise for us: a dessert! We had an apple! Incredible! We hadn't seen an apple in ages. We were so impressed that we just kept the apple in our hands. We smelled it, warmed it in our clean hands.

I asked Joe, "What do you want to do with it?"

"Eat it, of course!" he answered, wondering why I'd ask such a silly question.

"I mean do you want to eat it all at once or half today and half tomorrow?"

"Let's see how it tastes!"

We shared everything with each other, so I said, "I'll give you half of mine if you give me half of yours."

"Okay. I think yours is a little bigger, so this way it will be fair."

Joe had a knife made from a spoon and so we divided the apples so that each of us got half of the other's. This way we had exactly the same amount. We cut very thin slices and ate them slowly to make them last as long as possible. The apple was delicious and reminded us of our childhood, when we used to climb the apple trees in our neighbourhood. After the trees in our neighbourhood were gone, we found other orchards, and we could choose between red apples, green, yellow, small or large, sweet or sour. We believed the old saying that "an apple a day keeps the doctor away" — believe it or not, it did! Our present situation was much different; what good could an apple a year do?

This one single apple had the power to bring back memories of times we had almost completely forgotten. Memories of our mother and father who introduced us to our first apple or applesauce, apple juice, apple pie, apple strudel — all this was locked up somewhere in our subconscious, and maybe it was better not to disturb those memories. We had enough problems as it was, and the memories were painful and heavy to carry.

Persecution and Escape
in Budapest

# Foreword

The Jews of Budapest were members of the second-largest urban Jewish community in Europe prior to World War II (after Warsaw, Poland) and constituted the largest remaining one by 1944. In 1944–1945, their brutal experiences differed in significant ways from those of Jews in the rest of Hungary. Based on Adolf Eichmann's preference, the perpetrators of the Holocaust in Hungary decided that the capital city — coinciding with district one of the Hungarian gendarmerie, the main executor of the deportations from the country — would be the sixth and last deportation zone. However, Regent Horthy finally halted the deportations from the country in early July 1944, just before the Jewish community in Budapest — after repeated deportations of some of its key members — would have collectively fallen victim too. By this time, deportations had been carried out all across the country and also in the immediate vicinity of Budapest (including locations that after the war became parts of the administration of the capital).

By early July, Jews in the capital city had been segregated into so-called yellow-star houses, which practically dotted the landscape of the entire city, rather than into separate ghettos. It had been decided that ghettos would be too difficult to create and would likely provoke negative reactions in a city where some 200,000 people were marked and persecuted as Jews. At the time, their deportation seemed imminent; however, developments of the larger war outside of Hungary luckily intervened. Yet, this delay soon resulted in a tragic twist for the Jews still in Budapest.

Shortly after Romania's successful attempt to switch sides in the war to join the Allies in August 1944, Regent Horthy decided to try a comparable feat for Hungary in mid-October, but his poorly prepared and weakly supported venture spectacularly backfired. After nearly a quarter of a century as regent of Hungary, he was removed from power. The Arrow Cross Party, a radical rightist and viciously antisemitic force led by Ferenc Szálasi — which had a partly overlapping agenda with, but was in opposition to, the authoritarian establishment of the country — grabbed power through a Nazi-backed coup. Ignoring the immense (and easily foreseeable) costs for the country in human suffering and material destruction, the Arrow Cross enacted an agenda that continued the Axis "crusade against the Bolshevist menace."

Although the majority of Hungarian Jews outside of Budapest had been murdered by the Nazis and their Hungarian collaborators in the spring and summer of 1944, this turn of events in the fall inaugurated a new chapter of profound suffering for the until-then relatively fortunate Jews of Budapest. Their mobilization for forced labour was intensified in an utterly cruel manner. Mass deportations to camps in the Reich were resumed, but no longer to Auschwitz-Birkenau, which was about to be liberated by the advancing Red Army. Extensive death marches were organized within Hungarian territory too. The Arrow Cross forced the masses of Budapest Jews — who had been segregated into individual buildings until then but not into separate areas of the city — into two separate ghettos at this stage. The two ghettos were colloquially known as the great ghetto and the international ghetto, the latter of which held Jews in the possession of some kind of protective paper issued by neutral powers (*Schutzpass* in German).

In December 1944, as the Red Army was making further gains and approaching Budapest, the Arrow Cross leadership decided to move to the western, Transdanubian part of the country. Whatever semblance of order still remained in the capital after mid-October now broke down as Arrow Cross thugs, who were often very young, started to terrorize the citizenry. They randomly murdered thousands of the surviving minority of Hungarian Jews, mostly by shooting them into the icy Danube River. Next to the imminent threat of death from illness or starvation, the continuation of Allied air raids constituted another source of constant danger for the Hungarian Jewish remnant — a danger shared with the other inhabitants of Budapest.

All of this was eventually exacerbated by a prolonged siege, which developed into one of the largest urban battles of World War II. In January 1945, the Red Army liberated the centrally located ghetto (into which the international ghetto had just been merged) with its 68,000 survivors. Against the fierce resistance put up by German and Hungarian forces, the Soviets eventually conquered the entire ruined city by February 13, 1945. As several of the stories in this anthology attest, the liberators of the "racially persecuted" (to employ a favoured expression of the times) and the entire country from fascism could not bring real freedom to the Hungarians. The liberators themselves lived under the tyrannical regime of Joseph Stalin, which was about to be imposed on half of the European continent, including Hungary.

Unlike in the rest of the country, where the ghettoization and deportation measures faced little resistance from non-Jewish (or Jewish) forces, by the time the worst atrocities of the Arrow Cross were being perpetrated in Budapest, resistance to the genocide took various forms. The metropolitan environment of Budapest and the fact that Hungarian state authorities were evidently collapsing created a more conducive environment for the development and occasional successes of rescue attempts.

Jewish resistance networks, often led by Zionist activists, cooperated with the embassies of neutral countries still active in Budapest, such as Switzerland and Sweden, to produce protective papers in order to to help numerous persecuted individuals escape. Because of the anarchistic circumstances, possessing such papers (some of which were admittedly forged) offered no real guarantee, but they would often prove useful and even decisive. As the memoirs excerpted here reveal, despite the grave dangers involved, some non-Jewish Hungarians in Budapest, including members of the Christian Churches, helped Jews hide and survive. More controversially, a few of the Zionist activists, most notably the famed Rudolf Kasztner, were also ready to negotiate with the Nazi perpetrators to help some Jews survive. Such often heroic acts and their sometimes successful outcomes add colour to a very dark overall picture.

More generally though, proactive cooperation with the German occupying forces — the country's long-standing allies — was the decisive fact in the Hungary of 1944–1945. Significant segments of the Hungarian state apparatus and numerous members of society were implicated in the genocide against Hungarian Jewry in various but often crucial ways. While we ought to be fully cognizant of this devastating overall picture, resistance was not entirely absent during the last, almost fully apocalyptic stages of the war, and achieved several notable small victories.

# Shattered Dreams
## Dolly Tiger-Chinitz

Spring came early in 1944. On March 19, the world as we had known it suddenly ended. Dr. Anna Faragó came in during recess to pick up her daughter Panni, who was in grade school. We ran to her, and she squatted down and spread her arms to embrace us. We were all sobbing hysterically. There was no need for explanations. There was a lot of growing up right then, as reality condensed in one panicky moment.

And so it all started.

It was on March 19, 1944, that the German forces occupied Hungary. Historians will quibble over this definition for many generations: apologists for Hungary will call it an "occupation"; those who condemn Hungary's role in the war will say that the German troops were invited. It does not really matter. The spectre of antisemitism — implied, whispered, feared, unfathomable — suddenly became the focus of our lives: ever-present in every breath, menacingly staring from placards, newspapers, movies, theatres. It was everywhere, and everything else was dwarfed in comparison.

The school year came to a hasty end. Unbeknownst to us, serious negotiations had taken place between our mother and Mother Superior for the possibility of accepting us and sheltering us at their mountain retreat as servants, students or whatever else, in exchange for a large sum of money. Mother Superior refused.

Our parents moved to Budapest and rented a room in the Hotel Lukács. A semblance of our life started again. I remember most the daily tedium of going for short walks, but also of sitting in the room, listening to the radio, calling room service (the waiter's name was Armand) or standing by the circuit breaker in the hotel's corridor and switching back the breaker every time Vinyi's attempts at cooking in the room overloaded the power supply.

I also remember how difficult this time was: the hushed conferences at night and the crying; Apu's constant efforts to soothe and reassure; his absences during the day; Vinyi's vigil by the window. We took up a position to see what she was watching so intently every afternoon, smoking one cigarette after the other, hands trembling. We saw a tall, dark, handsome stranger standing across the street under the window. We confronted her. She tearfully confided in us. "No matter who asks you about him, you never saw anybody or anything! My life and reputation are at stake. You realize what Apu would do if he found out that this man was my lover and that we met each day."

We were excited. Romance and adventure, like in a movie, brought a ray of colour to our drab, fear-filled days. Later, much later, we found out that the man was the brother of Aunt Zuli's butler. He was a farmer who had been hiding Zuli and Imre bácsi since March 19 in the attic of their farmhouse where, to avoid arousing suspicion, they were not even allowed to move about during the day. Imre bácsi offered them, in writing, in case they survived, the Gyömrő property. The man who came to the hotel nearly every day brought messages and requests. The requests were always the same: Imre bácsi wanted cyanide to end it all.

Events unfolded at a maddening pace. We received falsified documents and were drilled to remember our new names, birthdates and birthplaces. Luckily, the two years of convent school left us proficient in Catholic prayers. We were also warned about two fairly large black attaché cases: no matter what happened, those two valises had to be rescued. If Vinyi and Apu were to disappear, if there was a bombing raid and things got destroyed, the most important thing in the world apart from having each other was hanging on to the black valises — irrespective of what was actually in them, which we simply did not know.

The summer was hot. We were discouraged from using the pool or any public facilities. We even avoided going to the shelter during air raids. We were "in hiding." Our life was in danger, not from the war, not from the bombs, but because we were the prey and there were hunters all around. On a very rare foray to the city, we were crossing one of the busiest thoroughfares of Budapest, hanging on to Vinyi from both sides, when one of the nuns from the convent saw us from across the street. "Why aren't the little girls wearing the yellow star?" she shouted over in lieu of a greeting. Mother looked at us and just said, "Run." We boarded a tramway that had just pulled in and sat in petrified silence, our hearts pounding in our throats.

Apu's many forays to the German headquarters with suitcases full of bricks of gold resulted in a deal: if the Tiebergers come out of hiding, they will get on the train with the wealthiest Hungarian Jews headed for Switzerland. The deal was negotiated with Eichmann himself, and since the Tiebergers were one of the wealthiest Jews, the price was high. Zuli's thirty-five carat diamond ring had to be turned in as soon as the first official order came through for all Jews to turn in their valuables. The diamond was in the world's official diamond registry and far too well-known to try to hide. The hazelnut-sized ring used to be on Zuli's finger at all times. When we went swimming in the good old days, she used to pin it with a safety pin inside her bathing suit, between her breasts. We were intrigued by the size of that diamond and by the obvious affection she had for it.

It took days of anguished meetings and nights filled with whispers and tears. "How could he say that to me," Vinyi sobbed, "I thought that the Diamants were our friends. He even told me, wait till they torture your precious twins at the Gestapo, you will remember where Elza and Imre are hiding." They finally decided to come out of hiding and did go to the railroad station at the appointed time. Hundreds of Jews were ready to board the train destined for Switzerland. As the names were read, family after family came forward with a small bundle of personal belongings. Zuli, Imre bácsi, and their children, Babi and Gyula, stood anxiously among them. Another official suddenly came forward and read another list: the list of those who would not be permitted to board the train for freedom. The Tiebergers were among them.

A taxi was summoned, their cover blown. They returned to a room in the yellow-star house, a small room on the fifth floor. Imre bácsi walked out to the balcony and, with an athlete's ease and assurance, in one graceful movement dived off the low parapet. After the "troubles" started, we had often heard him talk about the epitaph he wanted for his tombstone: "He lived fifty years." I never saw his tomb, but I understand that this is indeed all it says, "Imre Tieberger. He lived fifty years."

There is no way to describe the agony and the chaos of the following days. A million deaths is a statistic; one death is a tragedy. We were still counting deaths one by one.

~

The war became the background noise to our anguish over the persecution of Jews. The bombings continued, escalating in frequency and power, but the news from the front was positive: the Allies were advancing. One bright Sunday morning, October 15, 1944, Regent Horthy spoke on the radio. His message was astonishing: Hungary will right away capitulate, or words to that effect. I am sure the entire event and the entire speech is part of history books today. Our reaction was delirious jubilation. Apu sounded a note of warning though. "Very difficult days lie ahead," he said. "It is not going to be that simple." By evening Horthy's attempt was over and he was now under house arrest. Ferenc Szálasi, a leader closely aligned with Germany, took over. The Jews were warned of even heavier penalties.

Armed gangs started roaming the city on trucks and on foot, flushing out scared Jews from hiding places, shooting them, pillaging and generally creating havoc. I am not going to write about it: historians can do a better job. But it was the background noise to our everyday existence and it is important to our story how these events touched our lives.

One morning we heard the dreaded knock on the door: Mrs. Paul was under arrest. Documents were produced while we cowered in our beds, and the police took Vinyi away. Apu left almost immediately, but first he told us to call Júlia's son, Gyuri Szentirmay, pack a suitcase with some clothes and leave the hotel immediately with the attaché cases.

We did as instructed. Gyuri came and took us to his apartment. "You are my little cousins from the countryside," he instructed us. "We cannot go down even to the air raid shelter from now on. Do you understand? Do you have your documents?" We were surprised to find Zuli's butler living there. A few weeks followed that sometimes come back in dreamlike shreds to haunt me. One memory is of a sick woman in a hospital bed, Julika néni, shrunken to the size of a child, hugging us, barely able to speak; the other is of the dark anonymity of movie houses, theatres, operas, where the three of us would go through the rain-slicked, dark, shiny streets, huddled together against the cold, against the fear.

The long tear-filled nights, when Gyuri started taking us to his bed. What was he doing to me? His reassuring whispers, "I love you, I am going to marry you, I am not doing this to Mari, only to you." My mind went blank, all I felt was the warm pleasure of his embrace, the cozy, warm bed, his caressing, searching hands, and sometimes I even managed to stop the shivering, stopped being frightened, stopped yearning for my mother.

You can get used to anything. One eats, one takes a bath, one goes out, comes in, and it becomes a routine of sorts. We visited Julika in the hospital. On November 1, we remembered Zuli. It was her birthday. Was it really only one year ago that Imre bácsi threw such a lavish party for her? When János and I, bored, dodging the over-dressed and overfed crowd, decided to count the orchids? When in the war-torn Europe of November 1943, Zuli Tieberger received 103 orchids for her birthday? When her husband gave her an incredible machine, a large box that you plug in that makes ice from water in a special little compartment, and in the rest of the box you can keep food cold without having to put ice in it? János tried to explain to me how this miracle took place, but I frankly doubted whether he really knew.

The ominous knock at the door in the middle of the night again. I was sleeping with Gyuri, and he went to the door. Two uniformed Szálasi men with guns came in. We were to produce documents. I sat in an armchair and my teeth chattered. Gyuri went to fetch another quilt and tucked it in around me. I sat glassy-eyed and answered questions. Yes, we came from Subotica and are his nieces. We don't know where our parents are right now (which was true). They point-ed a gun at us. The neighbours suspected that we were Jews in hiding since we never went down to the shelter during air raids. Why don't we? We are not afraid, we reassured him, teeth chattering. So why are we afraid now? They wanted to know. We are very sleepy. A physical altercation ensued between them and Gyuri when they wanted to ap-proach us roughly. Finally, they left.

On nights when things were quieter, we listened to the rumblings of the distant guns, the Katyusha rocket launchers, the deep, rum-bling explosions of the large cannons. The Soviets were coming. It can't last long anymore, we thought.

In the middle of December, Apu called and told us to come to Zuli's apartment in Buda. Fearfully, we crossed the Danube River, at-taché cases and small suitcase in hand. The bridges were festooned with dynamite, cigarette-package-sized bundles fluttering in the wind, glistening in the setting sun. Only a few weeks previously an-other bridge was blown up, supposedly by accident, at the height of

rush-hour traffic. The day after the explosion we saw tramways gro-
tesquely hanging in the abyss between bridge and water. Hundreds of
lives were lost, more casualties of war.

It was a tearful reunion at Zuli's apartment. Many explanations
followed. Vinyi had decided to go into hiding after getting out from
a brick factory. She had tied a kerchief around her head, borrowed
some old raggedy clothes and knocked at the door of the apartment
Zuli had owned, offering her services as a maid. No one in the building recognized her. The high-ranking officer living in the apartment
felt that this good-looking maid fresh off the farm could be helpful to
his paralyzed wife. She was hired on the spot.

As she was telling us the story, she made jokes about her feelings:
she planned heroic deeds, to poison the entire dinner party assembled one night around the table, high-ranking officers still deluded
with the possibility of victory while defeat could be heard a few miles
away. Her plans came to naught, but she asserted herself splendidly
when the officer decided to flee to the west and started packing Zuli's
best silver. She "advised" him about what looked more valuable and
more worthwhile to take. She took a big risk: how would a peasant
girl know the value of antique sterling silver? Yet many fine pieces
ended up being saved this way.

Apu made arrangements in the shelter of the building where
Imre Tieberger's office was to let us stay during the inevitable siege
of Budapest. It was late December when, bundles in hand, we started
out to cross the bridge from Buda, where Zuli's apartment was and
where we had all lived together for a few days, to the office on the Pest
side. After walking for about an hour (vehicular transportation was
out of the question), we realized that we would never make it, and we
also realized that it might not matter where we stay during the few
dangerous days the siege was going to last.

We returned to Zuli's apartment and set up two beds in the corner
of the shelter, which was underground, took down food and cooking
utensils and waited. There were about forty, maybe fifty other people

in the building — tenants, servants, the janitor's family, refugees, some very prominent people (I remember a judge), several small babies and, including us, five teenagers: two boys and three girls. The shelter was built to wartime specifications of reinforced concrete, deep underground. It was the safest spot, but there were several other rooms on the basement level: the laundry room, the furnace room heaped high with coal and a row of lockers the size of large closets, assigned to each tenant.

In our locker, Vinyi tried to bring a semblance of normalcy to our lives. The ever-clean, genteel Vinyi conjured a table with a tablecloth, proper eating utensils and napkins. Here in this cramped little place, the four of us sat down three times a day, surrounded by shelves of bric-a-brac and some zealously guarded food, and ate our meals. The dishes were cleared and a basin was located where we could even wash them.

The relentless bombing and shelling went on day and night. The building was heavily damaged. Zuli's apartment became uninhabitable, the furniture exposed to the elements. I could see the white lace curtains billowing back and forth through the wall where windows once framed the beautiful view. We did not go up very often.

Romances flared up, sputtered and died. I earnestly kept a diary, mostly dreaming of meals I would like to have. A semblance of life returned when we got a phonograph and danced in one of the dark cubbyholes. There was no gas, no electricity and no water. We fashioned candles out of tallow and rags for wicks. Sanitary conditions became unbearable. We melted snow for cooking and washing our hands. We never undressed anymore.

The days turned into weeks. Apu sat at the stove in the furnace room, wide-brimmed hat on his head, peering over steel-rimmed glasses, resting his chin on his walking stick and guarding Vinyi's last remnants of coffee, which everyone eyed with jealousy. We had potatoes and a large case of sardines. Some flour too. Vinyi baked something we called bread.

The tedium led to daily fights, and the high-class people developed scabies. Radios no longer functioned, batteries wore out. We lived by rumours. Where were the Soviets? We heard that Pest had already fallen to them, but that they had to continue fighting house to house to conquer Buda too. It was very cold, and we shivered even with all our clothes on under the eiderdown comforters. Vinyi gave us each three hundred pengős to put in our shoes. What trust and how grown-up we felt!

The Germans dragged in a few badly wounded soldiers. There was lots of blood, moaning and screaming. I could not look. They took off their uniform jackets and with little sharp pocket knives removed all their insignia, the epaulets, and built a small bonfire on the concrete floor and burned them all. Something was indeed starting to change.

# The Light in a Dark Cellar
## Susan Simon

A new law came into effect after the German army occupied Hungary in March 1944. Jewish families in the Mátra Mountains were ordered to move to the nearby small town of Gyöngyös. This was the first step of discrimination that affected us, and we naively hoped that it would be the last.

Before we left the mountains, we went on an excursion in the forest behind our house. We knew every path and chose to go towards one of the lookouts. Mother carried a bag with a metal box and a short shovel. Before the path widened to the lookout, we stopped. Next to a huge oak tree, Father dug a hole for the box and buried it. Mother made sure no one was near. She whispered to Rozi and me that the box contained the family jewels and asked us to remember the trees around it, so we could find it when we come back to fetch it. We jumped around on the soil to pack it down, then covered it with a bunch of grass.

Back home, we packed and rented a bungalow in the pretty garden district of Gyöngyös. To me, this still felt like an adventure. Jewish children were now forbidden to go to school, and I was happy to play with the other children all day.

During the years that followed, Mom reminded me of the cocky rhyme I made up: "Since I am smart, not a fool, I don't need to go to school." I chanted these defiant lines often, or switched to my favourite romantic tune: "In the month of May, in the month of May, everyone falls in love."

We were in the month of May; spring was in the air, romance in my heart, as well as a wish to grow up, to become beautiful, adored and loved. I was free to play, sing and dream all day with the other Jewish children.

This interlude ended quickly, when we were ordered to move into the ghetto. My parents' faces were careworn. They didn't know what to do. We had the option to return to our home in Budapest, though it was a prime target for the bombs of the Allied forces. To avoid the bombs, we moved into the Gyöngyös ghetto. On the day of our move, it was pouring rain. Shuffling through an ocean of mud, hardly able to see the shacks waiting for us, we found neither running water nor a bathroom. Mom burst into sobs and couldn't stop. She knew how the lack of sanitation led to epidemics. Father stood around for a while, then, looking at Mother, he made up his mind. We left the ghetto, only a few minutes before the gates got locked. His decision saved us; I doubt that anyone returned from the camps that followed the Gyöngyös ghetto.

On the train to Budapest, I kept my eyes on the ground, afraid to look at people, praying silently to get home. An hour in the ghetto was enough to make me understand that we were being persecuted.

∼

Because our building in Budapest had been turned into a "Jewish house," it filled up with Jewish families. Not being permitted to go to school, the children played together. Board games, like checkers, were popular and easy to take to the cellar during air raids. This was not the case with Monopoly, a challenging game, but it was waiting for us upstairs. Losing in a game was so hard for me that I spent hours plotting my strategy to win, forcing others to wait. Often they let me win out of frustration.

Our games helped us to forget, at least temporarily, the threats

mounting around us. Most of my relatives in the country were collected into ghettos, but we didn't know yet that they were going to be
deported to death camps. Father was conscripted to a forced labour
camp, and Grandpa was imprisoned by the Nazis. Mother sent cakes
to Grandpa, hiding money and letters in them. The aroma of these
cakes made us hungry, but we couldn't even taste them; our consolation was that Grandpa would be allowed to enjoy them. We had no
cakes anymore, but still enough food to keep hunger at bay.

On Friday evenings, when the sacred Sabbath enters the Jewish
homes and hearts, Mother continued the tradition of lighting candles
in our splendid silver candlesticks. She also lit them for additional
prayers whenever we heard that a family member or friend was in
danger. As threats grew and multiplied, the candles were lit most evenings to enhance the power of our prayers. Mother extinguished them
afterwards to make them last longer, since we couldn't buy new ones
anymore. Listening to her say her prayer, her hands resting on our
shoulders, we stood there, Rozi and I, with our palms together, just
like children on a sentimental religious postcard. Our feelings, however, were genuine, and their intensity is engraved into my memory:

Dear God, look down upon us. We stand here forlorn, forsaken, torn
from the men we love. We seem to be travelling on a flimsy boat,
lost at sea, our sails fluttering in the storm. Please guide us to shore,
to find each other again. Please give us hope and strength. And if
you can grant us another wish, please, oh please save the world!
Dear God, let people become kind and human again!

Rozi and I listened fervently, opening our souls to Mother's
prayer. Who could resist such a prayer? Three souls rising in unison.
We felt a divine presence in our hearts, lighting the deepening darkness around us.

Our trials started with practice alerts, which were repeated day
and night with sirens booming all over the city, warning us to collect

our bags and rush to the cellar. The sirens grew deafening. We panicked often, forgetting our packages as we ran down the stairs from our second-storey apartment.

Father was with us before he had to go to a forced labour camp, and he kept repeating that there was nothing to worry about. He ambled down the stairs in his socks and night shirt to demonstrate that there was no reason to dress up. In his optimistic view, it was all a charade, and we were sure to go back soon to continue our sleep. Unfortunately, all this only made Mom more anxious.

When it all started, I was more afraid of the sirens than the bombs. The drawn-out, high-pitched blast seemed to land right inside my head, seeping down to invade my heart till it froze in terror. As the war progressed, sirens were followed by explosions, and I learned to reserve my fears for the latter. Eventually there were no sirens at all; life turned into a perpetual night in underground cellars, where the sound of bombs and buildings crumbling were all we could hear.

In the early stages of the war, with sirens alerting the public, Rozi and I had to grab a bag filled with food, drink, a first-aid kit and toys and run as fast as we could. If I was in the washroom, Mother waited for me. When the sirens were not enough to penetrate my childish sleep at night, she woke me up and urged me to hurry. In the cellar we gave silent thanks for arriving in one piece.

Windows were covered with black paper, and cracks were filled with caulk to shroud our house in darkness at night. Rumours circulated about cellars collapsing, as well as the buildings above them, but Mother didn't pass on such gossip to us so the threats would not ruin our hopes.

We had to wear a yellow star above our hearts to identify us as Jews, and we were allowed to leave our homes for an hour or two at certain times to buy food. Scared to walk with our stars, our heads buzzing with horror stories about how Jews were killed on the streets, we rarely stepped outside. It didn't help that Nazi propaganda was spread on huge posters, glaring from rooftops. One of them showed a little girl covered with vivid splashes of blood, holding a toy that had exploded in her hands. This shocking scene blamed the Allied forces for throwing down explosives in the shape of toys from their airplanes. In truth, only the Nazi imagination could invent such crimes. Confused, Rozi and I thought of this disturbing picture before we fell asleep, particularly because the little girl on the poster had a sweet baby face with big blue eyes, just like Rozi. This likeness terrified her.

The Arrow Cross, the Hungarian party closely allied with the Nazis, took over the government on October 15, 1944. Shortly after this event, they passed a law ordering the Jews in the capital to move into a ghetto.

My family had already escaped a ghetto in the small town of Gyöngyös; Mother didn't want to enter another one. She decided that we should hide. Before we left our home, I had to hand our festive silver candlesticks to her, while she stood on a ladder in our living room to stash them away on the top shelf of a floor-to-ceiling cupboard. As I lifted them, one at a time, I was surprised by how heavy they were. They also made a faint tinkling sound that I hardly noticed.

When Mom had to leave with Rozi and me, Father found us a place in a convent, next to the barracks on the outskirts of Pest where he was stationed. He paid for us to be accepted, and on a balmy autumn day, we moved in. Golden leaves covered the grounds, but we had to stay in the building with other mothers and children to hide from view.

Bathroom facilities were limited, as there were more families than the convent was prepared for. Hoping that hygiene would protect us from infections, Mom woke Rozi and me at dawn to get washed in ice-cold water, in absence of an alternative. Another annoyance was that the nuns expected us to attend religious services every day, and we had to kneel at the appropriate times. They explained that converting to Catholicism meant updating our Jewish faith, rather than leaving it behind. Their missionary efforts were ill-timed, as it felt like coercion when being a Jew was already punishable by death. No one dared object to the nuns, however, since we were at their mercy; no one, that is, except me.

Whenever we had to kneel, I remained standing, to demonstrate how strongly I felt about my religion. Mom kept pulling my skirt anxiously, but I stood my ground — both in the literal and the symbolic sense. This righteous defiance had less to do with heroism than with my ignorance of the dangers we were facing. As the war continued, both my arrogance and my innocence were replaced by a more cooperative attitude and a better understanding of the threats around us.

At this stage of the Nazi occupation, I was still the pampered, know-it-all child with a sharp critical attitude. Sharing close quarters with many families, I compared the mothers. There was a Mrs. Gold, whom I admired because she appeared calmer than my poor mom, who was visibly struggling to cope.

Hiding Jewish families in the convent had been organized by Sister Anna. She had a remarkable presence, coal-black eyes in a long white face expressing intelligence, compassion and composure. Her tall, slim figure, all clad in white, and her quiet, efficient movements revealed power of the benign, angelic kind. She attracted my attention when I noticed that Mom liked and respected her.

Father's forced labour camp was separated from our convent by a fence. When the order came to move his battalion to the front, Father tried to escape. He was caught and locked up for the night, to be shot at dawn. An armed guard stood in front of his door, while Father sat in a makeshift, unheated wooden shack, trembling from cold and fear. He recited every prayer he could think of, both in Hebrew and Hungarian. He contemplated how he could break the door but realized that even if he managed to do so, the guard would shoot him. Father decided to beg for mercy. He raised his voice to be heard through the locked door and told the guard that he had a family to raise, that his life was precious to them.

Mother tossed and turned all night, sensing a calamity. A loud explosion woke us up before dawn. Mother jumped out of bed, recognizing that what we had just heard was a shot from across the fence, where Father was stationed. The rest of the day she walked up and down in a frenzy, flailing her arms, sighing frequently, hardly noticing us. At last, Sister Anna came to her with good news. She told Mother what had happened to Father, adding that his begging had not fallen on deaf ears. His guard had let him go with the words, "Run away! I don't want more blood on my hands!" Father climbed the fence and jumped down into the convent garden. He hurt his left foot but wasn't injured otherwise. His guard fired a shot after him, but only to protect himself by pretending that he attempted to kill the run-away Jew.

Sister Anna took my limping Father into the convent and led him out through the back door. We couldn't meet him, but when Mother heard that he had escaped, her composure returned. Rozi and I were blessedly ignorant of all this until much later when Mother was ready to tell us what had happened.

A few days after this event, the news spread like wildfire that the Nazis were at the gates of the convent to search for Jews. Sister Anna kept her cool and led all the families to the barn behind the convent. She made sure that we were well covered with straw. I can still smell the peculiar scent of that straw: dry, dusty, yet fragrant. Under it, fear turned my body to stone, restricting my chest as I struggled for air. Only my hands were alive, squeezing Mother's for courage. Lying there for a long time, eventually my breathing calmed down and my body felt like my own again. "Please God, don't let them find us" was the mantra I kept repeating silently, endlessly.

Suddenly I heard voices, and our protective darkness lit up. Rozi burst into a sneeze, and my heart stopped. So did time. The interval that followed seemed to last forever, and I wasn't sure if I was still alive. Does death feel like this, I wondered. Eventually I heard voices, then the blessed darkness and silence returned. My relief was immense.

Mother found out later that the straw covered us well, in spite of the bright flashlight of the Nazi who searched the barn. He had heard Rozi's muffled sneeze, but Sister Anna convinced him that the noise had come from outside. She also managed to get rid of the Nazis, but they told her that they would be back at dawn. We had to leave right away.

Years later Mother heard that Sister Anna survived the Nazis, but while trying to protect the novice nuns, she was raped and then murdered by Russian soldiers. She died a true martyr, in the spirit of her faith. Mother never forgave God for allowing this to happen.

We stepped out of the convent at night, shrouded in darkness. The first snow of the winter was floating about, turning to water as it settled on the pavement. We seemed to be the only people alive on the black, silent street. With eyes heavy from lack of sleep, Rozi and I let Mother pull us along with her brave, determined hands that stopped trembling to give us strength. A big scarf covered most of her face to hide her curved "Jewish nose," which she thought could give us away. As dawn broke and the streets grew lighter, we tried to keep to the shadows. We knew that Jews found on the streets without yellow stars were shot on the spot, but with the stars on us the outcome could still be the same. Our lives depended on not being noticed.

Mother's big problem was where to go. We had lost touch with Father and had no one to turn to. She hoped to find an acquaintance who would take pity on us and give us a hiding place. We shuffled on, our hearts beating in our throats, until we arrived at the house of a salesman who had worked in our furniture store before the war. He didn't dare to hide us, but was in touch with Grandpa, who was looking for us. After six months in prison, Grandpa was let out; we never knew why the Nazis let him go, just as we didn't know why they locked him up in the first place.

His freedom at that time was a godsend, as he found us an apartment where he could join us too. Four or five Jewish mothers and their numerous children were staying there already, but they accepted us. Like Anne Frank, we had to live a noiseless, invisible life; if any one of the children uttered a sound, or a toilet was flushed, we would be in mortal danger. Food was brought to us in secret, and Mother sighed with relief whenever it arrived.

Grandpa's presence was a saving grace. He entertained the children with pantomime, silent games, stories he whispered and with toys he fabricated from whatever he could find, including dry beans, the staple food of the time. Having him to play with was like sunshine breaking through a black cloud.

Unfortunately, we could only stay in this apartment for a week, because a Nazi had spotted one of us. Although all the windows were covered with black paper and closed, the one in the bathroom was slightly open. This window, as all the bathroom windows of the building did, opened to a shaft, with an opening in the roof for air. A Nazi used the bathroom across from ours, and we noticed that he carried his gun even to the toilet. The problem was that he heard one of us, a child, flushing the toilet. Only the adults were allowed to do this when the other bathrooms seemed empty, but the child forgot the rule. Soon the wife of the superintendent arrived to warn us that the Nazi wanted to search the apartment. Her husband pretended to look for the key to give us time to disappear.

We were back on the street again. Grandpa gave us a big hug and, to my dismay, walked away. I wanted to run after him, but Mother's firm grip and the fear in her face stopped me. At least I didn't know yet that we would never see my beloved Grandpa again, and Mother would never forgive herself for letting him go.

Grandpa had left to avoid becoming a burden to us; he thought that we would have a better chance to survive without him. His grief for Grandma made him feel too old and sad to fight for his own life. He was only in his early fifties, healthy and strong. Years later, Mother spoke to a man who had witnessed Grandpa's death. He was shot on the spot when he slapped a young Nazi who pushed him to obey his orders. Not afraid of death, he died with courage, standing up for himself.

As I grew older, I couldn't accept this account of his last day. There was always an element of uncertainty in war stories, and I had been clinging to the hope that he was still alive. Years after we had separated, I was still waiting for his return, running after men who reminded me of him. He came to me in a dream, twelve years later, after I had left my family for Canada. He stood between the silver candlesticks, which in my dream were as tall as he was. His smiling face was lit up in the candlelight. He opened his arms for me in this strange new country where I felt lost, and his welcome made me feel at home.

On the day we said goodbye to Grandpa, we were on the street again, clutching Mother's hands and searching for a place to hide. It was early December, and the Nazis and their Hungarian collaborators were not the only threat we faced. Air raids were so frequent that people stayed in their cellars. We hardly noticed the crumbling buildings and demolished stores, as we had to watch our footsteps among the rubble and broken glass covering the streets of Pest.

Walking carefully, concentrating on where to place my foot, a stunning sight stopped me in my tracks. A young man and woman lay on the pavement to my right, in eternal embrace. This was the first time I saw corpses, and I stood there bewildered, observing their bare limbs and the rigid expressions on their faces. It took a while before I understood that this young couple was dead.

Mother couldn't protect me from the dread and revulsion as I witnessed the horrific juxtaposition of youth and death. All she could do was grab my hand, pull me to walk faster, to run, to escape the nightmare of the war-torn streets, where, with every step, we took the chance of turning as rigid as the young couple on the sidewalk.

Mother soon found a house protected by Sweden — Sweden issued documents so that the Nazis would leave the Jewish residents in peace. We moved into the coal cellar of this house, while the Allied bombings continued relentlessly. They could now be launched so suddenly that there wasn't any time for warning sirens.

The coal cellar was dark, though a tiny window let in a bit of day-light. At least forty mothers with children tried to build their nests on the sooty cement floor, and some managed to drag down a mattress or two. We couldn't find any, so Mother sent me to an acquaintance close by to ask for cushions. I went without my yellow star, feeling important, aware that she counted on me. Running across the street, I was confident that as the "chosen one" I was invulnerable. When I arrived, I was told that they had no pillows, so I asked for blankets, rags and whatever else could be spared. They filled a bag for me and Mother's face lit up when she saw it. We managed to keep warm on the rags, sleeping pressed against each other.

Although Mom did what she could to maintain the ritual of wash-ing us in icy water, she couldn't get rid of the soot in the coal cellar; our skin and clothing were covered. Fortunately, we still had water, but there was less and less food. Mom spent her days desperately searching for nourishment, until a kind, soft-spoken young priest ap-peared. He came to us regularly at noon, dragging along a huge pot of hot soup, which he ladled out with a gentle smile. His soup kept us alive; nevertheless, my dreams were filled with images of bread, milk and fruit.

A couple of weeks later, sitting on the cement floor with our stom-achs grumbling, Mother gave in to temptation. She opened a tiny can of pineapples, our last treasure, which was meant to save us from starvation. I can still feel the heavenly taste of that fruit. I wanted so much to swallow, but I resisted the urge for a long time, turning the sweet golden delight around in my mouth without biting it. We sat there, Rozi and I, savouring our treat, conjuring up happy times gone by, such as our dining-room table, laden with fruit and cake. We hardly noticed that Mother didn't even taste the pineapple.

One day when the kind priest brought us soup, he also gave me a book. It was the first novel I proceeded to read on my own. The hero was a dog, sacrificing his life to save his master. My heart went out to this animal, reminding me that goodwill, caring and devotion did exist, though it had gone into hiding — as we had.

Paradoxically, the dog in the novel kept my faith in humanity alive. It strengthened my hope that the madness around me would end, allowing us to return into the daylight, safe and sound. In the meantime, I rushed to the tiny window each morning and stayed there, glued to my book, escaping from the world around me until our soup would arrive.

There was another diversion Mother invented for us. She used her skill in fashion design to draw paper dolls with a variety of elegant paper robes. We had only sooty, threadbare clothes to wear, but our paper dolls were dressed like royalty. I didn't realize how fortunate I was that as a child I was able to get absorbed in play; neither did I give credit to Mother at the time for making such an escape from my surroundings possible.

One cold winter morning brought a new crisis. A group of Arrow Cross officers appeared to herd Jews into the ghetto, even from houses like ours that were protected by Sweden. The Hungarian Arrow Cross had no scruples about breaking contracts and promises.

We had no strength left to escape. Gathering our few belongings, we climbed the stairs to the street and stood there with the other families, blinded by daylight, shivering with cold and fright. Rozi and I held Mother's hands, striving to steady ourselves. Mother was afraid of the explosions around us, but even more of being killed by our guards. She had heard how often the Arrow Cross took their victims to the banks of the Danube, where they shot them into the river instead of taking them to the ghetto.

Mother didn't share these fears with me, and I didn't recognize where we walked, but I knew the general direction we took from Mother's hand: towards the Danube her grip tightened, away from it, her hand relaxed. While she trembled for our lives, I could afford to be preoccupied with my brown leather school bag containing my precious book, our treasured paper dolls, papers and coloured pencils.

When we heard the order to leave all packages behind, Mother asked me to drop my bag. I couldn't let go of it, and the guard next to us heard Mother's quiet, insistent pleading. He mumbled to her that I could keep my bag. His hardly audible words, like the story in my novel, like the slightest compassion we received from anyone, warmed my heart and kept alive my faith in humanity. These events also confirmed my belief in my own good fortune and my hope that the love and security of my early childhood would return. I clung to this hope, as I clung to my schoolbag, a present from the past, from my lost paradise; it was tangible proof that this paradise had really existed.

Often my feelings oscillated between the extremes of blind faith and overwhelming terror, probably needing the former to offset the latter. I remember my inner struggle to maintain my sanity. I aimed to keep my sense of terror at bay by focusing on the loving, secure environment of my pre-war years. I didn't always succeed. Mother, however, saw me as the "chosen one," and this gave me a sense of protection by a personal God, a sort of guardian angel for whom my fervent, silent prayers were louder than bombs.

Our walk to the ghetto seemed to last forever. It didn't help that my toes were frozen and squished, since I had managed to outgrow my shoes, even while the rest of me was shrinking from starvation. The ghetto was an enclosed part of the city, with buildings that were no different from many others in Budapest. Mother, Rozi and I settled in one of them, again in the coal cellar, this one even more crowded than the one we had left. Nevertheless, we were relieved to be alive, not at the bottom of the freezing Danube.

Too weak to wash, we didn't care that there wasn't enough water anymore. Consumed by the effort to feed us, Mother watched people and listened to them talk about where she might find a few scraps of food. My hunger had disappeared, but it was replaced by nausea. Mother managed to round up a piece of dry bread with pork fat and garlic, but my stomach turned when I smelled it. I saw the concern on her face at my refusal to eat but I didn't fully realize how ill I was.

Hardly able to move, burning with fever, my imagination came to my aid. It made me conjure up our cozy armchair at home, covered in soft purple velvet and glowing in the light of the fireplace. Safe, like Noah in his ark, adrift on turbulent waters, sweeping away the rest of humanity, I too felt secure in this armchair, which grew big enough in my mind to hold my entire family. When I felt cold, thirsty or afraid, I would just close my eyes and see my all-embracing armchair, which made me feel loved, warm and safe.

Eventually, this magical armchair grew wings and flew to my rescue through air raids, explosions, dark cellars and other realities of the war. It turned into the harbinger of a happy future, returning our past to us. As darkness, hunger and my illness dragged on, I kept daydreaming about the moment when the horror would end, when it would appear only as a nightmare from which I would wake up to my pre-war life.

# Rowing on Ice
## Kathleen (Kati) Horvath

In the fall of 1943, we had the opportunity to buy an unfinished house in Túrkeve, where my husband, Pál (Pali), had his workshop for manufacturing hand-woven towels. I moved there with my little son, Ádám, to avoid the daily scares and trips to the cellar. Pál came every weekend to be with us. The weeks passed entirely peacefully, as if war didn't roar just a few kilometres away. There was a large uncultivated lot that belonged to the house, and the house had two rooms in habitable shape. The bathroom was unfinished, so we had to use the outdoor one, but the kitchen had a fireplace, and we used dry corn husks for fuel. We had chickens who laid eggs and rabbits for meat, but we had to buy milk. Túrkeve was a small village, close to the Romanian border, which we crossed to get salt in exchange for other goods.

I had brought exclusive seeds with me from Budapest. With my friend's help we created a garden of vegetables and flowers, of a kind not seen before in Túrkeve. It was a refuge from the storm around us. Jews were not treated much worse than the rest of the population there at that time. There were restrictions, food coupons and other wartime issues, but everyone had to bear it and no one complained. Túrkeve was definitely a much better place to be than Budapest. I was happy as a lark, enjoyed being with my son and worked in my beautiful garden.

It was on March 15 — the national holiday of Hungary — that

my son complained of a sore throat. By the evening he was running a low-grade fever. The next day I wanted to call the local doctor, but it turned out that the doctor had been conscripted, and there was no doctor left in the village. By the evening Ádám still hadn't gotten better, so I decided to take the next train to Budapest (a three-hour trip) to see our pediatrician, who was my husband's cousin, and his wife, my schoolmate.

We arrived the next afternoon and spent the weekend with the family. Ádám got treated and was soon well again. After spending some time in the cellar, due to air raids, I wanted to return to my idyllic escape in Túrkeve on March 20, 1944. Though I had read and heard over the radio that the Germans had marched in and occupied Hungary the previous day, I did not concern myself with it too much, as I thought that in practice they already ruled anything and everything in Hungary anyway. To my mind, the fact that they were now there physically would not make too much of a difference. I felt safe as long as I could get back to Túrkeve.

But to my great surprise, from the moment the Germans arrived no Jews could travel, except to return to their permanent home. I was stuck in Budapest, shut out from my gorgeous peaceful Garden of Eden. I phoned my friend, frantically asking her to spare no expense to get me the necessary papers proving that I was a permanent Túrkeve resident. I would have done anything to get back to Túrkeve to save me from the nightmare of living in a cellar with my little son. However, all my crying and trying did not help. I was stranded in Budapest.

Little did I understand then that fate had not let me and my little son perish! Six weeks later, the whole Jewish population of Túrkeve was forced onto a train to Auschwitz and, with the exception of very few, were murdered there.

In Budapest, it was a time of hunger, a time to hide and a time to survive until the next day. When the restrictions against the Jews forced us to live in designated houses that we could leave for only a few hours each day, I went to work to sew shirts for the army in a converted state factory. Working in one of these factories meant I could enjoy the privilege of being allowed to stay out for twelve hours, and we also got some soup to eat. I took my two-year-old son with me, so he could at least have some soup. The factory was on the fifth floor of a building at Deák Ferenc tér, a major intersection in Budapest, where my friend's parents originally had an elegant and expensive clothing store. I worked there for only a short time, just until I got an official paper that allowed me to stay out longer. It was imperative that I find some place to hide, some place where we were not known.

For days and nights I hid in the basements of different houses, stealing food wherever I could. When I had no food, I smoked dried chestnut leaves in old newspaper wrapping. It had a terrible taste, but quenched my hunger. I had my son bound in a blanket on my front or sometimes on my back. I spent most nights in the underground metro stations, until someone told me that these places did not offer protection from the bombs.

On one occasion it was too late for me to get home on foot with my son bound on my back. In previous weeks Jews could only travel at the end section of the tramway or buses. From then on Jews could not use public transportation anymore at all. I was able to get to my husband's family house, at 11 Vörösmarty Street, where my father-in-law acted as the house commander responsible for the residents' compliance with the latest ordinances. There were only two gentile families in the house, and all the others were members of the Grünfeld family — my husband's grandfather and his wife, and their four children with their respective families. The apartment house belonged to Fülöp Grünfeld, my husband's maternal grandfather.

I asked my father-in-law to let me and my son spend the night with them, as I was not able to get back home in time to beat the curfew. He did not let me in! I could never forgive him for that. He put me and his grandson in a life-threatening situation, just for his own possible personal safety.

On October 15, the Hungarian Arrow Cross fascist party took power and ruled as an active hunting unit. Arrow Cross brigades broke into Jewish houses marked with yellow stars and collected the inhabitants, regardless of age or state of health. They marched them to the banks of the partially frozen Danube River, lined them up on the very edge and shot them point-blank so they fell into the icy river. The ones who did not die instantly from being shot froze in the cold water. There were babies and elderly people among the murdered. The Arrow Cross members did not shoot their victims all at once. These murderers enjoyed seeing their fright. The news of the atrocities filtered to us slowly from the very few who by some sort of miracle managed to escape. But at the time we did not believe them. It felt so horrific that it simply could not be true, we thought.

The Arrow Cross brigades usually conducted their raids at night or in the wee hours of the morning: they dragged people from their beds, not giving them time to get properly dressed, which kept them in shock. Then they marched them through the streets and started shooting indiscriminately. The wounded were left where they fell, or others were forced to carry the victims. I personally did not see this being done; I just saw the results and heard from those who survived.

I have few memories of the worst period during the occupation of Budapest. The news on the radio was coded. There was total chaos, with the bombs and sirens creating unbelievable noise. We were hunted by the Arrow Cross and the police. The bombs came whistling down, and houses collapsed like playing cards. We didn't even know if it was daytime or night, because the windows were covered, so no light could enter. There was no day or night in the cellars either. There was no electricity and no radio, and we seldom dared to go out to look for food.

News arrived from someone who had been forced to go out to hunt for food: the big grain mill had been directly hit by a bomb and there was flour on the ground. We ran with sacks and boxes to collect some usable food from the burned-out ruins. On a different occasion, a stranger arrived shell-shocked and dropped the news that on Almássy square fresh horse corpses were available, dead for only two days. We ran to carve a piece.

In the end, it was my mother who saved us. She heard about a Swede named Raoul Wallenberg who gave out identity documents, *Schutzpässe*, to the Jews. One afternoon in November 1944, while I was not home, my mum put her grandson and some food in his carriage and left the house. She went and stood in line at the Swedish consulate for hours. The consulate closed at 6:00 p.m., and they told her to come the next day. She insisted and told them that if she left now, she would be shot on sight with her only grandson because the curfew for Jews had started. She begged the clerks to listen to their consciences, and they let her in. She not only got *Schutzpässe* for herself and for me and my son, but they even drove her and Ádám to the Jó Pásztor (Good Shepherd) cloister on the Buda side of the Danube River.

My mother sent word — I do not know how — to our house commander, Mr. Berzeky, a tailor and the only gentile still living in our house, to tell me to come to the cloister in the Óbuda district of Budapest to join her and my son. Berzeky was a nice person and was very apologetic when he had to apply the restrictive regulations ordered by the regime. On this occasion he came to me with good news, but since by this time Jews were not permitted to use public transportation, he also risked his life by using his wife's papers to accompany me to the hiding place.

Óbuda is on the other side from Pest, so we had to cross the Danube on one of the bridges. Just two weeks later, no bridges were left across the river, and there was no way to cross from one side to the other at all: the Siege of Budapest was in full swing. At that time, the Jó Pásztor cloister was housing young women aged twelve to twenty who had been in trouble with the law — underage prostitutes — sentenced by the state prosecutor to be incarcerated or reformed. There were two classes of nuns in the institution. The ones we referred to as

Márias wore full white habits and were educated; they were the teachers. The other group, who we often called Magdalénas, dressed in full black and did all the physical work to support the establishment.

There were also nuns who taught trades, like shoe repair or plumbing. For the girls who were judged not to have the capacity to learn and grow intellectually, there were classes to teach them a practical profession, such as cooking, cleaning or gardening. The nuns owned a huge wall-enclosed lot. In the front was the big chapel, with a refectory to the left and right of it. There was a large courtyard that contained a huge vegetable garden, instead of the flowers that were there in times of peace. On both sides there were classrooms and dormitories for the inmates, followed by cells for the nuns (one side for the Magdalénas, the other for the Márias). And finally, at the opposite end, there was a pantry and a huge communal kitchen and dining room.

There were a few more refugees hidden in the cloister, I was told, but we never met them; or if we did see them, I was not aware that they were also refugees. We were dressed as Magdalénas, and we tried to be helpful with chores. We were given background stories, though these stories would have been unlikely to hold up after even three minutes of interrogation, but memorizing them helped to overcome our feelings of insecurity. My story was that I was a prostitute with an illegitimate child and so had returned to the cloister where I had been a resident before I became pregnant.

The big danger I brought to the nuns was my circumcised son, because in Europe only Jews practised circumcision. It was considered a dead giveaway that we were Jewish. On one occasion while I was there, the Arrow Cross came to inspect the premises. The warning signal from the front of the cloister came immediately. The routine was to make the refugees disappear, hiding them as well and as far away as safety permitted. We gave Ádám a sleeping pill, put a small porcelain dish over his head and bandaged his head with a bloody tissue. The story was that he had a serious head wound and could not be moved or even touched. We even put soiled diapers on him, so there would be no inspection. The alert seemed to last forever, though in reality it probably lasted for no more than fifteen minutes.

Around Christmas, the nuns' chicken coop was hit by shrapnel fragments, and we had paprika chicken for four days in a row. Imagine what a feast this was after living on the most meagre, makeshift sustenance for almost a year! My mother volunteered to prepare it. She had plenty of helpers to pluck the chickens and remove the embedded pieces of shrapnel.

# Frightful Days
# Katalin Kenedi

On March 19, 1944, we got the same answer from whomever we asked: the German troops entered Hungary and there was no resistance, absolutely none, and they were on their way to the capital. My husband, whom I called Bandikám (my little Andrew), knew exactly what would happen, which meant he was not optimistic at all. Every day brought some new sign of problems for Jews, new regulations, new anti-Jewish orders. On April 5, a strict order came that every Jew had to wear the yellow star, which was to be sewed onto the left side of every garment worn outside, such as a dress or a coat.

That same evening there was an air raid. The sirens were wailing, and as the warden of our building on Andrássy Avenue, I had to make sure everybody went downstairs into the shelter, which was built from our pantry. The Tóths were downstairs, as were the Patakis and other families. Dr. László Tóth was there, who was the head of the press club. He had a friend of his there too. He came to Bandikám and me and told us, "You don't know how ashamed I feel that you and my many friends have to wear the star." His friend Sándor Endrődi was a famous poet, and he had the same opinion. I will never forget that night; they were all so kind, and there were no bombs yet. I arranged with Lyan Tóth that night that she would take over the command of the house from me, because I thought it was not appropriate to keep this position as a Jew.

On April 9, Bandikám's draft call arrived, and he left for the countryside. It was impossible to go see him. But he was again lucky, since his superiors were nice people who recognized quickly that they could work less in the office if Bandikám organized their jobs. So he was in the office full-time and had many privileges. He could get mail illegally and had better working hours. He had a hard time when they all had to go to empty houses and take the belongings of the Jewish people who had been deported. What they saw and what they heard was heartbreaking. He was asked to take care of ancient documents, and he brought back a lot to Budapest when he came home for a short holiday in October. This turned out to be a life-saving event for him.

The summer months of 1944 passed fast. In August we got a new prime minister, Géza Lakatos, who was a true human being and made life easier for the Jewish population of Budapest. However, the summer had been terrible in the countryside outside of Budapest. From even the smallest places where Jewish people lived, they were forced to move from their home to a closed ghetto. Then we heard the horrible news about the deportations. All the Jews from the rest of the country had already been deported. Then it followed with the suburbs of Budapest, and we heard that the gendarmerie would be sent to the capital, too, to arrange for deportations, but thank God they had not enough time to execute that.

We received a cable from the Swedish government, on behalf of our business friend Mr. Björkman. Our whole Kopstein family was to travel to Sweden, and the Swedish government would support all of us till the end of the war. I ran with my daughter, Judit, to the Swedish Embassy, which was located on Gellért Mountain. There were thousands of people all fighting for their lives. We tried to get close to the entrance. For one minute the door opened, but only to tell the crowd of people not to wait in vain.

Then Vili Forgács saw us and reached out to pull us inside. It was a fantastic moment for us, but we were sorry that so many did not have the access we had. Vili was a family friend who worked at the embassy at that time. We gave the cable to Vili and he showed it to everybody because it was unique. Then he told us what he needed to get us our Swedish passports and told us to bring him papers for the whole family. So we signed up for my mother-in-law, Sári mama, my sister-in-law, Dici, Judit, Bandikám and I; Laci, Dici's husband; and Laci's mother, Irma néni. When we got all the papers together, we had to go back to the embassy. It was again heartbreaking to see people begging for help; it is still heartbreaking just to write about it.

We were dreadfully stressed, and it remained difficult to live from one day to the next, but life went on. We had to plan who could go and where to shop in the few hours we could get out of the house. There were many big air raids and bombings that summer. I always had the nightwatch from 6:00 p.m. to midnight. I was in a little room on the main floor with a radio and had to listen constantly for any warning. I always took time to write my daily letter to Bandikám, and I waited every day for mail or any other news from him.

There were many air raids, which always caused lots of anxiety. Whenever the sirens came on, everybody had to go down to the cellar with no more than a totebag. I had a bigger one because I was also in charge of first aid. We never knew from one minute to another if we would see the sun shining the next day. But God helped us all the way.

Hiding in the cellar one night, we thought that our house got hit, but it was actually a house two blocks away from our apartment building. The bomb had gone straight down to the cellar and exploded there. There was a feather warehouse there, so everyone suffocated. A young couple we knew died together in that cellar. When the sirens went off, signalling that the raid was over, the house commander instructed everybody to go to the building that had been struck to help clear the rubble. They knew nobody was alive. I declined to go or to let Judit go. I had a long argument with her, but we did not go.

We had moved by now and were pretty well off living at Hunyadi tér (square), and only Bandikám was missing. I knew he was treated well, but he was far away. As Irma néni was still living at the same place as when she first moved to Budapest when she got married in the early 1900s, she could still shop with her old butcher, who served her well but mostly under the counter. With more people to feed, she now needed more flour. There was a place where we bought geese with her help every week. We also had places to buy fruits and vegetables. Irma néni received good service everywhere; she was a kind person and everybody loved her. There was even a dairy store where we got everything we needed.

Many efforts were made to get Bandikám's whole labour camp regiment to Budapest before Bandikám finally arrived back on October 13, 1944. In the wee hours of the morning we would have visitors, many comrades from Bandikám's regiment. An officer named Vörösmarty bicycled for hours from the town of Várpalota to ask for help. Just a few days before Bandikám got back, I got a request to visit a general in the Sashegy neighbourhood and ask him for help. I never got there, because before I could reach his villa there was an air raid and I had to run to the first shelter. It was in the convent Notre Dame de Sion, on the top of the mountain past the Gellérthegy. I had a good many kilometres to walk in a hurry. I arrived there, and it was full of soldiers; the convent had been emptied for use by the army. I would blow my "big Jewish nose" constantly, thinking that this was a way to hide it. After the air raid was over, I tried hard to accomplish my task, but I wasn't successful. I found out that the general was out of the city.

I rushed home by foot and arrived at five o'clock, just in time. We were already living at Hunyadi tér. There was a curfew, and Jewish people could only be out of the house between 11:00 a.m. and 5:00 p.m. So I had to take risks many times. It was dangerous, but I just went and God helped me.

I visited many of the close relatives of the comrades. I brought them illegal mail and took mail from them to give to the men who frequently came in the morning hours to Hunyadi tér to take the mail back to the labour camp. Bandikám was sending letters to be distributed, as well as food. I got close to some relatives and we maintained our friendships afterwards.

When Bandikám arrived for three days, October 13 to 15, we were happy. We got a separate room in the neighbourhood, so we had a little privacy. Then on October 15 at noon we went to meet the soldier who would escort him and two of his comrades, close friends of ours, back to the town of Várpalota. On the way we heard that Regent Horthy made a speech. All windows were open and the radios were blaring. He made a truce with the Soviets, agreeing that from then on Hungarians would fight with the Soviets against the Germans. It almost cost him his life, but it was wonderful to hear that. He also stated that Jews shouldn't be afraid anymore. After this, Bandikám's escort did not show up, so we went home. The first thing we did was to take down the yellow star from the door post.

However, in the evening the gong sounded not for the air raid but for soldiers who came to take away the Jews. We all had Swedish passports already, so after a long argument, they left. The next morning, after I purchased some apples, I went to Andrássy Avenue and spoke with the house superintendent. I told them that they should help us, and that we would like to come back and stay for a short time in the Patakis' place on the third floor, as they had left to hide in the countryside. They agreed.

So in October 1944 we — Sári mama, Dici, Bandikám, Judit and I — were for the time being living at the Patakis' place. The door had been broken by a bomb and was fastened only temporarily. We all had a place to sleep and could even speak on the phone with Kálmán Vándor, who was at the city's army command. He could speak from there undisturbed too. The superintendent became increasingly afraid of hiding us and told us to leave. Kálmán called us back later and told us to go to some friends' place for the night. By then, a command had been given on the radio that anybody who sees a Jew should report them to the police. The next day, Sári mama, Dici, Judit and I went to an area of Budapest called Rózsadomb to stay with friends.

Bandikám stayed behind at the Patakis' place. He was in real danger there, because that same night an ambulance was blown up on Andrássy Avenue. The police and many soldiers came to look at every inch of the house. The main floor's door was sealed. It was the place we had left a month earlier. Then they went to the second floor, where the nuns and the old priest were living. The police and soldiers then wanted to open the Patakis' place where Bandikám was standing inside the door. The housekeeper reassured them that it was in ruins, and finally they went upstairs to the Tóths' closed residence. A man we didn't know was living next to the Tóths', and at the nun's place two German men were staying too. They saw Bandikám leave the next morning, but they looked away on purpose and did not report him. The house superintendent and his wife were so kind and generous that they even brought us supper, a whole duck. But he told us that he was sure we would not survive. "I'm working with the police. I ought to know," he added. The next time we saw them was in January 1945, after the siege, when we moved back to our place on Andrássy Avenue.

On October 17, 1944, Bandikám went to the so-called International Army, where they gathered all the men from the different labour camps with foreign passports. He got to Jókai Street, where a section of the Swedish Embassy was. Dici, Sári mama, Judit and I were with Magda Petneházy at the time. A neighbour of hers named Bánkiné realized that she was hiding Jews and wanted to immediately call the police. I stopped her and asked her to phone Kálmán Vándor. He told her not to worry and to just leave us alone. At our friends' place, we had a few pieces of our own furniture and we could stay overnight in our big blue armchairs. They let Judit, who was not even fifteen yet, sleep in their bed. We left in the morning.

Sári mama and Dici went back to Hunyadi tér. I went with Judit to my mother's villa, though I knew that she had had to leave with Uncle Sándor, my stepfather and János to live in a Jewish house on Akadémia Road, a building marked with a big yellow star. The house superintendent looked happy when I told him that I would like them to keep us there for a few days. I told him that I would pay him generously. Kálmán Vándor told us on the phone that the Soviets were near, which was true, and it would be only a few days till they would enter Budapest.

We then went to 51 Zárda Street. We were there for only a short time. The house superintendent told Judit that he had known me since I was a young girl and didn't want to take any money for keeping us. Éva Linksz, my only cousin, who lived in the house, came and brought a pair of socks for Judit and some cookies. After a short time, a few officers and about two hundred soldiers arrived on trucks. They surrounded the house. They took Judit and me. As we walked down the hill between armed guards, we saw a woman pushing her bicycle upwards. The officer asked me if I knew this woman. I told him, sure I do. Madi was our French nanny. My mother had given her a home when she did not even have a spoon. All that she had, my mother had given to her. Then the officer told us that she had gone to the police station and reported that we were hiding.

We were taken to a police district office. We were lucky to speak to a senior officer who wasn't an antisemite. The whole time he tried to persuade us to go to Christian friends to hide. Then he told us that he would keep us there for a while, since he knew that at another police station Pál Jávor had been beaten half-dead, and he didn't want that to happen to us. Pál Jávor was a Christian actor who had married a Jewish woman. We heard later that another bunch of Jewish people who got caught were shot to death on Széna tér, not far from the police station where we were being kept. During the night, the police officer came to our cell and brought us bread and butter to eat. It was uncomfortable there, it was cold, and we ended up sitting the whole night. When I went to the bathroom, one police officer was at the open door watching. In the morning we were taken with some others to the main police station. We were jammed in a few rooms without any food or anything else. There were many interesting people there, such as Margit Bethlen, the wife of the late Prime Minister István Bethlen, and many actors, including Márton Rátkai with his Christian wife.

We were eventually taken to the Mirabel. It was a condominium building in the Svábhegy (now Széchenyi-hegy). The entrance was on the fourth floor. When we got there, everybody had to give their money, watches and wedding rings to the police officer and then we were escorted to our rooms. Judit and I were placed into a small room, some three by three metres, with ten other women. The room had no furniture and it was so tiny that we had trouble even sitting. We did not get much to eat, just a little piece of bread with a bowl of soup for the whole day. The soup was simply the liquid in which the noodles for the police staff had been cooked. It was very salty. I was spending my birthday there, and Judit wanted to give me her lunch as a birthday present.

One day we were all, one after the other, called to a room where a detective was sitting at a typewriter and was taking down our information. I was standing in line when a woman came in and seated herself halfway on his table. He got up and smacked her in the face. He told her that she should know where she is: it was the headquarters of the Hungarian Gestapo. She was the wife of the owner of Nagy és Eichner, a wonderful butcher store, where we frequently bought special sausages, corned beef and other kinds of meat. Then I saw Judit standing in the doorway. The officer looked up and asked, "Why are you here?" Judit answered, "I am strong and when you take my mother to work I want to go too." But he sent us both back to where we had been held before.

We were surprised to get back all our belongings — all the money, my watch and wedding ring, and even our precious Swedish *Schutzpässe*. We had to get into two big police riot vans, each of which could hold forty people, but we were 120. Then we left, and as usual nobody knew where we were going. We drove a long way. There was a big air raid and they stopped the vans. The drivers said that both vans had ruptured tires. We waited and waited until they fixed them. After the air raid was over, they drove us to the big gathering place called Tattersall. Luckily, there was nobody there, as all the guards had run away and everything was closed. We were then driven back to Svábhegy and our small room. I looked out of the windows and saw a man who I knew from Hunyadi tér. I screamed his name, Linden. He was a chauffeur for the police. He finally noticed me, as our window was on the same level as the entrance to a little bridge. He came in and asked the police officer to let us speak. I spoke with Linden, who went back and told Sári mama and the others that Judit and I were alive.

The same day the detective who had spoken with us earlier came around to our room. Judit was laying on the floor in her winter coat. He asked me if she was sick. "No," I said, "she is hungry." The next day at two o'clock we were called to the office of the senior police officer. They said that since we were Swedish citizens we were entitled to leave. We left in a hurry, because we had only a few hours to get home before five o'clock. We were scared that somebody would arrest us again. We looked terrible. We hadn't had a shower for many weeks.

When we arrived at Hunyadi tér, we rushed upstairs. Everybody was relieved to see us. First thing I asked about was Bandikám. They told me that he was sick at the Vilma királynő Road orphanage. It had been bombed, and when I ran over there the next morning, as soon as I could, I found him lying on a bunk under the blue sky; there was no roof left. He was in really bad shape, depressed, but he recovered quickly knowing that Judit and I were okay. He had been told many different stories about us — for instance, that we were out of the country working in a gun factory near Vienna. Bandikám then went back to Jókai Street.

A few days later we got an order to move to a Swedish protected house. We packed our belongings, which we had little of, and went to Pozsonyi Avenue. We got rooms on the seventh floor, which was not so good for Sári mama and Irma néni, who were in their sixties.

Women in their sixties at that time were already considered old, and we were concerned because we had to frequently walk downstairs to the air raid shelter. The elevator did not work any more.

One day Bandikám appeared, escorted by a young officer with a white armband, which meant he was a Jewish convert to Christianity. His wife was Jewish and she had been my schoolmate for a couple of years. She was in the same room with her mother, her father, who was a judge, and two sisters. Bandikám could stay there for the night. Some thirty-eight of us stayed outside the big room till the morning, when Bandikám had to go back.

The next day I went over to Jókai Street to look around, but by that time Bandikám had gone to Tátra Street, where Wallenberg set up a new section of the Swedish Embassy. When I arrived home I saw our belongings on the floor of the hall. Sári mama, Irma néni, Dici and Judit came down to tell me that we had to move. So we moved to 5/c Tátra Street. The embassy's new section was just across the street, at 6 Tátra Street, very close to Bandi's workplace. He had two jobs. One was distributing new housing for hundreds of people — Wallenberg offered blocks of houses in the same district. But mostly he was involved in rescuing people in the "life-saving" department. That meant that he had to negotiate many times with the Arrow Cross and pay them off in return for individuals who had been captured. It was heartbreaking to hear afterwards that he would pay the money and then find out they had already been killed. But Bandikám saved a lot of lives by giving away so many *Schutzpässe* to friends and even to people he didn't know.

In one of the first days he worked at the embassy a young comrade of his from the labour camp named György Steiner showed up. Bandikám naturally gave him a *Schutzpass* from somebody who didn't need it any more and told him to stay at home. Instead of staying home, he contacted his girlfriend and went strolling along the shore of the Danube River. He was stopped by the Nazis, who took him away and killed him.

The end of the war was close, but life got even more dangerous. The siege started around Christmas and everybody had to stay in the cellars. It was uncomfortable sitting on a chair for so long, often for twenty-four hours, but that was all we could do. When I wasn't in the cellar, I was always on the go because I was the house administrator and also in charge of first aid. Whenever the Arrow Cross came to check the number of people who were on the list of this house, there had to be a perfect match with those present. I always had a knot in my stomach during such checks.

Nonetheless, we had a few happy moments at Tátra Street. Each day, Bandikám came home in the early evening hours. We were the only ones who slept upstairs. Bandikám explained to me that if he couldn't straighten out and have a good night's sleep, he couldn't perform his stressful job.

Around this time, our good friends' daughter, Zsuzsi, showed up. She had been taken to a labour camp in Vácbottyán in early November. She was working there with many of her former classmates. They were told that they would soon be deported. The day before the planned deportation, the Hungarian Arrow Cross guards all got drunk and decided to kill the girls rather than deport them. They made them dig their own large grave and made them stand on its edge. They started shooting and the girls fell into the grave one after the other. Zsuzsi was desperate. She knew she had only moments left. She jumped into the grave before getting shot and she lay under the dead bodies of her former classmates until the guards left them for dead. She was the only one left alive. She crawled out and cleaned herself of the blood of her friends. In a brave move, she hitchhiked with a German truck driver, who did not know she was Jewish. She claimed that she was running away from the Soviets. She came to our place, and Bandi arranged for her to be adopted by Sári mama as a minor. That meant she could be on Sári mama's *Schutzpass*. She was saved.

On Tátra Street, we had three rooms. One room was shared by

Sári mama, Irma néni, Dici, Judit and Zsuzsi. This was luxury compared to the heartbreaking news we heard of the ghetto. The conditions were terrible there, with many people squeezed together, at times around forty-five to fifty people in the same room. The food was much less than what was needed. At least in the cellar, we had bathrooms and a first-aid room. Yet, there were times when we had no water to drink or even just to clean our mouths. Judit and Zsuzsi would go out to the street and gather snow. Zsuzsi carried bricks and made a fireplace on the floor to melt the snow. They even used my favourite books for fuel. At the last minute I took my favourite James Hilton book out of the fire, so it got burned only slightly.

Bandikám told me every day about the terrible rumours he was hearing at the embassy. He heard that everybody was going to be killed; that everybody would have to go to the ghetto; that every house would be evacuated separately and everybody would be taken to the Danube and shot. Such horrible rumours often proved to be true. We were saved by God and maybe sheer luck. The horror stories circulated every night but were not spoken during the day downstairs in the cellar.

Bandikám came home many times totally exhausted after meeting with the Arrow Cross to negotiate. We would hear the Arrow Cross come to our door. We had a big sign on the door indicating that the house was under the protection of the Swedish government. The soldiers still came in, and then I had to show them our book with the names of all the people in our building, and everybody had to show their *Schutzpässe*. They would conduct a large search regardless, hoping to find people hiding without a *Schutzpass*. We had a few young men hiding in the cellar, who were in the resistance movement. They were wonderful young men who risked their lives every day.

Every day brought new misery till Bandikám came home. The constant uncertainty of life and the everyday struggle to stay alive for just one more day took its toll. Thank God Bandikám's nerves were strong, since mine were not. He was capable of making big decisions in seconds and of keeping his eye on all the relevant details. This is why he was able to have his position beside Wallenberg at the embassy. His presence was felt even while he was across the street at the embassy and had a positive effect on everybody. He made me feel strong and capable of fulfilling the demands and needs of so many different people.

There were many unforeseen events. As time passed, tensions grew ever greater. We would look out the glassless windows and try to remain invisible. We first heard and then later saw people shot from the house right across from ours. It was terrible to see. Many mattresses were thrown out of the windows from the higher floors and then some of the people were too. They were lined up to be escorted to the ghetto. It was an apartment building protected by the Red Cross, but the bandits didn't care. We could see how ruthless the Nazis and Arrow Cross were. They were using their guns to beat people. We heard that on their way to the ghetto, anyone who got out of the line or slowed down was simply shot. Everything was uncertain, and this uncertainty was the worst part. I am describing only the facts of the situation, because if I tried to write about the emotions, the fear for our lives and for our loved ones, I would never be able to complete my story.

We were more than lucky to survive these times. I always say that God and good luck were with us all the time. I promised, and I kept my promise, that when our little family, Sári mama, Bandikám, Judit and I, survived, I would not report on Madi, the French bitch who reported us to the Nazis. Judit and I could easily have been deported. We now know all about the deportations, which very few people survived. We were also lucky with our Swedish *Schutzpass*, even though we were told many times that even with our *Schutzpass* we would eventually be forced into the ghetto or be taken to the Danube River to be shot. Thank God we survived it all.

When on January 16, 1945, the Soviet soldiers finally arrived at our place, Bandikám heard them speaking Slavic. We were happy. We thought that after so many years of oppression we would now be able to live a normal life again. But we had to experience a terrible disappointment from which we would never recover. We couldn't just pick up our life where we had left off, since everything was different now. Only the feelings within our family hadn't changed. I continued to worry about many aspects of our life: about Bandikám and his health; about Judit, who was so young and yet looked older because she was so tall; and about Sári mama, who was not so young any more. But everybody continued to help everybody, and so it was easier for all of us to survive the years ahead too.

# To Start off as a Christian but to Arrive as a Jew
## Eva Kahan

On March 19, 1944, the Germans occupied Budapest. It was a Sunday, and we heard the news on the radio. We couldn't foresee the consequences. However, that day we had a visitor, a cousin of my father's who had lived through the Anschluss in Vienna. I remember him saying that we had no idea what this news meant. At the time we thought he was exaggerating — after all this was Hungary, and besides, my father had fought for this country and had several World War I medals to prove his merit.

Well, just a few days later new laws and proclamations started to be announced by the day, almost all of which concerned the Jews. We increasingly became outcasts in the eyes of others. We learned bitterly that the nation was very willing to enforce these rules. We started to recognize the severity of our situation, yet couldn't imagine, not even in our wildest thoughts, what lay ahead of us.

Among the first restrictions was that no Jewish household could own a radio. (Obviously the Germans didn't want us to know what was going on in the world.) This was hard on my father, because he liked to listen quietly, behind drawn curtains, to the BBC from London. We had a big radio that we buried in the rabbit house, thinking that we would take it out when possible. We also buried some of our jewellery in the cellar.

About two weeks after the Nazi occupation came the law for Jews to wear a yellow star. Our food supply was also restricted. We received coupons for bread, lard or oil, sugar, flour and meat, including chicken and fish. Mind you, these items were on ration coupons for everyone, but our coupons had a large J on them and our portions were smaller.

At that time, staying home was the safest thing, so I hardly went anywhere. A friend of mine lived nearby and we were together a lot. One day she suggested we visit a boy in the labour camp near her house. The camp had at one time been an old vinegar plant; now these boys lived there and from there they went on foot to work at a chemical factory at the other end of the city. We went there, and among many other boys, I met Lajos. He took an instant liking to me and decided that we would survive through this mess together. He and a few other boys started to come to our house (they found a shortcut through the factory's fence), bringing news of what they heard in the city.

One day Lajos told my father that he would save me, and he talked about his plan. He had Christian friends from the street (not very law-abiding boys) who would sell their identification papers, as they could obtain duplicates for themselves. Armed with these documents, we would go live in another part of the city as Christians who had lost their home in the bombings. My father didn't know what to do. He agonized over putting my fate into Lajos' hands, not knowing how much sense of responsibility Lajos had. At the same time, he just couldn't bear the risk of keeping me, a young girl, at home. I know what a hard decision that was for him. I remember a friend telling him that if one Jew was going to remain alive at the end, that would be Lajos. My father was still reluctant to let me go and suggested to me that Lajos and I get married, just on paper, at least for the time being.

I thought that this wouldn't be fair to Lajos, besides the fact that I really liked him and his optimistic spirit gave me a sense of security. I wanted to belong to him, so I told my father that I would marry him in the usual way and that I trusted he would take good care of me. My father contacted my grandfather for reassurance, and he did not object. From then on Lajos came to our house often, always bringing me some little gifts, like a piece of pastry or other hard-to-get things. (Jews were not allowed to enter pastry shops, but he just removed his armband and walked in.)

I recall a tragicomical incident, when we walked near our house on a small side street. I was wearing the yellow star, of course, but Lajos had removed his armband because he didn't have his leave pass. One woman looked out of a window and motioned to Lajos to approach her. She said to him, "I don't mean anything bad, but why are you going around with a Jewish girl? It's not right."

The next law against Jews was that they could live only in houses that were appointed to them. These were so-called Jewish houses, with a huge yellow star on the front. The announcement was posted by the city hall as to which houses were designated as Jewish houses. People were given five days to find a place and move. We were lucky (or so it seemed then) that our house was already on the list, so we all just had to move into one room to make room for others. It was up to us whom and how many to take in. Jews were going from house to house begging for a room or even just part of a room. We ended up with sixteen people in our house, where only the three of us had lived before. It was terrible to turn away all the people looking for a place once we were full.

Our wedding in the City Hall of Óbuda took place at that time. I was sad that we couldn't even go there together. I was wearing the yellow star (as always, because many people knew me in Óbuda) but Lajos had removed his armband because he couldn't obtain a pass to leave (he climbed over the fence to get out for his wedding).

It was safer not to be seen together, so we walked on opposite sides of the street. In the City Hall Lajos put on his band since no stranger could see it anyway. Only my father and one other witness were present at the ceremony. At the end the judge announced that the bride, despite being married to a Hungarian, would not receive Hungarian citizenship. We were considered homeless, which surprised all of us — mostly Lajos. But I couldn't have cared less. I had come to the conclusion a long time before that no matter how much I was taught to love my country, I had no emotional attachment to it.

I was happy to be married to Lajos and felt safe when he was around. Under the German occupation, Hungary was now a frequent target of Allied bombings, but being with Lajos, I wasn't scared, not even during air raids. When the planes were flying overhead, we went up to sleep on the terrace and watched. He was gentle, caring and full of love. We were happy and trusted our luck.

After the Jews had to move into designated houses, Lajos thought it was time for me to leave home, because it was no longer safe there. We already had our false papers. We became Mr. and Mrs. Gozon. My name was Anna (I added Éva as a middle name, for safety); his name was Kálmán. I left home just a few days after our wedding, and from then on Lajos was managing my destiny.

One of his so-called friends, who knew we were Jews, rented us a room in a terrible place, which was formerly a whorehouse. It was full of bedbugs — we couldn't sleep because of them. This was supposed to be our honeymoon. Lajos was still in the labour camp and he visited me whenever he could get away. I was terrified when he was not around. I was mostly afraid of the people in the house around me. I knew, and they sensed, that I was not one of them. The wife of Lajos' friend was slowly stealing my things, wearing them openly because she knew I couldn't do anything about it. I was scared to stay in the apartment but had nowhere else to go. I sat on a street bench for hours or walked to a nearby church, thinking that nobody would bother me there. I lived for the moment of seeing my husband again.

The sirens began to scream more and more often. To be in the shelter with these real low-class people made me feel lonely and scared. We could hear the planes overhead with the terrifying whistling sound of the falling bombs and then the enormous explosions. I actually welcomed these heavy attacks, hoping that they would bring the end closer. Still, I was scared to face all of this alone.

One day, when Lajos was with me, there was a huge air raid and as soon as we came out from the shelter we went to see what had happened to his family. The Jewish house where they lived was in ruins, so we got worried. However, we heard that many people had been pulled out and placed in another house. We found his whole family there. No one was hurt, they were just shaken.

As for us, it was time to move on. Luckily, through an ad we found a couple who rented their kitchen to us. I should say, rather, that we rented only a single bed in one corner of the kitchen because the woman came in to cook sometimes. They had no idea that we were Jews, of course. We told them that we came from the countryside and had just gotten married and that Lajos was working in a firearm factory and had to be on guard at night. This story had to be given to everyone in answer to the questions, why isn't he a soldier and where is he at night? We lived a double life, which was nerve-wracking at times, but we slowly got used to it.

The factory where Lajos supposedly worked was quite a frequent target for bombing. After an air raid, when we heard on the radio that the factory was attacked, everyone approached me with sympathy and I played the role of the worried wife. When he came home I ran to kiss him and quickly whispered in his ear the news. He nodded to me, showing that he knew and was ready to tell the people what had happened there. He let his imagination run free and told them satisfactory stories. He had answers to every question — he was brilliant! He was friendly with everybody and did small favours for them. People liked us.

The problem was that we had no income, so I decided to go to work. There was a small factory nearby that made bottle tops and needed workers. I took my papers, studied all my "Aryan" ancestors and applied for a job. At that time, you had to prove your Christianity with documents of non-Jewish ancestors, going back to great-grand-parents. I got the job, which was terribly boring, but at least I earned a little money. At lunchtime I had to socialize with the workers and I listened quietly to their political views, their opinions about Jews, deportations, Hitler and the war. I was afraid I might raise suspicions by defending the Jews, and of course I wouldn't talk against them — which was what they expected of me — so I kept quiet and was very sad.

Lajos had been thinking about deserting the labour camp but he feared causing trouble for the others. He started to have problems with his frequent absences and the boys found it unfair that they had to cover for him. One reported him for being out without a pass, and he was punished with solitary confinement for ten days. I nearly went out of my mind until he sent a message telling me where he was. I just had to see him, but it was dangerous for me to go to Óbuda. To walk around the streets, even with false papers, was a risky undertaking. Vehicles were stopped and identification was demanded. Spot checks on pedestrians were common. Anyone who was found suspicious was taken in for further investigation. The authorities had little problem with men, as in Hungary only Jews were circumcised. Such spot checks were frequently performed in doorways.

To visit my husband, I had to start off as a Christian and arrive in Óbuda as a Jew. I sewed a star on a sweater that I folded over my arm. I carried a flat parcel that covered my chest. Before I got on the street-car to Óbuda, I walked around a bit and casually put on my sweater, covering the star with the parcel for a while. This way, if someone spotted me, they couldn't see the change; however, it was against the law to cover the star. I arrived without a problem and was lucky to be able to talk to Lajos. Every afternoon he was sent to the backyard of the building, to water gasoline barrels and cool them down. We talked briefly there and he promised to come as soon as he could. For a while after that, he just came for short visits — he couldn't stay overnight.

The couple with whom I lived were friendly to me, but I was very lonely without my family and friends. I lost contact with my father (there was no mail and no phone). Air raids became even more frequent. The sound of the sirens was frightening, especially at night, when all the tenants of the house had to go down to the cellar with their little suitcases and their crying children. I tried to convince myself that the bombs dropped from American or British planes were actually good for us.

One time I went to a market for some food when the sirens started. We had about eight minutes to reach a shelter and I realized that by running I might be able to reach the house where Lajos' family lived. I wanted to be with them rather than with strangers. The boys (Zev, Józsi and Akiva) liked me and maybe the others did too. They were happy to see me. The raid passed quickly and we went up to the apartment. The building was designated as a Jewish house and was very crowded with entire families in each room. Akiva was sick and I was sitting on his bed, talking to him, when a member of the Hungarian Arrow Cross came in and started questioning my mother-in-law. We all had to be ready to show identification papers. I had both Jewish and Christian ones on me. I slowly turned away, took out my false papers and slipped them under the bedsheet, thinking that in a Jewish house it was safer to be Jewish. I almost fell off the bed when I heard my husband's name mentioned. The man was actually looking for Lajos Kahan. I started to tremble, but my mother-in-law was brilliant. She said, "Are you saying Lajos? I don't have a son by that name. Oh, you probably mean my oldest son, Ignác, who is on the Soviet front. Look at his picture — that's him." And she went on and on talking about her oldest son, until — I think — they got tired of her. Luckily they didn't ask for my papers, because my document in Hungarian said Lajos Kahanné, which would have shown that I was married to the person they were looking for. To this day we don't know how they got his name and why they came for him. But it was an ominous sign.

On October 15, Regent Horthy made a proclamation to the Hungarian nation. He said that the Germans didn't keep their promises, and therefore we were breaking our military agreement with them. He asked for help from the Allies. This proclamation had a great impact on the Jews. They began to hope that now everything would be normal again. They were celebrating — some even removed the yellow star from the Jewish houses. Soon enough this proclamation was annulled and the Arrow Cross leader Szálasi took over. He made public his intention to annihilate the Jews of Budapest.

Following that, there was anarchy in the city. The situation seemed completely out of control. The cruelty of the Arrow Cross members sometimes surpassed even that of their counterparts, the German SS. Under the Arrow Cross, deportations from Budapest were intensified. We knew people who were dragged from their homes at any and every hour of the day. Any resistance or escape attempts were followed by executions. People who tried to help Jews faced the same punishment. But we didn't know where these people were taken. There were rumours going around about death camps, but we really didn't believe them. We assumed they were taken to work without pay for the Nazis, like the boys in the forced labour camps. My father was strong and healthy, so I wasn't overly worried about him. Besides, before we left, Lajos had also given him false documents, which he planned to use when necessary.

Lajos decided that the time had come to desert the army. He simply didn't go back anymore. He acquired a document that showed we had lost our home due to bombing, and he put in a claim at a government office for a place to live. Soon they allocated us a partly furnished apartment, which formerly belonged to a Jew. We took it with mixed feelings but then we said to each other that this way we would at least take care of his belongings. This was our first apartment. Even if it wasn't really ours, it was a haven where we could hide from the terrible world outside.

The designated houses made all age groups into easy targets for deportation. In the Kahan family, first Lajos' mother was taken; after that, his two older sisters, Irén and Dóra. When they took away his mother, Tibi (Zev), the youngest, was following the group and saw that they were led to a brick factory. This factory was no longer making bricks. It was like a large gathering place from where the deportations were carried out systemically. Miraculously, Lajos was able to bring his mother out from there and she came to live with us temporarily.

While she was with us we received a note from Irén and Dóra that said, "They are taking us towards the border on foot, we are at Sutó village. Save us!" Lajos instantly decided to go. We begged him to stay, saying, it's impossible, it's crazy. But he didn't listen. I asked what his plan was, what could anybody do? He said he had no plan, he will see when he gets there. The next morning he left. He was away for three days, while his mother and I were worried sick. The end result was that he didn't find his sisters but brought back ten other Jewish women who had escaped from the troops and were hiding in a stable. One of them was the mother of one of his friends. He covered them with a canvas and when the authorities stopped him on the way back, he said he was taking vegetables to the city. They arrived safely. These women were convinced that God had sent him to save them.

Irén and Dóra ended up in a concentration camp. Soon Lajos saw that he had to somehow secure the safety of the remainder of his family. He acquired false papers for them, and then he rented a little house in a suburb. The house was in the middle of a field and consisted of a single room. We took members of the family out there on a streetcar. My father-in-law, a religious Jew with a beard, had Christian papers! This was dangerous for all of us, but there was no other way.

In order to help people, Lajos was risking his life every day. In the beginning, I didn't know that he was connected with the underground. They were forging different documents, rubber stamps, certificates. The so-called *Schutzpässe* — which Wallenberg, the great Swedish diplomat gave out to save lives — were also forged by the underground, and consequently far more turned up than was the legal allotment. Unfortunately, such passes didn't save lives for long.

Later on, I also helped fill out birth certificates, but I never found out who Lajos' link was in the organization, nor where and when he picked up his connections. It was better not to know, because anyone arrested on suspicion of being associated with them was tortured for information.

By the end of November, all the remaining Jews in Budapest were forced to live in the newly formed ghetto, which was a large designated area surrounded by barricades and three-metre-high walls. It was cut off from the rest of the city and its gates were soon guarded; no one was allowed out and hardly any food was allowed in. The area was overcrowded and poor hygiene conditions caused terrible illnesses to spread.

One morning we heard that the Red Army was just hours from the city. The Germans were holding on. They would have rather burned the city down than surrender. We were worried about people in the ghetto. I suspected that all my relatives were there. As time went on, living conditions became more and more unbearable. There was no more food, no heat, no electricity. People were dying by the hundreds there. Compared to them we were lucky. I lived far from the ghetto and had no idea at the time about the terrible living conditions there. I was too preoccupied with my household. We took in Akiva and Józsi as the house of my in-laws was just too small. Piri and Anna were also hiding as Christian maids somewhere in the city. Housekeeping was all new to me. It was the first time in my life that I had to take care of four people — to clean, cook, wash and iron for them. Washing everything by hand was the hardest, as my skin would rub off from my hands, showing the raw flesh. Once it healed, I already had a new load of laundry to do.

Around Christmas 1944 the Red Army encircled the city. We had so many air raids that it wasn't worth going up to the apartment anymore. Besides the planes, they were shooting the city with cannons, so all the tenants moved down to the shelter. They built bunk beds all around and there was a little stove in the middle. At first we didn't go to this crowded shelter, just occupied an empty store space at ground level. It wasn't as safe as the shelter, but it was more private. A few times German soldiers came in, just to sit and talk to us. I was uneasy about these visits, but I guess they were just as tired of the whole war as we were.

By that time there was no more public transportation in the city, most of the bridges were blown up and nobody went to work any longer. My in-laws were starting to have problems with neighbours who suspected that they were Jews. It was time for them to move on. Thanks to our good relationship with the janitor (brought about with a few loaves of bread), he allowed my in-laws to come into our house and live temporarily in the laundry room. So the whole Kahan family was together again, except for the four girls. We hoped they were alive somewhere.

Food had the greatest value at that time. We always had enough, but there was not much variety — mostly dried beans, split peas, lentils. We had margarine, a little flour and sugar. But our greatest asset was bread that Lajos brought from a friend, who had a bakery that was no longer open to the public. Nobody else had bread in the house.

The Red Army was all around Budapest. We didn't see them, but sure could hear their cannons. We hoped the end was close because our lives were hanging on by a thread. I wondered how long our luck could continue. We all knew the siege of the city would be terrible. The street-level store was no longer safe, so we had to move to the basement with the other tenants. It was crowded there; we were sitting or lying most of the time on our beds, one single bed to each couple.

Lajos went out often to acquire some food or just to talk to people, but he always stayed in the neighbourhood. One day he came home with a new hat that looked to me like part of some kind of uniform. Combined with his boots and leather jacket, it looked okay. I didn't ask where he got it, as I didn't know much about what he was up to. He made connections with people, and as a result of that he would always bring some food home. There were now seven of us to feed. One day a young Hungarian soldier came to our shelter carrying the thigh of a horse. The meat, cut from a horse killed by machine gun on the street, was meant as a gift. He said he had brought it for Sergeant Gozon. I was right there but didn't move. The word "sergeant" confused me, until one of my neighbours tapped me on my shoulder, saying, "Hey, he is looking for your husband!"

When Lajos came home I pulled him aside and confronted him angrily. "At least you could have told me you were a sergeant before I made a fool of myself! You know I'm not familiar with these military ranks and uniforms!" Lajos just laughed, but I thought the situation could have been serious.

# A Time of Fear
## Alexander Eisen

The summer of 1943, I went to Békéscsaba to visit my grandparents. By then, the Hungarian government had called up young Jewish men to what they called "work battalions" on the Soviet front. They called up one of my uncles too. We knew he was on the Soviet front with the Hungarian army. My grandmother was frantic with worry about him. She had not received a word from him since his induction. One day a postman came to the door with a telegram. The expression on my grandmother's face when she received the telegram was one of sheer horror. She turned white. She handed the telegram to me and said, "Read it to me." I opened the telegram and read, "This is to notify you that your son…" I hesitated to go on.

"What? What?" she cried out.

I finally read the word "died."

I believe that emotional pain can surpass any physical pain. The pain on my grandmother's face was frightening. All I could think was that I was alone with her and must do something. I ran as fast as I could to the store where one of my aunts worked. I dragged her home, and soon everybody gathered around my grandparents.

All attempts to find out the circumstances of his death met with failure. We never found out when or how he died. As far as we know, no one from his group returned alive.

Later, we heard that the Hungarian army treated the Jewish soldiers in the most vicious way imaginable. They used them for target practice or let them freeze to death naked in the Russian winter.

In the fall of 1943, I left Békéscsaba and returned to Budapest. Budapest remains a grey city in my memory; I cannot recall any colour. The buildings were made of grey stone. The water flowing down the Danube always looked grey. Little bits of sunshine peeked past the high buildings and narrow streets. The mood both at home and on the street was ominous.

I turned thirteen years old. I was supposed to be a man, but I was a frightened kid. I was frightened of the Christian kids who chased me and who would beat me up if they caught me. I was frightened of the Germans. I was sure they were coming to kill us all.

I was not interested in school, but I studied. I was a poor student and had almost no friends to speak of. So I daydreamed. I dreamed that American and British soldiers would come in planes and parachute down to save us all. I dreamed of my father and wished with all my heart to be with him. I also immersed myself in books and whatever I could learn about electronics. I stood in front of radio store windows, familiarizing myself with the parts of a radio, and I was constantly looking for a book about the theory of electricity and electronics I could actually afford to buy.

But I also had to face reality. I observed how my mother struggled to support us and how my oldest sister got involved with left-leaning youth. We were always cold and hungry and suffered from frozen feet. We didn't have good shoes. Mine always leaked and I had to wrap my feet in newspaper for insulation.

As I was struggling to pass my exams, I was listening to the news and trying to anticipate the future; the approach of the winter of 1943–1944 was frightening to me. We were short of everything. I kept growing, which created a demand for clothing, specifically winter garments. Food was still scarce; good items were available for an enormous amount of money, totally out of our reach. The cheap staples were limited to locally grown items. I saw that everyone was in the same situation and mood. Occasionally, we went to the movies. For an hour or two, I could forget about the real world around me.

Spring arrived, the spring of 1944, and it wasn't so cold anymore. I continued to tinker with electricity. I zapped myself a few times with 220 volts of electricity but I quickly learned to be cautious. I became fairly knowledgeable in electronics and had accumulated radio parts and tools, so by the spring I had constructed a radio that actually worked. It was primitive, but I was happy. I fiddled with my radio constantly, and I immersed myself in adventure books.

The state exams were approaching, and I was worried. My health was not great. I suffered from a moderate fever, and my mother worried about my lungs. I added to her worries with a good dose of my own hypochondria. I tried to cram into a few weeks the studying I had neglected to do throughout the year. I never got to do the exams in full. On what exams I did take, I ended up receiving low grades. My mind was on the world situation.

The latest news in the synagogue was mixed. I went there daily to listen. I went from group to group, listening to the men discuss all the rumours in great detail. The Soviets were advancing and rumour had it that Prime Minister Kállay was negotiating with the Allies. This news was exciting, but I could not understand how it would be possible to implement it, as the Germans were all around us.

At the beginning of March 1944, no one knew what the situation was, but by March 19 it became clear — we woke that morning to the German occupation of Hungary. Kállay was gone; the new prime minister was Döme Sztójay, a well-known antisemite. Hitler had also heard the rumours about Hungary's secret negotiations with the Allies. Fearing that Hungary would declare neutrality or, worse, join the Allies, the Nazis had occupied the country. Regent Miklós Horthy, who came to power after World War I, remained in his position, but the Nazis effectively created a puppet government with Döme Sztójay as its leader.

At this time, approximately 825,000 people were categorized as Jewish in Hungary, with about one-fourth of them living in Budapest. Adolf Eichmann and his special unit arrived to handle the "Jewish problem" in the country.

When we went to school the morning of March 19, the principal sent for our teacher. When he returned, his face was ashen. He told us to gather our books and belongings, go home and never come to school again. It felt like a giant cloud had descended over the world, and I lost all sensation and feeling. I saw everything in deep grey. To this day, I remember that time only in grey or black. My sisters and I came home from school that day and then we sat in silence, just looking at each other for a while. Since I was the most pessimistic of the family and listened to most of the rumours about the Jews in Poland and Czechoslovakia, I started to speculate. The problem was that I speculated out loud. My mother stopped me promptly. We began to talk about how to keep in contact with our families in Békéscsaba and Pápa. Hungary had a well-organized postal system, and we wondered whether it would still be easy to send letters.

The new Hungarian government immediately executed a series of anti-Jewish orders. One of the laws was that every Jew had to wear a yellow star on their outer garments. We all scurried to find yellow material for the Star of David patches we had to wear. They had to be regulation size and worn in the right place. We heard the name of Adolf Eichmann again and remembered only too well hearing about him in Vienna and what his name meant.

We learned the names of the members of the newly created Jewish Council, which the Germans called the *Judenrat*. Its members consisted mostly of prominent wealthy Jews. The *Judenrat* was one of the Germans' most sinister deceptions. They established these councils to make it easier, much easier, for them to murder the Jews. The Jewish Council members believed that they could help protect Jews by doing the Nazis' bidding. This was not so. Without the help of the *Judenrat,* it would have been almost impossible for the Germans to organize a fluent way to disseminate orders or to collect names. Of course, these Jews thought that, in their position, they could save themselves and their families. Sometimes it worked and sometimes it did not. It worked in Budapest but it worked perfectly for the Germans elsewhere.

April 1944 was a terrifying month. We could see the terror on the faces of our Jewish neighbours. The fear certainly must have shown on my own face too. It went immediately to my stomach; I stopped eating. Communication to and from our relatives in the country stopped altogether. This was a very worrying sign.

By the beginning of May, the rumours were substantiated by people who had somehow managed to escape and make it to Budapest. The stories were just awful. We heard about the Hungarian gendarmes rounding up Jews in football fields or brick factories and transporting them to so-called labour camps in Poland. My mother worried frantically about her parents and siblings in Békéscsaba.

I was scared to go out on the street. When I saw a uniform, my stomach turned sour. My mother and I decided to change our appearance to a more modern look that would make us appear less obviously Jewish. I shaved off my side curls and started growing hair on my shaven head. My mother took off her *sheitl*, her wig. We had to wear a yellow star when we left our home. Penalties were very strict if a Jew was caught not wearing such a star. This usually consisted of a beating and then deportation. We did not know about Auschwitz. In our minds, the destination of the deportations was just an abyss.

Towards the end of May a new law was passed. László Endre, the State Secretary in the Ministry of the Interior, ordered all the Jews in the city to be concentrated into designated buildings that would be marked with a large yellow Star of David over the main entrance.

The building where we lived was designated as one of the all-Jewish buildings. All non-Jews living in our building had to leave. Two of our boarders were not Jewish and were sorry to go. We were sorry too, as they were nice people. We were fortunate to be able to stay in our own apartment.

There was an influx of Jews into our building, which was a truly sorrowful sight. These people had been dislocated all of a sudden; arguments and fights arose all over. They came poorly equipped for this ordeal, lacking what they needed most. In the hurry of moving, they left behind almost all their belongings. In all this chaos, personality differences between the dislocated Jews and the hosts they were forced upon could easily become a source of friction. The severe lack of food added to the terrible suffering.

In early June 1944, we received a letter from the Swiss Embassy in which we were notified that our father had arranged an entrance certificate to Palestine for us. We were stunned. We had no idea until then whether he had reached Palestine or not, as we'd had no way to communicate with him since he had left. He had managed to send us this certificate through the Swiss Red Cross.

We heard that Rudolf Kasztner, a lawyer originally from Kolozsvár (Cluj) and an opportunist, was negotiating with Eichmann, assembling a transport of Jews to Switzerland in exchange for money and gold. My mother went to see Kasztner and showed him our certificate. He promised to put us on the list for this transport.

My mother came home happy and hopeful. We had the full right to be on the train. We were exhilarated. Two weeks later, we heard that the train had left. Our seats had been sold to some high-paying individuals. We were heartbroken. My mother went to see someone who had stayed behind and all she got was a speech saying how only true Zionists got on that train. We knew plenty of non-Zionists who were on that train — very wealthy non-Zionists.

We couldn't do a thing with our entrance certificate to Palestine. There was no way out of Hungary.

One day, I had to go out on an errand and use the streetcar. At one of the stops, a police officer boarded the streetcar, came over to me and motioned for me to follow him. He took me to the police station and told me I would be deported the next day. I panicked. I tried to convince him to let me go. I said to him, "Look what a Hungarian patriot I am!" I showed him my Hungarian-style school cap and lied, telling him I was only twelve. I asked him, did he not have kids? He interrupted me once and said, "What difference does it make? Tomorrow all of you will be deported." I did not stop talking for at least half an hour. He finally looked at me and said, "Go to hell. I can't listen to you anymore."

I was lucky. Had he been a gendarme, he would have shut me up with a rifle butt. You have to count your blessings. My entire future was to depend on such lucky accidents.

My older sister, Jitti, was not so fortunate. She and a friend of hers came up with a very stupid idea. They decided to try to join the Slovak partisans, as Hungary did not have any partisans (not many Hungarians objected to the alliance with Germany). They boarded a train with false identity papers to Munkács of all places, which was close to the Slovak border. They were arrested almost immediately at the train station. Both of them were packed into a deportation train that was passing through on its way to Auschwitz-Birkenau.

The following week, a notice appeared in a daily newspaper in Budapest. The article said that two Jews had been arrested in Munkács with false identity papers. We knew right away that the article referred to Jitti and her friend. We knew the general direction of their travel. My mother decided to seek help from Adolf Eichmann. Of all people! She took the certificate we had received from our father via the Red Cross and went to see Eichmann. She could not get in to see him personally, but she managed to see Himmler's deputy, Kurt Becher. Kurt Becher was very polite and understanding and promised her that he would find out about Jitti. He said that if she were still in Hungary, he would free her. He told my mother to return the following day.

The next day my mother went back to see Kurt Becher, and he, pretending to feel great sorrow, told her that my sister was no longer in Hungary.

New hardships engulfed us. We were only permitted to leave the building for a few hours a day. Our food rations were halved. A period of hunger started that only became worse as time passed. The days stretched longer and longer as we sat at home with nothing to do but speculate about the future.

Friends of my older sister from the group she belonged to came to visit us and arranged false identities for us. It was encouraging to know that we had not been forgotten. In two weeks, we had our false papers. My Hungarian name was to be György Máli.

With great difficulty, we made it to October, when we heard that Regent Horthy was severing Hungary's alliance with the Germans and was negotiating a separate peace with the Soviets. The Jews were literally dancing with joy. My sister Litzi and I were devastated. We could not understand how people could not see the ramification of Horthy's move.

The next morning, the Germans forced Regent Horthy to appoint the Arrow Cross Party leader as the de facto prime minister of the new Nazi-puppet Hungarian state. His name was Ferenc Szálasi.

The Arrow Cross terror started immediately. Teenage boys and men with Arrow Cross armbands roamed the streets of Budapest looking for Jews. This was their only interest: to find Jews. It took only one with the courage to shoot a Jew; the rest followed wildly. They came into the yards of the Jewish buildings marked with a yellow star and shot into the apartments. Luckily, they were not given much ammunition — not because they wanted to save Jews, but simply because bullets were scarce. The terror escalated, and the streets were soon strewn with bodies of Jewish men, women and children. They were left where they fell.

The winter closed in quickly that year, so the bodies decomposed slowly. One day, I had a horrifying shock when I dared to go out for some food. A girl's body lay prone on a patch of grass. She was stark naked, her eyes open — she must have been about eighteen or twenty years old — with a small bullet hole under her left breast. People just rushed by, trying not to look at her. Nobody dared or thought to cover her. When I got home, I was sick. My mother asked me what was wrong, but I could not answer. I have not been able to talk about it until now. She must have been killed a very short time before I saw her, for she still had normal skin tone and her body must have still been warm. The sight has never left me.

The Allied bombings intensified, and dead bodies of non-Jews also started to accumulate on the streets.

The Szálasi government issued an order requiring all Jewish men and women above a certain age to report for labour camps. This led to the infamous death marches of late 1944. Thousands of mostly Jewish women (not many men were left in Hungary, as most were in the forced labour service already) under Hungarian guards were marched to the Austrian border and beyond. Very few survived this march. Anybody who faltered was shot without pity and left by the side of the road.

I was under the required age and did not have to report, but my mother and sister had to do so. I happened to be infected just then with a virulent flu and had a high fever. To be alone and very sick was the most frightening situation I could imagine, and it put me into a state of panic. I remember my mother starting to prepare for the march. She sewed warm clothing and organized what they needed to take. They were supposed to report the next day. Then my mother's uncle came over with instructions from her grandfather that under no circumstances should my mother and sister report for the march. To my greatest relief, they followed those instructions and did not.

Having heard that the Swiss and Swedish embassies issued so-called *Schutzpässe*, protective papers to Jews, my mother decided that as soon as I got better all three of us would go to the Swiss Embassy to ask for *Schutzpässe*, bringing along our Palestinian certificate from the Red Cross.

We made it to the Swiss Embassy and were told to go home and come back the next day to receive our passes. This was not to happen, since as we exited the embassy we were arrested by the Hungarian police and taken to the police station. We were then taken into separate rooms for interrogation.

A detective wanted to frame me, accusing me of discarding false identity papers on the floor in the corridor. Luckily, we had decided not to take our false identity papers with us, so I could be very indignant about the accusation.

All I remember is that they let us go. When we arrived home, our mother told us the strangest story about what had happened to her. The chief detective who interrogated my mother had asked to see her passport. In her passport there were Swiss visitor visas from much earlier, when my parents had agreed to take a young Jewish boy to Switzerland in exchange for a fee, as they had been desperate for money. The detective looked at my mother, who was very beautiful, and exclaimed loudly so that the other detective would hear, "But you are a Swiss citizen!" and gave the order to let us go.

We were afraid to return to the Swiss Embassy.

As the carnage continued, we grew desperate. Szálasi ordered a wall built around the Jewish neighbourhood to confine the remaining Budapest Jews in a ghetto. The ghetto wall was coming up fast and we did not want to be stuck within it. Our building was only three buildings away from the edge of the ghetto, so we could see the wall's construction advancing.

We heard that my aunt Lili had managed to get into a Swiss safe house with her two sons. Both the Swiss consul and Swedish consul had declared certain buildings in Budapest as foreign diplomatic territory and permitted Jewish women and children into these buildings as their citizens. A decision had to be made. The wall was fast nearing completion and any movement in or out of the ghetto would soon be impossible. One night, during a British air raid, and just about a day or two before the sealing off of the ghetto, my mother, Litzi and I made our move. We removed our yellow stars, rubbed off any signs remaining from them and left our apartment, not taking any bags with us or saying a word to anyone.

We headed to the outskirts of Budapest, to an area called O T I Telep, which had been built by the National Institute for Social Security and consisted of small, detached houses mostly inhabited by working-class people. We went by foot and it was a long way. Watching the British bombs falling and knowing that most people were hiding in shelters, we rushed. With nothing but our new identity papers in our pockets, we wanted to reach a friend of my older sister's, a Christian woman who had a home in the area.

When she saw us arrive, she was literally shaking since she was afraid of being arrested for her leftist views. The next morning she had an idea. She approached an elderly neighbour, Mr. Murin, who was living alone in a small building down the road. She asked him if he could house us poor refugees from the south of Hungary. She told him that we were escaping from the Soviet advance and had come to Budapest. Mr. Murin took us in; whether he believed our story or not, we will never know.

The condition in the streets and the city was horrendous. The Red Army was at the outskirts of the city; they pounded Budapest with what sounded like ten thousand artillery pieces. The most terrifying of these were the Katyushas. Rockets fired six at a time with different noises and colours. Fighter-bombers were constantly in the air strafing anything that moved. The lack of food made us totally desperate. We had to go out and brave the artillery, brave the strafing of the fighter-bombers, but mostly brave the horrible and deadly Arrow Cross bands. They were solely interested in catching Jews and murdering them. They would murder Jews on the spot or take them to the Danube, make them take off their shoes, shoot them and dump them into the river. Sometimes, to save ammunition, they would line up two Jews, one behind the other, and shoot them both with a single bullet.

Scouring for food was especially dangerous for me, for no gentile Hungarian male was circumcised. To find out if a boy was Jewish, all that was necessary was to pull down his pants and look. I was in extreme danger several times; if anyone looked at me for longer than a few seconds I knew I was under suspicion and that I had to act. I found that the best way to de-escalate the situation was to approach the individual and engage him or her in a discussion using street language. The tactic usually worked provided I kept calm — which took some effort, for on the inside I was shaking from fright.

Finding food was a matter of chance. A lucky find was a horse that had been hit by shrapnel or bullets. A crowd would form around the carcass and fight to chop off pieces of meat with kitchen knives. Once we heard that dried peas could be found in a railway car nearby. My sister and I hurried to the place and indeed managed to grab a sack of peas. We carried that sack between us, bombs falling all around us, but it was a find of enormous value. The problem was that it became too heavy for us in our weakened condition. To our great sorrow, we had to dump half the sack's contents before we got home. My mother tried to cook the peas and after a few hours of cooking, they were still as hard as pebbles. She finally ground them and made patties.

When we were very hungry, we would go to bed at four in the afternoon and start talking about food. The best conversations were always the ones about potatoes with onions — that was our favourite dream.

Then one morning in the first week of January 1945, I woke up and went to the front door, opened it, and right in front of our door there was an artillery piece pointing toward downtown Budapest, operated by three Soviet soldiers. We were free.

I ran inside, shouting, "The Soviets are here!"

I heard Mr. Murin mumble to himself, "Now Hungary is lost."

After liberation, Mr. Murin declared that he had always known we were Jews. Whether that was really the case or not, we owed him an enormous debt of gratitude and we expressed it in later years by helping him financially.

Litzi and I decided to go back to investigate our apartment. We retraced our steps in an entirely different mood from the one we were in during the fateful night of our escape. The walk seemed endless, even more so than on that night. Weak as we were, we went with lots of anticipation. In the distance, artillery fire and bombing sounded constantly, for the Germans were still fighting in Buda, the western part of Budapest on the other side of the Danube.

What we found in our apartment made us sick. In our absence, the people in our building had used our apartment as a morgue. Our apartment was full of bodies in a terrible state, mostly elderly adults, children and babies. All of the bodies were emaciated from sickness or hunger. The Soviet authorities ordered the burial of all bodies within forty-eight hours. They decreed heavy penalties if it was not done in the allotted time. It was January, the ground was frozen, my sister and I were weak and we had to clear our apartment of bodies. The terrible thing was that they had to be carried down the circular stairway, and many times the bodies would slide onto my neck. The bodies were collected and carried by handcarts to a nearby garden, where we had to help bury them.

Somehow, we eventually established ourselves back in our apartment. The war still raged on for another month until the Soviets took Buda.

# My Escape to and from Hungary
## Victor David

At the beginning of the German occupation, I was afraid that the new regime would go after the Polish refugees, and for two weeks, I did not sleep at home. My friend Mrs. Bobo Szensky allowed me to sleep in her store, where I was locked in. During this time, I ran into an acquaintance from my high school who told me that he had come from Budapest to look for a guide to cross the border to Romania, where Jews were still living freely. I asked my friend Willy Lengyel if he could help me find a guide, and two days later, he found one. My friend had by then returned to Budapest. In the meantime, small groups of Hungarian youngsters belonging to Zionist organizations were coming to Nagyvárad and escaping to Romania.

A few weeks later, I was woken by the police in the early morning hours and taken to their head office. There, I found other Polish refugees. After a short interview and visual inspection of my penis, to see if I was circumcised, I was arrested and taken to the basement. In the cell, there were some twelve other prisoners, all sleeping on one big bunk. The food was awful.

My neighbour, a Hungarian gentile named Elek Kovács, who was the secretary of the Communist Party, became very friendly with me thanks to my knowledge of the Hungarian language. Every day, his wife would bring him food, and I noticed that he was getting letters from her too, hidden in the thermos bottle, and was sending her back notes the same way.

I asked him if I could send a letter to my friend, and he readily agreed. I sent a letter to Mrs. Szensky telling her what had happened to me, and I received a letter from her a few days later. She was very sympathetic to my fate, but unfortunately, she couldn't visit me because all the Jews had been restricted to a ghetto. But Vilma, who worked for her in the store, was able to come and visit me. I had managed to smuggle in all the money I had with me, so I surreptitiously gave her most of the money I had and she arranged for my meals to be sent to me from a restaurant.

Some three weeks later, we were taken to a railway station and sent to Budapest. I told my friend Kovács that my intention was to escape, that I would not allow them to send me back to Poland. Should I need any help, he had a brother-in-law in Budapest, he said, and gave me his address; if I returned to Nagyvárad, his wife would be ready to help me.

In Budapest, after about two weeks in the prison on Mosonyi Street, we were put on a passenger train toward the Austrian border. The prisoners were eight to a compartment, and with the police in the corridors we occupied a whole car. We were not allowed to open the windows, and when visiting the toilet, we had to leave the door open so that the police officer could watch us. Next to me sat Romek, a Polish boy my age, and next to him was a fairly good-looking girl from Yugoslavia. We told her that we intended to escape and asked her to go into the corridor and flirt with the police officer to distract him, which she did.

The train was going quite fast. On the side where the window was located, there was a second pair of railroad tracks, so we would have to jump quite far to land on the ground. My companion opened the window and jumped first, but when I sat on the window ledge and tried to push my foot away from the train, I broke the windowpane and my body slipped to the ground. I lost consciousness from the impact. Fortunately, my companion followed the direction the train was going, found me and dragged me over to the side, into a wheat field. I was very badly shaken from the fall, had trouble breathing, chipped my tooth, and my posterior hurt me very badly. I spent an entire day hiding in the field, trying to recover. Towards evening we walked away from the tracks. I could hardly walk but luckily, we soon found a suburban train station.

I was able to buy train tickets to Budapest. While I was waiting for the train to arrive, I fainted again but luckily for only a short time. We arrived in Budapest after midnight, and Romek decided to go back to the town he had lived in, where he had a gentile Hungarian girlfriend. I waited until the morning and then went to the address given to me by Kovács. I was received with sympathy, given a room to rest and some food, and I remained there for twenty-four hours. Then I went to a Jewish hospital for a checkup. I was told that I might have broken two ribs, but that was all.

I wrote to Vilma to send money to Budapest, giving her the address of Kovács' brother-in-law. A few days later I received the requested amount. I spent my time in Budapest trying to recuperate by hiding in the movie theatres and swimming pools. About three weeks later, I felt well enough to try to escape to Romania. One day, I met a Jewish acquaintance from Nagyvárad on the street. I told him that I intended to go to Romania and he told me to come the next morning to a certain synagogue, where I would receive money for the trip. The next day I received one thousand pengős.

Another Polish refugee, hearing that I was planning to escape to Romania, decided to join me and we took the afternoon train to Nagyvárad. We separated on the train — he stayed in one car and I in another. I also noticed a group of youngsters whom I recognized as Jewish trying to escape to Romania. A few hours later, two detectives came in with my companion and he pointed me out to them. They took us to a sleeper car without looking at our documents, but told us to take our slacks down. Again, being circumcised was enough to condemn us.

We were dropped off at the next railway station, and the detectives handed us over to the police officer who was in charge of the railway security system. I tried to convince the police officer that Poles and Hungarians had been friends for centuries and that my problem was caused by the German occupation of Hungary. After a long conversation with the police officer, during which my companion disappeared, the officer let me go. I boarded the next train to Nagyvárad.

I went to the house of Elek Kovács and introduced myself to his wife, who already knew everything about me. She got in touch with Vilma, who came to see me and brought me the remaining money that I had left with her. I told them about crossing over to Romania and asked Vilma to get me a good pair of walking shoes and to contact Willy's father, who had contacts with smugglers. Willy, his sister and his mother had been taken away alongside all the other Jews to Auschwitz, but the father, who was a Hungarian gentile, had been left behind. Willy's father took me to his house, where I remained in hiding for a few days, until he got in touch with the smugglers and established a date for crossing the border to Romania. He hired a horse-drawn carriage to take us to the village of the smugglers, which was located some five kilometres from Nagyvárad.

There I found an elderly Jewish woman with two grown daughters who came from Budapest; they were also trying to escape to Romania. We crossed the border during the night and met with a prearranged horse-drawn wagon carriage that was full of hay we could hide in. They took us quite a distance to a railway station, where the guide bought us tickets and put us on the train to Arad, the closest city where the local Zionist organization would take care of us.

In the middle of the trip a group of police officers came on board to verify documents; we were arrested and taken off the train in a small town called Belényes (Beiuş in Romanian). Some fifteen Jewish refugees were caught and transferred to the police station. When the Jewish residents heard about us, a group of them came to the police station; they spoke to the commandant, offering to take care of us in their homes until our departure, and they guaranteed that we would not escape. Having received a considerable bribe, the commandant released us to the Jewish residents, who distributed us into several private homes. Having saved us from the horrors of imprisonment, our hosts then told us that we should not be afraid or worried, that we would be interned in a camp called Târgu Jiu, a village in central Romania, where we would remain until the end of the war. The Soviets were nearing the Romanian border and had already liberated parts of eastern Poland.

# The Sorrows of Liberation

# Foreword

Strangers hugging each other, shedding tears of joy: these are the images commonly associated with the moment of liberation. However, as Dan Stone argues in *The Liberation of the Camps*, liberation is better understood not just as a joyous moment but also as a fraught process with many complications and numerous further personal tragedies.[1]

With the conclusive defeat of the Axis powers by May 1945, there remained two notable groups of Jewish survivors from Hungary: those liberated from Nazi camps (or at the end of death marches leading out of them) and those who survived the last stages of the war in Hungary — in the ghetto or in hiding, surviving the murderous violence of the Arrow Cross and the Soviet siege of Budapest. Upon their liberation, members of these two groups had comparably difficult but slightly different challenges ahead.

Badly undernourished and often suffering from multiple illnesses, survivors had to first regain their physical strength. After extended physical torments, many of them proved unable to do so and passed away upon their "liberation." If they survived this first phase of recovery, their earliest thoughts were usually directed towards aiming to find their relatives, many of whom were no longer alive, and the few

---

1  Dan Stone, *The Liberation of the Camps: The End of the Holocaust and its Aftermath* (New Haven: Yale University Press, 2015).

who had survived often proved difficult to reconnect with. Survivors often felt shattered when they realized the full scale and systematic nature of the Nazi murder campaign and their own irreparable personal losses, which tended to largely overshadow their experiences of liberation.

Those who were liberated abroad, mostly from Nazi camps, had to decide whether to return to Hungary (and their previous places of residence may not even have belonged to Hungary in the postwar era, since the territorial enlargements of the country achieved between 1938 and 1941 were annulled with the defeat of the Axis) or look for possibilities to emigrate more permanently to the West or Palestine/Israel. If they intended to return after their deportation, survivors could typically count on little to no help from the supposedly new and democratic Hungarian authorities.

Those who managed to make it back to Hungary had to re-establish their existence there: get registered, undergo examinations and often also medical treatment, reacquire or acquire new accommodation (often the latter, since the former proved unfeasible due to resistance by those who had benefitted from the anti-Jewish persecution and were taking up residence in their homes), find a stable source of income, and maintain a daily routine. They had to try to reintegrate into a society whose political representatives had expelled them just the year before with the clear intention of having them murdered and with rather limited opposition expressed against this by members of gentile society. A slight majority of survivors from Hungary probably initially chose to reintegrate (due to the complex history of border changes and the lack of a central database, it is impossible to offer exact figures here). The benefits of such a choice could be substantial, but the personal and psychological costs were never negligible and were often long-lasting.

As mentioned, those tens of thousands of the "racially persecuted" who were liberated in Budapest had many similar problems to confront, but they also tended to have somewhat different considerations. They had just suffered deep traumas in the very place where they were meant to continue their lives. Key parts of the city and often precisely those most closely associated with Jewish life and the Jewish religion became indelibly associated with their persecution — their very own streets and houses had often been the setting of immense tragedies. Survivors in the capital might also have encountered their tormentors in a neighbourhood cafeteria, on the tram or at the post office.

Despite such frightening possibilities, the largely anonymous environment of the only Hungarian metropolis allowed survivors to begin new lives without necessarily being constantly reminded of the worst horrors in ways that smaller localities could not. Alongside different levels of integration prior to the war, this helps explain why the already heavily Budapest-based community of survivors tended to stay in greater proportions than their counterparts from the rest of the country, making post-war Hungarian Jewry a predominantly metropolitan entity.

Regaining basic rights as citizens might have appeared to be a self-evident matter after the defeat of fascism, but even partial compensation for the most egregious injustices often proved out of reach for Hungarian Jews after the war. Restitution policies in Hungary were generally insufficient. The political and broadly cultural recognition of the devastating experiences of Holocaust survivors was inconsistent and at best half-hearted, especially when it came to the acknowledgement of the substantial share of Hungarian responsibility. The imposition of a Stalinist dictatorship crushed within a few years the promising signs of a national renewal and the hopes regarding the development of a free and democratic society (the country, after all, conducted its first-ever general elections in 1945, and the communists were still far from fully dominant at the time). Human rights and private property would continue to be violated on a mass scale with the full support of the Hungarian state apparatus, and Holocaust survivors, if anything, were disproportionately affected.

Many survivors who decided to attempt to restart their lives in Hungary upon liberation therefore chose to leave in subsequent years. Some of them inevitably proved more fortunate than others in their post-war pursuits; however, irrespective of whether they decided to live in the newly founded State of Israel or emigrate to the West, these émigrés could later count on greater societal openness and sensitivity towards their wartime experiences than what was experienced by the survivors who stayed in Hungary or its neighbouring Eastern bloc countries. The centres where the Holocaust in Hungary has been remembered thus migrated with them.

All of these complications make memoirs of Jewish survivors from Hungary composed in the West — and all of the survivors in this anthology eventually immigrated to Canada — uniquely valuable, especially concerning the fraught process of liberation. These memoirs tell the stories of their authors' liberation by the Soviets without ideology, which would have been very difficult to do in post-war Hungary. The stories here highlight both the hopes and new sorrows the end of the Nazi genocide brought. The authors recall the often downright brutal treatment they received by members of the Red Army, their nominal liberators, including acts of gendered violence (another taboo topic in post-war Hungary), and the often insensitive or even malevolent approach to their recent past by other members of Hungarian society and the emerging communist establishment. They paint a complex and nuanced picture of liberation.

# Rowing on Ice
## Kathleen (Kati) Horváth

Before the end of 1944 we had to leave our safe haven at the Jó Pásztor cloister. The Siege of Budapest was in full force, and German soldiers were helping the Hungarian army to senselessly defend Budapest from the advancing Soviet army.

One day a Soviet soldier was shot dead in the back as he knelt in front of the altar and crossed himself. The nuns were shocked and outraged, and the chapel had to be resanctified. A few days later, a young boy who was maybe thirteen entered our bunker asking if there were any Soviets here. The musket he carried was taller than he was, there was no sign of facial hair on him and he wore a grown man's jacket as an overcoat. The nuns felt sorry for him; we took his musket, and the nuns gave him some civilian clothes and told him to find his way home.

This was a serious warning sign to me: the cloister was now "no man's land," and it was time to leave Budapest, possibly move back to Túrkeve, where there would be no more German soldiers and their rules wouldn't determine our fate. Túrkeve was close to the Romanian border and, according to the news we'd gathered through the grapevine, had already come under Soviet occupation. My assumption was that some sort of an order would be in place there for civilians.

I told my mother we had to leave. We had found out from the boy soldier that the Soviets were at the northern tip of the nun's property, just a short walking distance away. When I told the nuns that we were leaving to join the Soviet-occupied part of Hungary, they were leery to join us because of the stories of rape and other atrocities that preceded the advancing Soviet army. However, some six or eight of them joined us the next afternoon.

There were several inches of freshly accumulated snow on the ground. The building in the back, which the soldier boy told us was the Soviet front line, was less than two hundred metres from the cloister. The nuns dressed in white started the trek and we followed in a single row, their footsteps creating our path. The whole trip did not last more than fifteen minutes or so, but it must have been highly visible for both sides (the German and the Soviets) when nuns dressed in black were moving on the freshly snow-covered ground.

Soon shots came from the German side, and two nuns were shot dead and another was wounded. I had my son bound in a warm blanket over my chest and belly, ready to fall to protect him. I started to panic when big red spots began to accumulate in the snow under us, and I ran towards the building where the Soviets were supposed to be to get help for my bleeding son. As soon as I arrived, I started screaming for help; to my relief I found out that he was unharmed. It was a finger on my left hand that was grazed by a bullet, most likely from the German side.

The Soviet soldiers were extremely helpful, courteous and friendly. They even procured milk for my son! We had not seen milk in more than a year, and they gave us directions so we would have a good chance to get behind the front lines and cross the Danube River as safely as possible. The conversation consisted of sketchy phrases of Yiddish, Latin, French and German, but mostly just hand signals. We spent the night there on the floor. I was leading a group of four nuns, my mother, my son and two seventeen-year-old delinquent girls. I had to figure out a way to cross the Danube and find our way to get close to the Romanian border, an area that had by then been occupied by the Soviet army.

I can't remember the name of the rowing club we broke into to get a skiff to cross the Danube. But I do remember that it took forty-eight hours to remove a safely secured skiff from the storage space above that had four rolling seats and was fitted with a sufficient number of oars. The clubhouse did not have any food reserves except tomato juice. We lived on that for those two days. I can still feel the burst of acids in my stomach from the tomatoes, which had been kept in plain aluminum containers.

Next, we pushed the skiffs out into the partially frozen Danube, which was breaking up with great blocks of drifting ice. It was an incredibly dangerous situation, but the fact that there was no other way gave us courage to try. We didn't even consider the potential consequences; we just saw it as a way to escape. It did not take too long to cross the Danube. I pushed the blocks of ice with the oars and my own hands to get to the other side. We started in daylight, and it was dusk when we landed on the other side. There was a Soviet patrol waiting on the Pest side. No one took a shot at us, even though we were in plain sight. This too was a miracle, which I didn't even realize at the time.

A Soviet officer demanded my watch, and I gave it to him, then asked him for shelter for the night. If I remember correctly, he let us sleep in an army vehicle. We then hitchhiked on Soviet army vehicles from village to village till the city of Szolnok. Sometimes, when we could not find a Soviet army convoy to give us a lift, we walked on the highway, which was covered with snow up to our knees. While the nuns were part of our group, we slept in parishes. After they found homes with relatives and friends, and only my mother, my son and I remained on the road, we tried to find accommodations for the night wherever we saw light in someone's window. My mom had packed schmaltz (goose fat) before we left the nunnery in a jar for basic sustenance, as well as a bottle of rum for disinfection.

My son had caught whooping cough, and my mother and I carried him on our backs, alternating the load with our goods. Whenever we could hitchhike, I explained to the driver that I had syphilis to avoid being raped, which would have been the usual price for taking a ride with a front soldier. It worked.

In Szolnok I befriended a Soviet soldier, who ordered a couple out from their bedroom to let me sleep in their bed. I had not slept in a bed for a long time and had been walking along the cold January highway with my son on my back for over two weeks by then. Ádám was coughing badly. This nameless soldier went to the army doctor and described Ádám's cough to him and brought back a full bottle of cough medicine. My guess today (sixty-six years later) is that I got all this help from the Soviets because I always started my request by pointing to myself and saying "Yid." They must have seen the atrocities the Germans committed in the Soviet Union and felt pity for me. From Szolnok, we got a freight car to Mezőtúr and then hitchhiked on a horse-pulled hay cart for the last sixteen kilometres to Túrkeve.

It was difficult to get back to normalcy. Other citizens looked at us like we were from outer space. Only a single Jew returned from Auschwitz at first, and he was distraught at not finding anyone who had come back from his family. He waited for one whole week for someone to return. When no one did, he hanged himself. Two days later, his wife and daughter arrived looking for him. It was indescribable, and even the otherwise hostile local population deemed it to be tragic.

But the general population of Túrkeve was not happy and did not welcome the few returning Jews — to say the least. The return of Jews meant to them that they had to give back the stolen goods which, after using them for a year, they considered rightfully theirs.

The occupying Soviet forces treated the village population, well-to-do peasants, as their servants. They raped the young girls, imposed a curfew on the village and limited everyone's freedom in many ways. The villagers saw the very few returning Jews as an extra burden. They treated these Jews the way they had learned to treat them from the Germans and were unhappy to be forced by the Soviets to return stolen goods. There was a warehouse where goods from the Jewish homes were collected, and only their rightful owners could reclaim them. However, if no one made a claim to a certain item, returning Jews were allowed to "borrow" them until the rightful owner hopefully returned too.

Though we were not welcomed, no one bothered us. It was a standoff with the general population, but as far as Soviet military control was concerned, I had as much freedom as everyone else. We could only drive with written permission from the occupying forces and never after dusk. But that felt like total freedom after what we had been through.

In the late fall, we sold the house in Túrkeve and moved back to Budapest. Our old apartment downtown at 5 Wekerle Sándor Street had been taken over by strangers who were unwilling to move out and give us back our home. When we applied to the authorities, we were told that even though it was our apartment, and the couple occupying it had moved in illegally without our consent, the new Communist regime would not put anyone out onto the street. As the present government had no free apartments at its disposal to house the occupying couple, we were made personally responsible for finding another suitable location for them.

We were learning that the only change in regime was in the colour — it was not the yellow star or the black arrow cross anymore, but the red flag with the star and the sickle was no better! Our rights continued to be denied.

# To Start off as a Christian but to Arrive as a Jew
## Eva Kahan

One morning we finally saw the first Soviet soldiers. We were relieved and happy to reach the day we had been waiting for so long. Unfortunately, these soldiers turned out to be a great disappointment. They were wild, unreliable and cruel. I was just as afraid of them as I had been of the Germans. Of course, we understood that they were fighting for their survival and hated all Hungarians (Jewish or not). After being on the front lines for years, they suffered and saw so much that they forgot how to be human. Stealing, raping, killing meant nothing to them. The war was still far from over. We lived in the northern part of Pest, and the Germans were still holding on downtown, where the ghetto was located.

One day Lajos and I decided that we would try to get to Óbuda to see what had happened to our house; maybe we would hear something about my father too. For this we had to cross the Danube. We started to walk northward towards a bridge that we heard was still in one piece, but it was open only for military traffic. The river was frozen solid and we found a way to walk across.

It was afternoon when we arrived at the house. It was empty and deserted. The gate was open, the windows all broken or missing, the floor covered with dirt. In one room, however, I found a bunch of family photos on the floor, which I picked up and saved.

On the way back it was already dark when we arrived at the bridge. This time we asked the Soviet soldiers to take us over on their truck. Don't ask how we communicated with them, but we made ourselves understood. Anyway, as we crossed and reached the Pest side, we suddenly found ourselves in the middle of a battle. Enemy planes flew low, firing machine guns. The soldiers jumped off and were hiding under the truck. We got off also and lay on the ground, holding on to each other. Around us in a semi-circle the air-defense artillery cannons were firing at the planes. Never in our lives had we been in such a dangerous situation. The whole attack was so sudden and it didn't last as long as it appeared to us at the time. When I think back now, I can't understand why we took such chances — how come we had the courage to go on an excursion like that, when people hardly dared to go out from the shelters? One had to be young and foolishly optimistic.

Soon, after we heard that the Soviets had liberated the ghetto, we went to see my grandfather. He was okay because he was with his sons and their families all along. I heard from him that my father was in the ghetto in the house of the Jewish Council. We were surprised. Why would he be in the ghetto when he had false documents? Well, we immediately went there and found him sick, lying on a wooden bench. We wanted to take him with us but he was too weak to walk. We promised to be back for him. The next day we borrowed a sled and took a bagful of food with us and went back to the ghetto. I will never forget the children on the street begging for food; as we gave some to one or two of them, a whole bunch kept on following us. Also engraved in my memory of the ghetto is the heap of corpses in a yard, bodies of mostly old people and children in their underwear, on top of each other.

We pulled Father to our house on the sled and gave him a bed in the laundry room next to my in-laws. He was sicker than I had realized. He couldn't eat at all and had constant diarrhea. He slowly told us what had happened to him. When the Arrow Cross came to power, they broke into our house. He tried to escape by jumping from the terrace to a friendly neighbour's garden and through his gate to another street. He didn't get far: someone called a German soldier's attention to him, saying that he was a Jew without the star. (This was a neighbour of ours, who had to serve a jail sentence after the war.) My father was captured and taken to forced labour — gathering corpses from the streets and battlefields. One day he had an opportunity to escape and came back to Budapest.

I didn't mention before that my mother's family owned an apartment house, with around eighty dwellings in it. My father was managing that house before the war. The janitor came to us every month, to give accounts of the rents, bills and problems. He was a nice, decent man who owned a grocery store in the house. My father, not knowing where I was, had no place to go. He decided to go to the janitor, who hid him in an empty apartment and brought food for him every day. He was there for weeks, until for some reason the janitor got afraid, or ran out of food, and told him to leave. He had no choice other than the ghetto, which was more than full by that time. There was no place for him, just the office of the Jewish Council without a bed and with little more than a bench. His greatest problem was food. One plate of soup a day was all he would get from the community kitchen, no more. He quickly lost weight and all his energy was gone. When the Red Army liberated the ghetto, the Jews could leave, but he stayed on.

I tried to give him different foods — whatever was available — but he didn't want to eat. If he did try, it went right through him. He was thin like a child. Lajos brought a doctor, but he couldn't help him. He would need baby formula, milk maybe, which was non-existent in Budapest. The war wasn't finished yet and there were no open stores, no transportation, no hospitals in operation. The city was in ruins.

About two weeks after we brought him to us, he died of starvation. Lajos buried him in a nearby field, wrapped in a sheet. At his grave there was only a wooden marker with his name on it. Several months later the city collected such corpses and buried them in a common grave in the cemetery.

The Jewish owners of our apartment came back and we gave them back their home. We were still living in the shelter anyway. I still didn't want to reveal my identity to the people in the house and tell them we were Jews. Somehow I was ashamed that we had lied and deceived them all along. Basically I am an honest person, and it was always hard for me to lie and pretend to be someone I am not.

# My Surprising Escapes
# Benedikt Korda (Kornreich)

By this time, our German supervisors and the German army had more urgent concerns than to care whether we reported to work or not. They didn't need us any more. Our Hungarian guards were preoccupied with saving their own skins. They were soldiers of a defeated army. Most of them were not bad guys, just ordinary folks who wouldn't hurt us. We moved about freely in Baia Mare (Nagybánya in Hungarian) and made some acquaintances. Some people immediately left for home. It was a questionable decision. Some succeeded and some had problems — they were hunted by members of the Arrow Cross.

The main problem for me was distance. Munkács was not too far, about 140 kilometres away, but given the circumstances, hitch-hiking wasn't an option. We also had to eat and sleep along the way. So why not take a train? One had just moved slowly into the station. We jumped on it and were ready to go. It was evening and already cool. "Boy, shut that window there," someone on the train said. I closed it, but it didn't help, as the glass was missing from the window. We started playing cards, since the bloody train wouldn't move. A conductor arrived. "When are we going to move?" He looked at his watch: "Well, I am not sure. Maybe in two, maybe in three months." The point was that the Germans had already planned their retreat from Baia Mare and started blasting the rails at different points. This train was not going anywhere. Perhaps at some point further west we could still have caught a train. But why rush? One would have had to move on German-occupied territory. True, the German military didn't pose any danger at that time; they had other problems to cope with. But what about the Arrow Cross goons? They did their best, indeed, to hunt down Jews.

We all longed for home. But where was our home? I frequently pondered this question. I realized that nobody would be waiting for me in Munkács. Who knew whether I would be allowed to enter my own house? About the whereabouts of my wife, Bozenka, I had only guesses. The Soviets were already knocking on the door. It was a question of a day or two, we thought, before the Soviets conquered Baia Mare, so why not wait there? That's what the majority of us did. What we did not realize was that danger was lurking not only from the Nazis and Nazi sympathizers, but from the opposite side too. The embrace of the Soviet bear turned out to be very dangerous too and in some cases even fatal.

We were not alone with our preparations for the final move. After we had departed from him, commandant Gyenge was busy too. But he wanted to play it safe and to make it safe for us as well. His first concern was to get rid of the frame, our guards. There were various characters among them, some of them big "patriots" who could denounce us and others who could put us in danger by their sheer stupidity. Old Gyenge knew his folks very well. He was apparently a good psychologist. He summoned first the two worst ones. Looking at their papers, he said, "Hmm, you haven't had a furlough, let me see, that's more than a year. Well, I could grant you four weeks." You can imagine the reaction of the two guys. What a miracle, to be out of the danger zone in the last minutes.

They thanked him, grabbed their papers and ran as fast as they could. No sooner did they leave than others arrived begging, "Lieutenant, I hadn't had a furlough for almost two years." "Lieutenant, my wife is expecting." He played it like a comedy with them. At first, he was quite benevolent and made exceptions. Then he pretended to be hesitant and even rude while still granting furloughs. To the last ones he curtly said that there was no way he could give more furloughs or he would be court-martialled. Then he took pity on them: "You know what, you can go on your own. I'll turn a blind eye to it. If somebody catches you, just say that in the chaos you lost contact with your unit." It took him less than an hour to get rid of the whole bunch. He then went to one of his new acquaintances to get rid of his uniform, to change into civilian clothes.

The air was clear for action and it was high time to make a move. Since for all practical purposes our labour battalion no longer exist-ed, we stopped wearing armbands or any other symbol of the labour service. We were on our own. I had a very close friendship with Ernő, the barber, Dezső, the tailor, and István, a druggist apprentice. With the first two I shared our common leftist religion, and István I some-how adopted. He was a young, muscular fellow who was very scared. He needed somebody to reassure him.

We got accommodation in the house of a Romanian Orthodox priest. It was a big house, and our room was nice. It was Ernő's acquisi-tion, and I still don't know how he talked it over with the priest. None of us four spoke Romanian, and the priest knew only Romanian and some French. But he was a nice guy and I guess that, in those tumul-tuous hours, he was glad to have four additional men in the house.

The arrival of the Soviets in Baia Mare was imminent, according to our reliable sources of information: German officers. Without any clothing or anything else making us look different from other civil-ians, we had the chutzpah to accost officers, have chats with them and ask about the situation. They thought we were local Germans (how else could we have spoken fluent German?) and they were quite frank with us: "We are packed and ready to go." It was news we were happy to hear. But we were cautious, because we did not know what these changes would bring. We played it cool and put on sad faces.

We got an unexpected visitor. Gyenge, in civilian clothes now,

appeared at our veranda where we were enjoying the fine, late afternoon sunshine. It was the same day he got rid of his brave soldiers. He
looked around at our living space. "Boys, you do have a good place.
How did you find it? It's only the four of you here?" How did he find
us? After all, we hadn't told anybody where we were staying. In situations like this it is better to stay in small groups. Did he drop in here
just by chance? No, as it turned out.

"Benő, I would like to talk to you."

"Sure, why not. Let's sit down out there." I pointed to the two
wicker chairs in the backyard.

"Benő, what I am going to tell you is strictly confidential. I never
talked about this even with members of my own family." He paused.
I reassured him, of course, and was quite curious what his secret was
going to be. "You probably noticed that I am not a Vitéz," he said,
referring to the Hungarian Order of Vitéz,[1] of which many government and military employees were members, "in spite of the fact that
I distinguished myself in World War I, as you could have seen from
the collection of medals on my uniform."

"Yes, we noticed and we discussed it, but didn't have a clue."

He looked at me inquisitively for a while, then started his shocking story: "I was born Schlesinger, a Jew. My parents converted when
I was in elementary school. To apply for a Vitéz membership I would
have had to produce personal documents, including my birth certificate, which I didn't want to do. I hope you understand why. So I

---

1  This Hungarian order of merit was in existence from 1920 to 1944. Members of
the Hungarian military were admitted into the order based on the medals they
earned. Membership came with many benefits, including land or a house, along
with an official title. During World War II, many government and military officials were members of the order, with members both supporting and opposing
the Nazis. After the coup in Hungary on October 15, 1944, the order was suspend-
ed, ostensibly to demonstrate that the order would not support the Arrow Cross
Party installed by the Nazis.

procrastinated. I had a good excuse for that procrastination. I was born near Kolozsvár (Cluj) in Transylvania, which after World War I was annexed by Romania, and as you know, Hungary and Romania had been on a war footing during the whole interwar period. So I kept insisting that I had not been able to get my birth certificate from Romania. Now, why am I telling you all this? I'd like some advice from you. I consider you a reasonable man and," he added with a sly smile, "I am old and experienced enough to know that you are not a Christian. I am sure that European Jewry will recover from this nightmare and will become influential again. What do you think, should I bring into the open my Jewish origins?"

Now, that was not only a bombshell, it was also a tall order for me to answer such a question. Though he was an old fox, I had no reason not to believe his story. But what advice could I give him? First, I was not so confident about the recovery of European Jewry, as he put it. More exactly, I had seen too much and knew too much and was quite despondent about the future. More importantly, how could I know what implications such a step might possibly have on an old man and his family. What kind of advice could I give him? I told him that as long as he felt some attachment to Judaism, it was fine to go public. Otherwise, I told him that I was not sure that it was ever going to be good for Jews in Europe. We shook hands and he left. Twenty years later, I heard that Gyenge died of starvation soon after the war.

~

When the Soviets arrived, they questioned us. I told them, of course, our story and, in order to gain their confidence, we added that we were communists. We shouldn't have said that. The fact that we spoke Russian was enough to arouse their suspicion. We were suspect, indeed, and they were prepared to dispatch us to a POW camp. Many of our comrades were indeed taken prisoner by their "liberators," a tragic and horrible irony. Allegedly, it was my answer to their last question that saved the situation. The question was, if everything I said were true, would I join the army to fight the Nazis? I answered without hesitation. "I would be happy to, just give me a rifle and show me how to use it. Though I have no military training, I'm a good learner."

For better or worse, we stayed with the Soviets as interpreters. For them it was a bargain, as they urgently needed somebody who knew Hungarian. Formally we were in limbo; we weren't on their payroll, we worked simply for basic sustenance. But who cared? A new chapter in my life opened. My "career" in the Royal Hungarian Army, which had sometimes seemed almost endlessly protracted and unbearable, came to a definite end. It was soon buried in my memory.

Now, in retrospect, as memories come back again, I feel I was quite lucky. After all, I spent only slightly more than a year and a half in that labour battalion, a relatively short period of time. Others, less fortunate ones, spent many years in jails and camps, if they survived at all. Also, the regime in our unit was much milder than in most other places of involuntary confinement. The main point: I survived in good health. Unfortunately, not everybody was so lucky. For a number of our comrades (and to this day I don't know exactly what number), the end was tragic.

# Beliefs under Shock
## Veronika Schwartz

It was getting quite late. We were extremely tired and my cousin felt sick. I begged her to continue walking. She turned to me and said, "Vera, you go on please. I can't walk anymore." She indeed collapsed. At that moment, I lay down next to her, telling her to pretend that we were dead. The first guard yelled at us to get up and keep walking. We stayed motionless. He poked, kicked, and pushed us with his rifle into the ditch. When the second guard came and wanted to shoot us, he told him, "They are dead, don't waste your bullets."

Motionless, we lay there until there was no more sound. I told Magda that we had to keep walking, otherwise we would freeze to death. Slowly we crawled out of the ditch. We walked slowly, with Magda leaning on me. Suddenly, we noticed a light, and we soon realized that it was coming from a house. At that point, we had no choice, we had to try to go inside. The door was unlocked. There were people sitting around a table, but no one said a word to us. We crouched under a bed and fell asleep there. In the morning, a man was poking at us with a broom, yelling, "Juden heraus!" (Jews out!) We crawled out. As we left the house he threw some bread crusts after us. I stopped to pick them up and we ate them all. I remember thinking that he still had some humanity left in him.

We continued walking. We walked by a more populated area and suddenly saw a police officer directing traffic. We quickly turned around and went into a house. One woman came to ask us if we would like some food. Of course we wanted food — we were starving. She came back with two servings of ham and mashed potatoes on porcelain plates with cutlery. We didn't exactly know why she was so considerate, but soon another woman came to tell us that the Soviets had entered the area. She asked us to tell the soldiers, if they came into their house, that they were good people, that they protected us and gave us food. Now we understood the situation. We were happy that we would finally be free soon.

Soviet soldiers indeed entered the house within just a few minutes. One of the men in the family was sitting with all his military decorations on his uniform. A Soviet soldier shot him instantly. We were scared. We didn't know what would happen to us. One of the women came to me, begging me to save her daughter, saying that a Soviet soldier had taken her into one of the rooms and that he would kill her.

Recalling how nicely the women treated us, I ran into the room. I was still very naive, not realizing that he was about to rape her. As I started explaining that these people had given us food, he was reaching for his gun. My cousin ran into the room, grabbed me, slapped my face and pulled me out. She was trembling. She asked me, "Don't you know the reason he took the girl into the room?" At that moment, I didn't know. I was trying to save a life and I was now in a state of shock. If it had not been for Magda, I would have been killed.

We realized that we were in danger as well. The freedom we were hoping for had not come. There was no law and order. We were on our own. When night came, we slept with our heads covered with a scarf to look less attractive. Even so, one night while both of us were asleep, a soldier woke me up. With his flashlight shining into my eyes, he ordered me to get up and go with him. I was terrified. I screamed and cried. My cousin tried to explain to him that we were in concentration camps, we are Jewish. He said that Jewish is good. Then Magda told him that I was only a child. At that point he got angry and told Magda, "You are not a child," and forced her to go with him. I was tormented, waiting, not knowing what would happen to her. She returned within a short time and told me that he was unable to rape her because she cried and screamed too much. He got angry and hit her with his rifle and let her go.

The fear continued every day. We kept searching for food. We met a mother and daughter who were of Polish origin. They found some potatoes and cooked them, and they insisted on sharing them with us. They were also survivors. I could never forget them.

Once we hid in a pile of hay to avoid some soldiers. They must have noticed us and they lit the hay on fire, so we had to get out. An older Soviet officer noticed us too. He told the young soldiers to leave us alone and they listened to him. This officer seemed to like us. He said I looked like his daughter. He kept companionship with a woman in the same house we were staying. We were lucky this officer understood the situation we were in.

The older Soviet officer became a good friend to us. Sometimes he brought us some food. I distinctly remember the beige-and-white winter coat and the shoes he gave me. More than anything, he probably saved our lives. One early afternoon, young people were rounded up, Magda and I among them. We were told to get into the army truck. Both of us tried to explain that we were not the enemy — that we were not Germans but were Jewish survivors — but it made no difference. We were forced into the truck. While waiting on the truck we noticed the Soviet officer talking with the soldiers, and right after they came to tell us to get off. Later, this officer told us that the other people on the truck were sent to Siberia to do hard labour. We just didn't know how to thank him enough. This man did have a heart. He understood our plight and just wanted to help us. He didn't expect anything in return.

There are several events that I will never be able to forget: One is that in Auschwitz, a woman was telling me that she was unable to eat the bread that we were getting so she traded it for a little bit of jam.

I told her to try her best to eat the bread since it was our main food. As she began to talk about her husband, she suddenly went out of control. She started slapping everybody around. She was taken away. Another is that during our train transport from one camp to another, a young girl — she was about my age, I was seventeen and I don't believe she was more than eighteen or nineteen years old — rushed to me, hugging and kissing me and telling me how happy she was that she found me. She told me that I was her sister and she begged me to promise her never to leave her again. One story from after our liberation really affected me: We met a young girl, also a survivor. She was from a very religious family. She told me how thankful she was to survive and that she hoped to find her family when she got home. Well, that didn't happen. A drunk Soviet soldier raped her throughout the night. The next morning the girl was dead; she had bled to death. The soldier was still next to her, drunk.

Lastly, right after the Soviet takeover, as we searched for food, we noticed a rifle in the bedroom of one of the houses we walked into. Magda and I looked at each other. Here was our chance to take revenge — "an eye for an eye," as they say. But, we never reached for that rifle. No, we were not killers. We were victims of planned genocide, and two wrongs don't make a right.

Sometime in the month of May, our friend the Soviet officer came to see us. He told us that the train tracks to Hungary had been repaired. He gave us the exact time when a train would be going there. He advised us to get on it and we took his advice. We knew he only meant well. We were eager to get back even though I was never able to call Hungary home again. It was my birthplace and I was in love with the beauty of the country, but I kept remembering the Hungarian government's cooperation with the Germans and their eagerness to carry out all the horrible atrocities against us.

We arrived at the train. It was difficult to get into the boxcar as there was no platform and we had to pull ourselves up. The car was filled with Soviet soldiers, many of them drunk and urinating on the floor. With our heads and partially also our faces covered, we looked nowhere except down to the floor. After several hours, the train came to a halt in a small town. We got off and transferred to a passenger train. As we walked in to look for a seat a woman spat in front of us and remarked, "These filthy Jews are coming back." At that moment I felt very happy that we had survived and that the antisemites felt defeated.

As I was sitting by the window, a young man knocked on it to get my attention. I opened it. He told me that he was my brother's friend and he had seen my brother in Újpest! However, he did not know where exactly he was staying. At that point I knew that all my efforts to stay alive had not been in vain. From that moment, my main concern was to find my brother and be reunited with him; nothing else mattered. Afterwards, I realized that my brother's friend had recognized me because he was the son of the rabbi in a nearby town, and he used to come to our home.

Magda decided to go to Kisvárda. We parted, hugging and kissing and wishing each other the best of luck, and promising that we would soon see each other again. I managed to get to Újpest. There were many people at the train station there, among them representatives of a Jewish organization that was formed to welcome and help out survivors. A young woman by the name of Márta Komáromi and her brother and sister-in-law approached me. They asked for my name and some other questions, then offered me accommodation since I didn't know anyone in Újpest. I was happy to accept the offer and I was thankful to them.

Also, a young man came over and offered me a voucher for a dinner at a restaurant. My mind was preoccupied with finding my brother so I declined, telling him that I didn't know Újpest and I didn't know where that particular restaurant was either. He introduced himself. His name was Miklós Mandel and he was very polite. He told me that he would also go to the same restaurant and we could go together, and that he lived nearby to where I would be staying. He offered to call on me. I accepted and appreciated his help.

Márta and the young couple took me to their apartment on Árpád utca. The apartment wasn't too big but it was very nice, and they put a mattress on the floor for me. I was wondering why they were doing all this for me, so I asked them, "Why are you inconveniencing yourselves? You don't even know me." Well, this is the answer they gave me: "What we are doing for you is nothing in comparison to what your brother did for us. He saved our lives." They told me that my brother had escaped the labour service by posing as a Hungarian officer and therefore he was able to save Jews. After the Soviet occupation, he was arrested. They were questioning him about his activities. Márta told me that the most important thing was to try to visit him.

The next morning I went to the prison with Márta. The Soviets questioned me on my own. After that, they took me into a small room. Then they brought in my brother. It was a tearful reunion. I tried very hard to be brave and not to cry. I would have liked to be cheerful and to reassure him that everything would be fine. We kissed and we hugged each other, then his eyes filled with tears. He asked, "What about Klára and Éva? Our parents?" I saw how tormented he was, so to avoid further questioning I told him what happened — that I was separated from them in Auschwitz and had not seen them again but that we should still continue to hope.

He told me not to worry, he was quite sure he would be released and then we would be together. Márta also felt confident that my brother would be released, and that's what happened. The next day he was free. The very first thing he did was to rent a store on István utca in Újpest. He started out by doing watch repairs. Neither of us had any money but thanks to my parents' foresight he had an excellent trade. The store went by the name "Zoltán Fekete" instead of his real name, Zoltán Schwartz. In Hungarian, *fekete* means black. Schwartz, in Yiddish, also means black. I guess he felt more comfortable with a name that sounded Hungarian rather than Jewish. How unfortunate. It threw a sharp light on the society we were living in.

I decided to go back to Kisvárda and went to our house. The family who had previously rented the lowest-priced apartment from my parents now lived in it. When I walked in they were stunned, as if seeing a ghost. They just stood looking at me without saying a word. I asked them if they had seen anyone from my family. They just shook their heads. Finally, they told me that they had been told that no one would be coming back, that we had all been killed.

I could not believe what I had just witnessed. Here I was with a Christian family and they were not expressing their sorrow. They were not telling me how happy they were to see me. They were behaving as if they were expecting me to apologize for being alive.

I asked if they had found any photos of my family. Once again, they just shook their heads. I went down to the cellar. Right away I noticed that the brick where my father had placed the jewellery had been removed. There was nothing, just empty space. Then I went up to the attic to search for some jewellery that my father had hidden there but everything had been stolen from there too. How cruelly everything was grabbed, things my parents had worked so hard for! I didn't go to see the rest of the house. I don't know what happened to our beautiful solid cherrywood dining room set, the walnut bedroom set, and all the little treasures such as knick-knacks and collectibles that my family valued so much and took such great care of.

My hopes were shattered. They had not seen anyone from my family and I didn't even have a picture of my mother, my father, my sisters, Klára and Éva, my beloved grandparents, uncles, aunts or cousins. I felt so betrayed, so helpless and heartbroken. I continued walking through the backyard. There was dead silence. All our tenants were gone. They were all Jewish except the ones who had moved into our home. All the apartments were now empty. The Posner family, the old man who used to deliver bread products door-to-door and who had a much younger wife and many children; the tailor who worked so hard and was so kind to everyone; the young couple with two children (I used to admire how beautifully she darned old socks); the blind old lady, Mrs. Gartman, who made ends meet by selling door-to-door shoe polish, stove polish and shoelaces. I was very fond of all these people. I missed them all so much.

I continued down the path to visit the families to whom my parents had entrusted our livestock: the beautiful horse, cows, sheep, goats, geese, ducks and chickens. Once again, I encountered people who were very much surprised to see me. None of them asked about the rest of my family. They only complained about the terribly difficult times they had been through and how, when the Soviets came in, everything was taken from them. In my eyes they were thieves. I had no respect left for them.

There was one more family friend I went to visit — our shoemaker. My mother had left beautiful satin material with his wife. From this material, my mother had planned to make a housecoat. When I entered the house, the woman was wearing a satin housecoat made from the material my mother had entrusted to her for safekeeping. Once more, I heard the same story: we were told nobody would be coming back.

It was a painful experience, so much so that I could not bring myself to go over to my grandmother's property, nor did I go to see our second house, which we used to rent out — the first house on Kis utca where we had beautiful nut trees.

I met up with my cousin Magda, who wanted to go back to Újpest with me. When we arrived there we walked down the main street, Fő utca. Our store was locked up and the street was deserted. I felt devastated. The reality set in more and more. I realized that Toska, the kapo in Auschwitz, had not exaggerated. She told us the truth, but at that time I refused to believe it. Now I had to realize that every word she said was true. Perhaps it is better that I did not believe her at the time, or else I would probably not be alive to tell the truth about the most senseless, cruellest and most systematic killing of six million innocent Jews in the twentieth century.

# Amid the Burning Bushes
## Helen Rodak-Izso

We heard some noise from the bushes, but nobody dared to look up. One of the girls turned to me and said, "For you it doesn't matter anymore, so go and see!" She was right, as we all knew what terrible shape I was in. I lifted my head and saw a grey horse with a Soviet soldier on it. The miracle we had dreamed of finally arrived! We were liberated, at the last minute. As unbelievable as it sounds, what we had wished for became a reality.

We jumped up from our despair and hugged the soldier, even his horse. I love animals, but usually from a distance. This was something else. A more beautiful scene was just not imaginable. After a brief, happy welcoming, the soldier urged us to leave the forest because they had to comb through the whole place looking for civilians. He sent us to the farm. We were reluctant and afraid to go, but he assured us that the situation was different now. We were not eager to meet those Germans again.

The situation had changed, but now there were new complications and problems. We went back to the farm and found an abandoned two-storey furnished home. Some of the girls stayed downstairs. My aunt Clara, my sister, Olly, and me and four friends with their young daughters, who were about fourteen years old, occupied the second floor. In the room was only a double bed and an iron stove. Our room-mates were from our town, and we lived through everything together.

My sister is and always was a very able and adventurous girl, so she volunteered to look around for some food with another girl. Very shortly she was back with a bag of sugar in her hands, but unfortunately two Soviet soldiers had followed them and they were not exactly sober. The wooden stairs creaked under their heavy and strong steps and heavy boots. The doors opened, and there they stood with a machine gun. They didn't use their hands, only those ugly guns, which were really frightening. They looked under the bed, where we had hidden one of the very young girls. When they reached for her she gave out a shriek full of fear and somehow they let her go. The other young girls disappeared under their mothers in the double bed. I didn't see my sister but was hoping that she was hiding with the other girls.

Nobody was concerned about me and I was left lying on the floor. In the shape I was in I never dreamed that I could have a problem with a soldier. But one of the soldiers came to me and called me out. I answered in Slovak that I was old. I really felt like a very old and aged person. I was sure that he would leave me alone. He checked my face with his flashlight and said in Russian that this was not true and started to pull me. I tried with all my might to cling to the leg of the iron stove with one hand, and with my other free arm I was grasping his boots and begging him to leave me alone. He was kneeling beside me; he looked so strong, like a giant. Of course, I was already very frightened.

I tried to talk to the Soviet soldier, telling him how long we had been waiting for them to liberate us. I could not believe that after so much struggle, after constantly dreaming of this day, he wanted to destroy me. He wanted only to "take me out for a while," he said. The other soldier lost his patience and said to him, "Why are you asking her? Just take her out and afterwards toss her through the window." Under the window was a big lake, where ships were visible.

Now he grabbed me with force, and I became agitated, crying and gasping for air. I was terrified! I begged him to leave me alone, yelling please, please! I felt like I was suffocating, and I started to cough as I gasped for air. While sobbing and desperately crying for help, I suddenly blurted out, "Please, I am sick, I am sick!" I wasn't exaggerating. I don't know where I found those words, but unfortunately it was the truth.

The word "sick" worked like magic on him. He became panicky and let me go immediately. He shouted at me angrily, asking why I didn't tell him before. I know he was thinking of a different kind of sickness, something contagious, but who cared? I was saved, and this was a good lesson for us. Because this type of danger was always around us. It also helped a bit that Clara mentioned the word Kommandatura,[1] which implied that my death would have been reported to the new authorities in Berlin. This sobered him up, as they were terrified of their superiors.

I was hoping that my sister was safe, but she had had a similar experience. Thank God, she also escaped. It was a frightening experience for both of us. The girls downstairs, unfortunately, were not so lucky and had even more terrible experiences. The next morning, everything was quiet. The Soviet soldiers disappeared, and we tried to rest, believing that the road going home would soon be open for us.

We were liberated on May 2, 1945, in Muritz, a town not far from Hamburg, which the Russians instantly renamed Malchow. The picture of such a place is indescribable. We had won our freedom for which we had longed for such a long time, but it was difficult to handle. We would come and go, then stop and pointlessly gaze about, still in rags. Our hair started to grow, but we still looked awkward, strange. We didn't have guards anymore, but the whole place was like an ant's nest, swarming and in constant agitation from all sides, uncertain comings and goings.

After our experiences on the roads, on farms and in barns, finally

---

1 The Allied Kommandatura (in German, Alliierte Kommandantur) was the governing body for the German capital city of Berlin after Germany's defeat in World War II. This body was subordinate to the Allied Control Council, which governed all of Germany after the war.

we were in a city, not quite aware yet what was going on around us and with us. On our wandering tour we had lived through so much, in the open air, that it was unbelievable to walk on sidewalks among houses, where people lived their ordinary lives. We were bewildered when we saw a milling crowd, where everybody spoke a different language.

The streets were full of such semi-conscious people like us, who had not yet awoken. People were excited, but everyone reacted differently. Some became very quiet, not knowing what had happened around them. Some were loud, intoxicated with the sudden joy. Others were distrustful but tried to believe that all of this was real and true.

We walked slowly, looking around, not believing that nobody was behind us with rude remarks, cruelly shouting at us. We tried to start a new life, which was still a big puzzle for us for a long time. We were trying to find ourselves, somebody, something, which had unfortunately disappeared, vanished forever. We didn't belong to anybody, to any place.

~

We went on with our journey until we reached Krakow, Poland. We went straight to the Red Cross building, where we hoped to get some help. Instead, we were bitterly surprised, disappointed to realize that even after liberation our long period of difficulty would continue. Everybody was trying to find ways to stretch out and rest their tired bodies. I found a place on the table, which was fine. But at midnight they threw us out into the darkness, because we were Jewish refugees. There was no place for us. We didn't hide who we were or where we had come from, although nobody inquired, but their solution for what to do with us was simple and quick.

The only place to go in the middle of the night was the railway station. We thought it must be somewhat safe since it was a busy place. We lay down on the station's asphalt sidewalk and fell asleep.

Early the next day a police officer woke us. He said this was not a safe place for us to sleep and mentioned that there was a Jewish Council office already open. When we got up, we discovered that while we were asleep, someone had stolen our meagre belongings. The items we had collected on our journey and had been able to carry were gone. Olly had some books, but a piece from our dear mother's scarf, our biggest treasure, which we had cherished as a talisman through the whole year, was gone. It was an immense blow to us.

Before we left our previous place, Muritz, we had received identification papers, allowing us to travel freely; these documents were renewed at every major station. The Jewish Council office was already crowded with refugees, but the workers in the office there really tried to help every way they could. Tables stood along the length of the room, and food was offered to everyone. We met other people who were in the same situation, so we could talk and share our experiences with each other. We understood each other. We didn't feel like strangers, but instead like terribly wounded souls meeting. Everybody asked the same questions, which mostly meant inquiring about lost family members.

There was nothing else for us to do but wait. We decided to go out and look around in the city. Krakow is very old and beautiful, with ancient civic buildings and churches. Something pulled us like a magnet. We couldn't believe our eyes: There was a military truck speeding by with soldiers from our country and our flag, our colours! We followed the Czechoslovak truck and approached the driver and the others when they stopped. We spoke in our language with them. What excitement! They were all from our country.

We tried to tell them in a few words about our predicament, asking whether they could perhaps take us along. They regretted that they were not returning until later. After some thinking and discussion among themselves, they came to an agreement and asked for our papers, which we proudly showed them.

They seemed to be understanding and trusting and offered to take us to the border. This offer was more than we could have hoped for, and we thanked them profusely. We explained to them where we were housed so they could find us, not letting ourselves believe that their promises were serious. After this experience, we went back to the building and told our story to everyone who was interested.

We had hardly returned when we were called to the front door. To our sincere surprise and astonishment the truck was standing there waiting with the soldiers. Everyone knew that this truck had come for us. We could hardly believe that they had kept their word. But there it was, our wonder car, waiting for us! We were the first lucky ones to be picked up, to be helped to go home. The group we left behind looked at us with mixed feelings. The air was full of emotion, including fear of reality.

We took our seat at the back and were trying to think and even hope. The road was beautiful. It was a sunny day, and we were travelling towards home on a country road bordered with fruit trees. This time we were overjoyed to see them in full bloom.

Once we got close to the border, they let us go, and we walked the rest of the way to the station. After a short walk, we came to a town called Český Těšín at the Polish-Czechoslovak border. As we were nearing it, some local people approached us. They were waiting for people like us. These Czech village people received us with humanity. They were holding a huge homemade loaf of bread; we were simply speechless and reduced to tears. We just looked at each other. It looked as though our dream had become real. They also had tears in their eyes as they escorted us to the gate that led us to the station, where we found ourselves on our side of the border. One cannot forget such a simple yet human, heartfelt welcome.

Back in Košice, we found ourselves on Bocskay Road, where my father's plant used to be. A familiar shape started to emerge before our foggy eyes. It was our brother Leslie, who hurried towards us on the cobblestones on a broken-down, shaky bicycle. He had tried to meet us earlier at the station, but didn't feel able to. It is difficult, perhaps even impossible to describe the next minutes and hours. We spotted each other from afar, but in our impoverished state none of us could utter a word.

On our way home from the station we first went to the home of one of our fellow former prisoners named Lenka Sinai. She was optimistic by nature, but I don't know whether she really expected to find her husband and son at home or just tried to console herself with that possibility. She asked us to wait for her in front of her home while she looked through the house, which stood wide open and empty. Shortly she emerged with the news we all feared so deeply. Although we were not surprised, it was still dreadful to receive such a confirmation.

From there we went to our home, to which my brother escorted us. As we turned the corner onto Bajza Street, the picture of our never-forgotten home emerged before us. Its heavy steel front door opened easily. With solemn and heavy hearts, we started to climb the well-known stairs to the second floor where we used to live. We were suddenly standing in front of our home, our dear parents' home.

The little bronze name plate, unchanged, was still on the white door: Márk Friedmann. This sign stated the truth about the residents in this home. This was part of our past and shows the world that we had had a home where we had hoped and waited for a better future.

Although the door opened for us, there was nobody waiting there. The sombre look of the house gave away the grave situation as we walked through the abandoned rooms. All hell had broken loose. We had no strength left or need to cover up anymore.

The dining room with its broken locks, the bare walls and the whole emptiness was just too much to bear. The silence loudly complained about what had happened in those rooms. The grand piano was upside down and stuffed with hay. The dining-room furniture had been too heavy to move, but the beautiful carpets, as we heard later, had been taken away through the window.

Before we had to leave, we had given away our things for safe-keeping to a few people whom we had trusted. We now discovered our things were with strangers who used them shamelessly. Those strangers had been our neighbours, or acquaintances of some kind. We had not been expected to come back, so our return was an unpleasant surprise for them. We tried hard to be a mensch again, but it took us a long time, longer than we had anticipated.

The balcony was still there with open doors waiting for us. This place was once a cozy, friendly corner with flowers all around, even hanging on the walls. Facing the street, but built a little bit into the building, the balcony, hidden from the outside world and noise, had provided us with privacy. This had been our dear mother's favourite place with all her plants and flowers, which she tended with patience and special feeling.

One day while we were still at home, a bird came to visit and to our delight it stayed and built a nest among our mother's flowers. We watched her build a home, to which she brought her family. The flying in and out was such a cheerful sight! According to an old common saying, a bird's nest brings luck. So we were hoping for good luck but unfortunately in vain. Nothing and nobody could have helped with what was to come.

I still have that bronze name plate.

# The Miracle of Our Survival
## Yittel Nechumah Bineth
## (Kornelia Paskusz)

Oblivious to the plight of the innocent, the sun rose in her splendour, and morning arrived. The tame animals in our barn welcomed us more warmly than any of the humans we had encountered during the last year. We did not fear them, and they did us no harm. We knew, though, that we had to keep moving. This was not a place for us to stay.

We searched for the mayor of this small town. Mother, in her eloquent German, begged him to give us a permit to stay, but he refused, advising us instead to walk another ten kilometres, where we would find the American army. He reassured us that in the next town the white flags of surrender were already hanging, and we would be safe there. He was nice enough to give us some food.

The thought that we were walking towards freedom made everything seem much easier. We walked with ambition and excitement. Along the way, we met other refugees, who were also walking eagerly towards their freedom. At this point, many of us refugees had already received some meagre items of clothing, food and a bit of money from the town authorities under American protection.

We arrived at the next town. The American soldiers gave Mother and me a room on the second floor of a lovely apartment, next door to two other refugee girls. Peace, however, was not yet destined for us. The place was swarming with Soviet soldiers. They had helped liberate us from the Nazis, but now these soldiers posed a very serious new threat. At fifteen, I really did not know why we had to fear them, but the terrified look on Mother's face when any soldier approached us clearly indicated that these soldiers were to be dreaded.

While sitting in that lovely apartment one day, we suddenly heard screams from the room next door. The two girls were yelling at Soviet soldiers, begging them to leave them alone. "We are sick, we just came from the concentration camps!" they shrieked. Mother held my hand very tightly, led me to the window and said, "Katikám, if these Soviet barbarians break our door, we will immediately jump out this window." We stood there hugging each other and saying *tehillim*, psalms, by heart. *Hashem Yisborach* was with us, for in a very short time — although it seemed hours — we heard the front door being slammed. Quiet followed, and we knew that the Soviet beasts had left. We sighed with relief as another huge stone had just fallen off our hearts.

Mother decided that it was not wise to stay in this apartment any longer. We collected ourselves and organized the few pieces of linen and clothing we had. We found a small abandoned carriage, loaded our belongings onto it and set out, walking side by side as we had done so often in the past weeks. Most of the time I was the one to push the carriage. We found lodgings in the homes of families along the way. Mother had received some coins from the Americans and was able to pay for our accommodation, so we had no problems finding places to sleep.

Our next apartment was in a village close to Dresden, where we rented a room. There was a huge public kitchen, where food was being distributed to the refugees. The people who lined up for this food looked more like skeletons than living human beings. One day, while the food was being distributed, a young Italian man suddenly appeared out of nowhere and approached us. He did not know our language, and we did not understand his, but we gesticulated and communicated in a slightly comical way. He seemed to be telling us that tomorrow the shops would be giving away free merchandise to war refugees. He explained that he would come for me and take me to get free clothing, linen and shoes. It sounded very tempting.

Night came and we closed our door to settle in for some sleep. Just as we were drifting off, a Soviet soldier suddenly entered our room, stating that he needed to stay with us for the night. Seconds later, the Italian lad came in and dragged him out. The Soviet soldier did not resist; he had come in as a wolf and left as a lamb. We were convinced that the Italian lad who came to rescue us was none other than the Prophet Eliyahu (Elijah) Hanavi. He disappeared afterwards, and we never heard from him again.

We walked on and finally reached Dresden, Germany. This once-beautiful large industrial city was razed to the ground during the war. It was difficult to find shelter for the night because the city was teeming with people, all searching for a place to stay. In the end we managed to find a huge school building that served as a shelter. We sat on alert all night, leaning against the wall. There were so many people in the shelter of such varied types that we were simply too afraid to close our eyes. We felt we couldn't trust anyone.

Morning came after a sleepless and tiring night. We could not afford to indulge our exhaustion; we had to move on. Germany had been very heavily bombed by the Allies. All the bridges and railway tracks had been destroyed, and so there were no trains running. The only way we were able to travel was on foot. We had to trudge onwards in the direction of Hungary, our home. In spite of our weariness, we were so relieved that the war was finally over that we continued enthusiastically, though anxiously.

The road, however, was still not destined to be a smooth one. A major obstacle appeared in our path when we came face to face with the Elbe River. There were no bridges, so what were we to do? We stood in front of the river pondering our next move. Suddenly, not too far away, we noticed a narrow board that had been placed on the river for pedestrians. There was no other choice — we had to walk across the river single file. Mother went first, I followed pulling the wagon, and behind me went one of the girls who had been with us since our evacuation. Again, we put all our faith in the Almighty *bashefer*, creator, fervently saying *tehillim* along the way. It was such a relief when we finally reached the shore on the other side.

On the other side of the river, we found a lovely empty house high up on a mountaintop, which we were able to rent for a week. We spent a wonderful and relaxing few days in this house. We were in desperate need of such a rest, both physically and emotionally. We were not yet mentally at ease, because we had not been able to find out anything about the whereabouts of the rest of our family. Mother, who was extremely concerned, managed to contain her anxiety, trying to maintain an optimistic mood.

On Sunday morning we left this comfortable house and started out once more. We continued walking all day and found new lodgings in the evenings. Finally, we crossed the Czechoslovak border and arrived in Bratislava, the capital city of Slovakia, one of the most ancient and important Jewish centres in the Austro-Hungarian Empire. This beautiful city — Pressburg to the Germans, Pozsony to the Hungarians — was set against a gorgeous panorama of rivers and mountains. This was the renowned city of Torah study, famous for its many rabbis, acclaimed yeshivas and *kehillos*, Jewish communities. Bratislava boasted having had the leadership of the *heiliger* (holy) *tzaddik*, the righteous Chasam Sofer and later his son, Shmuel Binyomin Sofer. Mother was very familiar with the city, since she had often come here on business trips.

We arrived at the Judengasse (Jewish Street), a famous street that had until the war been populated with Jewish people. The street now stood totally empty. The houses were abandoned and the yeshivas were no more; no shul had a *minyan*. It all looked so strange and tragic.

We headed towards the kitchen, operated by the American Jewish Joint Distribution Committee, a relief organization from America, where we were told kosher food was being distributed to refugees. Mother pointed to a girl in the crowd of refugees and said, "Katikám, I know that girl." No sooner had she uttered those words than Renee, my dear sister, was hugging her and crying tears of happiness. When she told us that dear Yozsa and dear Dóra were also in town we quickly forgot about food and hurried to meet our sisters.

In the middle of downtown Bratislava, a sensational scene unfolded. A mother and her daughters were reunited after more than a year of separation. The three girls were kneeling down and kissing Mother's feet. There was so much crying and hugging that a ring of curious onlookers formed around us, wondering what the commotion was about. When they learned that a family had just been reunited, there was not a dry eye in the crowd.

We were now a group of five. With joyful spirits, we continued walking. We crossed the Hungarian border and came to a train station where the trains were running. We asked for a train to Csorna, but the ticket agent told us that they needed a minimum of twenty-five passengers in order to proceed there. We would just have to wait until they had enough passengers. Since Mother was so anxious to get home, she paid for twenty-five tickets just to get the train going. We settled into our seats eagerly; we had so much to tell each other, so many tragedies to share, that we did not even notice when the train left the station. Suddenly, we were jolted back into the present by an abrupt stop. After passing three towns, the train could go no further because a bridge had been blown up.

We got off the train and found ourselves in the town of Mosonszolnok. Here we met Mr. Holzaple, who had been our manager before the war. He was very excited to see us and immediately invited us to his lavish home. He set the table in the dining room for an elegant meal. In spite of the fact that we were very hungry, Mother quickly offered her apologies. She said that we must decline the dinner invitation because we could eat only kosher food. Our host was so surprised. "Paskusz néni, it is a time of war," he said. Mother explained to him that at this point it was no longer a matter of life or death and that we would adhere to our kosher standards. She then asked Mr. Holzaple if he would do us another great favour and drive us to Csorna with his carriage and horse, as we were tired and eager to get home. He was very kind and quickly agreed. When we finally settled into the carriage, it was hard to believe that, at long last, we were really going home.

The sun was setting but it seemed as if a brand new day was ahead; we looked forward to a new beginning. Soon we were approaching our birthplace, our home. This was the place of our innocent childhood, where we had laughed, played and learned for so many happy years. Our hearts were throbbing with excitement. We imagined coming home to everything just as we had left it.

We jumped out of the carriage in front of our house and immediately found ourselves surrounded by twelve Jewish men. When they saw us, they cried unashamedly. They told us with bitter emotion that we were the first women or girls to arrive back in our town, and they were so happy to see us because they had thought that all the women had been murdered. We were their consolation that at least some women had survived and their hope that more of us might be on our way home. There was chaos, with everyone shouting at the same time. The men asked us if we had seen this one's mother, that one's sister or daughter, or another person's wife. They were filled with hope and anxiety, yearning to be reunited with their loved ones. But many would be disappointed beyond consolation; their loved ones had become victims of the most gruesome crime in all of history.

With great hesitation, we slowly ventured into our house. Our gorgeous home had been converted into a barn. The beautiful parquet floor, which we had so carefully shined in the past, was destroyed. Straw and animal waste were strewn all over. The house that used to impress everyone who entered was now a scene of total devastation. We stood there bewildered. We did not know where to start or what to do. All of us knew that our primary goals were to rebuild our home, find a means of livelihood and settle down to a family life, but we now realized that this would not be a quick process. We had to take one step at a time.

The men who had arrived earlier had already established a kosher kitchen in the home of our former neighbour, Mr. Kovatch. That house was unfortunately empty, because nobody in the Kovatch family had come back. The first thing Mother told us to do was to go to the kosher kitchen for a hot meal, which we indeed desperately needed. She had noticed our disappointment at the sight of our ruined home and wanted to revive our spirits. Sure enough, the delicious warm meal gave us new energy and we felt much better. In spite of the conditions in the town and in our house, it felt wonderful to be home again.

With serene faith in the *Ribono Shel Olom*, Master of the universe, we soon set out to work. We wanted to rebuild our house immediately. We hired somebody to do the heavy work of cleaning it up, carting out the dirt and polishing everything as best as possible. We then went around looking for our fine furniture, but the only things we found were some odds and ends — tables, chairs and beds. From these we were able to furnish four rooms and the kitchen. It was not nearly the same as it had been, but it was acceptable. After the ordeal we had all been through, our simple house felt like paradise.

The post-war period was not easy. Our financial situation was very difficult. The Hungarian pengő had become worthless, depreciating by the hour. My sister Renee went to the market to buy a wagonful of wood to heat the house and she gave a deposit on the purchase; by the time the wood was delivered, the pengő's value had decreased by half. It was almost funny to watch it drop.

This situation came to a point where the pengő was replaced by eggs as the most valuable means of exchange. The problem was that eggs go bad, and it was very difficult to know if an egg was fresh or spoiled. We discovered that if you shook an egg and heard a noise inside, it meant that the egg was spoiled; a silent egg was still fresh.

The market was quite a sight with everybody going about shaking eggs. This was a period in history when a dozen eggs were considered a very generous bar mitzvah gift. There was a very famous story going around of a man who sent a bar mitzvah boy a silver wine *becher*, a cup, for a gift. Along with the present he sent a letter apologizing for this gift, saying that unfortunately he owned no eggs, and this *becher* was the only thing he could find and afford at this time.

The people in Csorna busied themselves organizing and restructuring their lives as best as they could. We, too, threw ourselves into our daily activities, but not without heavy hearts — for we had still not heard anything from our brothers Binyomin, Meshulem and Shlome Meir. The last we knew was that Shlome Meir had two children, fourteen-year-old Elozor Akiva and thirteen-year-old Tzortl, and that he was living in Sopron. We had already heard about Lici, our oldest sister, who perished together with her three darling little children, *Al Kiddush Hashem*, to sanctify God's name. We mourned for her and worried about the others.

One morning, the mail carrier came at an unusual hour with a telegram from Switzerland. We could not read it fast enough. It was from our brother Meshulem, informing us that he was sick with typhus but that as soon as he recovered he would be coming home. We literally danced with joy and prayed for his recovery, happily anticipating his homecoming.

Hungary was now under Soviet occupation. This was not good; the Soviets were not used to living in freedom and did not respect the liberty of the people under their jurisdiction. They found out that we owned a four-room house, and without any explanation they demanded that we give them two of the rooms. We had no choice in the matter: Three Soviet officers moved into one room, and an elderly Russian Jewish tailor moved into the other. The tailor's name was Mr. Davidovitch, and he was a good man. He sat by his sewing machine all day, working very diligently.

The Soviet soldiers caused us a lot of hardship. They were extremely demanding in all respects. We kept our doors bolted at all times, because we could not trust them at all. We felt so insecure that at night we preferred to stay with families in other houses — we felt that it had become too dangerous to stay at home. Mother thought that this was just the necessary precaution. Naturally, we did not socialize with the Soviets in any way.

Mr. Davidovitch knew that we were constantly anticipating our brother Meshulem's arrival. One day, we heard him yelling, "Meshulem, Meshulem!" at the top of his voice. We opened our door and ran out. Sure enough, in walked our dear brother, looking like a wine barrel; he had eaten too much in Switzerland and had gained too much weight. We were so glad to see him. We spent endless hours together, talking and sharing all the troubles we had faced.

He told us that he had been with our brother Shlome Meir and his fourteen-year-old son, Akiva, in a labour camp in Germany. They had to carry heavy cement sacks back and forth all day long. Shlome Meir, only thirty-six years old, weak and starved, became ill. The Nazis took no excuses; his quota of work had to be done. Thus, for several weeks, Meshulem did all the work that Shlome Meir was supposed to do. He dragged the cement sacks back and forth very diligently and quickly to hide the fact that his brother was ill. Tragically, both Shlome Meir and his young son soon collapsed under the burden of this hard labour and their illnesses, and Meshulem had to witness their deaths. Meshulem, still a young teenager at the time, was traumatized, yet he even arranged for their burial under those horrible circumstances. We were heartbroken to receive the tragic news and we cried together.

Meshulem was now eighteen years old, and Mother was eager for him to resume his yeshiva studies. He had already missed so many months of learning. She started inquiring and learned that the Pupa *rav*, the leader of the Hasidic dynasty, Reb Yosef Grünwald, was heading a new yeshiva in Szombathely. She felt that going to yeshiva was the most important thing for Meshulem and made all the necessary arrangements. He left home again after only three months.

Several weeks later, Mr. Davidovitch was once again banging and yelling. This time he shouted that a beggar was at the door and he did not want to let him in. We looked out and were very shocked to see our dear brother Binyomin standing on the stoop, looking like a skeleton. We welcomed him with overflowing hearts, crying happy tears at being united once again. Binyomin was clearly in terrible health, but Mother carefully looked after him. Very soon, he got back to normal.

*Hashem Yisborach* was very good to us. We had survived a Holocaust unequalled in the history of the universe. Our family was almost complete. We would never forget our beloved sister Lici, nor our brother Shlome Meir, but our family was more fortunate than most, and we were grateful.

Many of our friends, relatives and neighbours came home with only a few family members or with none at all. There were mothers or fathers who had lost all their little children, and children who had lost both parents. There were *chasanim*, grooms, who had lost their *kallahs*, their brides, and *kallahs* who had lost their *chasanim*. There were wives who had lost their husbands, and husbands who mourned their wives. The tragedies were beyond comprehension; the grief was enormous.

The survivors were shattered, but they rose from the abyss of sorrow and started to rebuild their lives from the ashes. They began again from scratch, and little by little they picked up the pieces. But they could never forget and never will. Each year on the twentieth day of the month of Sivan on the Hebrew calendar, there are mass *yahrzeits*, commemorations of death, for the millions of martyrs who were sacrificed *Al Kiddush Hashem*, to sanctify God's name, in the Holocaust. The memory of these martyrs and what they endured will last and will be passed on from generation to generation until the full redemption of *Klal Yisroel*, the Jewish people.

# Hoping in Isolation
## Miriam Mózes

About three months after our arrival in Theresienstadt, the three of us were sitting on our beds in our Lager room when we heard unusually happy sounds from outside. People were singing and dancing outside our room. We did not know the reason for this unusual event, but we had the feeling that finally something good must have happened. A group of kids entered our barracks, jumping up and down and dancing around shouting loudly, "The Soviet army marched into Theresienstadt. We are free, and the Germans went to hell!"

I jumped out of my bed and, still in my pyjamas, joined the group of kids to convey this wonderful message around the camp. Everybody was happily hugging and kissing. We were all singing and dancing, shouting enthusiastically, "We are free, we are free, we are free!" We left the room and continued to sing and dance all morning to help everybody enjoy this happy moment. Even the poor souls lying on the ground in front of the barracks with typhoid fever forced some smiles and waved their weak hands, happy to be free.

We were all very much aware that we were among the few lucky ones to survive the horrible year after our deportation to Austria. It was an extraordinary moment to realize that the gloomiest year of our lives was over and that we were free again. We were all excited about the thought that we would be going home soon and would be able to pick up our lives.

~

When we arrived in Budapest, Mom found a gentleman who seemed to be helping travellers at the train station. He knew about Jewish organizations in the recently liberated city. One of them, the American Jewish Joint Distribution Committee, was established by American Jews to help war refugees to restart their lives. The gentleman was kind enough to phone the organization and reassured Mom that we would be picked up soon. Indeed, within an hour a small car arrived and the driver picked us up and took us to a huge hall, which was full of liberated Jewish refugees — that is, survivors. A very kind young lady welcomed us and handed out a few bags full of food. András and I just grabbed the bags, opened them up and stuffed our mouths with the delicious cheese buns, cakes, fruits and, last but not least, chocolate. Mom in the meantime talked to the lady, who found a place for us to stay overnight. She also gave us train tickets to Hódmezővásárhely. The next morning we were on our way home.

Unfortunately, my dream was never realized — my father was not waiting for us. Our house was also not the same as it was before the deportation either. It was empty — everything in it was vandalized and there was hardly any furniture left.

# Hiding from the Germans, Running from the Soviets
## Esther Davidovits

One day at the end of January 1945, the SS officers said that the Soviets were coming and that we had to leave right away. We were in an all-women's subcamp of the Stutthof concentration camp deep in the forest of Thorn (Toruń), Poland doing forced labour, digging trenches and sleeping in army tents on just a little bit of straw. We had been freezing cold, and walking the hours to work, on so little food, was exhausting. Now the Germans were running away and they didn't want to let us go free. Some of them burned the tents with the women prisoners trapped inside them because they didn't want to take them along but they didn't want to set them free either. Our SS officer took us with, saying that the Germans would win the war and we would still be their prisoners.

We were on a death march and close to one hundred women were murdered during the march. After several weeks of hiding out without food and shelter, they found an empty jail cell in the town of Krone (Koronowo). They decided to put us in the cell and lock the door. They said they would come back for us after they came out of hiding. We lacked food and water and thought we would die there.

It was one day later that the Soviets liberated us. They found us and let us out, but we weren't free to run away. They wanted to rape us and keep us as their prisoners. Some of the girls died while others managed to run away. One night I managed to escape into the woods with my sisters, Eta Raisa and Shava. We found a farmhouse and begged the family to let us in. They said we could sleep in the barn. They asked us if we were Jews. When we confirmed it, they said we could not stay there and made us leave. They didn't want to help us. We were cold and hungry. We ran from place to place, sleeping in the fields and begging for food. Eventually, in one city we found a Red Cross truck. The workers told us we could sleep in an old abandoned school for the night. The school was full of garbage and its floor was dirty.

My older sister, Eta Raisa, said that she would clean up the debris and dirt in one corner of the room so that we could sleep on a clean floor that night. Meanwhile Shava and I went to the Red Cross truck to get supplies and food. We were on our way back with some supplies and food when suddenly we heard an explosion and saw a crowd of people gathering. We ran over to see what was going on, why the commotion. It turned out to be my worst nightmare. My sister Eta Raisa had picked up a grenade when she was cleaning the floor and it had exploded in her hands. She didn't know that it was a grenade when she picked it up. A friend of mine was with her and she was hurt too. Her breasts were gone and her chest was open. My sister's hand and eyes were missing but she was still alive and conscious. She spoke to me and told me she was sorry for what happened.

The nuns took her and my friend away to the hospital. I didn't know where this hospital was. There was no transportation, and I couldn't speak enough Polish to ask for help. I walked for miles until I found the hospital. I found my sister lying in a bed and I kneeled down beside her. She asked me to get her water because she was thirsty. I didn't have water so I left and went to a house nearby and begged for a bottle of water. I brought it back to her and gave her some. A nun came into the room and started to yell at me, telling me not to give her water and that I must leave because they were going to operate on her in the morning. I left and came back in the morning before her operation and said farewell to her. The girl who was with her when the grenade exploded had died by then.

I never came back again because I was on the run with the others. We were running from the Soviets while hiding from the Germans. The war wasn't over and we wanted to find our way back to our hometown. I had to keep running and couldn't stay in one place for long. I couldn't stay behind by myself. There was no food, I had no money and I didn't know the language. I was planning to come back for my sister once I was safe and back home. To this day I don't know what happened to her. I never heard from her or saw her again. I tried to find her through the Red Cross but no one knows what happened to her.

# The Light in a Dark Cellar
## Susan Simon

In mid-January 1945, rumours spread that Soviet soldiers had crept
into the city, chased away the Nazis and were now occupying a section of Budapest. Before our hopes could rise, panic swept through
the ghetto that the retreating Nazis were shooting every Jew on their
path. Rumours also spread that the ghetto was mined. The next morning, we heard whispers about a strange quiet on the streets. Slowly,
with our eyes accustomed to the light and with trembling legs and
fluttering hearts, we joined a group of mothers and children peeking
out of a doorway. Could this silent emptiness be the glorious moment
of liberation we had dreamed of? Or is it the quiet before the storm,
before mass murder? Unable to answer those questions, we felt utterly paralyzed.

Then two women appeared with their children, their hands full of
bread. They waved to us, and the bread they carried was all the proof
we needed to believe that the nightmare was over.

With hunger kept at bay, we became increasingly anxious about
our missing men, praying fervently for our beloved father and my
grandpa. Lying in bed all day, I often heard knocks on the door that
no one else could hear. I also discovered the joy of reading novels.
On February 13, 1945, I was absorbed in a book, ignoring the bright
sunshine, which promised a new spring. Preoccupied, I didn't even
react to a real knock on the door. When I looked up, a big man stood

in front of me, his face hidden behind long, fuzzy black hair, a bushy black beard and a huge reddish moustache that matched neither his beard nor his hair. My eyes did not recognize him, but my heart made a leap, and I threw myself into Father's arms. My feeble heart seemed to thrive on this kind of jolt, because from the moment Father returned, I got out of bed and resumed the active life of a nine-year-old.

The rest of the day passed in ecstasy. We heated water for Father's bath — a luxury he hadn't enjoyed in months. He shaved off his beard and moustache, and praying that he would no longer need any disguise, Mom cut his hair and he began to look like himself. We celebrated with the canned meat and vegetables he brought, which was a real feast compared to our daily noodles and jam. Until we moved to our own home, Father assumed the job of providing food for all of us.

In retrospect, our experiences during World War II affected not only the years that followed, but also our pre-war memories. My early childhood acquired the glow of an almost unearthly paradise, an illusion fabricated by my internal magician, probably to compensate for the trials during the war. Another way my subconscious conjuror or mental trickster transformed the fear and suffering during the war into manageable hardship was to magnify the tiniest hope into a saving grace, the smallest bit of comfort into pleasure, even ecstatic delight. While starving, a bite of dry bread seemed a feast; when freezing, Mother's body was a furnace; threatened with death, Mother's hand meant total safety. When people notice this wondrous capacity of their minds, they might be able to develop it further. Endurance against terrible odds could depend on it.

Contemplating the inner forces that came to help us during our times of great trial, I must mention too how the misery we shared helped to unite us. The antagonism between Mother and me evaporated during the threats, and there were no fights among family members, no matter how limited the space they had to share.

Was my blessed background a significant factor in my survival? All I know for certain is that my sense of security, the love that was lavished on me in my early years and the tales that sprang from Grandpa's limitless imagination have been the mainstay for the rest of my life's journey.

You might wonder how people go on after so much tragedy and heartbreak. After Father returned, we hardly grieved for Grandpa; jubilant that Father had survived, we felt overwhelmed with gratitude. Most of the Jewish children we knew were orphaned, so having two parents alive was an incredible blessing. Grieving would have felt like blasphemy.

Among the ruins of the previously splendid Budapest, the "Pearl of the Danube," people felt a compulsion to clear away the rubble, build new lives and put all the horrors behind them. There must be a balancing tendency in human nature, so that after a period of despair, hope takes over. We tried to forget that the new life we were so eager to create was built on the graves of our loved ones.

Father had lost his mother, three brothers and their families, many cousins, aunts and uncles. Mother lost her father, and her three cousins were all widowed. With few relatives or friends left, we were reduced from a large, vibrant clan to a small, nuclear family. Our home, a veritable social centre before the war that often welcomed our relatives from the country, now had no visitors.

Yet we could neither cry nor grieve. The habit we were forced into during the war of running feverishly for our lives seemed to hurl us on. Still on the run this time, away from our memories, we felt forced to escape all the heart-wrenching pain. This attitude was relatively easy for us children, but our parents were not as forgetful as they wanted to be. Their grief would surface later, when their energy was less occupied with the immediate struggle for food and shelter.

# With Aching Hearts
## László Láng

Translated from Hungarian by Marietta Morry and Lynda Muir (2013)

I was standing by the banks of the Danube in front of the Ferenc József Bridge in Budapest. The bridge was underwater, with wood planks piled over it, and I was the last one to cross it. I could no longer see my two friends. The "floor" of the bridge gave out loud sounds under my feet, like the body of a giant violin, but I strode happily onward, feeling like a free man. It was the middle of May in 1945.

I crossed Váci Street, from where I turned into Kossuth Lajos Street, and continued on to Rákóczi Avenue. But really it was nowhere near as simple as that. Because of how I looked, I was stopped at every second step by someone who'd ask me where I came from and whether I knew this or that person. Many people pushed money into my pockets. It took me some four hours to reach Hungária Boulevard, and I received a lot of money on the way.

Hungária Boulevard was near Hermina Avenue, that is, near MIKÉFE. There was a short street where my old boss lived, the one who had taught me the trade. I was conscripted into the labour service from there and so that's where I returned — to his apartment. They received me with great joy. They told me I could stay with them, and I could decide later what I wanted to do. Their workshop was operational and if I wanted, I could start working there in a few days.

This sounded tempting but it felt more important to me to find my parents and my only sister first, or to at least learn what had happened to them. After the typhus fever, I was so tired and weak, both physically and emotionally, that I was simply not able to make a decision. My boss's wife, who was fond of me, prepared a good dinner and a bath for me, which I could really use by then. She threw out all the clothes I had brought along. We went to Teleki Square the next day and she bought me a nice suit, shoes and underwear.

A couple of days later, I told them I wanted to travel to the countryside to find out what had happened to my father, mother and sister. Thus I travelled to Fony, which was then in the county of Abaúj-Torna in what is Slovakia today. Four Jewish families used to live there. Out of those, only one man and my sister returned. We had a pleasant reunion. They didn't know that I'd managed to escape. Sadly, my parents were butchered by the Nazi henchmen in Auschwitz. My sister, Katalin, weathered those difficult times in Pesterzsébet, a suburb of the capital city. My foreman had procured her false papers and she took to wearing a large cross. True enough, it was easier for women to hide their Jewishness than it was for men.

Together Katalin and I tried to get back some furniture that, as "Jewish property," was previously auctioned off by order of the Hungarian government, or had simply been stolen in the process. There were some honest people who gave items back without a word, but there were those who refused, saying that they had paid good money for them. But these things didn't matter much anymore, because I knew and sensed that I would not be able to live in a country where the people considered Hungarians of the Jewish faith their enemy. Antisemitism was deeply rooted in the Hungarian Christian people, and it was impossible to rid them of it.

~

I suppose I don't have to say much else about World War II — we all experienced the antisemitism, the abasement, the deportation that the demented Hungarian government inflicted on intelligent and educated Hungarian citizens whose only crime was that their great-grandfather had been Jewish. It continued like this from generation to generation. None of us wanted to believe that the Jewish religion was a life-endangering offence, but first torture and then the gas chamber followed. It was full-scale annihilation.

When I returned from the labour camp, many in the village were surprised that I'd made it back. And no one squeezed my hand to express their sympathy with me after the unjust persecution I'd suffered. The Hungarian people sympathized with this policy and secretly applauded it. I felt that they rejoiced at the events that occurred during this tragic time. I still feel the same way. I was not religious, my parents were Reform Jews and we didn't pray much. My father didn't have a beard, and he had no expectations of me in terms of religion. My mother came from a more religious family. She tried to keep a kosher household as much as she could. I didn't have any Zionist beliefs, but to this day I have the feeling that the Hungarian people do not want us Jews, no matter if the individual is a great artist or specialist. Jews are considered a class enemy.

I was quick to catch on to this and decided that I would not be able to build my life among people who reject me. This accounted for 60 per cent of my reason for emigrating. The other 40 per cent was made up by the difficult economic situation after the war and an incident I experienced. I was living in Budapest, on Aradi Street, where I rented a small room. I started working in a machine shop, the one where I'd previously studied. The atmosphere among the workers was quite pleasant. There was high inflation and the salary was inadequate, but I had faith that the situation would improve. However, one day after I'd come home from work, I looked out the window and witnessed the following scene: a Soviet soldier was standing there with a gun in his hand, making a boy strip. He let him go once the boy had nothing on but his underwear. This was too much for me and forced me to make a decision. I asked myself, how can one live in a country where, in broad daylight, a member of the glorious Soviet army that had liberated Europe dirties his hands with such despicable acts? To what depths has civilization sunk? How could one ever get used to that?

The next day, I left my job and went to the horticultural campus where the Zionist organization Habonim Dror gave preparatory training for emigration. I immigrated to Palestine — Israel did not yet exist — at the beginning of 1946. I like Hungary; it's a fine country and a beautiful place. But I cannot forgive the Hungarian people for having adopted Hitler's fascist politics, which resulted in the deaths of six million innocent people — my father, my mother and fifteen of my relatives among them — who were all hounded to death. I wouldn't be able to live there! It's something I will never be able to forgive.

# Two Sorts of Homecoming
## Moishe Rosenschein

Translated from Yiddish by Vivian Felsen (2015)

On November 6, 1944, I travelled back to my hometown, Szolyva (Svaliava in Ukraine). How disappointed I was when I entered the house where we had lived and found an empty room without doors and windows. I felt a stab in my heart. I felt utterly cold. I started to cry like a child. I now saw my terrible misfortune, but desperate crying did not help. No one answered.

I went out of the house and walked over to see the neighbour, a non-Jewish woman. She told me everything about how my parents had been taken away. I went into town where I found boys whom I could ask about my siblings. No one knew anything about them. I felt miserable and angry. Everyone who returned home found at least a brother or a sister, but not me.

I went to a tailor and asked whether I could work for him and also learn the tailoring trade. He agreed. I was very diligent doing housework, but unfortunately I had very little time for tailoring. At 7:00 or 8:00 p.m. each night I would try my hand at sewing, but it just wouldn't work out for me. I usually felt very tired by the evening and would rather go to sleep or rest.

The life there was of no interest to me. Every day I was very sad when I went past the house where we used to live. I also had no close friends or relatives. The non-Jews here were also very unpleasant. I couldn't stand them.

Eventually, I got a notice to report to the Soviet army, so I left and ended up in Szatmár. I was eating in a restaurant there when the door opened and a close childhood friend of mine, Eliezer, whom I had not seen for three years, came in. We were very happy to see each other and began talking. Suddenly he said to me, "You will now go home." I answered him by saying "No way," because I had no one to find there. To that he replied, "You will still go." And he pulled a letter from his bag and said to me, "This is from your brother Joseph."

As soon as I heard the word brother I hugged and kissed him. He could hardly push me away. I quickly paid for my lunch and ran out. I caught a coach and went right to the station. As luck would have it, not long afterwards a train arrived. I rode all of the next day to arrive back to Szolyva. I went inside, and my brother Joseph jumped on me. We kissed each other. After having survived so much pain and suffering to finally find each other, we both cried. We went out for a walk and shared our experiences. Before I knew it, it had grown dark. I called a few friends, and we went to a tavern where we drank until midnight. We came home and slept next to each other because we had so much left to tell.

～

In the morning of July 24, 1946, we crossed the French border. We arrived in Marseilles the next day, where we were taken to a place right at the seaport. We thought that we would be leaving the next day for Eretz Yisrael.

On Friday we made an Oneg Shabbat. We sat outdoors and ate supper. Then we danced the hora,[1] after which we sat on the seawall

---

1 An Israeli folk dance that is performed by a group in a circle and is traditionally danced on celebratory occasions.

and began singing the beautiful songs of the *chalutzim*, the pioneers in Palestine. At the time I was very fond of the *chalutzim* and kibbutz life, and I had made up my mind that I would only live on a kibbutz and pursue a communal life. We remained there until midnight and admired the splendour of the seashore. All around us electric lights lit up the moon and the stars. We danced again before going to sleep.

Life was wonderful there, including the cultural part of it. Every two or three days, various cultural lectures took place, as well as other talks about the problems in Palestine. Everything was very well organized. Our daily program looked as follows: We got up in the morning, did our exercises, ate breakfast, worked in the kitchen or laundry, had lunch, were given two hours of rest, then Hebrew lessons, supper and then everyone could do what he or she wanted, such as writing letters. We ended up spending almost three months there, and the entire time I visited the city only twice.

One Friday night a *shaliach*, an emissary, came and said that we should pack up, because the next day we were setting sail for Eretz Yisrael. We danced for joy and packed our belongings.

On Saturday morning at 7:00 a.m. when we were supposed to leave, our *shaliach* came and told us we had to go back with our bags because something had happened and that for the time being we could not travel. Deeply disappointed, we went back wondering what could have happened. But it didn't last long. Just an hour later trucks came and drove us to the port, where our ship, the *Latrun*, was waiting for us.

We had barely boarded the ship when it suddenly started to move, since it had been betrayed by British spies. Hence, our accommodation could not be properly organized and I could hardly sit anywhere. An hour after the ship had set sail, people started to feel sick and began vomiting. I spent the first three days lying down and couldn't even turn over, partly because I was very weak but also because there was simply no room. I had no food during those three days. On the fourth day, we were given two boiled potatoes and some cooked food that was so hard it could have broken our teeth. On the fifth day, I got up and felt better. We cooked something salty for lunch. We got half a litre of water every day, which was unfortunately very warm.

The next day our ship was struck and had some leaks, so that day and night we had to bail out the water. I slept in the coal cellar where the air was so stuffy that I almost choked. When someone stood in front of the door, everyone else started shouting, "Comrade, go away, there's no air here!" The ship also rocked from side to side. When it tilted to the right, people had to run to the left. And as soon as we got to the left side, we had to run back. The entire time that the ship was tossed by the waves, I was in the toilet only twice. It was so filthy you couldn't go in there.

On the eighth day, water got into the machine room, and the ship remained at a standstill. For the whole night we bailed out water. The next day the ship gradually began to sail on to the Adriatic Sea. There we encountered terrible storms and were in grave danger. On the eleventh day we threw all our rucksacks into the coal cellar. We sailed for a total of fourteen days, but on the twelfth day, October 19, we were caught by the British. They lit up our ship with aircraft for the entire night. Then they came with warships. They bumped up against our ship and began to throw tear gas bombs. Half an hour later, British soldiers were on our ship. We tried to fight them off, but it was pointless. We had only bottles while they had weapons. A couple of men were wounded.

On November 1, as soon as we got off our ship in Haifa, we saw two rows of armed soldiers along the entire length of our ship and theirs. My heart almost stopped when I saw that. After all the trials and tribulations I had endured, I was now in my homeland but armed soldiers were standing next to me just in case, heaven forbid, I try to escape. We shouted at the British soldiers, "Fascists! Auschwitz!" They barely responded. All of our bags were searched for weapons. Then we were forced to board their ship. It was much more comfortable than the one we came on, yet on our broken ship I felt heartened because I always had the hope that we would be able to disembark without the British catching us. But on their ship, I knew that I would only get to Cyprus.

I bathed, because for the fourteen days of our voyage I had only washed myself twice. In the evening they gave us something to eat. It was Friday night. When I lay down to sleep it felt like I was in a real bed. On Saturday we danced a hora on the ship and showed the British that, even though they were taking us to Cyprus, we were not defeated.

# As a Free Man
## Mark Lane

The winter of 1944–1945 was a horrible winter in Auschwitz-Birkenau. And then in mid-January 1945, the SS arrived, a special group in black uniforms. They came and roused us with yells of "Schnell!" and started to chase us out of the barracks. We were to be taken on a death march because the Soviets were coming and so they wanted to evacuate the camp; we had already heard the cannons and artillery of the Soviet front, great explosions from a distance.

We walked through the day and night. A lot of people couldn't make it; they died. It was a terrible situation. We walked for three days along with Soviet prisoners of war. The Germans machine-gunned some of the Soviet P O W s right on the road. When we arrived at a railway station, cattle cars were waiting for us again. We didn't know where we were going, but after a day and a half the doors were opened and we were in Prague, Czechoslovakia. Standing there were people from the Czech Red Cross. They gave us tea and bread, and one of the women from the Red Cross took off her sweater and gave it to me, and I wore it under my striped uniform. We travelled for a couple of days before the doors opened again, and then we were lined up and we walked for a few kilometres until we arrived in a camp: Mauthausen, in Austria.

With its huge gates, it was built as a fort originally. The barracks were added later on. Absolutely horrible place. With so very little food, we were skin and bone. We worked in a quarry, going down 186 steps to break stones and then having to carry rocks on our shoulders back up those 186 steps. And every twenty paces there was a guard with a truncheon beating us over the legs, yelling at us to go faster. And then even after we came back into the barracks, we were given a brick with rags around it to polish the wooden floor of the barracks.

We were there from January to the beginning of March; then again we had to line up in fives for walking, and where we were going, nobody knew. We were in a city called Wels, and I remember that the sun was shining and stores were open and there was a lady who came out from a butcher shop with a shopping bag and I said to her in German, "Madam, would you be kind enough to give me some food? I am very hungry." But she did not even look in my direction.

We marched until we came to an unfinished camp called Gunskirchen. The camp was in a dense forest, with trees everywhere except the space where the barracks had been built; the floor was earthen. The sun was shining, the snow had started to melt a little bit, and the floors were muddy. There were no facilities of any kind. The barracks were just a frame with no doors, and it was terribly cold. Hardly any food was given there and to this day, I do not remember what I ate or if I ate. It was a horrible place.

And then on the blessed day of May 5, 1945, we heard the rumbling of engines. Before, the rumblings were always coming from the sky, with thousands of planes flying overhead. Now we could hear the rumblings on the ground, and soon we saw the stars of the American army tanks. One of the tanks had a loudspeaker and announcements were made in all different languages, saying, "This is the American army and you are free. We have come to liberate you." Tanks arrived with five stars and black faces looking out from the turrets. We had no black people in Czechoslovakia so I did not know what to think. But it was the 761st Black Panther Brigade under the command of General Patton, and this was the first camp that they had helped to liberate. The American soldiers started to throw us chocolates and chewing gum. We didn't know what gum was, except that we could not swallow it. When the soldiers liberated us, they had never seen camps, and they had tears in their eyes. But we were free!

We had friends who were dying and we begged them, "Do not die. The Americans are here." But a lot of them could not hold out. Thousands of people died in Gunskirchen, but nobody was buried. There was nobody to bury them and so the bodies were just left in the woods, and the smell was horrific. This was how we lived. This is how we, I should say, existed.

During the time in the camps, I never knew from one second to the next whether I was going to live or die. When I saw a German with a gun, I didn't know if he was going to kill me. How in the world could the most modern, most advanced, most technically proficient people in the world be converted into a nation of murderers? They built factories to kill people. And it wasn't only Jews they killed. But I survived. I almost didn't believe it. After what I had gone through, I was free! Only people who have lost their freedom can appreciate it.

My father could never talk about the Holocaust. When you lose a wife and three children, it's difficult to talk about that. He seldom spoke about my mother or the rest of the children. Some people couldn't, and I understand it; I have friends who could not or would not talk about it. I have one friend who came from a Hasidic home who turned away from religion entirely. Right after liberation, in Austria, my friends and I were discussing whether we should stay Jews — why should we stay Jews, and was there a God? If there was a God, we asked, how could he have allowed the atrocities to happen? To this day, when we discuss these things, it's hard to understand.

For me, if I had stopped being a Jew, with my background of both religion and Zionism, then Hitler would have won the war. Besides, to me, a Jew is a Jew is a Jew. We say in Hebrew, "Ein somchim al ha'nes," we do not rely on miracles, but by the same token, I think people should still believe in miracles.

All these years, I never wanted to go back to Eastern Europe. Many times, I was asked to go on the March of the Living to Auschwitz and Majdanek and other Nazi camps. I did not want to go there. The one thought I had concerned Mauthausen: "I'm going into those gates as a free man and will come out as one." This thought stayed with me all those years.

Eventually, my wife and I decided to go there on our way to visit our granddaughter in Israel. We stopped for three days in Vienna and then took the train to Mauthausen. When we got up to the gates, I was overcome as memories came flooding back. Nowadays, I think Mauthausen is operated to make money in Austria — there were tourist buses from all the different countries of Europe. I walked in with my wife and to the person at the gates I said in German, "124 922," the number that was on my wrist at Mauthausen. There was no charge for us.

I went through the gates with tears flowing from my eyes, and it took me a while to get my blood pressure back to normal. Most of the barracks in the camp were demolished, but my barracks, number 11, was still standing. There were memorials dedicated to all the different prisoners from all the various countries.

I went to the quarry. Above the steps where I used to work there was a display, all overgrown with moss. I remember going up and down those steps, but I have absolutely no idea what happened to the rest of the rocks or if they were ever of any use to anyone. But when I came out of the camp a free man, I imagined addressing Hitler himself: "See, I have made it. I won, not you."

# Fate and Fortune
# Leslie Fazekas

In the Saurer-Werke tank factory, I documented this important period of my life in a diary, and I wrote to Judit when I could.[1] By reading the diary and the letters that Judy and I exchanged with each other, one would think that our deportation wasn't so terrible after all. The fact is that in June 1944 about 20,000 Hungarian Jews were deported to Vienna and its vicinity. For some reason, these people were treated differently from other Jews, and most of them survived. We were part of these 20,000 Jews. We survived partly because of the special treatment we received and partly, I think, because we escaped from the Lager as the Soviets were approaching it.

Most of the people we had lived with for ten months remained in the barracks. They were detained by the Germans and eventually perished, another one hundred unfortunate souls, victims of human evil. These friends of ours were counting down the days until the end of the war, full of anxiety and happiness that the war would soon end and they would be able to go home. For them, it didn't happen that way.

At that point we were already in the cellar of a liqueur factory with

---

1  Leslie's diary and letters to Judit will be published by the Azrieli Foundation in 2020 under the title *In Dreams Together*.

other deportees, mainly with people who came from the neighbouring Lager. They had arrived via Auschwitz. They told us what they
had been through, and only then did we realize what had happened
to the Jews of Europe. Some of these people had lived through many
concentration camps, had to survive in them for three or four years.

My father was in the Jewish hospital in Vienna at the time, where
he had to undergo a serious operation. As soon as we were liberated
by the Soviets we left for Hungary to get out of the war zone. We were
afraid of the returning Germans and the wild Soviet soldiers.

Three weeks later my fifteen-year-old brother, George, asked for
a lift on a Soviet truck, went to Vienna and brought back our father,
who up until that point had been convinced that we were among
the murdered. My father felt unimaginable joy and delight when he
caught sight of his child entering the ward. He believed that George
saved his life. The truth is that our father saved ours. If he had been
with us in the Lager and had not been strong enough to leave with us
at the right moment, we would have shared the doom of our Lager
mates.

My diary of our Lager life now strikes me as unbelievably naive.
When I wrote it, I didn't know what was happening in other Lagers,
what life was like in other parts of Europe or about the terrible fate of
the six million European Jews who would be killed. I was absolutely
convinced that we were in a very bad situation. It was not true. We received special treatment in the factory where we worked, in the Lager
where we stayed for ten months and in the city of Vienna, where we
were allowed to move freely towards the end of our captivity when we
had to walk to the factory, which was far from the Lager.

Aside from being ignorant and naive, I was also nineteen years
old, with all the implications of this age: I was full of sentiments, ex-
citements and enthusiastic expectations concerning the future after
the war. I didn't doubt for a moment that we would eventually be
liberated from our precarious situation.

Finally, there was my sweetheart whom I loved, with whom I

arranged a regular correspondence, which occupied our lives and kept our spirits high in the most difficult days of our captivity.

My diary contains discrepancies in the ways it describes the food, the difficulties, the night shift, my relationship with other people. In the ten months during which I wrote the diary many things changed — just as I did. I always wrote what I felt at any particular moment, independently of what I might have written a few days earlier. My sincerity took precedence over consistency.

We knew that we were living in the last phase of the war, and our survival would be the beginning of a new life. That, alongside my optimism, explains why I felt it was so important to study even in the Lager: I was preparing for the future.

In retrospect I find that, in spite of the constant dangers and insecurity, one can find very little reference to God in my diary. Sometimes I relate to the Roman goddess Fortuna, or to Fate or to the sheer Luck that protected me in those difficult times. It was difficult to trust in God when He had abandoned us and pushed us away. *Eli, Eli, lama sabachtani?*[2] (My God, my God, why hast Thou forsaken me?) How sad and tragic it is that this Evil wasn't satisfied that it took away our liberty, took our loved ones and our lives. It also took away our God, our faith and all the spiritual values that kept us through the millennia.

After liberation and my return to Hungary, I stopped keeping a diary for a long time. I was busy starting a new life. From that period, all I have left is my letters addressed to Judit. In January 1955, I lost both my father and my brother within one week. That somehow made me return to writing again.

In May 1955, I restarted my diary — my life. I have an entry for almost every day, which I have done for more than sixty years. There is a notebook for each year — many, many notebooks carefully lined

2   Matthew 27:46, based on Psalm 22:2.

up on my desk. They are all written in Hungarian, except for the diary of my deportation, which I translated into English.

As far back as I can remember, I always kept a diary. When I thought that something important had happened to me, I would write it down. I used to record my thoughts in a separate notebook. All my pre-war notebooks got lost in the conflagration. Here in Canada I marvelled at the fact that objects survived many generations and were handed down from parents to children. There is no break in continuity. My grandson inherits my son's teddy bear. Photos of my son's childhood are looked at by his sons. Things from thirty-five years ago still exist — the buildings where we once lived, our furniture, the books.

All that was left from my father was a small pocket knife, and from my mother, a worn-out handbag in which she kept a note with the anniversary dates of my father's and brother's deaths according to the Jewish calendar, but our Hungarian past is otherwise gone without a trace. The house where we used to live before the war doesn't exist anymore, and no other physical trace of our lives remains either. Only the memories.

Here in Canada there is continuity, an unbroken sequence passing from father to son, from son to grandson. There, my youth was brought to an end by the war and deportation. There, my adulthood was interrupted by emigration, after which a whole new life started. From that point on, everything that had happened in Hungary became history. Not just personal history, but the history of the whole family. After Spain, Turkey and Hungary, my family will continue in Canada and that's how the story of my life becomes a turning point in my family's history.

If a misguided bomb had killed me, or the SS soldiers had shot me with their machine guns, if I had perished in this war along with millions of other victims, I would not have been the only one who had died. My sons, Peter and George, wouldn't be here either, and neither would Thomas and Andrew, our grandchildren, nor all those who will follow them.

The long chain of my ancestors that takes me back uncountable millennia would have been broken. My forefathers who had to flee from country to country, who were hiding and suffered terrible fates to save their lives, and thereby also mine, would have suffered in vain.

But they didn't suffer in vain. They prevailed over their persecutors. I hope for yet many more generations. Amen.

# Shattered Dreams
# Dolly Tiger-Chinitz

During the night, the Soviets arrived. There was a lot of shooting, and then we were face-to-face with them. Huge, high-cheek-boned, burly men in a different uniform, yelling and yelling and then yelling some more, all the while brandishing their machine guns.

All of a sudden a small, frightened German soldier was kicked down the stairs leading into the shelter. He was alternately holding his hands high in the air in the international sign of surrender and shielding his head from the kicking boots of the Soviets. It felt like a slow-motion movie. No one understood what was going on. The Soviet officer kept repeating *shpion*, a spy, and that we were harbouring him and would all have to die now.

He pulled out a hand grenade from his belt, removed the pin and raised his hand to toss it down. Vinyi lay down on top of us and told us not to look. We shivered and sobbed uncontrollably. Like in a movie, an arm reached out from behind, slowly, ever so slowly removed the grenade from the officer's hand and told us in Hungarian to relax, we were not going to be killed. A handsome Hungarian officer who defected to the Soviets weeks ago took control of the situation.

Chaotic days followed. It was over but it was not over. There was nowhere to go, and it was terribly cold. The Soviets were menacing. Rumours of rape and pillage were common, and the men were constantly being ordered out to work. We started to hear Russian phrases like *malen'kaya rabota* (little work); *day mne svoi chasy* (give me your watches), and *zhenshchiny* (women), which became part of our language. Vinyi painted red dots on our foreheads with her lipstick, braided our hair, put us to bed and told us not to move. Every time a Soviet soldier came in, she told him that her children were sick, very sick. They started bringing us huge pails of cooked horse meat. They broke into our locker and drank everything that they could find in bottles: imitation rum extract, imitation vanilla extract, cough medicine, Chanel No. 5 cologne. And what they did not drink, they wantonly destroyed. The floor was littered with broken bottles, cans and ripped suitcases stomped to smithereens by raging, frustrated Red Army soldiers.

Then one day some high-ranking Soviets approached Apu. He is a "Bourgeois," a jeweller, so where was his hidden jewellery? He has to hand it over. Apu feigned not to understand. One of them held a gun to his temple as another hit him with the butt of his rifle. Where are the jewels? Where are the watches?

We were in bed, shivering under the covers but Vinyi remained calm. "Give it to him, please give it to him." Apu pulled out one of the attaché cases from under the bed. He opened it. There were three hundred gold Patek Philippe watches neatly packed in the attaché case. We looked on dumbfounded while the Soviet soldiers stuffed them all into their pockets. More soldiers came in and pinned Apu's hands behind his back. More, they said, give us more, where is more of the jewellery? Apu pulled the other attaché case out from under the bed. They opened it. It was full of unset diamonds neatly packed in glassine paper. A suitcase full of diamonds. There was also some gold jewellery on the bottom, chains and bracelets. A king's ransom. They packed it all into their pockets. More, they demanded, more — we were told you buried some in the garden. They led him out of the door. Vinyi carefully smoothed her hand over the covers. She pulled a small lace handkerchief out of her pocket and filled it with about a dozen stray diamonds that had scattered around when the Soviets tried to open the little envelopes.

Vinyi worked calmly, quietly, and no one said a word. The neighbours cowered, seemed to retreat from the private burden and agony of one family; we were marked, unclean. She carefully folded and knotted the handkerchief, made a little bundle out of it. She beckoned a Hungarian officer, who was observing all this in silence. "Here," she said to him, with a charming smile, "take it, I'd rather you have it than them." The officer first refused it, then scrawled a number on a piece of paper. "When you get out of here, call me," he said. "I live in Pest. I will give it back to you. I will keep it safe for you." Vinyi smiled and she eventually did get it back!

Apu dug out a small jar with a few trinkets in the garden. He returned as a broken, old and tired man, with a red circle deeply etched on his temple where the pistol had been held. He and Vinyi both sat down heavily on the bed, looked at us, and Vinyi said, "Now no one can say any more that I married you for your money." The next morning her hair was white. She had troubles with her passport: no one believed that the picture was only a year old. Vinyi was forty-one years old when the war ended.

～

A crisp, cold morning we — Zuli, Babi, Mari and I — arrived back in Subotica. A trusted maid protected Babi's apartment and miraculously, nothing was stolen or damaged. Subotica changed hands yet again, with minor scrapes and bruises only, and was again part of Yugoslavia. There was something eerie, unreal in the air. It took us a few days to discover that practically everyone was gone. We did not meet one familiar person, we did not see one familiar face.

And yet, we settled into an almost normal existence. We walked, talked and ate. We were coming out of a long nightmare.

It was suddenly May, and the burst of flowering trees scented the air. We were standing at the end of the Korzó facing the train station and licking our ice cream cones when we saw them. A bedraggled column of people coming down the street. Some were supporting each other, some women were bald, all of them extremely emaciated. What was this? A crowd gathered to look at them, these ghosts. "They are coming back from the concentration camps," someone whispered. There was an eerie silence. Of course, by now we had heard rumours about the concentration camps. But seeing these people was different.

We saw two friends with their mother. We ran towards them. "Greti, Olga!" we shouted incredulously, "what happened?" Their mother started crying. We urged them to come up to our place right away, as we lived just a few steps down the street. They did. Our mothers were hugging each other and crying. "Where were you?" We talked and ate. They bathed and dresses were exchanged. Names, names, names were rattled off, most accompanied by a shrug. "I don't know," or the phrase that became a common euphemism: "She will not return." The words "died," "killed" or "perished" were never used. No stories were exchanged. No one discussed anything. There were silences, and there was a regrouping of energy. There was a terrible effort to forget, to get on with life.

~

Ženska Gimnazija was only slightly damaged; some of its windows were broken, and shell holes like giant pockmarks disfigured the face of the building. But it was still the old school, with benches that bore the hundreds of engraved initials, painstakingly done during long, boring sessions of geography or history or while trying to focus on a difficult math assignment.

We were an odd assortment of girls on that first school day. One girl in uniform towered above us all. She was rumoured to be very old. "She is seventeen," my friends whispered in awe. "She fought with the resistance in the forest since she was thirteen."

A shy black-haired girl with two fingers missing on her left hand stood alone. She seemed extremely self-conscious, trying to hide her hand between the folds of her skirt. "Sarah was in Auschwitz," someone remarked. "She would not say what happened, but I heard…"

Snippets of conversation reached me, "…and where were you?" and "…that's nothing, let me tell you…"

In all that hubbub, it dawned on me. We were exchanging adventures. Not the usual adventure stories told on the first day of school — the farm vacation, the lake, the mountains — but about the "Great Adventure" that marked us all, some not quite as visibly as Sarah, but irreparably nevertheless. We were exchanging stories about a horrid time we could not comprehend, into which we had been dragged unprepared, and from which not even the most loving mothers could shield us. Some of us carried dreadful secrets deep inside and were silent, while some talked incessantly because the burden was too great for them to carry.

The school bell rang and we stood at attention to greet our teacher. She sat down behind the desk and adjusted her glasses, smoothing out a sheet of paper in front of her. She started calling names: "Abel" — "Present" — "Ackerman" — "Present" — "Barta" — "Present"; she droned on, and I watched a fly on the broken windowpane. There was a hushed excitement in the air. Expectation, joy, a new school year had started, and we could try to be children once again.

We did not have counsellors or psychologists waiting at the end of the war to guide us through the minefields of our memories, to help us digest them and cope with the enormity of it all. We were — fortunately — thrown back into life: It was "sink or swim." There were no self-help books written about the Holocaust and how to deal with its aftermath for those first ten years after the war. Later, the floodgates of memories were opened. Suddenly, it was all right to remember and to try to live with those memories.

# Glossary

**Aktion** (German; pl. *Aktionen*) A brutal roundup of Jews for mass murder by shooting or for deportation to forced labour, concentration and death camps.

**Allies** The coalition of countries that fought against the Axis powers (Germany, Italy and Japan, and later others). At the beginning of World War II, in September 1939, the coalition included France, Poland and Britain. After Germany invaded the USSR in June 1941 and the United States entered the war following the bombing of Pearl Harbor by Japan on December 7, 1941, the main leaders of the Allied powers became Britain, the USSR and the United States. Other Allies included Canada, Australia, India, Greece, Mexico, Brazil, South Africa and China.

**American Jewish Joint Distribution Committee (JDC)** Colloquially known as the Joint, the JDC was a charitable organization founded in 1914 to provide humanitarian assistance and relief to Jews all over the world in times of crisis. It provided material support for persecuted Jews in Germany and other Nazi-occupied territories and facilitated their immigration to neutral countries such as Portugal, Turkey and China. Between 1939 and 1944, Joint officials helped close to 81,000 European Jews find asylum in various parts of the world. Between 1944 and 1947, the JDC assisted more than 100,000 refugees living in DP camps by offering retraining programs, cultural activities and financial assistance for emigration.

*Anschluss* (German; union) The annexation of Austria into Germany in March 1938, as part of the Nazi plan to unite all German peoples into a Greater Germany. A plebiscite held under strict Nazi supervision on April 10, 1938, was 99.7 per cent in favour of the *Anschluss*. Austria was renamed Ostmark and ceased to exist as a separate nation until 1945.

**antisemitism** Prejudice, discrimination, persecution or hatred against Jewish people, institutions, culture and symbols.

*Appell* (German; also *Zählappell*) Roll call. In Nazi camps, roll calls, the practice of gathering inmates to count who was present, were part of a series of daily humiliations for prisoners, who were often made to stand completely still for hours regardless of weather conditions.

*Appellplatz* (German; the place for roll call) The area in Nazi camps where inmates had to assemble to be counted, often in dire weather conditions for hours at a time.

**Arrow Cross Party** (in Hungarian, Nyilaskeresztes Párt — Hungarista Mozgalom; abbreviation: Nyilas) A Hungarian right-wing extremist and antisemitic party founded by Ferenc Szálasi in 1935 as the Party of National Will. The newly renamed Arrow Cross Party ran in Hungary's 1939 election and won 15 per cent of the vote. The party was fought and largely suppressed by the regime in the coming years, but re-emerged as a major force in March 1944, when Germany occupied Hungary; in August 1944, the party was temporarily banned. Under Nazi approval, the party, led by Szálasi, assumed control of Hungary from October 15, 1944, to March 28, 1945. The Arrow Cross regime instigated the murder of tens of thousands of Hungarian Jews. Starting on November 6, with the last group leaving on December 11, 1944, approximately 70,000 Jews were rounded up and sent on death marches towards Greater Germany. Tens of thousands died or were murdered along the way, and some 50,000 survivors were handed over to the Germans. Between October 1944 and January 1945, the Arrow Cross murdered thousands of Jews in Budapest. *See also* Budapest ghetto; Szálasi, Ferenc.

**Aryan** A nineteenth-century anthropological term originally used to refer to the Indo-European family of languages and, by extension, the peoples who spoke them. It became a synonym for people of Nordic or Germanic descent in the theories that inspired Nazi racial ideology. "Aryan" was an official classification in Nazi racial laws to denote someone of pure Germanic blood, as opposed to "non-Aryans," such as Slavs, Jews, part-Jews, Roma and Sinti, and others of supposedly inferior racial stock.

**Auschwitz** (German; in Polish, Oświęcim) A Nazi concentration camp complex in German-occupied Poland about 50 kilometres from Krakow, on the outskirts of the town of Oświęcim, built between 1940 and 1942. The largest camp complex established by the Nazis, Auschwitz contained three main camps: Auschwitz I, a concentration camp; Auschwitz II (Birkenau), a death camp that used gas chambers to commit mass murder; and Auschwitz III (also called Monowitz or Buna), which provided slave labour for an industrial complex. In 1942, the Nazis began to deport Jews from almost every country in Europe to Auschwitz, where they were selected for slave labour or for death in the gas chambers. In mid-January 1945, close to 60,000 inmates were sent on a death march, leaving behind only a few thousand inmates who were liberated by the Soviet army on January 27, 1945. An estimated 1.1 million people were killed in Auschwitz, approximately 90 per cent of whom were Jewish; other victims included Polish prisoners, Roma and Soviet prisoners of war. Starting in May 1944, over 420,000 Hungarian Jews were deported to Auschwitz in mass transports, with smaller groups arriving through October 1944. The majority of these Jews were killed immediately in the gas chambers. *See also* Birkenau; death march.

**Auxiliary Labour Service** (Also referred to as forced labour battalions or forced labour service) Units of Hungary's military-related labour service system (in Hungarian, *Munkaszolgálat*), which was first established in 1919 for those considered too "politically unreliable" for regular military service. After the labour service was made compulsory in 1939, Jewish men of military age were recruited to serve; however, having been deemed "unfit" to bear arms, they were equipped with tools and employed in mining, road and rail construction and maintenance work. Though the men were treated relatively well at first, the system became increasingly punitive. By 1941, Jews in forced labour battalions were required to wear an armband and civilian clothes; they had no formal rank and were unarmed; they were often mistreated by extremely antisemitic supervisors; and the work they had to do, such as clearing minefields, was often fatal. By 1942, 100,000 Jewish men had been drafted into labour battalions, and by the time the Germans occupied Hungary in March 1944, between 25,000 and 40,000 Hungarian Jewish men had died during their forced labour service.

**bar mitzvah, bat mitzvah** (Hebrew; literally, son/daughter of the commandment) The time when, in Jewish tradition, children become religiously and morally responsible for their actions and are considered adults for the purpose of synagogue and other rituals. Traditionally this occurs at age thirteen for boys and twelve for girls. A bar mitzvah or bat mitzvah is also the synagogue ceremony and family celebration that marks the attainment of this status, during which the bar mitzvah boy — and in more liberal Jewish communities, the bat mitzvah girl — is called upon to read a portion of the Torah and recite the prescribed prayers in a public prayer service. Variations of this ceremony for girls are often held in Orthodox practice as well.

**British Broadcasting Corporation (BBC)** The British public service broadcaster. During World War I, the BBC broadcast radio programming to Europe in German and the languages of the occupied countries. Allied forces used some of this programming to send coded messages to resistance groups. It was illegal to listen to these broadcasts, but many people in Nazi-occupied Europe turned to it as the most reliable source of news.

**Becher, Kurt** (1909–1995) SS lieutenant colonel who was the commissar of concentration camps in Germany and also held the position of Chief of the Economic Department of the SS Command in Hungary during the 1944 German occupation. As economic chief, he was involved in negotiations on behalf of SS authorities Heinrich Himmler and Adolf Eichmann with Jewish representatives to extort wealth from Jews in exchange for saving the lives of some Hungarian Jews; the best-known example is what became referred to as "Kasztner's train," which led to the survival of 1,684 Jews. After the war, Becher was not tried as a war criminal due to Rudolf (Rezső) Kasztner's testimony on his behalf. *See also* Kasztner, Rudolf (Rezső).

*beys midrash* (Yiddish; Hebrew, *beit hamidrash*; house of learning) A Jewish religious study centre.

**Birkenau** Also known as Auschwitz II. One of the camps in the Auschwitz complex in German-occupied Poland and the largest death camp established by the Nazis. Birkenau was built in 1941, and in 1942 the Nazis designated it as a killing centre, using Zyklon B gas to carry out the systematic murder of Jews and other people considered "undesirable" by the Nazis. In 1943, the Nazis began to use four crematoria with gas chambers that could hold up to 2,000 people each to murder the large numbers of Jews who were being brought to the camp from across Europe. Upon arrival, prisoners were selected for slave labour or sent to the gas chambers. The camp was liberated in January 1945 by the Soviet army. An estimated 1.1 million people were killed in the Auschwitz camp complex, most of them in Birkenau and the vast majority of them Jews. *See also* Auschwitz.

**Blechhammer** A forced labour subcamp of Auschwitz established by the Germans on April 1, 1944, in a village of the same name in Poland (now Blachownia Śląska). Under the command of the Auschwitz III-Monowitz concentration camp, Blechhammer held 4,500 prisoners over its time in operation, men and women from fifteen European countries, making it the second-largest Auschwitz subcamp by prisoner population. In the nine and a half months Blechhammer existed, approximately 250 prisoners died in the camp. On January 21, 1945, the Germans evacuated the 4,000 prisoners in the camp and marched them to Gross-Rosen concentration camp, killing about 800 prisoners on the way.

**British Mandate Palestine** The area of the Middle East under British rule from 1923 to 1948 comprising present-day Israel, Jordan, the West Bank and the Gaza Strip. The Mandate was established by the League of Nations after World War I and the collapse of the Ottoman Empire; the area was given to the British to administer until a Jewish national home could be established. During this time, Jewish immigration was severely restricted, and Jews and Arabs clashed with the British and each other as they struggled to realize their national interests. The Mandate ended on May 15, 1948, after the United Nations Partition Plan for Palestine was adopted and on the same day that the State of Israel was declared.

**Buda** The western part of Budapest, situated west of the Danube River. The area comprises about one-third of Budapest and is mostly hilly and wooded. *See also* Pest.

**Budapest ghetto** The area of Budapest in which Jews were confined, established by Hungary's Arrow Cross government on November 29, 1944. On December 10, the ghetto was sealed off from the rest of the city. Jews who had held "protected" status first moved into the separate ghetto known as the international ghetto, which was merged into the main one in early January 1945. By that point, the population of the overcrowded ghetto reached close to 70,000, and people lacked sufficient food, water and sanitation. Supplies dwindled and conditions worsened during the Soviet siege of Budapest, which began in late December 1944. Thousands died of starvation and disease. The ghetto was also vulnerable to Arrow Cross raids, and thousands of Jews were taken from the ghetto and murdered on the banks of the Danube. Soviet forces liberated the short-lived ghetto on January 17, 1945. *See also* Arrow Cross; Danube River; ghetto; Pest.

**cattle cars** Freight cars used to deport Jews by rail to concentration camps and death camps. The European railways played a key logistical role in how the Nazis were able to transport millions of Jews from around Europe to killing centres in occupied Poland under the guise of "relocation." The train cars were usually ten metres long and often crammed with more than a hundred people in abhorrent conditions with no water, food or sanitation. Many Jews, already weak from poor living conditions, died in the train cars from suffocation or illness before ever arriving at the camps.

***chalutzim*** (Hebrew; pioneers) A term used within Zionist youth movements outside of Palestine to refer to its members who hoped to immigrate there. *Chalutzim* were also agricultural immigrants who moved to Palestine to establish settlements and build self-sustaining communities, primarily associated with the wave of immigration known as the Third Aliyah (1919–1923) that followed in the wake of World War I and the establishment of the British Mandate in Palestine.

**cheder** (Hebrew; room) A traditional Jewish elementary school in which religious studies and Hebrew are taught.

**circumcision** Removal of the foreskin of the penis. In Judaism, ritual circumcision is performed on the eighth day of a male infant's life in a religious ceremony known as a *brit milah* (Hebrew) or *bris* (Yiddish) to welcome him into the covenant between God and the People of Israel.

***csendőr*** (Hungarian; gendarme, pl. *csendőrség*; gendarmerie) A member of the military forces in rural Hungary that were responsible for maintaining law and order. During the German occupation of Hungary, the pro-Nazi *csendőrség* operated under the jurisdiction of the government of Hungary and undertook a major role in facilitating the ghettoization and deportation of Jews to Nazi camps.

**Dachau** The first Nazi concentration camp to be established, in March 1933, located about sixteen kilometres northwest of Munich in southern Germany. At first Dachau held primarily political prisoners, but over the course of its existence, all the groups persecuted by the Nazis — Jews, Jehovah's Witnesses, homosexuals, Poles, Roma and others — were imprisoned there. From 1933–1945, approximately 190,000 prisoners were held in Dachau and its numerous subcamps, where they performed forced labour, mostly in the production of armaments for the German war effort. As the American forces neared the camp in April 1945, the Nazis forced 7,000 prisoners on a gruelling death march. It is estimated that over 40,000 people died in Dachau.

**Danube River** The second-longest river in Europe, running through ten European countries, including Hungary. It is an important source of drinking water and mode of transportation for millions of Europeans. During the winter of 1944–1945, members of the Arrow Cross rounded up Jews from the streets and the nearby Budapest ghetto, marched them to the shore of the Danube and shot them so that their bodies would fall into the river to be carried away. A memorial consisting of sixty pairs of rusted cast-iron shoes was erected on the site in 2005. *See also* Arrow Cross Party; Budapest ghetto.

**death march** A term that refers to the forced travel of prisoners who were evacuated from Nazi camps near the advancing military front to camps within Greater Germany in late 1944 and early 1945. Amid the chaos as the end of the war neared, the death marches prevented prisoners from being freed by liberating Allied armies and kept them under the Nazi regime to be used as slave labour for as long as possible. Prisoners often had to walk hundreds of kilometres under difficult conditions and at least 250,000 prisoners died of starvation, exhaustion, exposure, or at the hands of SS guards if they collapsed or could not keep up with others on the march. Between November 6 and December 11, 1944, approximately 70,000 Jews were rounded up by the Arrow Cross in Budapest, Hungary, and sent on death marches towards Greater Germany; tens of thousands died or were killed along the way, and the remaining 50,000 survivors were handed over to the Germans.

**Eichmann, Adolf** (1906–1962) The head of the Gestapo's Jewish Affairs department, which was responsible for the implementation of the Nazis' policy of mass murder of Jews. Eichmann was in charge of transporting Jews to death camps in Poland and coordinated deportations from Slovakia, the Netherlands, France, Belgium, Greece, northern Italy and Hungary. After the war, Eichmann escaped from US custody and fled to Argentina, where he was captured in 1960 by Israeli intelligence operatives; his ensuing 1961 trial in Israel was widely and internationally televised. Eichmann was sentenced to death and hanged in 1962.

**Einsatzgruppen** (German; task force) Units of Nazi SS and police that were charged with securing the territories occupied by Nazi Germany after the invasion of the Soviet Union in 1941. These mobile death squads, with the support of local collaborators, were responsible for rounding up and murdering over a million Jews and many others in mass shooting operations. They were a key component in the implementation of the Nazis' so-called Final Solution in Eastern Europe.

**Endre, László** (1895–1946) The antisemitic extremist secretary of state who headed the administrative section of the Hungarian Ministry of the Interior under Andor Jaross in 1944. Endre eagerly collaborated with the Nazis in the ghettoization and deportation of Jews to concentration and death camps and was Adolf Eichmann's major Hungarian partner in crime. After the war, Endre was tried and executed in 1946 in Budapest.

**Eretz Yisrael** (Hebrew; Land of Israel) The traditional Jewish name for Israel.

*Feldgendarmerie* (singular, *Feldgendarme*; plural, *Feldgendarmes*) Military police units of the German armed forces that were active in World War I, disbanded after the war and reintroduced by Nazi Germany. *Feldgendarmerie* units were usually active in German-occupied territories, where they worked closely with the SS and were known for their brutal disciplining of German soldiers who were deserters or otherwise violated military law. *See also* SS.

**forced labour service** *See* Auxiliary Labour Service.

**gendarme** (pl. gendarmes; derived from French, *gens d'armes*, people of arms) Member of a military or paramilitary force, or gendarmerie, in France and, during World War II, in Hungary.

**Gestapo** (German; abbreviation of Geheime Staatspolizei, the Secret State Police) The Nazi regime's brutal political police that operated without legal constraints to deal with its perceived enemies. The Gestapo was formed in 1933 under Hermann Göring; it was taken over by Heinrich Himmler in 1934 and became a department within the SS in 1939. During the Holocaust, the Gestapo set up offices in Nazi-occupied countries and was responsible for rounding up Jews and sending them to concentration and death camps. They also arrested, tortured and deported those who resisted Nazi policies. A number of Gestapo members also belonged to the Einsatzgruppen, the mobile killing squads responsible for mass shooting operations of Jews in the Soviet Union. In the camp system, Gestapo officials ran the Politische Abteilung (Political Department), which was responsible for prisoner registration, surveillance, investigation and interrogation. *See also* SS.

**ghetto** A confined residential area for Jews. The term originated in Venice, Italy, in 1516 with a law requiring all Jews to live on a segregated, gated island known as Ghetto Nuovo. Throughout the

Middle Ages in Europe, Jews were often forcibly confined to gated Jewish neighbourhoods. Beginning in 1939, the Nazis forced Jews to live in crowded and unsanitary conditions in designated areas — usually the poorest ones — of cities and towns in Eastern Europe. Ghettos were often enclosed by walls and gates, and entry and exit from the ghettos were strictly controlled. Family and community life continued to some degree, but starvation and disease were rampant. Starting in 1941, the ghettos were liquidated, and Jews were deported to camps and killing centres.

**Gimnázium** (Hungarian; in German, *Gymnasium*) A word used throughout Central and Eastern Europe to mean high school or secondary school.

**Glöwen** A forced labour subcamp of Sachsenhausen located between Berlin and Magdeburg, Germany. Established in the summer of 1944, the camp was located at a munitions and machine storage area of the Dynamit Aktien Gesellschaft (DAG) facility, one of the three most important producers of explosives in Nazi Germany. The camp, which held only Jewish prisoners, had a population of more than 770 men and women kept in separate camps. Although conditions in the camp were harsh, the mortality rate was fairly low. The men's camp was dissolved in February 1945, and the women's camp was dissolved in April 1945. The men were sent on multiple transports to other camps, some to the Sachsenhausen subcamp at Rathenow, some to Bergen-Belsen (where most died of starvation) and a third group back to Sachsenhausen, from where they were forced on a death march. The women were marched to the Ravensbrück subcamp at Malchow, where they were liberated by the Soviets on May 2, 1945.

**Gross-Rosen** A labour camp established in 1940 located in and named after the Gross-Rosen village in western Poland, now named Rogoźnica. Prisoners were forced to construct camp barracks and work in a nearby quarry. As the camp was expanded to include armaments production, Gross-Rosen became classified as a concentration camp and was the centre of a complex of at least ninety-seven subcamps. As of January 1945, 76,728 prisoners were held there, of whom about one-third were women, mostly Jews. Liquidation of the subcamps began in January 1945 and Gross-Rosen was evacuated in early February 1945, with 40,000 prisoners, including 20,000 Jews, being forced on death marches. The camp was liberated by the Soviet army on February 13, 1945. An estimated 120,000 prisoners passed through the Gross-Rosen camp complex; 40,000 died either in Gross-Rosen or during its evacuation.

**Habonim Dror** (Hebrew; the builders of freedom) A Labour-Zionist youth movement formed through the merging of two previously independent Jewish socialist Zionist youth groups, Dror and Habonim Union, in 1982. Dror originated in Russia in 1915 and moved to Poland after the Russian Revolution. By the 1930s, Dror had spread throughout Europe and to South America. Dror prepared Jewish youth to immigrate to British Mandate Palestine and was active in resistance activities during the Holocaust, including the Warsaw Ghetto Uprising. To foster the Hebrew language, Jewish culture and pioneering in Palestine, Habonim was founded in the United Kingdom in 1930 and became the Habonim Union in 1958 when it merged with similar groups in various other countries. Habonim Dror exists today in seventeen countries.

*Häftling* (German) Prisoner.

**Haftorah** A portion from the biblical books of the Prophets that is chanted after the Torah reading at synagogue services on Sabbath, festivals and fast days. The Haftorah is sometimes chanted by a youth who is celebrating a bar/bat mitzvah.

**Hasidism** (from the Hebrew word *hasid*; pious person) An Orthodox Jewish spiritual movement founded by Rabbi Israel ben Eliezer (1698–1760), better known as the Baal Shem Tov, in eighteenth-century Poland. The Hasidic movement, characterized by philosophies of mysticism and focusing on joyful prayer, resulted in a new kind of leader who attracted disciples as opposed to the traditional rabbis who focused on the intellectual study of Jewish law.

**High Holidays** (also High Holy Days) The period of time leading up to and including the Jewish autumn holidays of Rosh Hashanah (New Year) and Yom Kippur (Day of Atonement) that is considered a time for introspection and renewal. Rosh Hashanah is observed with synagogue services, the blowing of the shofar (ram's horn) and festive meals during which sweet foods, such as apples and honey, are eaten to symbolize and celebrate a sweet new year. Yom Kippur, a day of fasting and prayer, occurs ten days after Rosh Hashanah.

**Himmler, Heinrich** (1900–1945) The most senior officer of the Nazi Party. Himmler oversaw the SS and the Gestapo and was directly responsible for implementing the "Final Solution" — the mass murder of the European Jewish population. Himmler orchestrated the establishment of the Nazi concentration camp system in which millions of Jews, Roma and others considered "undesirable" under Nazi racial policies were either murdered or kept imprisoned under brutal conditions. Himmler committed suicide on May 23, 1945, while in custody of the Allies.

**Hitler, Adolf** (1889–1945) The leader of Nazi Germany from 1933 to 1945 and head of the Nazi Party from 1921. In 1933, Hitler was appointed chancellor of Germany, and the Nazi Party came to power. In short order, Hitler destroyed his political enemies, established a dictatorship and implemented antisemitic domestic policies and expansionist foreign policies that led to the start of World War II and the Holocaust. Hitler committed suicide in April 1945 as the Soviet army reached Berlin.

**Horthy, Miklós** (1868–1957) The regent of Hungary during the interwar period and for much of World War II. Horthy presided over numerous governments that were aligned with the Axis powers and pursued antisemitic policies. After the German army occupied Hungary in March 1944, Horthy served primarily as a figurehead to the pro-Nazi government led by Döme Sztójay; nevertheless, he was able to order the suspension of the deportation of Hungarian Jews to death camps in the beginning of July 1944. Horthy planned to withdraw his country from the war on October 15, 1944, but the Nazis supported an Arrow Cross coup that same day and forced Horthy to abdicate. *See also* Arrow Cross Party; Sztójay, Döme.

**Jewish Council** (in German, *Judenrat*) A group of Jewish leaders appointed by the German occupiers to administer the ghettos and carry out Nazi orders. The councils tried to provide social services to the Jewish population to alleviate the harsh conditions of the ghettos and maintain a sense of community. Although the councils appeared to be self-governing entities, they were actually under complete Nazi control. The councils faced difficult and complex moral decisions under brutal conditions — they had to decide whether to cooperate with or resist Nazi demands, when refusal likely meant death, and they had to determine which actions might save some of the population and which might worsen their fates. The Jewish Councils were under extreme pressure and they remain a contentious subject.

**Jewish houses** (in Hungarian, *sárga csillagos házak*) In June 1944, three months after Germany occupied Hungary, the Nazis and the collaborating Hungarian government ordered the Jews in Budapest to move into designated buildings marked with a yellow Star of David. More than 200,000 Jews were assigned to fewer than two thousand apartment buildings. They were allowed to leave the buildings for two hours in the afternoon, but only if they wore an identifying yellow Star of David on their clothing. *See also* ghetto; Star of David.

**Jewish ghetto police** (in German, Ordnungsdienst; Order Service) The police force that reported to the Jewish Councils, under Nazi order. The Jewish ghetto police were armed with clubs and carried out various tasks in the ghettos, such as traffic control and guarding the ghetto gates. Eventually, some policemen also participated in rounding up Jews for forced labour and transportation to the death camps, carrying out the orders of the Nazis. There has been much debate and controversy surrounding the role of both the Jewish Councils and the Jewish police. Even though the Jewish police exercised considerable power within the ghetto, to the Nazis these policemen were still Jews and subject to the same fate as other Jews. *See also* Jewish Council.

*judenrein* (German; free or cleansed of Jews) A pejorative term used by the Nazis to describe an area from which all the Jews had been removed (either deported or killed). *Judenrein* deliberately carried connotations of cleanliness and purity, maliciously suggesting that the presence of Jews defiled a location.

**kapo** (German) A concentration camp prisoner appointed by the SS to supervise other prisoners in exchange for special privileges, like extra food or better sleeping arrangements. The kapos were often cruel to their fellow prisoners.

**Kasztner, Rudolf (Rezső)** (1906–1957) A Hungarian Jewish Zionist activist known for his controversial efforts on behalf of Hungarian Jews during the Holocaust. As the head of the Budapest Relief and Rescue Committee, Kasztner negotiated with Adolf Eichmann in what became known as the "blood for trucks" deal in an attempt to save Jewish lives in exchange for goods, and he is most infamously known for "Kasztner's train" — the release of 1,684 Hungarian Jews to the neutral country of Switzerland in 1944. After the war, Kasztner's role in the negotiations was analyzed acutely: some viewed him as a collaborator while others applauded him for saving as many lives as he could under the circumstances. Kasztner was assassinated in Israel in 1957 after a widely publicized libel trial, the purpose of which had been to defend accusations against him but instead turned into a moral, politicized examination of his actions during the war. Although most of the guilty verdict was overturned in 1958, the original judge's oft-quoted ruling, that Kasztner "sold his soul to the devil," is still the subject of much debate.

**kibbutz** (Hebrew) A collectively owned farm or settlement in Israel, democratically governed by its members.

*kiddush* (Hebrew; sanctification) The blessing over wine that is recited on Shabbat and other Jewish holidays. *See also* Shabbat.

**kosher** (Hebrew) Fit to eat according to Jewish dietary laws. Observant Jews follow a system of rules known as *kashruth* that regulates what can be eaten, how food is prepared and how animals are slaughtered. Food is kosher when it has been deemed fit for consumption according to this system of rules. There are several foods that are forbidden, most notably pork products and shellfish.

**Lakatos, Géza** (1890–1967) A general in the Hungarian army during World War II who was appointed prime minister of Hungary by Miklós Horthy, replacing the government of Prime Minister Döme Sztójay, and who served in this position from August 29, 1944, to October 15, 1944. Lakatos's government did not resume deportations of Hungarian Jews, which had been halted in July 1944. Lakatos was forced to resign after the Arrow Cross Party's coup. *See also* Arrow Cross Party; Horthy, Miklós; Szálasi, Ferenc; Sztójay, Döme.

**Leitmeritz** A subcamp of Flossenbürg concentration camp located in the German-annexed Czech lands on which construction started in the spring of 1944. The camp included two construction sites, which were intended to become factories producing tank engines and cables for the aircraft industry, with several thousand concentration camp prisoners in work detachments doing slave labour at these sites. The 2,800 prisoners in Leitmeritz in August 1944 grew to nearly 5,000 in November 1944, almost 6,660 in February 1945 and reached around 9,000 in April 1945. The camp included all types of prisoners held in Nazi camps, from all over Europe, both men and women, including a large number of Jewish prisoners. Of the almost 18,000 concentration camp prisoners who had been held in Leitmeritz over the course of its existence, only 4,500 survived. In 1945, the camp became a collecting point for prisoners from other camps, including subcamps of Buchenwald, Gross-Rosen and Flossenbürg concentration camps. Leitmeritz was never liberated and continued to exist even after the liberation of the main Flossenbürg camp. Leitmeritz was finally dissolved after Germany fully capitulated to the Allies on May 8, 1945.

**Majdanek** A multipurpose Nazi camp in Lublin, Poland, that opened when its construction began in October 1941. People from twenty-eight countries were incarcerated at Majdanek, with Jews and Poles being the largest groups. Between the fall of 1942 and late 1943, mass murder operations by poison gas were in effect in the camp. Both a death camp and a concentration camp, Majdanek served different functions at various points of its existence — it used prisoners for forced labour; it held suspected Polish insurgents; it operated as a transit camp; and it acted as a storage centre for personal belongings taken from Jews before their deaths in other death camps. Tens of thousands of Jewish prisoners were killed at the camp. Majdanek was liberated by the Soviet army in July 1944, although fewer than 500 prisoners remained in what was then merely a remnant of the operational camp.

**March of the Living** An annual two-week program that takes place in Poland and Israel and aims to educate primarily Jewish students and young adults from around the world about the Holocaust and Jewish life before and during World War II. On Holocaust Memorial Day (Yom HaShoah), participants and Holocaust survivors march the three kilometres from Auschwitz to Birkenau to commemorate and honour all who perished in the Holocaust. Afterwards, participants travel to Israel and join in celebrations there for Israel's remembrance and independence days.

**Mauthausen** A notoriously brutal Nazi concentration camp located about twenty kilometres east of the Austrian city of Linz. First established in 1938 shortly after the annexation of Austria to imprison "asocial" political opponents of the Nazis, the camp grew to encompass fifty nearby subcamps. By the end of the war, close to 200,000 prisoners had passed through the Mauthausen forced labour camp system and almost 120,000 of them died there — including 38,120 Jews — from starvation, disease and hard labour. Mauthausen was classified as a Category 3 camp, which indicated the harshest conditions, and inmates were often worked to death in the brutal Weiner-Graben stone quarry. The US army liberated the camp on May 5, 1945.

*Megillah* The scroll of the Book of Esther, which is traditionally read during the holiday of Purim. *See also* Purim.

**Mengele, Josef** (1911–1979) The most notorious of about thirty SS physicians in Auschwitz. Mengele was stationed at the camp from May 1943 to January 1945, first as the medical officer of the Birkenau "Gypsy camp" and later as chief medical officer of Birkenau. Mengele was one of the camp doctors responsible for deciding which prisoners were fit for slave labour and which were to be sent immediately to the gas chambers. He was also known for conducting sadistic experiments on Jewish and Roma prisoners, especially twins.

**mensch** (Yiddish) A good, decent person, someone having honourable qualities; mensch generally refers to someone who is selfless or who has integrity.

*mezuzah* (Hebrew; doorpost) The small piece of parchment containing the text of the central Jewish prayer, the Shema, which has been handwritten in ink by a scribe. Some Jews place this parchment on the doorposts of their homes, often in decorative cases.

**mikvah** (Hebrew; a pool or gathering of water) A ritual purification bath taken by Jews on occasions that denote change, such as before the Sabbath (signifying the shift from a regular weekday to a holy day of rest), as well as those that denote a change in personal status, such as before a person's wedding or, for a married woman, after menstruation. The word mikvah refers to both the pool of water and the building that houses the ritual bath.

*minyan* (Hebrew) The quorum of ten adult male Jews required for certain religious rites. The term can also designate a congregation.

**Neu-Dachs** An Auschwitz subcamp in Jaworzno, Poland, established on June 15, 1943. The camp grew from its first 100 prisoners in June 1943 to 3,664 prisoners when it was evacuated in January 1945. Although the subcamp was an independent administrative and management unit with its own warehouses, kitchen and hospital, the terrible living conditions in the camp were the same as those at Auschwitz. The prisoners came from Auschwitz to work in the nearby coal mines and at the Wilhelm power plant. When the camp was evacuated, the prisoners were marched first to the Blechhammer labour camp and then a day later to Gross-Rosen concentration camp, before being taken by train to Buchenwald concentration camp. The Soviets liberated 400 seriously ill prisoners who had been left behind in Neu-Dachs on January 19, 1945. *See also* Auschwitz; Blechhammer.

**Oneg Shabbat** (Hebrew; Joy of Sabbath) A Friday evening or Saturday social gathering to celebrate the Sabbath, often with singing or group discussion.

**Organisation Todt** A construction and civil engineering group named for its founder, engineer and architect Fritz Todt (1892–1942), that undertook major civilian and military projects under the Nazis. Organisation Todt began in the Nazi period as a quasi-governmental agency, but in 1942 it was absorbed by the German government, becoming part of the Ministry of Armaments and War Production under Albert Speer after Todt's death. The Organisation Todt made extensive use of forced labour during World War II.

**Orthodox** The religious practice of Jews for whom the observance of Judaism is rooted in the traditional rabbinical interpretations of the biblical commandments. Orthodox Jewish practice is characterized by strict observance of Jewish law and tradition, such as the prohibition to work on the Sabbath and certain dietary restrictions.

**partisans** Members of irregular military forces or resistance movements formed to oppose armies of occupation. During World War II there were a number of different partisan groups that opposed both the Nazis and their collaborators in several countries. The term partisan could include highly organized, almost paramilitary groups such as the Red Army partisans; ad hoc groups bent more on survival than resistance; and roving groups of bandits who plundered what they could from all sides during the war.

**Passover** (in Hebrew, Pesach) An eight-day Jewish festival that takes place in the spring and commemorates the exodus of the Israelite slaves from Egypt. The festival begins with a lavish ritual meal called a seder, during which the story of the Exodus is told through the reading of a Jewish text called the Haggadah. During Passover, Jews refrain from eating any leavened foods. The name of the festival refers to God's "passing over" the houses of the Jews and sparing their lives during the last of the ten plagues, when the first-born sons of Egyptians were killed by God.

**pengő** The currency of Hungary between January 1, 1927, when it replaced the korona, and July 31, 1946, when it was replaced by the forint.

**Pest** The mostly flat, commercial eastern part of Budapest divided from Buda by the Danube River. It comprises about two-thirds of the city.

*peyes* (Yiddish; in Hebrew, *peyote*; sidelocks) Among certain Orthodox Jewish communities, males refrain from cutting the hair at the edge of the face, in front of the ears. The practice of growing these distinctive locks of hair is based on a strict interpretation of the biblical verse "You shall not round off the side-growth of your head, or destroy the side-growth of your beard" (Lev. 19:27).

**Purim** (Hebrew; lots) The Jewish holiday that celebrates the Jews' escape from annihilation in Persia. The Purim story recounts how Haman, advisor to the King of Persia, planned to rid Persia of Jews, and how Queen Esther and her cousin Mordecai foiled Haman's plot by convincing the king to save the Jews. During the Purim festivities, people dress up as one of the figures in the Purim story, hold parades and retell the story of Haman, Esther and Mordecai.

**rabbi** A Jewish teacher, scholar or leader of a congregation.

**Red Army** (in Russian, *Krasnaya Armiya*) A term used from 1918 to 1946 for the Soviet Union's armed forces, which were founded when the Bolshevik Party came to power after the Russian Revolution. The original name was the Workers' and Peasants' Red Army, the colour red representing blood spilled while struggling against oppression.

**Red Cross** A humanitarian organization founded in 1863 to protect the victims of war. During World War II, the Red Cross provided assistance to prisoners of war by distributing food parcels and monitoring the situation in POW camps and also provided medical attention to wounded soldiers and civilians. Today, in addition to the international body, the International Committee of the Red Cross (ICRC), there are national Red Cross and Red Crescent societies in almost every country in the world.

**Roma** (singular male, Rom; singular female, Romni) A traditionally itinerant ethnic group originally from northern India and primarily located in central and eastern Europe. The Roma, who have been referred to as pejoratively as gypsies, have often lived on the fringes of society and been subject to persecution. During the Holocaust, which the Roma refer to as the Porajmos — the destruction or devouring — Roma were stripped of their citizenship under the Nuremberg Laws and were targeted for death under Hitler's race policies. It is estimated that between 220,000 and 500,000 Roma were murdered in the Holocaust. Roma Holocaust Memorial Day is commemorated on August 2.

**Rosh Hashanah** (Hebrew; New Year) The two-day autumn holiday that marks the beginning of the Jewish year and ushers in the High Holy Days. It is celebrated with a prayer service and the blowing of the shofar (ram's horn), as well as festive meals that include symbolic foods such as an apple dipped in honey, which symbolizes the desire for a sweet new year.

**Shabbat** (Hebrew; in Yiddish, Shabbes, Shabbos) The weekly day of rest beginning Friday at sunset and ending Saturday at nightfall, ushered in by the lighting of candles on Friday evening and the recitation of blessings over wine and challah (egg bread). A day of celebration as well as prayer, it is customary to eat three festive meals, attend synagogue services and refrain from doing any work or travelling.

***Schutzpass*** (German; pl. *Schutzpässe*; protective pass) A document that identified the holder as a Swedish subject. Swedish diplomat Raoul Wallenberg issued these passes to at least 15,000 Hungarian Jews, thereby saving them from deportation. *See also* Wallenberg, Raoul.

**Siege of Budapest** Also known as the Battle of Budapest. The 50-day encircling and conquest of Budapest by the Soviet and Romanian armies toward the end of World War II, starting in late December 1944. Pest was liberated by these armies on January 17, 1945, but Buda remained under Nazi control until the Hungarian and German troops defending the city surrendered unconditionally on February 13, 1945. One of the deadliest sieges of the war, with high numbers of military casualties on both sides, the Siege of Budapest also resulted in the deaths of 38,000 civilians from bombings, sickness and starvation, and it destroyed the largest part of the city. *See also*: Buda; Pest.

**SS** (abbreviation of Schutzstaffel; Defence Corps) The elite police force of the Nazi regime that was responsible for security and for the enforcement of Nazi racial policies, including the implementation of the "Final Solution" — a euphemistic term referring to the Nazis' plan to systematically murder Europe's Jewish population. The SS was established in 1925 as Adolf Hitler's elite bodyguard unit, and under the direction of Heinrich Himmler, its membership grew from 280 in 1929 to 52,000 when the Nazis came to power in 1933, and to nearly a quarter of a million on the eve of World War II. SS recruits were screened for their racial purity and had to prove their "Aryan" lineage. The SS ran the concentration and death camps and also established the Waffen-SS, its own military division that was independent of the German army. *See also* Gestapo.

**Star of David** (in Hebrew, *Magen David*) The six-pointed star that is the most recognizable symbol of Judaism. During World War II, Jews in Nazi-occupied areas were frequently forced to wear a badge or armband with the Star of David on it as an identifying mark of their lesser status and to single them out as targets for persecution.

**Stutthof** A concentration camp established on September 2, 1939, near Danzig (Gdańsk), Poland. Initially its inmates were predominantly Poles, though the camp population also included Jews, political prisoners, criminals and others. In the late summer of 1944, tens of thousands of Jews arrived from the ghettos in the Baltic States and Poland, as well as from Hungary via Auschwitz, and the population of the camp became predominantly Jewish. Altogether, Stutthof held around 110,000 prisoners, of which at least 65,000 died, mostly from overwork, disease, malnutrition, abuse and, especially toward the end of the war, lethal injection or gas. The 66 subcamps of Stutthof held at least thirty thousand prisoners by 1944. In January 1945, with the approach of the Soviet army, many prisoners were sent back to the main Stutthof camp and thousands of others were forced on death marches.

**Sukkot** (also Sukkoth; Hebrew; Feast of Tabernacles) An autumn harvest festival that recalls the forty years during which the ancient Israelites wandered the desert after their exodus from slavery in Egypt. The holiday lasts for seven days, during which Jews traditionally eat meals in a *sukkah*, a small structure covered with a roof made from leaves or branches.

**Szálasi, Ferenc** (1897–1946) The founder and leader of the Hungarian fascist Arrow Cross Party, which actively collaborated with the Nazis in Hungary, notably in the persecution and deportation of Jews. Following the Nazi-orchestrated coup in Hungary on October 15, 1944, Szálasi was the leader of Hungary until March 1945 and continued Hungary's war on the side of the Axis. Szálasi had fled Budapest by the time the Soviet and Romanian forces had completely surrounded the capital city on December 26, 1944, and continued to rule over a shrinking territory in western Hungary. He was convicted of war crimes and executed in 1946 in Budapest. *See also* Arrow Cross Party.

**Sztójay, Döme** (1883–1946) Prime minister of Hungary from March 22, 1944, to August 29, 1944. A former general in the Hungarian army and Hungarian ambassador to Germany from 1935 to 1944, Sztójay had strong ties to Nazi Germany and played a pivotal role in the mass deportations of Hungarian Jews during his time as prime minister. After the war, Sztójay was found guilty of war crimes and executed in 1946 in Budapest. *See also* Arrow Cross Party; Horthy, Miklós; Szálasi, Ferenc.

*taschlich* (Hebrew; to cast) A ritual involving the symbolic casting off of sins through prayer beside a body of flowing water, performed on the first day of Rosh Hashanah.

**Theresienstadt** (German; in Czech, Terezín) A walled town in the Czech Republic sixty kilometres north of Prague that served as a ghetto, a transit camp and a concentration camp. Many of the Jews sent to Theresienstadt had been exempted from deportation to the east either because they were elderly, with veterans of the German army, or they were considered prominent. Despite the terrible living conditions in the ghetto, a rich cultural life developed that included artistic performances, clandestine schools and a vast lending library. The Nazis showcased Theresienstadt as a model ghetto for propaganda purposes, to demonstrate to delegates from the International Red Cross and others their supposedly humane treatment of Jews and to counter information reaching the Allies about Nazi atrocities and mass murder. In total, approximately 140,000 Jews were deported to Theresienstadt between 1941 and 1945. About 33,000 prisoners died in Theresienstadt, and nearly 90,000 others were sent on to death camps, including Auschwitz-Birkenau. The Soviet army liberated the remaining prisoners on May 9, 1945.

**Treaty of Trianon** One of the five treaties produced at the 1919 Paris Peace Conference organized by the victors of World War I. The Treaty of Trianon, signed in 1920, imposed a harsh peace on Hungary, newly independent from the dissolved Austro-Hungarian Empire, exacting reparations and redrawing its borders so that Hungary lost over two-thirds of its territory and more than half of its inhabitants.

**Wallenberg, Raoul** (1912–1947) The Swedish diplomat who was sent to Hungary in July 1944 by the US War Refugee Board and succeeded in saving tens of thousands of Budapest Jews at great risk to himself by issuing certificates of protection and bringing them under the flag of the Swedish government in more than thirty "safe houses." Wallenberg also organized food distribution, medical assistance and child care for the Jews of Budapest. Wallenberg was taken into custody by Soviet soldiers on January 17, 1945, when Budapest was liberated, and then disappeared; the circumstances around his disappearance and death have never been clarified. He was awarded the title of Righteous Among the Nations by Yad Vashem in 1963 and has been honoured with memorials and monuments in many countries worldwide.

**Wehrmacht** (German) The German army during the Nazi period.

**yellow star houses** *See* Jewish houses.

**yeshiva** (Hebrew) A Jewish educational institution in which religious texts such as the Torah and Talmud are studied.

**Yiddish** A language derived from Middle High German with elements of Hebrew, Aramaic, Romance and Slavic languages, and written in Hebrew characters. Spoken by Jews in east-central Europe for roughly a thousand years, it was the most common language among European Jews before the Holocaust. There are similarities between Yiddish and contemporary German.

**Yom Kippur** (Hebrew; Day of Atonement) A solemn day of fasting and repentance that comes eight days after Rosh Hashanah, the Jewish New Year, and marks the end of the High Holidays.

**Zionism** A movement promoted by the Viennese Jewish journalist Theodor Herzl, who argued in his 1896 book *Der Judenstaat* (The Jewish State) that the best way to resolve the problem of antisemitism and persecution of Jews in Europe was to create an independent Jewish state in the historic Jewish homeland of biblical Israel. Zionists also promoted the revival of Hebrew as a Jewish national language.

# Author Biographies
and Photographs

Yittel Nechuma Bineth, Montreal, 2019.

**Yittel Nechuma Bineth** (née Kornelia Paskusz) was born in Csorna, Hungary, on June 7, 1929. She was the youngest of eight children, and her mother, Lea Paskusz, was widowed six months prior to her birth when Yittel's father, Elozor Akiva Paskusz, died of pneumonia. Yittel was fifteen years old when the Nazis sent her to the infamous Auschwitz-Birkenau death camp. She survived due to the fact that she was protected by her mother throughout the year-long ordeal. At the end of the war, they met up with their remaining surviving family and ventured home.

Because of the chaos and danger from Soviet soldiers in Csorna, they escaped Hungary and crossed the border to safety in Austria. In January 1950, Yittel married Yaakov Bineth in Vienna. After the birth of their first child, they left for Melbourne, Australia. In Melbourne, their family grew to seven children. Although their life was comfortable, their most important aspiration was for their children to grow up Orthodox, as was their family tradition. They moved to Montreal, where there was already an established religious Jewish community. Their family was very successful in Montreal, establishing one of the first and biggest kosher bakeries and food establishments. Yittel raised nine children and many grandchildren and great-grandchildren, all of whom are Hasidic and fine people.

Even though Yittel Nechuma was born and raised in very difficult times, she was and is always upbeat, optimistic and positive. Yittel Nechuma lives in Montreal.

1 Victor David in Lwów, Poland, 1939.
2 Victor's driver's licence from Italy, where he was enrolled as a student after the war. Fano, Italy, 1946.
3 Victor and his wife, Ruth, in Montreal, circa 1965.
4 Victor, Montreal, 2014.

**Victor David** (né David Mojzesz) was born in Przemyśl, Poland, in 1922. During the early years of World War II, Victor lived and worked in Lwów as a forced labourer for the SS. After an SS officer he befriended suggested he flee to Hungary, which was considered safer at the time, Victor escaped across the border in September 1942. In Hungary, struggling to adapt and learn the language, Victor eventually secured false identity papers and sought shelter in the Jewish communities of Budapest and Nagyvárad before fleeing once again, this time to Romania, when the Germans occupied Hungary in 1944. In Romania, Victor was interned in the Târgu Jiu camp for about ten weeks, until Romania surrendered to the Allies and he was liberated.

After the war, Victor lived in Budapest and Bucharest before smuggling himself into Italy, where he lived in Fano, met and married his wife, Ruth, and worked for the Jewish Agency, later the Israeli consulate. Victor then worked as El Al airline's first employee in Italy. In 1951, Victor and Ruth immigrated to Montreal, where he operated a travel agency until his retirement in 1985. Victor speaks nine languages and has been a major donor to both Yad Vashem and the Montreal Holocaust Museum. Victor David lives in Montreal.

1

2

3

1  Esther and her family in Remete, Romania, circa 1940. Back row, left to right: Esther's brother Herschlipe (Herman); her sister Eta Raisa; her sister Bassa; her mother, Lia; her brother Raphael; her father, Baruch; her brother Itzhak Yacov; and her brother Shloime. In middle, her sister Gitza. In front, her sister Shava (left) and Esther (right).

2  Esther after the war. Ústí Nad Labem, Czechoslovakia, 1946.

3  Engagement photo of Itzik and Esther. Falknov nad Ohří/Falkenau, Czechoslovakia, circa 1946.

**Esther Davidovits** (née Basch) was born in Remete (now Remeți), Romania, on December 25, 1930. The youngest of nine children, she grew up in a close-knit family with her siblings and her parents, Baruch and Lia. In 1940, her village came under Hungarian rule and her family began to suffer from anti-Jewish restrictions. In April 1944, Esther was sent to the Técső ghetto; one month later she was deported to Auschwitz-Birkenau, where she struggled to survive. In the fall of 1944, she was sent on a transport to the brutal Stutthof concentration camp and then on to a subcamp in Thorn (Toruń), Poland. Esther was liberated in March 1945 from the nearby city of Danzig (now Gdańsk, Poland) with two of her sisters; tragically, one of her sisters died soon after liberation.

After returning to Remete, Esther reunited with Itzik, a childhood friend of the family. They married in 1947 and lived in Ústí nad Labem, Czechoslovakia, until 1949, when they fled the Communist regime with their new baby, Isi, and arrived in Austria. Esther and Itzik raised their first two children, Isi and Sam, in displaced persons camps in Austria until they could immigrate to Canada. In March 1951, they journeyed to Toronto; their daughter, Leah, was born in October that same year. Esther lives in Toronto and is very proud of her three children, nine grandchildren and six great-grandchildren.

1 Itzik's family before the war. Back row, left to right: his sister Esther; his mother, Feige (Fanny); his brother Simcha; and his sister Ruchel. In front, left to right: his sisters Brauna (Betty), Henia and Frieda, and Itzik. Remete, Romania, circa 1932.

2 Itzik in his Czech uniform, after becoming a part of the 1st Czechoslovak Army Corps. Krosno, Poland, November 1944.

3 Itzik and his wife, Esther, circa 1956. Toronto.

4 Esther and Itzik at their granddaughter's wedding. Toronto, 1997.

**Itzik (Ike) Davidovits** (1920–2015) was born in Remete (now Remeți), Romania, a village in Transylvania. Itzik was the sixth of nine children born to Yzuel and Feige (Fanny) Davidovits and grew up working on his family's farm of apple and fruit orchards. In 1940, Remete came under Hungarian rule, and in 1941 Ike was conscripted into the Miskolc viith forced labour battalion as part of Hungary's labour service. Ike toiled in the service for four years, defying death on several occasions; he ended up becoming a Soviet prisoner-of-war and then a recruit of the Czechoslovak army. Ike spoke six languages and his translation skills helped keep him alive. After the war, Ike reunited with his four surviving sisters, Brauna, Frieda, Henia and Sarah. His mother, grandmother, sisters Ruchel, Esther and Hannah and brother Simcha perished. He also reunited with Esther, whom he knew before the war, and they married in 1947.

In 1949, after their first son, Isi, was born, Ike and Esther escaped the Communist regime in Czechoslovakia. In a refugee camp in Linz, Austria, their second son, Sam, was born. In March 1951, the family journeyed to Toronto, where their third child, Leah, was born later that year. In Toronto, Ike opened up a roofing and sheet metal business with his brother-in-law Deshi. Ike was independent and living at home until he unexpectedly passed away on June 6, 2015.

1 Sandor (Alexander Eisen). Budapest, Hungary, 1940.
2 Alex under the false identity of George Mali. Budapest, Hungary, 1944.
3 Alex in his air force uniform with his fiancée, Renata. Israel, 1950.
4 Alex at a Yom HaShoah ceremony in Toronto, 2017. Photo by Michael Rajzman.

**Alexander Eisen** was born in Vienna, Austria, in 1929 into a middle-class family with two older sisters, Jitti and Litzi. In 1938, when Hitler annexed Austria, Alex's family fled to Hungary, where both of his parents had been born. Alex's father, Abraham, was arrested for carrying foreign currency, but before he was jailed, he managed to escape to Palestine. Alex, his mother, Rozsi, and his two sisters remained in Budapest.

During the German occupation of Hungary, Alex's paternal and maternal families were deported to Auschwitz-Birkenau, as was his oldest sister, Jitti. Alex, his mother and Litzi were held in the Budapest ghetto. They managed to escape and then hid on the outskirts of Budapest using false identity papers until liberation. After the war, they joyously reunited with Alex's sister Jitti, who had survived Auschwitz.

In 1946, Alex boarded an illegal ship bound for Palestine and his father. The British stopped the ship and interned Alex in Cyprus. He eventually reached Jerusalem, where his father lived. Alex joined the Haganah and then the Israel Defense Forces; he fought in the battle for Jerusalem during the War of Independence.

Alex met his wife, Renata, in the Israeli Air Force. In 1952, Alex and Renata immigrated to Toronto, where Alex was employed as a design engineer, first at Motorola and then at General Electric. Renata and Alex have been blessed with two children and five grandchildren. Alex Eisen lives in Toronto.

1 Leslie at eighteen years old, after enrolling in university. Debrecen, Hungary, 1943.
2 Leslie and his fiancée, Judy, after the war. Debrecen, Hungary, 1947.
3 Leslie (left) with Judy, his brother, George, and their parents, Andor and Flora, after the war. Debrecen, Hungary, circa 1950.
4 Leslie and his wife, Judy. Toronto, circa 2010.

**Leslie Fazekas** was born in Debrecen, Hungary, in 1925. He grew up surrounded by a vibrant cultural life with his younger brother, George, and his parents, Andor and Flora, who instilled in him the importance of education. In 1943, Leslie began dating Judit (Judy), who would become his wife after the war. After Germany occupied Hungary, Leslie and his family were held in the Debrecen ghetto, from where they were deported to Vienna, Austria. He and his family were sent to do forced labour at the Saurer-Werke camp, where Leslie worked the night shift manufacturing tank engines. Leslie wrote the details of his life in captivity in a diary and in letters to Judy from August 10, 1944, to April 2, 1945.

After the war, Leslie and Judy reunited and married on May 19, 1949. Their son Peter was born in 1951, and their son George in 1955. Leslie earned a degree in mechanical engineering from the Technical University of Budapest and spent seven years as a plant engineer at a steam engine factory. In 1956, during the Hungarian Revolution, the family fled and immigrated to Toronto. Leslie worked two years as a draftsperson and then for a management consulting company, first as a computer programmer, then as a systems analyst and consultant. In 1968, he was hired by the Ministry of Health to organize and program OHIP, where he worked for twenty years until his retirement in 1988. Leslie lives in Toronto and has two grandchildren and two great-grandchildren.

1 Passport photo taken for entry into Palestine, 1935. From left to right: Sandor (Sam) Grad, his mother, Frida, and his older sister, Eva.

2 Sam in Israel, circa 1955.

3 Sam and Josette's wedding photo. From left to right, Josette's parents, Gustave and Sura Malka Sosiewicz; Josette; Sam; Sam's stepmother, Gizella; and his father, Armin. Toronto, May 16, 1961.

4 Sam, Toronto, circa 2015.

**Sandor (Sam) Grad** was born on March 14, 1931, in Újfehértó, Hungary. His parents, Armin and Frida, decided to move to Palestine in 1935 with him and his older sister, Eva, but returned to Hungary in 1936 after Eva died from pneumonia. Sam's three brothers, David, Herschel and Irwin, were born after their return. In what should have been the year of his bar mitzvah, 1944, Sam, his family and other Jews in his town were rounded up and sent to a nearby ghetto. From there they were sent to Auschwitz-Birkenau, where his brothers and mother were murdered. Sam survived only because he was sent to a forced labour camp after lying about his age. From there he endured a death march and multiple concentration camps, including Gross-Rosen and Theresienstadt, where he was liberated by the Soviets.

After the war, Sam reunited with his father, and in 1949 he left Hungary for Israel, where he served in the military and worked in various industries. In 1957, Sam immigrated to Toronto to be with his father and stepmother. He married Josephine (Josette) Sosiewicz in 1961 and started an electronics distributing company called Prudential Distributors. Sam lives in Toronto and has three children, Cynthia, David and Alan, eight grandchildren and one great-grandchild.

1 Kathleen (Kati) at age sixteen, dressed up for a ball. Budapest, Hungary, circa 1935.

2 Kati and Paul (Pali) on their wedding day. Budapest, Hungary, 1938.

3 Kati on her wedding day. Budapest, Hungary, 1938.

4 Kati, age ninety. Montreal, Quebec, 2009.

**Kathleen (Kati) Horváth (née Spitzer)** was born on December 9, 1919, in Budapest, Hungary. Strong-willed and independent, Kati spent an adventurous childhood and carefree youth in Budapest, the suburb of Svábhegy and the village of Ercsi. Kati lived with her parents, Margit (Manci) and Herman Spitzer, and her older brother, Ivan. Her father died by suicide in 1932. Kati married Paul (Pali) in 1938; their son, Adam, was born in 1941. As anti-Jewish restrictions increased, Kati and her new family moved to the town of Túrkeve. One day before the Germans occupied Hungary, Kati and Adam were in Budapest; luckily, they were unable to return to Túrkeve, thus avoiding the deportation that sent all the Jews there to the Nazi camps. Kati, her son and her mother survived in Budapest in hiding in a nunnery, under false identities and with *Schutzpässe* from Raoul Wallenberg.

After the war, Kati reunited with her husband, who had been deported to Auschwitz-Birkenau. They had twin daughters, Éva and Gabriella, in 1946. Tragically, Pali died in 1948. Kati found work as a "draftsman" for Budapest's city hall, the first woman to hold the position. During the 1956 Hungarian Revolution, she and her children fled Hungary; they arrived in Montreal in December 1956, where Kati worked as a draftsperson for Steinberg's grocery retail chain for twenty-two years. Kati has three children, five grandchildren and eight great-grandchildren. Kati lives in Montreal.

1  Julius in Kolozsvár, Hungary, 1941.
2  Julius at his 80th birthday party. Mississauga, 2002.

**Julius Jakab** (1923–2014) was born in Cluj, Romania, which became Kolozsvár in 1940 when the city came under Hungarian rule. In 1944, at the age of twenty, Julius was drafted into the Hungarian army to perform forced labour. On the night before he left, his father, Isaac, gave him one piece of advice that would ultimately save his life — escape. After Julius was captured by the Nazis, he endured two sub-camps of the Dachau concentration camp, including the Kaufering concentration camp. It was from a death march to Dachau that Julius eventually made his escape, surrendering to nearby American soldiers. Julius's knowledge of several languages, including English, served him well in life after liberation.

After the war, with no family left in Hungary, Julius moved to Argentina, where he met his wife, Vilma, and had a son. They immigrated to Canada in the 1960s, where Julius reunited with his brother, Louis. Ever a creative spirit, Julius painted and wrote poetry throughout his life. He enjoyed spending time with family, including his grandchildren and great-grandchildren.

1  Eva Kahan and her family before the war. Left to right (in back): Eva's paternal grandmother, Etel; her brother, Gyuri (George); her father, Alfred; and her
   mother, Katalin. Eva is seated in front. Óbuda, Hungary, circa 1935.
2  Eva (right) with her father, Alfred, and her father's girlfriend, Mariska, holding
   the white angora rabbits her father had started to breed when he lost his job.
   Óbuda, circa 1943.
3  Eva and her fiancé, Lajos, during their engagement. Óbuda, 1944.
4  Eva at her grandson's wedding. Montreal, 2004.

**Eva Kahan** was born in 1922 in Budapest, Hungary, where she grew up with her parents, Alfred and Katalin, her grandparents and her brother, Gyuri (George). Eva's mother died unexpectedly in 1937, and in 1942, George was drafted into a forced labour battalion, never to return home. After the Germans invaded Hungary in 1944, Eva met Lajos (Louis) Kahan, who was an inmate in a labour camp near her home. They soon married, after which Lajos obtained false papers and they began to live a double life, as Jews around them were being deported. After they were liberated by the Soviets, Eva was reunited with her father, but he died two weeks later.

When the Hungarian Revolution started in 1956, Eva and Lajos and their daughter, Kathi, escaped with one small suitcase, sneaking across the border into Austria and then making their way to Montreal in January 1957. There, Eva worked at several jobs, often simultaneously, learning bookkeeping while working as a seamstress in a factory. Eva exercised every day, even up to the age of ninety, and enjoyed playing the piano for the other residents of her retirement home. She had two grandchildren and two great-grandchildren. Eva Kahan passed away in 2016.

Katalin Kenedi near her 95th birthday. Winnipeg, October 2004.

**Katalin (Kitty) Marianne Kenedi** (1909–2004) was born in Budapest, Hungary. During World War II, her resourcefulness in obtaining provisions sustained the lives of her family through precarious times. While her husband, Andor (Bandi), worked with Raoul Wallenberg as the head of the Schützling-Protokoll Department dedicated to saving Jews from deportation, Katalin worked as a medic in the international ghetto in Budapest and as such was instrumental in saving many lives. Her family was one of the fortunate to have survived by virtue of the heroism of Raoul Wallenberg. Katalin lost her brother Laci, as well as countless other relatives during the Holocaust.

In 1945, Katalin opened a boutique specializing in high-quality custom-designed knitwear. Forced to close the boutique in 1949 to prevent its confiscation by the Hungarian Communist regime, Katalin was able to secure employment as a translator with a state-controlled import/export company because she was fluent in Hungarian, English, French and German.

Katalin immigrated to Canada in 1970 with her husband, Andor. She became a very proud Canadian citizen and was happy to be surrounded by her daughter, Judith, son-in-law, Erwin (Weiszmann), and grandchildren, Ann and Paul. After Andor's death in 1973, Katalin returned to work in the fashion industry, where she was proud to continue part-time until she was eighty years old, while also actively volunteering in her community. Katalin truly had an indomitable spirit. She lived independently until her early nineties and celebrated her 95th birthday to great fanfare with her family and friends in October 2004. Katalin Kenedi passed away on December 7, 2004.

1 Benedikt (Benő) Kornreich with his siblings. In back: Benő (far right) with, from left to right, his brothers Stephen, Bela (Bert) and Joska (Joe). In front (left to right) is Benő's sister Sula (Sarah), his half-brother, Andor, and his sister Blanka. Munkács, Hungary, early 1930s.

2 Benedikt (Benő) and his wife, Bozenka. Edmonton, 1990.

**Benedikt (Benő) Korda** (né Kornreich) (1914–2010) was born in Munkács, Hungary (now Mukachevo, Ukraine), the sixth child of observant Jewish parents. His diverse education led to his multi-lingualism, and he spoke Hungarian, Yiddish, German, Ruthenian, Czech, Russian, French, Latin and English. Benő studied mathematics and physics in Prague and was there when the Germans invaded on March 15, 1939. He remained, marrying Bozenka (who was not Jewish) and teaching Jewish children who were banned from schools. In 1942, he was able to leave Czechoslovakia for Hungary, considered safer at the time. However, in 1943 he was drafted into the Hungarian forced labour service. In 1944, the Soviets liberated the region he was in, and he stayed on with the Soviet army, his knowledge of many languages making him useful as an interpreter, interrogating prisoners of war. In 1945, he returned to Munkács, learning that much of his family had perished in Auschwitz.

Benő eventually reunited with Bozenka and they returned to Prague, where they survived the years of Communist rule. Their daughter, Zita, was born in 1953. Benő worked as a statistician in the mining industry and then became the chair of the Department of Statistics in the School of Economics. When the Soviets invaded Czechoslovakia in 1968, he and his family fled to Edmonton. He was a professor at the University of Alberta for many years. Benedikt Korda died peacefully at the age of 96 on December 16, 2010.

1 Mark, Israel, 1948.
2 Mark, Israel, 1948.
3 Mark, Toronto, 2015. Photo credit: Elliot Sylman for the Neuberger Holocaust
  Education Centre.

**Mark Lane** was born August 3, 1929, in a small village called Olenovo in eastern Czechoslovakia (now Olen'ovo, Ukraine). When the area was ceded to Hungary in 1939, his family experienced rising anti-semitic persecution and struggled under various restrictions. As a young boy, Mark went to Hebrew school in the city of Munkács. In 1944, under the Nazi occupation, Mark and his family were forced into a nearby ghetto and then deported to Auschwitz-Birkenau, where his mother, two brothers and sister were murdered on arrival. Between January and March 1945, Mark endured death marches to the Mauthausen and Gunskirchen concentration camps, where he was finally liberated by the American army on May 5, 1945.

After the war, Mark reunited with his father and they restarted their lives in the Bad Windsheim displaced persons camp in Bavaria, Germany. In 1948, Mark left for Israel, where he fought in the War of Independence, volunteering to serve in the Negev Brigade. Mark immigrated to Canada in 1951 because his father lived in New York and wanted him to come to North America. In Toronto, Mark started a new life with his wife, Ruth, and ran his own business, selling furniture and appliances for thirty-four years. He also became an advocate for Holocaust education, speaking for the Neuberger Holocaust Education Centre and to students at Crestwood School. Mark lives in Toronto and has two children, five grandchildren and one great-grandchild.

1  László Lang, age sixteen, during the war. Budapest, Hungary, circa 1941.
2  László outside the MIKÉFE building. Budapest, Hungary, 1942.
3  László with a friend from MIKÉFE. Budapest, Hungary, 1942.
4  László, Israel, circa 2010.

**László Láng** (1925–2015) was born in Abaújszántó, Hungary, to Béla and Olga (née Fried) Láng. He had one sister, Katalin. During his childhood, his family lived in Büttös, Forró, Encs and the village of Fony. In 1940, due to increasing antisemitic restrictions in education, László's father suggested he learn a trade. He became an apprentice with the Magyar Izraelita Kézmű és Földművelési Egyesület (MIKÉFE, the Hungarian Jewish Craft and Agricultural Association) and earned his journeyman's certificate in metalwork. In 1944, László was drafted to the forced labour service; he toiled in Vác, Mosonmagyaróvár, Szőny and Sopron. Next transferred to Austria, he worked under German command in Windisch-Minihof, building tank traps. After liberation, László journeyed home to discover that fifteen family members, including his parents, had been murdered in Auschwitz. He reunited with his sister, Katalin.

In 1946, László left Hungary for pre-state Israel, where he lived on kibbutz and worked in a machine shop. Over the next decade, he served in the Israeli navy, married and had two children. Tragically, in 1960 both his wife and first daughter died within six months of each other. László married Eva, who had three children, and they had another child together.

He and his family immigrated to Canada in 1974, where László continued working in machine operations and design, eventually owning his own business. László also became an artist, using scrap metal to create hundreds of sculptures. László Láng passed away in Israel in 2015.

1 Miriam and her husband, Laci. Israel, circa 1950.
2 Miriam and her husband, Laci. Israel, circa 1951.
3 Miriam soon after joining Ontario Hydro. Toronto, 1972.
4 Miriam, Toronto, 2019.

**Miriam Mózes** was born in the town of Hódmezővásárhely, Hungary, in 1931. She grew up in a loving family with her parents, Tibor and Manci (née Brown) Rottman, and her younger brother, András (Andrew). During the war, Miriam's father was sent to a forced labour battalion; he never returned. During the German occupation of Hungary, Miriam, her mother and her brother were deported to Austria, where they worked in a labour camp. In March 1945, they were sent on a death march to Theresienstadt, from where they were liberated.

Miriam left Hungary for Israel in January 1950; that spring, she married Laci (Ze'ev; Leslie), and in the fall she was accepted into the Technion University for chemical engineering. In 1966, Miriam and her family moved to London, England, where she had been awarded a scholarship to earn her PhD in physical chemistry at the Queen Mary University (then College) of London. It was there, in the mid-1960s, that she first began to practise yoga, a pastime she became passionate about and still enjoys.

In 1970, Miriam and her family moved to Toronto, where she became head of the Pollution Abatement Research Group at Ontario Hydro, the first female engineer in the research division. An avid environmentalist, Miriam had a successful twenty-five year career at Hydro. Miriam has three children and six grandchildren. She lives in Toronto.

1  Helen at age seventeen. Košice, Czechoslovakia, 1932.

2  Family portrait in Kassa, Hungary (now Košice, Slovakia). In back, left to right: Helen's sister Olly, brother Alexander (Laci) and Helen. In front: Helen's parents, Terez and Marcus. 1943.

3  Helen after the war. Place unknown, 1945.

4  Almost fifty years later — Helen with her granddaughters: Rina (in back); Michelle (centre), Jillian (front left) and Terri (front right). Toronto, 1993.

**Ilonka (Helen) Rodak-Izso** (née Friedmann) (1915–1998) was born in Abaújkér and raised in Košice, Czechoslovakia (now Slovakia), which became Kassa, Hungary, during World War II. She was the daughter of Marcus and Terez and sister to Olly, Shani and Laci. Under the Nazi occupation of Hungary, she and her family were deported to Auschwitz-Birkenau on June 2, 1944. Together with her sister Olly, Helen survived stops in twelve concentration camps, a death march, the journey back to Košice after liberation and a move across the ocean to Toronto, Ontario. There, Helen became fluent in English and worked as a library assistant at the University of Toronto's Robarts Library for twenty years.

She was extremely devoted to her family, feeding their spirits with the purest love and their bellies with desserts from her youth. With her grandchildren, she would sing the entire soundtrack of *The Sound of Music* as it played on her record player. When she heard them laughing, she would ask what it was that was so funny, because, as she would explain, "I want to laugh too!" Ilonka passed away in 1998 at eighty-three years young. She left behind two sons and daughters-in-law, five grandchildren and seven great-grandchildren, who all love to laugh, know every word to the *Sound of Music* soundtrack, bake their grandmother's pastries and who are all very proud to be her legacy.

1 Moishe in Israel after the war. Rehovot, Israel, September 1947.
2 Moishe and Vera at their wedding. Montreal, 1958.
3 Moishe and Vera. Montreal, 1995.
4 Moishe with his brother Yossi (Joseph) at the wedding of Moishe's granddaughter. This is the last time the brothers saw each other. Israel, 2006.

**Moishe Rosenschein** (1922–2011) was born to Sara Weisz Rosenschein and Nosson Rosenschein in Szolyva, Czechoslovakia (now Svaliava, Ukraine), and grew up in a large, warm, poor religious family. He had two brothers and two sisters. In the fall of 1943, Moishe was sent to a labour camp and did forced labour in both Hungary and Poland, where he endured brutal conditions. As the Soviet army approached, Moishe escaped the forced labour unit, finding shelter in a Hungarian peasant's barn and in the forest until the area was liberated.

An orphan after the war, Moishe was isolated and depressed. Fortunately, his two brothers survived, which gave him tremendous encouragement. Determined to reach Palestine, Moishe endured many difficulties, including several months of detainment in Cyprus. When he finally arrived in pre-state Israel, he fought in the Arab-Israeli War. Moishe left Israel in 1951 and went to France for a short while before immigrating to Montreal, where he built a family.

He married Vera Neizer in 1958 and had two children, Nathan (Fanny) and Julie (Aharon), nine grandchildren and nineteen great-grandchildren. Moishe spoke six languages and worked as a teacher and bookkeeper. He enjoyed cantorial music, watching hockey games, playing cards, attending synagogue and spending time with his family. Moishe Rosenschein passed away in 2011. May his memory be a blessing.

1 Veronika and her dog before the war. Kisvárda, Hungary, early 1940s.
2 Veronika and her husband, Miklós Mandel, after their marriage in the Bad Windsheim displaced persons camp. Bavaria, Germany, March 1947.
3 Veronika and Miklós. Montreal, circa 1948.
4 Vera, Montreal, 2003.

**Veronika (Vera) Schwartz** (1927–2017) was born in Kisvárda, Hungary, where she lived with her parents, Mór and Eszter, two sisters, Klára and Éva, brother, Zoltán (Zoli), and extended family. In April 1944, she and her family were forced to move to the town's Jewish ghetto. A month later, Vera and her family were transported to the Birkenau death camp. Separated from her parents and sisters, Vera was sent to the main Auschwitz concentration camp. In Auschwitz, she met her cousin Magda Klein, with whom she survived the Auschwitz and Stutthof concentration camps, forced labour camps and a death march in the winter of 1945.

After liberation, Vera returned to Hungary, where she reunited with her brother, Zoli. While still in Hungary, she met the love of her life, Miklós Mandel, to whom she was married for over sixty-five years, until his death in 2012. Vera and Miklós left Hungary with Zoli in 1946 and lived in displaced persons camps until immigrating to the US and then to Canada in 1947. She and Miklós settled in Montreal under the assumed names of Miriam and John Stone. They built a happy family, with five sons and ten grandchildren. Vera wrote her memoir when she was sixty-seven years old out of a keen sense of duty to the family she lost and the family she built. She passed away on September 12, 2017, after a long battle with Alzheimer's disease.

1 Susan (front, left) on vacation with her family in Siófok, Hungary, early 1940s.
2 Susan (front, right) with her mother, Elizabeth, and her sister, Rozi. Budapest, Hungary, circa 1940.
3 Susan before the war. Budapest, Hungary, circa 1943.
4 Susan, Toronto, 2005.

**Susan Simon** was born in Budapest, Hungary, on December 13, 1935. She grew up in a close-knit family with her parents, Elizabeth and Paul, and her younger sister, Rozi. Before the German occupation of Hungary, Susan and her family were in the Mátra Mountains to escape the air raids in Budapest. In May 1944, they were sent to the Gyöngyös ghetto, but they managed to escape to Budapest before the ghetto was closed off and train travel became restricted. Susan's father was conscripted for forced labour, while Susan, her mother and sister hid in a convent and then sought refuge in a Swedish-protected house. They eventually ended up in the Budapest ghetto, from which they were liberated in early 1945.

Susan later enrolled in engineering at the Technical University of Budapest. She met her future husband, Tim, in 1955, and after fleeing the 1956 Hungarian Revolution, they reunited in Vienna, Austria, before immigrating to Montreal, where they married in 1957. Susan and Tim had two children and three grandchildren. In 2017, Susan published her memoir, *The Mystery of the Precious Candlesticks*, an intricate exploration of a dramatic childhood, a rebellious youth, family dynamics and the love that held her life together. Susan Simon lives in Toronto.

1  Dolly (left) with her cousin Babi and sister, Mari. Bled, Yugoslavia
   (now Slovenia), 1940.
2  Dolly (left) and her sister, Mari. Svábhegy, Budapest, Hungary, 1943.
3  Dolly. Yugoslavia, 1947.
4  Dolly and her partner, Larry Frisch. Jerusalem, Israel, 2019.

**Dolly Tiger-Chinitz** was born in Budapest, Hungary, in 1930 to a single, working mother, Johanna (Vinyi). She and her twin sister, Mari, spent their idyllic childhood surrounded by a large, affluent, loving family. After the 1938 Anschluss, their mother decided to marry a gentile man and move to Subotica, Yugoslavia, for their safety. When Yugoslavia surrendered to the Axis forces and their city was annexed to Hungary, Dolly and Mari's mother sent them to a convent in Budapest, again for their safety. Unfortunately, that did not prove safe enough after Germany occupied Hungary in 1944, and the entire family had to go into hiding with false papers. Dolly's mother was arrested, and Dolly and her sister were hidden by a young family friend, eventually enduring the Arrow Cross coup and the Siege of Budapest.

After the war, Dolly lived briefly in Yugoslavia, where she met Janos; they married in 1948 in Paris and then immigrated to Venezuela. After she and Janos divorced, she married Joe Tiger and moved to Canada in 1961. Dolly has four children, eight grandchildren and five great-grandchildren. In 2008, Dolly immigrated to Israel and married a widowed rabbi, Jacob Chinitz, whom she had met in Montreal. He passed away in 2012. Dolly now lives in a retirement home in Jerusalem with her partner, Larry Frisch.

1 Peter with his father, Vilmos. Budapest, Hungary, circa 1942.
2 Peter and his wife, Maria, on the occasion of their 25th wedding anniversary. Côte Saint-Luc, 1988.
3 Peter and his family at the wedding of his son, David. From left to right (in back): Peter's daughter-in-law, Diane, his daughter, Sandy, his son-in-law, Israel Remer, and his son, David Vas. In front, Peter and his wife, Maria. Montreal, August 1, 1999.
4 Peter and his grandson Dov. Montreal, 2003.

**Peter Vas** (né Fried) (1940–2004) was the son of Elisabeth Ungar and Vilmos Fried. In 1943, his father was taken by the Nazis to a forced labour camp in Bor, Serbia, operated by the Siemens Construction Union; in 1944, he died on a death march. Peter and his mother survived the Holocaust in a Red Cross safe house in Budapest. His mother remarried in 1948 to Dr. Marcel Vas, who legally adopted Peter.

In the aftermath of the 1956 uprising against the Communists, Peter escaped Hungary. He fled to Austria and then joined his aunt and grandparents in Montreal. In his youth, Peter was an avid speedskater and bodybuilder, as well as an accomplished wrestler and boxer. He met and married Maria Kramer in 1963 in Budapest.

Peter worked in Montreal's clothing industry and eventually opened his own company. He treasured the freedoms offered by Canada and proudly sent his two children, David and Sandy, to Jewish schools. He deservedly took immense pride in the success of his children, in whom he instilled the value of higher education. As his children became adults, he became their best friend and travel companion. In an effort to work through some of his childhood trauma, he took to writing, which is how his thirty-page poem, excerpted in this anthology and titled "The Unending Past," came into being.

1 Imrich before the war. Budapest, Hungary, date unknown.
2 Imrich while serving in the Czech army-in-exile during the war. Place unknown, circa 1944.
3 Imrich after the war. Bratislava, Czechoslovakia, circa 1950.
4 Imrich in Toronto, circa 1989.

**Imrich Vesely** (1917–1996) was born in the small town of Šurany near Bratislava, then part of the First Czechoslovak Republic (now Slovakia). In 1938, due to the rise of fascism and antisemitism in Slovakia, Imrich fled to Budapest, considered much safer at the time. One year later, he was drafted into a forced labour battalion, eventually sent to the Eastern Front to toil under gruelling conditions. In the face of violence and brutality, Imrich's wit, daring and bravery helped him survive. After escaping across battle lines to the Soviets, Imrich was taken prisoner of war but was eventually able to volunteer with the Czechoslovak army-in-exile as a pilot in the air force.

At the end of the war, after many heroic exploits, Imrich left the army and returned to Bratislava, reuniting with his mother and sister. He married in 1950 and worked as a hardware store manager. In 1973, he and his family left Czechoslovakia for Austria, where Imrich worked in the import/export business. Imrich arrived in Canada in 1980 to join his son, Peter. In 1983, Imrich wrote his memoir in Hungarian to commemorate his past, a story about the unbreakable human spirit. Imrich Vesely passed away in 1996.

# Index

Ágnes (cousin of Helen Rodak-
    Izso), 140
Ainsley (boyfriend of Veronika
    Schwartz), 172–73, 175, 178
air raids: in Budapest, 12, 14, 201,
    205, 214, 216, 222, 235, 237, 242–
    43, 252–53, 255, 259, 270; during
    death march, 146; in Košice, 138;
    in Romania, 108–9
*Aktionen* (roundups), 38–39
Allied Kommandatura, 313, 313n1
American Jewish Joint Distribution
    Committee, 323, 330
András (brother of Benedikt
    Korda), 105
Anna (relative of Eva Kahan), 258
Anna, Sister (nun), 218, 219, 220
antisemitism: by Arrow Cross, 111,
    200–201, 206–7, 217, 224–25, 230,
    232–33, 245, 246, 247, 255–56,
    268–69, 271–72, 294–95, 297,
    298; in education, 43, 49–50, 51,
    53–54; under German occupa-
    tion, 159, 216–17, 229, 235, 249–

50, 251, 264–66; by Hungarian
    state, 4–5, 23, 31–32, 69; Jewish
    fears of revenge, 60; Láng on,
    340–41; in soccer league, 44–45.
    *See also* Jewish houses; labour
    battalions; yellow star
Arrow Cross Party: ghetto forma-
    tion by, 200, 224–25; negotia-
    tions with, 244; violence against
    Jews, 111, 200–201, 206–7, 217,
    230, 232–33, 245, 246, 247,
    255–56, 268–69, 271–72, 294–95,
    297, 298
Auschwitz-Birkenau concentration
    camps: introduction, 132–33;
    death march from, 164–65, 349;
    deportation to, 138–41, 150–52,
    162, 173–74; forced farm labour,
    176–77; Jews saved from by
    Milakovics, 92; life at, 141, 152–
    54, 174–76, 177–78, 305–6; loss
    of family at, 105, 119; Neu-Dachs
    forced labour camp, 162–64;
    religious life at, 153–54; selection

process, 152–53, 175

Babi (cousin of Tiger-Chinitz), 9, 15, 206, 361

Baia Mare (Nagybánya; Romania), 110, 111, 297–98, 299–300

Baja (Hungary), 133

Bajcsy-Zsilinszky, Endre, 21

Bánkiné (neighbour of Magda Petneházy), 240

bar mitzvah, 140, 159, 326

Becher, Kurt, 267

Békéscsaba (Hungary), 261, 264, 265

Béla (brother of Benedikt Korda), 93, 105

Berzeky, Mr., 231

Bethlen, Margit, 242

Bineth, Yittel Nechumah, 59–62, 149–57, 319–28; burial and loss of family valuables, 60–61, 151; in Csorna ghetto, 149, 150; departure of brother for labour camps, 61–62; deportation to Auschwitz, 150–52; family reunions and losses, 322–23, 326, 327–28; farm labour in attempt to avoid deportation, 149–50; German occupation, 61; home invasion, 59–60; liberation and wanderings in Germany, 319–22; religious life and perseverance in camps, 153–54, 156–57; return home and post-war life in Csorna, 323–26; selection process at Auschwitz, 152–53; slave labour at Hessisch Lichtenau, 155–56; Soviet occupation, 326–27

Binyomin (brother of Yittel Nechumah Bineth), 61–62, 326, 328

Björkman, Mr., 236

Blechhammer forced labour camp, 165–66

Braham, Randolph L., 72

Bratislava (Slovakia), 322–23

British Mandate Palestine. See Palestine

Browning, Christopher: Remembering Survival, xviii

Bubi (friend of Tiger-Chinitz), 14–15

Budapest: air raids in, 12, 14, 201, 205, 214, 216, 222, 235, 237, 242–43, 252–53, 255, 259, 270; assistance for Jewish refugees, 40–41, 42; German occupation, 249–50; ghetto, 200, 224–26, 245–46, 258, 270, 294, 295; Jewish community, 19–20, 199–200; life after liberation, 284–85; pre-war memories of Tiger-Chinitz, 7–9; siege of, 200–201, 208–11, 230–31, 245, 258, 259–60, 271–72, 287; Soviet occupation, 201, 247–48, 272–73, 293–94

Carpathian Mountains, 74–75, 99–100, 101–2, 105–8

Chetniks, 12, 12n1

Christianity: baptism of Tiger-Chinitz and sister, 10; convent school in Budapest, 13–14, 16,

205; providing proofs of, 254; sanctuary in convent for Simon, 217–18, 219–20; sanctuary in Jó Pásztor convent for Horváth, 231–33, 287–88

"Christian" Jews, 25–26, 92–95, 244

Christmas, 191–92, 192–95

circumcision, 232–33, 254, 271–72, 275, 277

Clara (aunt of Helen Rodak-Izso), 140, 311, 313

Croatia, 21–22

csendőr. See gendarmes, Hungarian

Csorna (Hungary), 60, 61, 149, 150, 323–26

curfew, 60, 150, 229–30, 231, 238, 291

Czechoslovakia, 29, 97, 315–16, 349

Danube River, 13, 201, 208–9, 230, 231, 271, 288–89, 293, 339

David, Victor, 37–42, 275–79; arrest in Nagyvárad, 275–76; arrival in Budapest, 39–41; childhood and extended family, 37; escape from train and return to Budapest, 276–77; escape to Romania, 277–79; false identification papers, 42; in Lwów, 37–38; in Nagyvárad, 41–42; journey by foot to Munkács, 38–39

Davidovitch, Mr., 326, 327, 328

Davidovits, Esther, 331–33; in Stutthof subcamp, 331; survival during liberation, 331–33

Davidovits, Feige (Fanny; mother), 113

Davidovits, Itzik, 113–18; forced labour on Eastern Front, 114–15; induction into labour battalion, 113; mail from loved ones, 113–14; survival behind Soviet lines, 115–18

death marches, 134, 164–65, 166–67, 269

Debrecen (Hungary), 56–57, 133, 179–81

decimation, 13, 87–88

deportation: to Auschwitz-Birkenau, 138–41, 150–52, 162, 173–74; to Austria, 185–86; from Budapest, 257; farm labour in attempt to avoid, 149–50; from Munkács, 103–5; overview of, 131–32, 199, 236; of stateless persons, 23; to Strasshof, 179–81, 353

Dezső (friend of Benedikt Korda), 299

Dici (sister-in-law of Katalin Kenedi), 237, 239, 240, 244, 245

Dóra (sister of Yittel Nechumah Bineth), 152, 153, 323

Dresden (Germany), 321

Duci (friend of László Láng), 44–45

Durshansky (former colleague of Imrich Vesely), 28

Eastern Front: deaths in labour battalions, 85–88, 261–62; forced labour on, 86, 114–15, 123, 124; Korda's brother-in-law at, 24, 98–99; landmine clearing, 83–84, 88–89, 114; outdoor living conditions, 125

education: antisemitism at, 43,

49–50, 51, 53–54; Fazekas's university studies, 56–57; Mózes at Reformed Gimnázium, 47–52; Tiger-Chinitz at Subotica and convent schools, 10, 11, 13–14, 15, 16, 362–63
Eichmann, Adolf, 133, 199, 205, 264, 266, 267
Eisen, Alexander, 261–73; arrests by police, 266–67, 269–70; Arrow Cross atrocities, 268–69; attempt to get Swiss *Schutzpässe*, 269–70; Budapest memories, 262; death marches, 269; death of uncle on Eastern Front, 261–62; entrance certificate for Palestine, 266; false identification papers, 268; German occupation, 263–65, 267–68; in hiding on outskirts of Budapest, 270–71; Jewish Council, 264–65; Jewish house of, 265–66; life in Budapest pre-German occupation, 262–63; siege of Budapest, 271–72; Soviet occupation, 272–73
Eisen, Alexander, father of (Abraham), 266
Eisen, Alexander, grandmother of, 261
Eisen, Alexander, mother of (Rozsi), 262, 263, 264, 265, 266, 269, 270, 272
Eisen, Alexander, uncle of, 261
Eisen, Jitti (sister), 262, 267
Eisen, Litzi (sister), 268, 269, 270,

272–73
Eliezer (friend of Moishe Rosenschein), 344
Ella (aunt of Rodak-Izso), 137–38
Elozor Akiva (nephew of Yittel Nechumah Bineth), 326, 327
emigration, 284, 286, 341–42, 344–47, 356
Endre, László, 265
Endrődi, Sándor, 235
Eretz Yisrael. *See* Palestine
Ernő (friend of Benedikt Korda), 299
Ernő (husband of Helen Rodak-Izso), 63, 65, 66
Ernő (uncle of Veronika Schwartz), 171, 173
Ervin (cousin of Helen Rodak-Izso), 140
Eta Raisa (sister of Esther Davidovits), 331–32
Éva (friend of Miriam Mózes), 186
Éva (kapo), 175
Éva (sister of Veronika Schwartz), 171, 173, 308
Faragó, Anna, 203
farm labour, 149–50, 176–77
Fazekas, George (brother), 354, 355
Fazekas, Judit (wife), 56, 180, 181
Fazekas, Leslie, 55–57, 179–82, 353–57; in Debrecen ghetto, 179; deportation to Strasshof, 179–81, 353; diary and letters to Judit, 353, 354–56; on German soldiers, 181–82; in labour camp, 179; liberation from Strasshof, 353–54;

life prior to German occupation, 55–56; on loss of family continuity, 356–57; university studies as guest student, 56–57; visit to father in labour camp, 56

Fazekas, Leslie, father of (Andor Frenkel), 56, 354, 355

Fazekas, Leslie, mother of (Flora Frenkel), 56

Fekete, Mr., 170

Fekete, Zoltán. *See* Schwartz, Zoltán

Fisher family, 171

Fony (Slovakia), 340

food and hunger: Bineth on, 150, 152, 156, 320, 323–24; Davidovits on, 115, 117–18; Eisen on, 266, 268, 271–72; Grad on, 162, 163, 165, 166, 167; Horváth on, 229, 230–31, 289; Jakab on, 189, 190–91, 194–95; Kahan on, 250, 259, 260, 295; Kenedi on, 237–38; Korda on, 19, 20; Lane on, 350; Láng on, 120–21; Mózes on, 330; Rodak-Izso on, 142, 143–44, 146, 147–48; Rosenschein on, 123, 127, 345–46; Schwartz on, 171, 175, 304, 305–6; Simon on, 215, 221, 223, 226, 336; Vesely on, 86

food rationing, 19, 20, 250

forced labour: on Eastern Front, 86, 114–15, 123, 124; farm labour, 176–77; at Hessisch Lichtenau, 155–56; at Mauthausen, 349–50; at Neu-Dachs, 162–64; in Lwów, 37–38

Forgács, Vili, 236–37

Friedländer, Saul, 5

Friedmann, Helen. *See* Rodak-Izso, Helen

Friedmann, László, 120

Friedmann, Marcus (father of Helen Rodak-Izso), 135, 136–37, 139, 140

Friedmann, Terez (mother of Helen Rodak-Izso), 140, 146, 318

Fried sisters, 173

Fritz (guard of Julius Jakab), 190

Fulbrook, Mary, xviii

Gartman, Mrs., 310

gendarmes, Hungarian, 39, 64, 76–78, 84, 172, 180, 199, 236

German soldiers, 37–38, 181–82

Germany: continuation of war, 100; control of press and society, 21–22, 22n1; mass murder of Jews, 59, 132–34; occupation of Hungary, 61, 131, 159, 170, 183–84, 203, 228, 235, 249, 263; relationship with Hungary, 22, 24, 48, 73–74; war with Soviet Union, 79; wealth stolen from Jews, 151, 161, 180, 205. *See also specific concentration camps*

ghettos: in Budapest, 200, 224–26, 245–46, 258, 270, 294, 295; comparison between Hungary and Poland, 131; in Csorna, 149, 150; in Debrecen, 179; in Gyöngyös, 214; in Kisvárda, 171, 173; near Vásárosnamény, 160–62; in Theresienstadt, 168, 186, 329

*Gleichschaltung*, 22, 22n1

Glöwen concentration camp, 144–45

Goebbels, Joseph, 35, 36

Gold, Mrs., 218

Gonda, Dr., 55

Grad, Armin (father), 53, 159, 160, 162

Grad, David (brother), 160, 162

Grad, Frida (mother), 160, 162

Grad, Herschel (brother), 160, 162

Grad, Irwin (brother), 160, 162

Grad, Sandor (Sam), 53–54, 159–68; antisemitism in school, 53–54; awareness of world events, 53; bar mitzvah, 159; death marches and eventual evacuation to Theresienstadt, 164–68; deportation to Auschwitz-Birkenau, 162; eviction from home, 159–60; in factory ghetto near Vásárosnamény, 160–62; forced labour at Neu-Dachs camp, 162–64

Greti (friend of Dolly Tiger-Chinitz), 362

Gross-Rosen concentration camp, 167

Grünfeld family, 229–30

Grünwald, Reb Yosef, 327

Gunskirchen concentration camp, 350–51

Gyenge (labour battalion commandant), 101, 102, 104, 109, 110, 298–99, 300–301

Gyöngyös (Hungary), 213, 214

György (relative of Benedikt Korda), 105

Gyula (cousin of Dolly Tiger-Chinitz), 206

Habonim Dror, 342

Hajdúböszörmény (Hungary), 95–96

Hanukkah, 191–92. See also Christmas

Hartenstein, Pál, 120

Hashem ("the Name"), 62, 62n1

Hessisch Lichtenau concentration camp, 155–56

High Holy Days, 14–15, 156–7

Hitler, Adolf, 22n1, 35, 55, 100, 263, 352

Hlinka (Slovak military force), 28, 28n1

Hódmezővásárhely (Hungary), 49, 183–84, 185, 330

Holocaust: anthology's approach to, xix–xxi; comparison between Hungary and Romania, 6n4; documentation movement and survivor testimony, xvii–xix; drawing lessons from, xxiii; mass commemorations for dead, 328; memoir writing process, xx, xxi–xxiii, 286

Holzaple, Mr., 323–24

hora (Israeli folk dance), 344, 344n1, 347

Horthy, Miklós: antisemitism under, 4; attempt to withdraw from Axis powers, 110–11, 200, 206, 239, 256, 268; cooperation with Germans, 48; deportations halted by, 199; German occupation and, 263; hunting castle in Transylvania, 99; loss of faith in Germans, 25; territorial expansion into Yugoslavia, 12; trust in, 135

Horváth, Ádám (son), 227, 228, 229, 231, 232–33, 288, 289–90

Horváth, Kathleen (Kati), 227–33, 287–91; Arrow Cross atrocities and siege of Budapest, 230–31; escape to Soviet-occupied Túrkeve, 287–90; at Jó Pásztor (Good Shepherd) convent, 231–33, 287; life in Túrkeve, 227, 290–91; *Schutzpässe* from Wallenberg, 231; stranded in Budapest, 228–30

Horváth, Pál (husband), 227

Hotel Lukács (Budapest), 204

Hungarian army, 55, 69, 71, 79. *See also* labour battalions

Hungarian Jews: Arrow Cross violence against, 111, 200–201, 206–7, 217, 224–25, 230, 232–33, 245, 246, 247, 255–56, 268–69, 271–72, 294–95, 297, 298; assistance for refugees in Budapest, 40–41, 42; in Budapest, 19–20, 199–200; composition of, 3–4, 3n1; in concentration camps and death marches, 132–34; deportations, 131–32, 236; eviction from homes, 137–38, 159–60, 170, 184; under German occupation, 159, 216–17, 229, 235, 249–50,

251, 264–66; identification with Hungary, 5–6; Jewish Council, 264–65, 295, 315; life after liberation, 283–86; memoirs by, xx, xxi–xxiii, 286; reactions to news of atrocities, 59, 84–85, 135; resistance by, 201–2, 246, 257–58; restitution policies, 285; state antisemitism against, 4–5, 23, 31–32, 69; wealth hidden by, 60–61, 171, 213, 249; wealth stolen from, 151, 161, 180, 205, 309, 360–61

Hungarian Order of Vitéz, 300, 300n1

Hungarian pengő (currency), 325–26

Hungary: antisemitism by state, 4–5, 23, 31–32, 69; attempt to withdraw from Axis powers, 110–11, 200, 206, 239, 256, 268; Communist dictatorship, 285–86; comparison to Holocaust in Romania, 6n4; Czechoslovakia and, 97; food rationing, 19, 20, 250; life pre-German occupation, 18–19; Nazi racial beliefs and, 25; occupation by Germany, 61, 131, 159, 170, 183–84, 203, 228, 235, 249, 263; participation in deportations, 131–32; political situation, 21–23, 24–25; relationship with Germany, 22, 24, 48, 73–74; secret police, 25; territorial expansion, 3, 3n2, 12, 73–74

hunger. *See* food and hunger

identification papers, false, 42, 250,
   252, 254, 255, 257–58, 267, 268,
   340
Imre (Imike; cousin of Helen
   Rodak-Izso), 140
International Army, 240
Irma (relative of Katalin Kenedi),
   237–38, 243, 244, 245
Israel, 286, 352
István (friend of Benedikt Korda),
   299
Jakab, Julius, 189–95; birthday in
   camp, 189–90; Christmas in
   camp, 191–92, 192–95; hunger
   and food in camp, 189, 190–91,
   194–95; on telling Holocaust
   memories, 192
János (relative of Katalin Kenedi), 240
Jávor, Pál, 241
Jewish Council (*Judenrat*), 37,
   264–65, 295, 315
Jewish houses, 199, 214, 240, 251,
   255, 256, 265–66
Joe (friend of Julius Jakab), 189–90,
   193–94
Jolsva (Jelšava, Slovakia), 113
Jó Pásztor (Good Shepherd) convent, 231–33, 287–88
Jóska (brother of Benedikt Korda),
   105
Judaism: loss of faith, 177, 351, 355;
   sustainment through hardships, 14–15, 123–24, 125, 126–27,
   153–54, 156–57, 175, 215
Kahan, Akiva (brother-in-law), 255,
   258

Kahan, Dóra (sister-in-law), 257
Kahan, Eva, 249–60, 293–96; air
   raids, 252–53, 255; Arrow Cross
   atrocities, 256; on Budapest
   ghetto, 258; close call with
   Lajos's family, 255–56; double
   life using false identification
   papers, 252–54, 256–57, 296;
   father's survival and death in
   Budapest, 294–96; German occupation, 249–50; housekeeping
   work, 258–59; Jewish house of,
   251; marriage to Lajos, 250–51,
   251–52; siege of Budapest, 258,
   259–60; Soviet occupation,
   293–94; underground resistance,
   257–58; visits to Lajos in labour
   battalion, 254–55
Kahan, Eva, father of (Alfred), 249,
   250–51, 255, 256, 293, 294–96
Kahan, Eva, grandfather of (Beno
   Stern), 294
Kahan, Eva, mother-in-law, 255, 257
Kahan, Irén (sister-in-law), 257
Kahan, Józsi (brother-in-law), 255,
   258
Kahan, Lajos (husband): Arrow
   Cross search for, 255–56; bread
   acquired by, 259; burial of Eva's
   father, 295; community connections, 250, 260; double life
   using false identification papers,
   252–54, 256–57; Eva's visits to
   in labour battalion, 254–55;
   marriage to Eva, 250–51, 251–52;
   Soviet occupation, 293–94; in

underground, 257–58

Kahan, Zev (brother-in-law), 255, 257

Kaiserwald concentration camp, 141–42

Kállay, Miklós, 22, 25, 263

kapos, 144, 147, 156, 163–64, 175, 178, 192

Karsai, László, 132

Kassa (Košice; Slovakia), 65, 119, 141, 316–18

Kasztner, Rudolf, 202, 266

Kaufering concentration camp: Christmas at, 191–92, 192–95; life at, 189–91

Kenedi, Andor (Bandikám; husband): German occupation, 235; in hiding in Budapest, 239–40; illness, 243; Katalin's worry for, 248; in labour battalion, 236, 238–39; *Schutzpass* from Swedish embassy, 237; work with Swedish embassy, 244, 245, 246–47

Kenedi, Judit (daughter): air raid, 237; arrest by police, 241–43; in hiding in Budapest, 239, 240, 241; Katalin's worry for, 248; *Schutzpass* from Swedish embassy, 236–37, 247; in Swedish protected housing, 244, 245–46

Kenedi, Katalin, 235–48; air raids, 235, 237; arrest by police, 241–43; on deportations, 236; food sources, 237–38; German occupation, 235; in hiding in

Budapest, 239–41; husband in labour battalion, 236, 238–39; *Schutzpass* from Swedish embassy, 236–37, 242, 245, 246, 247; siege of Budapest, 245; Soviet occupation, 247–48; in Swedish protected housing, 243–44, 245–47

Kenedi, Katalin, stepfather of, 240

Kenedi, Sári (mother-in-law), 237, 239, 240, 243, 244, 245, 248

Kerekes (labour battalion master sergeant), 92–93

Kisvárda (Hungary), 169–70, 171–73, 307, 309–10

Klára (sister of Veronika Schwartz), 171, 173, 308

Klein, Magda (cousin of Veronika Schwartz), 173–74, 176, 303–5, 307, 310

Komáromi, Márta, 307, 308

Kopstein family, 236. *See also* Kenedi, Katalin

Korda, Benedikt, 17–26, 91–111, 297–302; airstrip construction in Hajdúböszörmény, 95–96; on antisemitism, 23, 24; attempt to leave Baia Mare, 297–98; in Baia Mare, 299–300; brother-in-law's experience on Eastern Front, 24, 98–99; as "Christian" Jew, 25–26, 92–95; Commandant Gyenge and, 298–99, 300–301; on deportation of Jews from Munkács, 103–5; dishonourable discharge from kitchen duty, 100–101;

on food rationing, 19, 20; on
Hungarians and Hungarian
Jews, 19–20, 96; Hungary's attempted withdrawal from Axis
powers, 110–11; induction into
labour battalion, 91–92; intentions to leave Hungary, 17; on
labour battalions, 23–24; loss of
family, 104–5; loss of personal
possessions, 91; on morality, 95;
march to Baia Mare, 108–10;
Margittai (military engineer)
and, 102–4; on political situa-
tion in Hungary, 21–23, 24–25;
road and bridge building in
Carpathian Mountains, 99–100,
101–2, 105–8; Soviet occupa-
tion, 301–2; train journey from
Prague to Budapest, 17–19
Korda, Benedikt, father of, 105
Korda, Benedikt, stepmother of, 105
Korda, Bozenka (wife), 96–97, 298
Kornreich, Benedikt. See Korda,
Benedikt
Kornreich, Mihály, 110
Košice (Kassa; Slovakia), 65, 91, 141,
316–17
Kovács, Elek, 275–76, 277, 278
Kovács, Mrs. (teacher of Miriam
Mózes), 49–50
Kovatch family, 325
Krakow (Poland), 314–16
labour battalions: introduction,
69–72; abandonment behind
Soviet lines, 115–18; airstrip con-
struction in Hajdúböszörmény,
95–96; basic training, 74;
"Christian" Jews and, 25–26,
92–95; conscription into, 53;
Davidovits on, 113–18; death of
Eisen's uncle on Eastern Front,
261–62; deaths in, 4, 70–71, 85–
88, 120–21; departure of Bineth's
brother for, 61–62; dismissal
of guards by Commandant
Gyenge, 298–99; escape attempts, 75–78, 127–28; factory
repair at Szőny, 119–20; Fazekas
on, 56, 179; forced labour on
Eastern Front, 114–15, 123, 124;
furloughs, 80–83; genocide
survival and, 71–72; Hungary's
attempted withdrawal from Axis
powers and, 110–11; illness and
near-death experiences, 121–22,
125–26; induction process, 73,
91–92, 113, 119; Kenedi's husband
in, 236, 238–39; Korda on, 23–24,
25, 91–111; Korda's brother-in-
law at Eastern Front, 24, 98–99;
landmine clearing on Eastern
Front, 83–84, 88–89, 114; Láng
on, 119–22; lumber conveyance in Carpathian Mountains,
74–75; mail from loved ones,
113–14; march to Baia Mare,
108–10; outdoor living conditions on Eastern Front, 125;
punishment for skipping work
for Purim, 123–24; road and
bridge building in Carpathian
Mountains, 75, 99–100, 101–2,

105–8; Rodak-Izso's visit to see husband, 63–66; Rosenschein on, 123–28; at Shipyard Island, 79–80; Simon's father in, 215, 216, 218–19; tank trap digging in Austria, 121; Vesely on, 73–89

LaCapra, Dominick, xxii

Laci (László; brother of Helen Rodak-Izso), 139

Laci (relative of Katalin Kenedi), 237

Lakatos, Géza, 236

Lane, Mark, 349–52; evacuation from Auschwitz and Mauthausen, 349–50; impact of Holocaust on, 351; liberation by Americans, 350–51; return to Mauthausen as free man, 352

Lane, Mark, father of, 351

Láng, Béla (father), 43, 119

Láng, Katalin (sister), 45, 340–41

Láng, László, 43–45, 119–22, 339–42; on antisemitism, 45, 340–41; apprenticeship in Budapest, 43–44; emigration to Palestine, 341–42; factory repair at Szőny, 119–20; illness and near-death experience, 121–22; induction into labour battalion, 119; loss of family and friend, 119, 120–21; return to Budapest and Fony, 339–40; soccer team and antisemitism, 44–45; tank trap digging in Austria, 121

Láng, Olga (mother), 119

Lăpusna (Moldova), 99–100, 101–2

Leitmeritz concentration camp, 167–68

Lengyel, Willy, 275, 278

Leslie (brother of Helen Rodak-Iszo), 316–17

Lévai (friend of Benedikt Korda), 98, 107–8

liberation, life after, 283–86

Lici (sister of Yittel Nechumah Bineth), 152, 326, 328

Lili (aunt of Alexander Eisen), 270

Lili (girlfriend of Imrich Vesely), 80–82, 83

Linden (friend of Katalin Kenedi), 243

Linksz, Éva, 241

Lodz ghetto, 131

Lwów (Poland), 37–38

Madi (French nanny of Katalin Kenedi), 241, 247

Magda (classmate of Miriam Mózes), 51

Major, Pál, 150

Mandel, Miklós (husband of Veronika Schwartz), 307–8

March of the Living, 352

Marci (uncle of Helen Rodak-Izso), 140

Margaret (friend of Miriam Mózes), 49, 50

Margit (aunt of Veronika Schwartz), 171, 173

Margittai (military engineer), 102–4

Mari (sister of Tiger-Chinitz), 10, 13–14, 14–15, 361

Mariska (aunt of Helen Rodak-

Izso), 140
Martin (uncle of Helen Rodak-
    Izso), 136–37
Mátra Mountains, 14–15, 213
Mauthausen concentration camp,
    120–21, 349–50, 352
Mengele, Josef, 152–53, 155, 175
Meshulem (brother of Yittel
    Nechumah Bineth), 59, 60–61,
    151, 326
MIKÉFE (Magyar Izraelita Kézmű
    és Földművelési Egyesület;
    Hungarian Jewish Craft and
    Agricultural Association), 43,
    43n1, 44, 45, 119
Miki (stepbrother of Benedikt
    Korda), 105
Milakovics (labour battalion cap-
    tain), 91–92, 93–94
Miskolc (Hungary), 152
Mojzesz, David. See David, Victor
Montgomery, John Flournoy, 131
Moskovitz, Miklós, 44
Mosonmagyaróvár (Hungary), 119
Mosonszolnok (Hungary), 323–24
Mózes, Miriam, 47–52, 183–87,
    329–30; deportation to Austria,
    52, 185–86; facing the thought
    of death, 186–87; German oc-
    cupation and eviction from
    home, 183–84; liberation from
    Theresienstadt, 329; at Reformed
    (Calvinist) Gimnázium, 47–52;
    return home to Budapest and
    Hódmezővásárhely, 330; in
    Theresienstadt ghetto, 186

Munkács (Hungary), 23, 38–39, 97,
    102–3, 103–5, 127, 267, 297
Murin, Mr., 271, 272
Nagybánya (Baia Mare; Romania),
    110, 111, 297–98, 299–300
Nagyvárad (Hungary), 41–42,
    275–76, 278
Neolog (Congress Judaism), 3, 3n1
Neu-Dachs forced labour camp,
    162–64
Ney, Blanka (sister of Benedikt
    Korda), 98–99, 105
Ney, Tamás (nephew of Benedikt
    Korda), 105
Ney, Tibor (brother-in-law of
    Benedikt Korda), 24, 98–99
Nicholas (cousin-in-law of Tiger-
    Chinitz), 15, 16
Nijinsky, Vaslav, 8
Norbert (relative of Benedikt
    Korda), 105
Novi Sad (Serbia), 13
Olga (friend of Dolly Tiger-
    Chinitz), 362
Olly (sister of Helen Rodak-Izso),
    139, 144–45, 146–47, 311–12, 313,
    315
Organisation Todt, 190
OTI Telep (Budapest), 271
Pál, Manci, 156
Palestine, 139, 266, 342, 344–47
partisans, 12, 267
Paskusz, Kornelia. See Bineth, Yittel
    Nechumah
Paskusz, Lea (mother of Yittel
    Nechumah Bineth): burial and

loss of family valuables, 60–61, 151; deportation to Auschwitz, 152; family reunions, 322–23, 327, 328; home invasion, 59–60; liberation and wanderings in Germany, 319–22; religious life and perseverance in camps, 153–54, 156–57; return to Csorna, 323–24, 325; son's departure for labour camp, 62

Pavlova, Anna, 8

pengő, Hungarian (currency), 325–26

Peter (friend of Miriam Mózes), 183

Pétervására (Hungary), 113

Petneházy, Magda, 240

Pinchas (friend of Moishe Rosenschein), 123–24

Piri (relative of Eva Kahan), 258

Piroska (relative of Benedikt Korda), 105

Poland, 131

Polish refugees, 41, 42, 275

Posner family, 169

Purim, 123–24

radio, 53, 55, 111, 169, 211, 249, 263

Rátkai, Márton, 242

Ravensbrück concentration camp, 146–47

Rechlin concentration camp, 143–44

Red Cross, 139, 247, 266, 314, 332, 349

religious faith. See Judaism

Renee (sister of Yittel Nechumah Bineth), 59, 151, 152, 153, 323, 325

Repenye (Repynne, Ukraine), 123, 126–27

resistance, underground, 201–2, 246, 257–58, 362

restitution, 285

Rodak-Izso, Helen, 63–66, 135–48, 311–18; arrest of father and uncle by Germans, 136–37; bar mitzvah of cousin Imike, 140; departure from Ravensbrück, 147–48; deportation to Auschwitz-Birkenau, 138–41; eviction of Jews from homes, 137–38; forced meal at Rechlin concentration camp, 143–44; at Glöwen concentration camp, 144–45; at Kaiserwald concentration camp, 141–42; in Krakow after liberation, 314–16; liberation and assault by Soviets, 311–14; loss of husband, 66; marriage to Ernő, 63; at Ravensbrück concentration camp, 145–47; on reactions to news of atrocities, 135; reflection on deportations, 142–43; return home to Košice, 316–18; visit to labour camp to see Ernő, 63–66

Romania, 6, 6n4, 110, 200, 277–79

Romek (friend of Victor David), 276–77

Rosenschein, Joseph (brother), 344

Rosenschein, Moishe, 123–28, 343–47; emigration to Palestine, 344–47; escape from labour camp, 127–28; forced labour on

Eastern Front, 123, 124; illness and near-death experience, 125–26; outdoor living conditions, 125; punishment for skipping work for Purim, 123–24; return home to Szolyva, 343–44; Yom Kippur, 126–27

Rosenschein, Moishe, sister of, 123

Rosh Hashanah, 156

Rothberg, Michael: *Traumatic Realism*, xxii

Rottman, András (Andrew; brother of Miriam Mózes), 184, 185, 187, 330

Rottman, Manci (mother of Miriam Mózes), 48, 184, 185, 187, 330

Rottman, Tibor (father of Miriam Mózes), 184, 187

Rozett, Robert, 69–70

Rozi (sister of Susan Simon), 213, 215, 216, 217, 219–20, 223, 224, 225

Sándor (Sanyi; brother of Helen Rodak-Izso), 139

Sándor (uncle of Katalin Kenedi), 240

Sára (relative of Benedikt Korda), 105

Sarah (Auschwitz survivor), 362

Schlesinger, Mr., 151

school. *See* education

*Schutzpässe*, 231, 236–37, 242, 244, 246, 258, 269–70

Schwartz, Veronika, 169–78, 303–10; in Auschwitz-Birkenau, 174–76, 177–78, 305–6; deportation to Auschwitz, 173–74; eviction and move to ghetto, 170–71; first boyfriend, 172–73, 178; forced farm labour, 176–77; marriage proposal at Auschwitz, 178; reactions to news of atrocities, 169–70; religious faith of, 175, 177; return home to Kisvárda, 309–10; return to Hungary, 306–7; reunion with brother in Újpest, 307–9; revenge contemplated, 306; survival during Soviet occupation, 303–5; unforgettable memories, 305–6

Schwartz, Veronika, father of (Mór), 169, 170–71, 173

Schwartz, Veronika, grandmother of (Eszter), 170, 171, 173–74

Schwartz, Veronika, mother of (Irén), 169, 170–71, 172, 173

Schwartz, Zoltán (brother), 170, 307, 308–9

sexual assault, xix, 207, 290, 304–5, 312–13, 331

Shava (sister of Esther Davidovits), 331–32, 333

Shenker, Noah, xviii–xix

Shipyard Island, 79–80

Shlome Meir (brother of Yittel Nechumah Bineth), 326, 327, 328

Simon, Susan, 213–26, 335–37; air raids, 216; Budapest ghetto, 224–26; encounter with death, 222; faith in humanity, 224, 225; father's escape from labour camp, 218–19; father's return home, 335–36; in hiding at convent, 217–18, 219–20; in hiding in Budapest, 220–21, 222–24; illness, 226; liberation of Budapest, 335; life in Budapest pre-Arrow Cross, 214–15, 216–17; loss of grandfather, 221–22; move to Gyöngyös after German occupation, 213–14; reflection on Holocaust experiences, 336–37; religious life, 215

Simon, Susan, father of (Paul), 213, 214, 215, 216, 217, 218–19, 335–36

Simon, Susan, grandfather of (Istvan), 215, 220–22, 337

Simon, Susan, mother of (Elizabeth): air raids, 216; Budapest ghetto, 224–25, 226; burial of family valuables, 213; communication with grandfather, 215; departure from Gyöngyös ghetto, 214; father's return and, 336; grandfather's death and, 221–22; in hiding in Budapest, 221, 222–23; in hiding in convent, 217, 218, 219, 220; religious life, 215

Sinai, Lenka, 317

slave labour. See forced labour

Slovakia, 22, 31

Smallholders' (Peasant) Party, 21

Sopron (Hungary), 120, 151, 326

Soviet Union: labour battalions and, 115–18, 301–2; liberation by, 128, 247–48, 272–73, 293–94; occupation of Túrkeve, 290–91; siege

of Budapest, 200–201, 208–11, 230–31, 245, 258, 259–60, 271–72, 287; violence committed by during occupation of Budapest, 304–5, 311–14, 320, 321, 326–27, 331, 341–42, 359–61; war with Germany, 79

Spitzer, Margit (Manci; mother of Kati Horváth), 231, 233, 288, 289–90

Stalingrad, Battle of, 55, 71

Steiner, György, 244

Stern, Gyuri, 44

Stigler (soldier), 38

Stone, Dan: *The Liberation of the Camps*, 283

Strasshof concentration camp, 133, 180–82, 353–54

Stutthof concentration camp, 331

Subcarpathia, 3n2, 4

Subotica (Yugoslavia), 9–13, 15, 361–62

suicide, 135, 169, 204, 206

Sukkot, 156

Suleiman, Susan Rubin, xx

Šurany (Slovakia), 29–30

Sweden, 201–2, 222–23, 231, 236–37, 244, 258, 269

Switzerland, 201–2, 205–6, 266, 269–70, 326

Szálasi, Ferenc, 111, 200, 206, 256, 268, 270

Szatyi (first love of Tiger-Chinitz), 13

Szeged (Hungary), 52, 133

Szemere, Tomi, 179

Szensky, Mrs. Bobo, 275, 276

Szentirmay, Gyuri, 16, 207–8

Szentirmay, Júlia, 16, 207–8

Szolnok (Hungary), 133, 289, 290

Szolyva (Svaliava, Ukraine), 343–44

Szőny (Hungary), 119–20

Sztójay, Döme, 111, 263

Târgu Jiu camp (Romania), 279

Theresienstadt ghetto and concentration camp, 168, 186, 329

Thorn (Toruń), Poland, 331

Tieberger, Elza (Zuli), 8, 13, 14–15,
16, 204, 205–6, 208, 361

Tieberger, Imre, 13, 14–15, 204,
205–6, 208

Tiger-Chinitz, Dolly, 7–16, 203–11,
359–63; air raids, 12, 14; Arrow
Cross atrocities, 206–7; attempt to negotiate freedom for
uncle and aunt, 205–6; early
childhood in Budapest, 7–9;
education experiences during
war, 10, 11, 13–14, 15, 16; first
love, 13; High Holy Days in
Mátras Mountains, 14–15; life in
Budapest after German occupation, 203–5; on memory and
personality, 7; move to Subotica
for safety, 9–13; refuge and sexual abuse by Gyuri Szentirmay,
207–8; return home to Subotica,
361–62; return to school after
war, 362–63; reunion with
parents and siege of Budapest,
208–11; sex education, 11–12,
15; survival of Soviet liberation,

359–61; war concerns by adults,
15–16

Tiger-Chinitz, Dolly, grandfather
of, 9, 11

Tiger-Chinitz, Dolly, mother of
(Johanna/Vinyi): arrest by
police, 207; convent school
and, 13–14, 203; in hiding in
Budapest, 209–11; High Holy
Days in Mátras Mountains,
14–15; life in Budapest before
German occupation, 8–9; life in
Budapest during German occupation, 204, 205; sex education
with, 11–12, 15; in Subotica, 9–10,
12–13; survival of Soviet liberation, 359–60; wealth stolen by
Soviets, 360–61

Tiger-Chinitz, Dolly, stepfather
of (Apu bácsi): on attempt to
withdraw from Axis powers,
206; in hiding in Budapest, 208,
209, 210; life in Budapest during
occupation, 204; life with in
Subotica, 9, 10, 11, 13; negotiations for Tieberger's release and,
205; Vinyi's arrest and, 207;
wealth stolen by Soviets, 360–61

Toska (kapo), 175, 310

Tóth, László, 235

Tóth, Lyan, 235

Transylvania, 3n2, 73, 74, 99, 301

Tripartite Pact, 5

Túrkeve (Hungary), 227, 228, 287,
290–91

Tzortl (nephew of Yittel Nechumah

Bineth), 326
Újpest (Hungary), 307–9
United States of America, 25,
 319–20, 350–51
University of Debrecen, 56–57
Vác (Hungary), 119
Vándor, Kálmán, 239, 240, 241
Varbai (classmate of Tiger-Chinitz),
 11–12
Vas, Peter: "The Unending Past,"
 xxvii–xxix
Vásárosnamény (Hungary), 159–62
Vesely, Imrich, 27–36, 73–89; on
 antisemitism, 31–32; arrival
 in Budapest, 30–31; deaths at
 Eastern Front, 85–88; employment in Budapest, 32–33, 33–34;
 escape attempts and interrogation, 75–78; forced enlist-
 ment in labour battalion, 73;
 furlough from labour battalion,
 80–83; at German Ball, 34–36;
 with girlfriend's family, 81–82;
 landmine clearing on Eastern
 Front, 83–84, 88–89; lumber
 conveyance and road building in Carpathian Mountains,
 74–75; on sense of relative safety
 in Hungary, 84–85; at Shipyard
 Island, 79–80; train journey to
 Budapest, 27–30
Vilma (friend of Victor David), 276,
 277, 278
Vilmos (uncle of Imrich Vesely), 30
Vízköz (Hungary), 124
Vojvodina, 3n2, 4, 23, 69

Vörösmarty (officer), 238
Wachsmann, Nikolaus, 134
Wallenberg, Raoul, 231, 244, 258
Weisz, Gyuri, 119–20, 120–21
Weisz, Smuél, 121
Wieviorka, Annette, xvii–xviii
Windisch-Minihof (Austria), 121
yellow armband, 25, 73, 251
yellow star: concealment of, 150,
 220, 270; non-Jew reactions to,
 51, 205; requirement to wear, 45,
 61, 137, 159, 216, 235, 250, 264, 265
yellow star houses. See Jewish
 houses
Yiddish, 163–64
Yom Kippur, 15, 126–27, 156
Young, Ella and Magda, 63–65
Young, James E., xxii
Yozsa (sister of Yittel Nechumah
 Bineth), 152, 153, 323
Yugoslavia, 12, 16, 22, 73
Zhulitse (Hungary), 127–28
Zsuzsi (friend of Katalin Kenedi),
 245, 246

The Azrieli Foundation was established in 1989 to realize and extend the philanthropic vision of David J. Azrieli, C.M., C.Q., M.Arch. The Foundation's mission is to support a wide spectrum of initiatives in education and research. The Azrieli Foundation is an active supporter of programs in the fields of education, the education of architects, scientific and medical research, and the arts. The Azrieli Foundation's many initiatives include: the Holocaust Survivor Memoirs Program, which collects, preserves, publishes and distributes the written memoirs of survivors in Canada; the Azrieli Institute for Educational Empowerment, an innovative program successfully working to keep at-risk youth in school; the Azrieli Fellows Program, which promotes academic excellence and leadership on the graduate level at Israeli universities; the Azrieli Music Project, which celebrates and fosters the creation of high-quality new Jewish orchestral music; and the Azrieli Neurodevelopmental Research Program, which supports advanced research on neurodevelopmental disorders, particularly Fragile X and Autism Spectrum Disorders.